THE MEN WITH
THE MOVIE CAMERA

To Laura, Esme, Anouk and Eden

THE MEN WITH THE MOVIE CAMERA

PHILIP CAVENDISH

THE POETICS OF VISUAL STYLE IN SOVIET AVANT-GARDE CINEMA OF THE 1920S

Berghahn**onfilm**

Published in 2013 by
Berghahn Books
www.berghahnbooks.com

© 2013 Philip Cavendish

Library of Congress Cataloging-in-Publication Data
Cavendish, Philip.
 The men with the movie camera: the poetics of visual style in Soviet avant-
garde cinema of the 1920s / Philip Cavendish.
   p. cm.
 Includes filmography.
 Includes bibliographical references and index.
 ISBN 978-1-78238-077-1 (hardback : alk. paper) -- ISBN 978-1-78238-078-8
(institutional ebook)
 1. Cinematography--Soviet Union--History. 2. Experimental films--Soviet
Union--History and criticism. 3. Silent films--Soviet Union--History and
criticism. I. Title.
 TR848.C38 2013
 777--dc23
                                                              2013020135

British Library Cataloguing in Publication Data
A catalogue record for this book is available from the British Library

Printed on acid-free paper

ISBN 978-1-78238-077-1 (hardback)
ISBN 978-1-78238-078-8 (institutional ebook)

Contents

List of Illustrations

Unless otherwise stated, all frame stills are reproduced with the kind permission of the Russian State Film Archive (Gosfil'mofond Rossii)

Acknowledgements

This monograph is part of a wider research project into the poetics of the camera and the creative role of camera operators during the silent era, one which was initiated during a period of sabbatical leave from 2001 to 2002. I am grateful to colleagues within the Russian Department at the School of Slavonic and East European Studies, University College London, for covering my teaching and administrative responsibilities during this absence, and also during two further terms' research leave in 2005 and 2010.

This project involved several months of research at the Russian State Film Archive (Gosfil'mofond Rossii) in Belye stolby, just outside Moscow. I would like to thank the employees of this archive for their friendliness and helpfulness, and for the efficiency with which they supplied me with viewing copies of the films which form the basis of this monograph. In particular, I would like to record my debt of gratitude to Valerii Bosenko, the Director of International Liaison, for facilitating the reproduction of frame stills from these viewing copies, the first time, I believe, that a foreign researcher has been permitted to make such reproductions; and to the Director-General, Nikolai Borodatchev, for kindly giving me copyright permission to reproduce these frame stills free of charge. I am also grateful to the British Academy for supporting my first research trip to Gosfil'mofond in February 2002 with a travel grant. The first chapter of this book appeared in the October 2007 issue of *The Slavonic and East European Review*. I would like to thank the editorial board for their permission to reprint it here, albeit in a revised and expanded form.

During the writing of this monograph, I have benefitted enormously from the advice and guidance of Professor Julian Graffy, my colleague in the Russian Department at the School of Slavonic and Eastern European Studies. He read and commented on the early drafts of the manuscript, and generously shared with me his unrivalled knowledge of Russian and Soviet cinema. I would also like to thank my former Ph.D. student, JJ Gurga, a specialist in Ukrainian cinema, for her invaluable help in transliterating Ukrainian film titles and names. This monograph would not have been possible without the purchase several years ago by UCL library services of a database which contains digital copies of the major Soviet film publications of the period. Although this database is not complete in relation to certain newspapers and magazines, it nevertheless constitutes an invaluable archival source. Lastly, I would like to thank my editors at Berghahn, Mark Stanton and Charlotte Mosedale, for their patience, professionalism and unstinting support.

Note on Transliteration and Conventions

I have transliterated according to the American Library of Congress system without diacritics. This applies to all Russian names which appear in the body of the text, the notes, the illustrations, the filmography and the bibliography. The names of those who considered themselves ethnically Ukrainian have been transliterated according to their spellings in Ukrainian, but these do not include those, like Nikolai Gogol', who published in Russian and are best known by this spelling of their name. Neither do they include those born in Russia with Russian-speaking parents who, for a variety of different reasons, were living and working in the Ukrainian Soviet Socialist Republic during the 1920s and 1930s. For those encountering the surname of Sergei Eizenshtein's cameraman for the first time (Tisse), it is pronounced as if it were French (Tissé or Tisset).

Russian film titles in the body of the text are given in the original throughout with English translations given on first mention only. The filmography gives both Russian and English translated titles in order to aid the non-Russian reader. Films released in the Ukrainian Soviet Socialist Republic in Ukrainian-language versions are given in their original titles followed by the translation in Russian and English. Where the film title consists of a name (for example, *Ivan*), it is assumed that the non-Russian reader will understand this. The titles of non-Russian foreign-language films have been given in the original with the English translation given on first mention. So, too, have the titles of foreign-language collections of essays or articles in newspapers and magazines which are mentioned in the body of the text. The titles of all foreign-language newspapers, magazines and journals have been given in the original without translation.

Unless otherwise specified, all translations from foreign languages are my own.

Abbreviations

ARK	Assotsiatsiia revoliutsionnoi kinematografii (Association of Revolutionary Cinematography)
ARRK	Assotsiatsiia rabotnikov revoliutsionnoi kinematografii (Association of Workers of Revolutionary Cinematography)
A.S.C.	American Society of Cinematographers
FEKS	Fabrika ekstsentricheskogo aktera (Factory of the Eccentric Actor)
GIK	Gosudarstvennyi institut kinematografii (State Institute of Cinematography)
GOSET	Gosudarstvennyi evreiskii teatr (State Jewish Theatre)
GTK	Gosudarstvennyi tekhnikum kinematografii (State Film Technical College)
Gulag	Gosudarstvennoe upravlenie lagerei (State Administration of Camps)
GVYRM	Gosudarstvennye vysshie rezhisserskie masterskie (State Higher Directing Workshops)
LEF	Levyi front iskusstv (Left Front of the Arts)
NEP	New Economic Policy
NKVD	Narodnyi komissariat vnutrennikh del SSSR (People's Commissariat for Internal Affairs)
RGAKFD	Rossiiskii gosudarstvennyi arkhiv kinofotodokumentov (Russian State Archive of Film and Photographic Documents)
RGALI	Rossiiskii gosudarstvennyi arkhiv literatury i iskusstva (Russian State Archive of Literature and Art)
VFKO	Vserossiiskii fotokinematograficheskii otdel Narkomprosa (All-Russian Photo and Film Section of The People's Commissariat for Education)

VGIK	Vsesoiuznyi gosudarstvennyi institut kinematografii (All-Union State Institute of Cinematography)
VKhUTEMAS	Vysshie khudozhestvenno-tekhnicheskie masterskie (The Higher Art-Technical Workshops)
VUFKU	Vseukrainskoe fotokinoupravlenie (The All-Ukrainian Photo-Cinema Administration)

Introduction

I am convinced that by visual means alone one can persuade the viewer to feel joy, to cry, to hate, to love, to experience agitation, to suffer. Everything depends on the passionate heart of the person who, through the eye of his camera, is the first viewer of the film.[1]

We came upon no ready-built city with central arteries, side streets running off to the left and right, squares and communal spaces, or little crooked lanes and cul-de-sacs, such as can be found in the stylistic cinemetropolis of today's cinematograph.

We came like bedouins or gold-seekers. To an empty place. To a place with unimaginably great possibilities, only a laughably small fraction of which have been realized even to this day.[2]

We must discover the visible world. We must revolutionize our visual thinking.[3]

This monograph is about the visual culture of Soviet avant-garde film during the 1920s, before sound technology and a shift in cultural policy towards Socialist Realism and 'a cinema understood by the millions' rendered the term 'avant-garde' ideologically suspect and thus obsolete. It is a study of the image in its various complex manifestations as a means of communication and stimulation, and treats the medium of cinema as a primarily photographic phenomenon which, in the case of the Soviet avant-garde, was characterized by a particular set of creative practices and aesthetic preferences. At the heart of this study lies a detailed consideration of camerawork, a term that encompasses a whole range of subsidiary phenomena pertaining to the presentation of screen material, but which in essence can be reduced to the poetics of composition and lighting techniques. This is a neglected aspect of cinema studies, and yet it is fundamental to the visual resonance of the filmic image.

On the rare occasions when issues of aesthetics arise in the writing about film, they are attributed largely to the creative intervention of the director and identified as part of his or her visual perception of the world. From a historical point of view, however, this is a simplification of a complex process that involves the creative endeavours of several individuals, the most prominent being the camera operator (in Russian, *kinooperator*), who has formal responsibility for the translation of dramatic or poetic ideas into visual images. In the case of Soviet cinema, this is demonstrated by the so-called '(camera) operator's scenario', which is drawn up in parallel to the director's scenario (*raskadrovka, montazhnyi list*), and contains a detailed description of the compositional mechanics and lighting arrangements that will be adopted in relation to a given screenplay or libretto; as the celebrated cinematographer Sergei Urusevskii once remarked (see the first epigraph above), by virtue of his position in relation to the viewfinder at the moment when filming takes place, the cameraman de facto constitutes the first audience of film material, albeit admittedly in unedited form. Although the names of the Soviet avant-garde camera operators are reasonably well known among specialists, their particular role in the creation of avant-garde cinema during the 1920s has remained relatively neglected. In part, therefore, this monograph is dedicated to the resurrection of these figures, for so long relegated to the margins of cinema history, and to their repositioning as co-authors of avant-garde productions during the silent era. It will challenge a number of myths about the avant-garde, many of them the product of directorial self-promotion and the auteur bias which informs so many studies of cinema, both past and present. If the history of avant-garde cinema in the Soviet Union during the silent era had been written, which it has not, this study would position itself as an alternative and competing version. It considers the works of the four main avant-garde units active at the time and examines the partnerships between the directors and camera operators that formed their core: Sergei Eizenshtein with Eduard Tisse; Vsevolod Pudovkin with Anatolii Golovnia; Grigorii Kozintsev and Leonid Trauberg (the so-called FEKS directors) with Andrei Moskvin; and Oleksandr Dovzhenko with Danylo Demuts'kyi.

As a study of the visual language of cinema in its most experimental forms, this monograph will also place Soviet avant-garde film within the context of the modernist revolution in the arts. Eizenshtein's recollection, cited above as the second epigraph to this chapter, suggests that the avant-garde was confronted with a *tabula rasa* when it first came to engage with the material of film. As will be shown in the chapters that follow, however, this is not quite the case. Nevertheless, the directors and camera operators of the avant-garde believed themselves to be engaged in a quest to revolutionize visual thinking. This was expressed concisely by the Constructivist artist Aleksandr Rodchenko (see the third epigraph above), but it was simply his own variation on the concept of 'making it new', one that united otherwise diverse factions within the international avant-garde. The story of cinematic experiment in the Soviet Union during the 1920s is partly the dialogue with and polemic against developments taking place in related fields, both within the Soviet Union and abroad. Through the reports of correspondents based in Berlin and Paris, their access to the films of the European avant-garde via showings at the ARK and other film organizations, translations of key theoretical treatises, and trips abroad, many of which included visits to film studios and international art exhibitions, Soviet directors and camera operators were relatively well informed about artistic trends and filmmaking practices in Europe.

Although it might be deemed provocative to insist on the auteur status of Soviet cameramen, it is important to stress that this was not a particularly radical position during the 1920s. As the first chapter will demonstrate, this decade was a 'golden age' for Soviet camera operators. Within the film industry as a whole, and to some extent even in the eyes of the film-going public, the cameramen of the 1920s were iconic figures: their creative initiative within the film-production process was encouraged; their names featured prominently alongside directors in posters and other publicity materials; the names of the most important camera operators were relatively well known among critics and industry observers; their individual styles or 'signatures' were discussed in the film press; and there was a burgeoning theoretical discourse around cinema as a visual medium that placed specific emphasis on the importance of cinematography. For the first time in the history of cinema, both in Soviet Russia and elsewhere, the camera operator was regarded as a creative artist rather than merely a technician or craftsman who executed the orders of others. This privileged status was the result of a number of factors: the collective principle adopted by the avant-garde units (the spirit of democracy and equality that prevailed within them and the distrust of the supposedly bourgeois concept of individual authorship); the importance accorded to documentary material and the associated idea of the camera operator as a media 'shock-worker' in the battle of ideas; and the fact that cinema, as an industrial and technological process, was hailed as the proletarian art form of the future. At the heart of this phenomenon, one with strong echoes in the theory and practices of Russian Constructivism, was the concept of the artist-engineer, someone who combined technical expertise with creative vision in the service of revolutionary and utilitarian art. The promotion of the engineer-constructor, encapsulated in El' Lisitskii's 1924 photo-montage entitled *Avtoportret (Konstruktor)* (Self-Portrait (Constructor)), was very much part of the discourse to which the camera operator belonged by virtue of his association with the moving-picture camera, itself an emblem of modernity because of its recent invention. The contributions of this first generation of Soviet camera operators, in terms of the films they photographed and their writings and pedagogical functions within the institutions that trained future industry cadres, laid the foundations for a system of thought that privileged the visual language of cinema and recognized the contribution of the camera operator to the evolution of its aesthetics. In effect, these cameramen succeeded in engineering their own myth, thus ensuring that the voice of their profession would be heard in future debates about the direction of Soviet cinema. The relative abundance of published material about Soviet camera operators, far more than exists in relation to their European or U.S. counterparts, is a testimony to this powerful, initial impetus.

The emphasis in this monograph on the creative role of the camera operator does not deny the importance of the director in the genesis of visual ideas. With the exceptions of Pudovkin and Trauberg, the directors who feature in this monograph were practising artists themselves and therefore clearly interested in visual concepts. It is important to stress, nevertheless, that those who did draw and paint were not formally trained in the arts. Furthermore, their artworks for the most part (with the exception, perhaps, of Eizenshtein's 'secret' drawings) do not suggest any particular originality. Detailed study of the sketches and designs produced before their move into film, as well as the drawings they executed as part of the preparations for their film productions in subsequent years, reveals on the one hand a set of rather traditional affiliations (their cartoons and caricatures), and on the other hand, a rather modish avant-gardism that was highly imitative (their costumes, set designs and paintings). It is important to distinguish here between the genesis of visual ideas and their realization in photographic form. With the exception of their portrait studies, which manifest themselves in sketches of friends and acquaintances, these directors produced artworks which, in the vast majority of cases, involve little or nothing in the way of direct observation of nature. While the existence of such works indicates sensitivity in relation to visual phenomena, there are important differences between the procedures of the sketch and those that pertain to cinematography. In particular, these would apply to the optical distortion of film lenses, even relatively conventional ones (40mm), when compared to the human eye; the fact that the orthochromatic film stock of the period perceived artificial and natural light in ways different from the human eye; and the fact that images in this era take the form of a gradation of tones ranging from extreme black to extreme white (although this is a neglected aspect of the writing on 1920s Soviet cinema, it would appear that, with the exception of

FEKS, the avant-garde rejected the practice of colour-tinting and toning). Memoirs from the period suggest that, with the exception of Pudovkin, who was actively involved in filmmaking from 1921 onwards, the directors of the future avant-garde had little or no understanding of the technical aspects of filmmaking until they received instruction at the hands of their camera-operating partners. Tisse, Moskvin and Demuts'kyi were amateur or professional photographers prior to their move into film; moreover, they understood how photography worked, and were familiar with recent international trends. They were, in fact, independent artists in their own right. With the passage of time, the creative alliances these figures forged with their partners became so close that they became inseparable, almost doppelgängers of each other.

Although the visual language of Soviet avant-garde cinema is routinely commented upon in studies of individual directors, it has not been systematically investigated in any meaningful sense. The nearest equivalent is the monograph by Jan-Christopher Horak which analyses the phenomenon of European and North American photographers who either became professional camera operators or experimented with the medium of film as a parallel field of artistic enquiry.[4] Apart from identifying some of the most significant figures who belonged to this tendency – alas, his discussion does not include Russian photographers – the importance of this monograph lies in the author's desire to subvert the boundaries of academic disciplines which, historically speaking, have tended to limit the scope of intellectual enquiry into the relationship between cinema and related art forms.[5] For the most part, this division also applies to studies of the cultural avant-garde in Soviet Russia, although recently there have been signs of a desire to overcome these artificial barriers. Margarita Tupitsyn's study of the painter Kazimir Malevich offers valuable insights into his interest in cinema, a subject about which he wrote on several occasions during the 1920s.[6] There have also been studies of the influence of Constructivism on the films of Eizenshtein and Dziga Vertov.[7] Tim Harte's recent monograph on the binding element of kinaesthesia within the avant-garde, and his analysis of the importance of montage and intra-frame dynamic in the experimental films of the 1920s, is a further welcome correction to the general neglect of cinema in discussions of Soviet avant-garde culture.[8]

Malevich's 1929 assertion that 'Kinetics by itself does not save the day and does not release cinema from the illusory status of painting' is an important insight into the areas of convergence within avant-garde culture in the Soviet Union and elsewhere.[9] Recognition of this symbiotic relationship explains why frame stills from avant-garde films (both features and documentaries) were included in the 1929 'Film and Photo' exhibition in Stuttgart, the Soviet pavilion for which was designed by El' Lisitskii; according to Tupitsyn, the Russian section was 'the only one to succeed in presenting the close links between film and photography'.[10] It is also the reason why, between 1926 and 1928, Rodchenko edited a special 'Film and Photo' section in the journal *Sovetskoe kino*, which treated frame stills from recent films as independent artistic entities comparable to works in the sphere of still photography.[11] In this sense, avant-garde cinema in the Soviet Union belongs to the phenomenon of experimental art at the beginning of the twentieth century, a period characterized by a radical assault on traditional modes of expression and the creation of new, hybrid genres. The vogue for kinaesthesia, for example, prompted by the advent of cinema, is clearly felt in the experiments of avant-garde painters and still photographers in the second decade of the twentieth century.[12] The temporal dimension notwithstanding, there is also a strong aesthetic kinship between the avant-garde film posters of the period, with their emphasis on the geometric and linear and their deployment of eye-catching blocks of colour, and the visual language of the films they advertise. Some of these posters actually exploit frame stills from the production in question; others incorporate photographic 'cut-outs' or hand-drawn illustrations that replicate images from the production stills.[13] An interesting meditation on the points of aesthetic convergence can be found in Rodchenko's photographic studies of the Constructivist sets that he designed for Lev Kuleshov's *Vasha znakomaia* (Your Acquaintance, 1928) in the second and third factories of Goskino. These offer unusual perspectives of the sets when compared to the finished film. Indeed, not only do they expose their artifice as 'constructions' (the compositions include the typical studio paraphernalia of the period, for example, the numbered, overhead arc lamps), they also constitute a meticulous enquiry into the material and spatial dynamics of the studios themselves, in particular their glass roofs and metal girders (both were modern architectural features in the sense that they had been designed in the early part of the century for the film entrepreneur Aleksandr Khanzhonkov).[14] The relative neglect of these photographs, in terms of both exhibition and publication, speaks volumes about the lack of interest in cinema's relationship with still photography during this vibrant and dynamic period.[15]

If the modernist project can be characterized broadly, and perhaps a little crudely, in terms of the estrangement of perception, then Soviet avant-garde cinema, no less than other experimental art forms, constitutes a statement on the impact of modernity on visual modes of thinking. Not all the avant-garde units examined in this monograph participate in this project with the same degree of commitment, but the movement as a whole is characterized by the democratization of rigidly codified aesthetic hierarchies and the poeticization of the commonplace. This strategy took the form of photographing objects and locations which, although they had appeared in documentary material in the pre-revolutionary era, had not featured previously within the sphere of feature film. In broad terms, a new landscape unfurls which privileges sites of heavy industry and technology, modern architectural forms and spatial dynamics, the textures of modern materials, boulevard culture and the kinetic energy of the crowd. The revolutionary context means that this landscape is often populated by death, violence, decay, disorder, disorientation, psychological and physical injury, hysteria and emotional extremes. Furthermore, in order to convey the extremes of (revolutionary) experience, there is a strong commitment to maximize the expressive potential of filmic images through recourse to innovative compositional mechanisms. These take a multitude of different forms: unconventional camera angles (known in Russian as *rakurs*), play with differential focus, optical distortion, activization of the frame periphery, truncation, dynamic lighting effects, *contre-jour*, the subversion of devices that had become conventional stylistic markers (the dissolve, iris, wipe and vignette), exploitation of multiple exposure for aesthetic purposes, use of the hand-held camera, the tilting of the camera, and in general a radical and crude departure from the canons of decorative 'tastefulness' that had characterized pre-revolutionary cinematography. Lighting techniques, the sphere that belonged exclusively to the camera operator during this period, are consistently interesting in the work of the Soviet avant-garde. In part these were prompted by the general interest in accentuating surface texture, but to some extent, especially in the case of portraiture, they were a response to the challenge of *typage*, i.e., the tendency to use non-professional actors, which reflected the desire on the part of the avant-garde to subvert the glamour conventions of 'bourgeois' cinema in favour of authentic, lived experience. While it may be countered that the democraticization of the visible world and the embrace of verisimilitude were not uniquely the properties of Soviet avant-garde cinema, these qualities were pursued with a vigour and determination that was exceptional and subsequently proved influential for the development of world cinema generally.

Following the example of John E. Bowlt and Olga Matich, the term 'avant-garde' is employed throughout this monograph to refer to the experimental tendencies that began to emerge in the visual arts in the first decade of the twentieth century.[16] The monograph is divided into six chapters. The first chapter charts the discourse that developed in relation to camera operation during the 1920s, in terms of both theory and practice, and the ways in which this reflected the influence of avant-garde aesthetics. The next four chapters examine the dynamics of the avant-garde teams that gravitated around Eizenshtein, Pudovkin, FEKS and Dovzhenko, with particular emphasis on the relationships that were forged between the directors and their respective camera operators. These chapters analyse the films produced by these partnerships from the point of view of visual aesthetics, but also those made independently by the figures concerned. Particular emphasis is placed on the pressure of dramaturgical imperative, the desire to develop new revolutionary genres and the aesthetic interests and artistic practices (if relevant) of the directors, but also the aesthetic inclinations of the camera operators and the evolution of highly individual 'signatures'. The conclusion pursues the emerging 'myth' of the camera-operating profession into the early-to-mid 1930s, a period when the shift to sound and new ideological strictures were bringing the existence of the avant-garde into question. This was a period when camera operators were seeking formal recognition of their authorship rights within the industry. As this chapter also makes clear, while at least three of the avant-garde units continued to work into the sound era, the films made by them, with the exception of Eizenshtein's *Ivan Groznyi* (Ivan the Terrible, 1944–46), cannot be called 'avant-garde' in the sense in which the term was understood during the 1920s. Those, like Boris Groys, who argue that Socialist Realism continued the ideological agenda of the avant-garde 'but by different means', have paid insufficient attention to the visual aesthetics of cinema. The radical differences between the two eras from the stylistic point of view can be demonstrated by reference to any of the films made by these avant-garde units during the 1930s and 1940s when compared to those of the 1920s.[17]

Notes

1.   'Vynuzhdennoe vystuplenie kak demonstratsiia protiv otsutstviia doklada ob izobrazitel'nom reshenii fil'ma', in Sergei Urusevskii, *S kinokameroi i za mol'bertom* (Moscow: Algoritm, 2002), pp. 173–75 (p. 173).

2.   'Sredniaia iz trekh', in S. M. Eizenshtein, *Izbrannye proizvedeniia*, ed. by S. I. Iutkevich, 6 vols (Moscow: Iskusstvo, 1964–71), V (1968), 53–78 (p. 54) (first publ. in *Sovetskoe kino*, 1934.11–12, 54–83).

3.   Aleksandr Rodchenko, 'Puti sovremennoi fotografii' [1928], cited (and translated) in Christina Lodder, *Russian Constructivism* (New Haven, CT: Yale University Press, 1983), p. 202.

4.   Jan-Christopher Horak, *Making Images Move: Photographers and Avant-Garde Cinema* (Washington, D.C.: Smithsonian Institution Press, 1997).

5.   Ibid., pp. 7–8.

6.   Margarita Tupitsyn, *Malevich and Film*, with essays by Kazimir Malevich and Victor Tupitsyn (New Haven, CT: Yale University Press, 2002).

7.   François Albera, *Eisenstein et le constructivisme russe* (Lausanne: L'Age d'homme, 1990); and Vlada Petrić, *Constructivism in Film: The Man with the Movie Camera: A Cinematic Analysis* (Cambridge: Cambridge University Press, 1987).

8.   Tim Harte, *Fast Forward: The Aesthetics and Ideology of Speed in Russian Avant-Garde Culture, 1910–1930* (Wisconsin: University of Wisconsin Press, 2009).

9.   Malevich, 'Zhivopisnye zakony v problemakh kino' [1929], in Tupitsyn, *Malevich and Film*, pp. 147–59 (p. 147).

10. Margarita Tupitsyn, *El Lissitzky: Beyond the Abstract Cabinet* (New Haven, CT: Yale University Press, 1999), p. 56. For examples of the works exhibited, see *Film und Foto der zwanziger Jahre* [catalogue of the 1929 'Film and Photo' exhibition in Stuttgart], publ. by the Württembergischer Kunstverein with articles by Ute Eskildsen and Jan-Christopher Horak (Stuttgart: Hatje, 1979).

11. For more on this initiative, see Chapter One.

12. Harte, *Fast Forward*, pp. 3–29. For the impact of kinaesthesia on photography, see the discussion of 'photodynamism' in Giovanni Lista, *Futurism and Photography* (London: Merrell, 2001), pp. 21–30.

13. Susan Pack, *Film Posters of the Russian Avant-Garde* (Cologne: Taschen, 1995).

14. Aleksandr Rodchenko, 'Khudozhnik i "material'naia sreda" v igrovoi fil'me: Beseda s khudozhnikom A. M. Rodchenko', *Sovetskoe kino*, 1927.5–6, 14–15.

15. For the most recent and largest retrospective, see *Alexander Rodchenko: Revolution in Photography*, ed. by Alexander Lavrentiev (Moscow: Multimedia Complex of Actual Arts/ Moscow House of Photography Museum, 2008).

16. See the introduction to *Laboratory of Dreams: The Russian Avant-Garde and Cultural Experiment*, ed. by John E. Bowlt and Olga Matich (Stanford, CA: Stanford University Press, 1996), pp. 1–14.

17. Boris Groys, 'The Birth of Socialist Realism from the Spirit of the Russian Avant-Garde', in ibid., pp. 193–218.

CHAPTER ONE

The Theory and Practice of Camera Operation within the Soviet Avant-Garde of the 1920s

Tisse is not a camera operator, he is a god.[1]

Introduction

THE ODESSA MIST sequence in *Bronenosets Potemkin* (Battleship Potemkin, 1925), an early-morning prelude to the images of the murdered sailor, Vakulenchuk, as he lies peacefully in a makeshift tent along the quayside, has been universally acclaimed for its atmosphere and poetic lyricism. The scenes of the harbour – ghostly ships lying at anchor, slow-moving yachts, a motley crew of motionless birds, and glinting water, all photographed *contre-jour* – are notable for their eerie sense of calm (Fig. 1). Eizenshtein had originally envisaged a 'port in mourning' scene that would be photographed out of focus, as if 'through tears'.[2] The impressionistic potential of the landscape that presented itself spontaneously to him and Tisse as they rowed around the harbour, however, quickly intruded. In his later reminiscence of the event, Eizenshtein evoked the uncanny mood of the scene: the mist 'clinging to the lens of the camera like wet cotton wool'; the quiet 'grumbling' of the apparatus, as if to say that 'such things are not supposed to be filmed'; and the ironic laughter coming from another figure in the vicinity (if he is to be believed, the pre-revolutionary camera operator Aleksandr Levitskii), an expression of scepticism that the scenes in question could be adequately registered given the relatively poor lighting conditions.[3] Such weather would normally bring filming to a halt. Instead, as Eizenshtein records, this 'found object' became the initial chords of what would later become a 'symphony' to the memory of the murdered sailor and the mutiny with which he would later become associated.[4]

The ecstatic response on the part of the screenplay writer, Nina Agadzhanova-Shutko, on seeing the rushes of these sequences, cited as the epigraph to this chapter, is doubtless hyperbolic. Inadvertently, however, it draws attention to a radical break in assumptions about the role of the camera operator in the post-revolutionary era: for the first time, instead of merely a 'hand that turns the handle', he is now saluted as the genius behind, and author of, the visual image.[5] This represents a fundamental, albeit perhaps unconscious, shift in the perceived relationship between director and camera operator, one which, in the case of Eizenshtein and Tisse, achieved a rare synchronicity. It went beyond recognition of Tisse's practical importance to Eizenshtein: his unflappability under pressure, his devilish speed and lightning-quick temperament, his painstaking approach to his work and the fact that, as the senior and more experienced of the two, he had personally vouchsafed Eizenshtein's transition from experimental theatre to avant-garde film director when they first started working alongside each other.[6] In the words of Eizenshtein, Tisse possessed that 'subtlest appreciation of the barely perceptible nuance, that "slight adjustment" [*chut'-chut'*] in the material which marks ... the creation of true art'.[7] The two men combined their respective roles with a rare understanding – as Eizenshtein noted: 'It is unlikely that anyone anywhere has ever encountered the kind of synchronicity of vision, feeling and emotional experience that binds Tisse and me.'[8] The film historian Jay Leyda, who had the privilege as a student of observing them working together on *Bezhin lug* (Bezhin Meadow, 1935–37), has described their partnership as 'one of the miracles of film history'.[9]

Miracle or not, this partnership was not an isolated event in the development of the Soviet avant-garde. The first decade after the October Revolution witnessed a series of creative alliances that blazed a trail of experimentation through the realms of cinema. Golovnia's camerawork for Pudovkin, Moskvin's life-long association with Kozintsev and Trauberg, and Demuts'kyi's prematurely interrupted but artistically fruitful collaborations with Dovzhenko were typical of this new type of partnership. If the formation of these relationships was initially fortuitous, they developed with the passage of time into profound creative alignments, as well as close personal friendships, the disruption of which provoked crises in the individuals concerned. Their significance in the context of avant-garde cinema cannot be underestimated. These camera operators were pioneers of Soviet cinematography, consummate technicians during an age that worshipped the machine, and at the same time artists who exploited their scientific expertise in the service of what they regarded as a new and revolutionary art. If it can be said that their formal influence waned in the early 1930s after the arrival of sound and the end of 'poetic cinema', their informal influence nevertheless persisted through their pedagogical functions and published writings. Successive generations of students were educated and trained by them at the camera operators' faculty of the GTK (later GIK, and then VGIK). It is little appreciated that, with the exception of Demuts'kyi, who died in 1954, these men continued to wield considerable influence into the 1960s, either teaching at VGIK (Golovnia and Tisse), or actively involved in film production (Moskvin). Despite the relative conservatism of their later years, it is doubtful that the Soviet 'new wave' of the 1960s would have taken place without them. More than the directors with whom they were associated, only two of whom were alive as the Khrushchev 'Thaw' began to gain momentum, they were actually the living link between revolutionary past and experimental present.

This chapter seeks to outline the changing status and perceptions of the camera operator during the post-revolutionary silent era. It will analyse the reasons why he was accorded a greater degree of significance as far as the filmmaking process generally was concerned, and why indeed he became something of an iconic figure. Not only were his creative impulses encouraged and respected, but the principle of the durable partnership with an individual director within a specific unit became a bedrock of Soviet filmmaking practice to the extent that, from the 1930s onwards, although ideological pressures and the politics of personnel could and very often did intervene, deviations from this norm were considered the exception rather than the rule. It should be emphasized that, while this was a peculiarly Soviet phenomenon, it was not without echo in the filmmaking practices of Europe and North America. The move towards unionization, prompted by the desire to protect camera operators from studio exploitation, gradually merged into the concept of professionalization, which in turn developed into concerted pressure for artistic recognition. The inauguration of the American Society of Cinematographers (A.S.C.) and the German Cameramen's Club in 1918 and 1919 respectively was accompanied by the publication of journals which not only discussed technical matters relevant to the development of cinematography, but also lobbied hard for a system of production in which the professional skills and creative initiatives of these societies' members were respected.[10] Despite this trend, however, it is undeniably the case that few film industries outside the Soviet Union produced partnerships as enduring as those of the Soviet avant-garde. The importance attributed to the art of the camera operator within Soviet film culture during the 1920s and beyond is reflected in both the quality and the quantity of the writing dedicated to it in the film newspapers and magazines of the period. Furthermore, general recognition of the creative importance of the camera operator gave rise to a complex dynamic between directors and camera operators in the Soviet Union which in some cases had far-reaching ramifications. According to Andrei Tarkovskii and Gleb Panfilov, two auteur directors who came to prominence in the early 1960s, this relationship was something akin to a 'marriage', one that was 'intimate, very complicated, capricious, vulnerable and tender'.[11]

This first chapter considers the broader issues that were common to the avant-garde units rather than the specific dynamics of individual partnerships. It seeks to chart the emergence of a new generation of camera operators out of the cauldron of revolution, and to analyse the ideological, psychological and cultural forces that shaped their ways of thinking. It will also examine the technological resources at their disposal, which influenced what they were able to represent on screen. In some senses, these men were fortunate to begin their careers at a time when theoretical debates around the essence of cinema were increasingly emphasizing its power as a visual medium of expression; indeed, because of his 'ownership' of the camera, the role of the camera operator within the production process became an important theoretical issue in its own right.

This chapter seeks to chart the evolution of this debate, but goes beyond abstract formulations to consider the actual practices of avant-garde cinematographers during the silent period and the degree of creative autonomy they enjoyed within even the avowedly collective dynamic of their units. In fact, it goes further and challenges the very notion of the auteur in relation to Soviet avant-garde cinema. It will be argued that the camera operator should be recognized as 'co-director', and thus co-author, of the many experimental classics of the post-revolutionary silent period. Furthermore, it will suggest that the history of film style is incomplete without due consideration of the aesthetic inclinations and cultural backgrounds of individual cameramen, or what some have described as their trademark 'signature' (in Russian, *pocherk*). Those who have written about Soviet cinematography from a professional point of view maintain that it is both possible and important to distinguish these signatures. The following assertion by Maiia Merkel', a camera operator trained at VGIK who in the 1950s moved into film criticism, might be regarded as typical:

> *Each operator has seen and expressed the world in his own different way. It is impossible to confuse the screen work of Moskvin and Volchek, Ekel'chyk and Magidson, Tisse or Gordanov. The appearance of each and every one of their works was a celebration which was invariably followed by controversy.*[12]

In turn, this has given rise to the idea of certain 'schools' or tendencies within Soviet cinematography which transcend the particular limitations of dramatic subject or genre and relate to the influences of certain camera operators on their apprentices, pupils or students. In certain respects, therefore, this monograph claims to offer the beginnings of a revisionist view of the development of Soviet cinema in general. It discusses film primarily as a photographic phenomenon, one in which the traces of multiple cultural influences are tangible, and treats the filmic utterance as a delicate negotiation between a series of diverse and sometimes competing pressures, the most important and compelling of which lies in the relationship between the director and camera operator. The fact that this relationship frequently collapsed – the history of Soviet cinema is littered with examples of this phenomenon, and the 1920s is no exception – suggests the potential volatility of its dynamics.

The Soviet Avant-Garde Camera Operator: Background, Training and Initial Work Experience

Despite their political radicalism and identification with the October Revolution, it would appear that none of the avant-garde cameramen who emerged in its aftermath were working class in terms of social origin. Furthermore, neither was formal training within the newly established GTK, or institutions elsewhere, relevant for the acquisition of their craft or the formation of their artistic views.[13] Tisse, for example, whose family origins are obscure, was born in 1897 and educated in a commercial school for mariners in the Latvian port of Libava (now Liepája).[14] While pursuing these studies, he attended evening classes at Professor Ernst Grenzinger's studio of painting and photography, where he trained and worked briefly as a photographer's apprentice. Having been entrusted with the studio's Pathé moving-picture camera in 1913, he moved into actualities and forged a distinguished career for himself as a newsreel photographer during the First World War, experiencing the rigours of a soldier's life and shooting a variety of material along a series of military fronts. By the time he was introduced to Eizenshtein in 1923, he had a wealth of experience behind him.[15]

His colleagues, by contrast, entered the industry in far less challenging circumstances. Demuts'kyi, for example, hailed from the Ukrainian intelligentsia and graduated from the law department of Kyiv University two years before the outbreak of war. Photography had been a childhood hobby that led in due course to his embrace of Pictorialism and membership of the prestigious Daguerre Society in Kyiv, which was promoting the latest trends in artistic photography. He joined the Odessa studios in the mid-1920s as a professional photographer and then progressed into camera operation via a brief apprenticeship under Oleksii Kaliuzhnyi, another Pictorialist photographer, who had moved into cinematography after the Revolution and forged a reputation for experimentalism in several projects during the early-to-mid 1920s, most strikingly in *Zlyva* (Liven', Downpour, 1929), which he shot alongside the former artist and sculptor, Ivan Kavaleridze.[16] Like Demuts'kyi, Moskvin also hailed from a professional background, but this time with a pronounced engineering and scientific bent: his father was director of the largest locomotive factory in Russia.[17] Moskvin's interest in photography also took the form of a private enthusiasm. From 1921 to 1924 he was registered as a student at the Petrograd Institute of Railway Communications, but at the same time he was informally attending classes on the art of photography held at the Higher Photo-Technical Institute; these had been arranged by his friend, Viacheslav Gordanov, who had been studying at the institute since 1923 in the hope of eventually finding work as a camera operator.[18] It was Gordanov who arranged for Moskvin to have work experience at Sevzapkino after his premature ejection from the institute, which led to his contact with Kozintsev and Trauberg and their invitation for him to shoot *Chertovo koleso* (The Devil's Wheel, 1926), their first full-length feature film. Alone among these future cameramen, although the circumstances are not clear, Golovnia found himself in the profession by accident. According to his memoirs, having arrived in Moscow in 1923, ostensibly to study agronomy, he apparently missed the deadline for the entry applications and instead answered an advertisement at the GTK for 'cinema engineers'; much to his surprise, having passed the exams, he found himself in the camera operation faculty.[19]

Despite the availability of formal schooling at this time, it was still apprenticeship that provided the most important source of training for the aspiring camera operator. Legend has made much of the GTK. As the first film academy in the world, this school, which opened in 1919, became famous for the workshops in directing and acting that served as an experimental laboratory for the methods of the avant-garde. As far as camera operation was concerned, however, its impact in these early years was relatively limited. When Golovnia enrolled, for example, the advertisement for the course did not even have a term for the profession, referring only to a course for 'film shooters' (*s"emshchiki*).[20] His memoirs explain that the courses were largely theoretical in content, with lectures in advanced mathematics, chemistry and photography, but with no moving-picture or stills cameras available for practical work.[21] Indeed, actual work experience was arranged in 1924 only after formal complaints on the part of the students. In Golovnia's case, this resulted in a brief spell of work for Kuleshov's film unit under the tutelage of Levitskii, after which he decided not to return to his formal studies but to continue working for the unit as an unpaid assistant; in due course, this gave rise to Pudovkin's invitation to collaborate on the making of *Mekhanika golovnogo mozga* (Mechanics of the Brain, 1926) and *Shakhmatnaia goriachka* (Chess Fever, 1926).[22] In Leningrad, the situation in terms of formal education and training was no better. According to Gordanov, the Higher Photo-Technical Institute was in a lamentable state. Despite boasting the 'cream of Russian photographic science' in the form of its academic staff, there was no money to pay the lecturers, the building was unheated, and no classes took place during the first year (1923). Reorganization followed in 1924, but the situation did not improve: for him and Moskvin, as for Golovnia, it was work experience that ultimately proved crucial.[23] In view of the generally impoverished conditions of the early 1920s, the haphazard organization of formal training should perhaps come as little surprise. The desperate shortage of professional camera operators meant that those who had not disappeared into exile were too busy with existing assignments to give lectures. As Gordanov points out, not without irony, the first cameraman to do so was none other than himself. This occurred as late as 1930, and in his view the training had improved very little.[24]

The Collaborative Principle within the Units of the Avant-Garde

The emergence of the avant-garde witnessed a radical shift in attitudes in relation to the art of cinematography and the role of the camera operator within the larger filmmaking unit. Unlike their U.S. or European counterparts, who could be invited to work at extremely short notice without prior knowledge of the script, the cameramen who worked within the Soviet avant-garde units, in theory at least, were involved at every stage of the production process. The division of responsibilities within the teams was fluid and the atmosphere essentially democratic. In a lecture to the German Cameramen's Club in 1927, Tisse stated his implacable opposition to what he termed 'the dictatorship of the director'.[25]

He offered an account of working practices within Eizenshtein's unit which placed special emphasis on the importance of collaboration. The production process started with a five-to-ten page libretto, rather than a (literary) screenplay, which expressed precisely and accurately the content of the film. This was then discussed among the members of the unit and expanded into a shooting script that worked out in detail the individual montage sequences and the overall design of the film in terms of its rhythms and visual architecture. Although each member of the unit was equipped with his own 'weapons', as Tisse describes them, the group essentially shared a common language. For this reason, it was impossible to define exactly the spheres of responsibility that distinguished the contribution of the camera operator from that of the screenplay writer, director or production artist.[26]

Even allowing for the fact that these remarks may have been motivated ideologically – in other words, by Tisse's desire to demonstrate the superiority of the emerging socialist model in the Soviet Union – they appear to have been an accurate reflection of avant-garde practices in general. Pudovkin, for example, was happy to place on record the extraordinary sense of unity that he experienced with Natan Zarkhi, the screenplay writer, Mikhail Doller, the assistant director, and Golovnia during the filming of his first feature film, *Mat'* (Mother, 1926) – as he writes:

> *We all remember the extraordinary harmony* [slitnost'] *of our work together, which makes it impossible now to establish with certainty who was responsible for what in the creation and assembling of the scenario or film.*[27]

This is confirmed by the knowledge that Golovnia co-wrote the screenplay for *Konets Sankt-Peterburga* (The End of St Petersburg, 1927) and was a moving spirit behind its conceptualization and realization.[28] In the work of FEKS, the principle of equality was also promoted. Kozintsev, for example, later admitted that 'shooting was always more than merely the practical realization of the directors' ideas'.[29] Furthermore, Moskvin's influence apparently extended to commenting on the quality of the acting and the arrangements for the mise en scène, spheres usually considered the exclusive preserve of the director; as he revealed at the 1935 All-Union Creative Conference of Workers in Soviet Cinema:

> *In my experience – I don't know how it is with others – it has never been the case that this is my sphere of responsibility ... [. T]hese are the boundaries which*

belong to Kozintsev, and these belong to Trauberg. If I am unhappy with the work of an actor, if I am unhappy with a particular episode, I will put my point of view across to the point of swearing and raising my fists, and as a result of discussion an agreed approach to our work is reached.[30]

In Dovzhenko's unit, which had been established after the success of *Zvenyhora* (Zvenigora, 1927), the emphasis again was very much on the bringing together of kindred spirits – in the words of the production artist, Iosif Shpinel':

He [Dovzhenko] always searched among his colleagues within the filmmaking unit not only for precise executors, but also for allies and like-minded people ... . It was while working on the film [Arsenal] that there emerged a subtle interdependence between Dovzhenko, Demuts'kyi and me: full understanding of our aims and tasks, and total clarity about what needed to be done.[31]

The Camera Operator as Iconic Soviet Figure

If camera operators benefited from the fact that socialist ideas and models of development, at least in theory, privileged the principle of collectivity, they also profited from their status as human 'accessory' to the camera. The post-revolutionary era was one in which the camera became an emblem of quasi-fetishized modernity. In part, this was the result of its associations with actuality footage and agitprop documentary as potential vehicles for the dissemination of ideology. The camera operator specializing in newsreel material, in particular in the context of military conflict, acquired iconic status by virtue of his courage, athleticism, daring and ingenuity. The film press of the period is full of images of cameramen in positions of potential danger, if not mortal peril, as a result of the places in which they were located or the inhospitable conditions under which they were working. Two images splashed across the opening pages of *Sovetskii ekran* for 13 April 1926 strikingly capture this popular myth in the process of formation. The first shows Vertov and Mikhail Kaufman, his camera-operating brother and founder member of the so-called Kinok (Ciné-Eye) group, ascending a steep staircase high above the port of Novorossiisk for the filming of panoramas intended for inclusion in *Shestaia chast' mira* (A Sixth Part of the World, 1926); and in the second, across the page, the reader is presented with a photograph of Petr

Novitskii, a newsreel specialist, wearing a gas mask while operating his camera during the First World War (Fig. 2).[32] In similar fashion, the cover of the first issue of *Sovetskoe kino* for 1927 shows Kaufman filming with a hand-held camera while on roller skates; and the second page of the second issue for the same year shows an unidentified cameraman strapped to the wing of a biplane at a dangerous altitude.

As various commentators observed at the time, the reputation of the Soviet camera operator specializing in actuality material depended to a great extent on his willingness to obtain adventurous shots, whatever the risks involved.[33] As the decade progressed, the mobility of the camera acquired a more directly geographical resonance as the political imperative for the production of ethnographic material involved teams of camera operators being despatched to the peripheries of the Soviet Union in order to show ethnic minorities 'liberated' from the imperialist yoke. As demonstrated by Vladimir Shneiderov and Georgii Blium's *Velikii perelet* (The Great Flight, 1926), a documentary that recorded their flight by aeroplane from Moscow to Peking, the myth of the modern camera operator could be said to have crossed into a sphere more readily associated with the explorer, aviator and wildlife filmmaker.[34] Reports and photographs from these treks to 'exotic' territories regularly filled the pages of the film press during this period. The culmination of this mythologizing process, *Chelovek s kinoapparatom* (Man with the Movie Camera, 1929), is an experimental documentary in which a cameraman (Kaufman) and a moving-picture camera (the French-made Debrie-Parvo 'L') become a single entity, an ubiquitous, omniscient and quasi God-like eye capable of recording a new kind of social and political reality. Not only is this mechanical eye able to perceive things that the human eye cannot, but the camera itself has become a 'Constructivist' object in its own right, a sleek blend of silver, metal design and utilitarian, ideological purpose. By being 'welded' to this machine, the Soviet camera operator became de facto a shock-trooper in the vanguard of progressive humanity, if not something of a twentieth-century seer.

Although distinctions must necessarily be drawn between the heroic recorders of documentary footage and the studio cinematographers associated with feature films, these were not deemed significant as far as the camera operators of the avant-garde were concerned. If not all of them had experienced a 'baptism of fire' on the fronts of the First World War and Civil War, they did nevertheless combine documentary and feature-film making as part of their routine professional duties during the 1920s and beyond. Furthermore, they belonged to units which, with the exception of FEKS, were fiercely committed to the doctrine of documentary-style authenticity. If the pre-revolutionary generation had been associated with the opulent studio interior, the image of the avant-garde camera operator, by contrast, was synonymous with gritty exteriors; in particular, factories, working-class tenement blocks and impoverished rural communities. Anecdotes from the period, repeated not without pride, are full of legendary exploits: Golovnia risking life and limb to secure close-ups of ice-floes floating down a freezing river for *Mat'* (he was suspended from a bridge and hanging within inches of the surface of the water);[35] Moskvin's bruising footage of a roller-coaster ride in *Chertovo koleso*;[36] his colleague, Evgenii Mikhailov, filming on horse-back with a camera strapped to his chest for the circus sequence in *SVD* (*Soiuz velikogo dela*) (The Union of the Great Cause, 1927);[37] and Demuts'kyi waist-deep with a hand-held camera in the rushing waters of the Dnieper for the opening sequences of *Ivan* (1932).[38] These stories directly echo the exploits of their counterparts in the sphere of actuality: Kaufman's filming of an ice-breaker on the polar ice cap (he was forced to leap away at the last moment to avoid the cracks in the ice that could have left him stranded);[39] shooting from the roofs of fast-moving trains;[40] and Vertov being struck on the forehead by a protruding girder as he was transported in a wagon suspended by cables high above the port in Novorossiisk (according to press reports, he momentarily lost consciousness and nearly fell out).[41] Even the *topos* within the documentary genre of the potential hazards of wildlife photography is echoed in the folklore of the avant-garde. Thus the anecdote that relates how, while filming the entrance to a bear's den in northern Russia, the Kinok correspondent Nikolai Konstantinov was forced to defend himself with his tripod from the aggressive attentions of its occupant has its direct counterpart in the legend, according to which Golovnia was rescued from the charge of an irate hippopotamus during the shooting of *Mekhanika golovnogo mozga* by a quick-thinking lighting technician who dazzled the beast with an arc lamp.[42]

Doubtless it is the principle of collective solidarity, coupled with the romanticism of newsreel photography, that explains the seriousness with which the figure of the cameraman is treated in the film-industry press of the 1920s. If his pre-revolutionary antecedent was the lynchpin of the film-production process – in certain respects he was more important even than the director – he was nevertheless for the most part an anonymous figure: his name did not feature in publicity materials; there was little discussion of his work in either trade journals or the popular film press; and the profession itself was largely shrouded in secrecy.[43] This is most emphatically not the case in the film magazines and newspapers of the 1920s. While it would be an exaggeration to claim that the status of camera operators was equal to that of directors, their portraits were routinely and prominently displayed in ways no different from directors or actors: see, for example, the portrait of Tisse that adorned the cover of the second issue of *Sovetskii ekran* for 1926; and the no less emblematic photo-montage composition by Petr Galadzhev, an artist but also one of the actors at Kuleshov's atelier within the GTK, which celebrated the first aerial shots of Moscow by Boris Frantsisson.[44] This critical largesse extended to both older and younger generations. Thus the series of mini-biographies penned by the director Leo Mur (real name, Leopol'd Murashko) for *Sovetskii ekran* in 1929 was devoted not only to the careers of Kaufman, Tisse and Konstantin Kuznetsov, all of whom had come to prominence during the 1920s (Kuznetsov had photographed Kuleshov's *Po zakonu* (By the Law, 1926) and *Vasha znakomaia*), but also to those of Levitskii, Louis Forestier and Novitskii, all of whom were 'veterans' of the pre-revolutionary epoch.[45] During this period, we also encounter the emergence of a critical discourse in relation to the 'signatures' of individual camera operators.[46] Short articles appear by cameramen themselves on their working methods and creative approaches.[47] Furthermore, there are reports on the position of camera operators in Germany and North America, with crucial distinctions drawn between their working practices and those of their Soviet counterparts (in particular, emphasis is placed on the relative openness of the latter and their willingness to share the 'secrets' of their trade).[48] Soviet cameramen were sufficiently well known internationally that they were occasionally saluted by their foreign counterparts.[49] In the fullness of time, moreover, there emerged a fully fledged theory of the Soviet cinematographer which made an important contribution to the debates about cinema as a visual medium in the 1920s. By 1933, at a special conference organized by the cinema section of Mosoblrabis (the Moscow Regional Workers of Art), camera operators were sufficiently confident of their position within the industry to demand authorial rights in relation to their work, payment for the drawing up of their 'operators' scenarios', and the right to join the ARRK as creative artists.[50]

The Camera Operator and Theoretical Debates about Film as a Visual Medium

The principles of Soviet cinematography emerged against a background of powerful ferment in related spheres of the visual arts. It was a period of rich cross-fertilization between genres and various forms of visual media, one that witnessed avant-garde painters in Europe not only being influenced by the invention of the moving image, but also themselves experimenting with the new technology. Fernand Léger and Dudley Murphy's *Ballet mécanique* (Mechanical Ballet, 1924), for example, was in some senses conceived as a showpiece for the technical possibilities of the camera. This was an era in which photographers also began to take a keen interest in moving pictures. Some, such as the American Pictorialist Karl Struss, moved directly into cinematography;[51] others, notably Paul Strand, Man Ray and László Moholy-Nagy, produced some of Europe and North America's first experimental films.[52] Previously marginalized and disparaged art forms, such as poster art and commercial design, began to take precedence over more traditional forms of artistic endeavour, to the extent that the boundaries between them began to be erased. Soviet cinema would reflect the impact of these developments and eventually come to rival them.

A good example of this synthesizing phenomenon is the work of Rodchenko, an artist trained in graphics and painting who subsequently, while employed as a professor and dean of the metalwork faculty at VKhUTEMAS, began to experiment with a range of different visual media, among them non-figurative, three-dimensional sculpture, photo-installation, photo-collage, photo-montage and still photography. His early works, conceived under the influence of Constructivism and Productionism, reflect the interests of these movements in technology, commercial and industrial design, and modern architecture. In time, he was also involved in a number of film-related projects. These took the form of cover designs for avant-garde brochures dedicated to recent film releases, for example *Bronenosets Potemkin* (1926) and Il'ia Erenburg's *Materializatsiia fantastiki* (The Materialization of the Fantastic, 1927);[53] film posters, most famously those commissioned in 1924 for the release of Vertov's *Kinoglaz* (Ciné-Eye) and the several offered to Goskino to promote the release of *Bronenosets Potemkin*;[54] portraits of prominent figures associated with the world of avant-garde or progressive cinema (Esfir' Shub, Vitalii Zhemchuzhnyi, Kuleshov and Dovzhenko);[55] and designs for film sets. At least two of Rodchenko's photographic series during the 1920s mirror the perspectives adopted on previous occasions by camera operators. His studies of light filtering through the glass and steel roof of the Briansk railway station (now known as Kyiv railway station) echo the perspective assumed by Kuznetsov for one of the scenes in *Vasha znakomaia*; and his 1930 series on Theatre Square, taken from the pediment of the Bolshoi Theatre, imitates the position adopted three years earlier by Grigorii Giber during the making of Abram Room's *Tret'ia Meshchanskaia* (Bed and Sofa, 1927).[56] It is symptomatic of the convergence between avant-garde cinema and photography during this period that several of Rodchenko's photographs were first published in a film journal, *Sovetskoe kino*.[57] Osip Brik's article on contemporary photographic trends, 'Chego ne vidit glaz' ('What the Eye Does Not See'), published in the second issue of *Sovetskoe kino* for 1926, not only introduced two of Rodchenko's early works, but also drew an analogy between his striving for unconventional angles of vision and Vertov's desire to show that which 'the ordinary eye cannot see'.[58] In the same way, some of Rodchenko's early photo-montages were first published in *Kino-fot*, a journal dedicated to the latest developments in film and photography that was edited by Rodchenko's Constructivist colleague, Aleksei Gan.[59] The hospitality of film publications generally towards related art forms can be gauged by the number of articles about the visual language of cinema by avant-garde painters;[60] the reports on international art and photographic exhibitions;[61] updates on events organized by the Russian Photographic Society;[62] articles (some translated from the foreign press) on recent developments within the international avant-garde;[63] analyses of the art of the film poster;[64] contributions on set design by production artists;[65] and discussions of the ways in which other performance-based arts, for example theatre, were beginning to exploit cinematic methods.[66] It is symptomatic of this general *rapprochement* that many of the covers of contemporary film magazines were designed by prominent Constructivist artists, most notably Gustav Klutsis, who designed three covers for *Kino-front* in 1926.[67]

The embrace of cinema at the beginning of the 1920s was universal on the part of Soviet avant-garde artists and progressive intellectuals. Although there were disagreements about, and perhaps even indifference towards, the issue of whether film could legitimately be regarded as an art form, its significance as a means of visual expression that could reflect the experience of modernity and the shift towards a mass-produced visual culture was unquestioned. Distinctions were necessarily drawn between the outmoded practices of pre-revolutionary melodrama, which were unceremoniously rejected, and the possibilities of a new cinema, which could reflect the revolutionary transformations of Soviet society.

For Gan, cinema was a technological phenomenon rooted in industrial culture; as such, it deserved to be regarded as a quintessentially proletarian art form.[68] Other contributors to *Kino-fot* placed emphasis on cinema as the harbinger of a new, mechanized era. According to the Imaginist poet Ippolit Sokolov, the 'synthetic language of cinema [is] the new international and visual Esperanto of the future'.[69] For Kuleshov, theatre, painting, literature and poetry represented a 'cul-de-sac' from which only cinema guaranteed a meaningful exit; for this reason, he urged that 'the expertise of learned men, the enthusiasm and energy of artists ... be directed towards the cinema'.[70] Similar appeals were made in relation to photography, a medium of expression with which cinema was regarded as naturally allied. In the second issue of *Kino-fot*, for example, the director of the Cinema-Technical Section of the GTK, Professor Nikolai Tikhonov, appealed for recognition of photography's agitational and educational potential, and stressed its 'inseparable' kinship with cinema.[71] Four years later, moreover, Brik urged all workers in the film industry to acquaint themselves with the latest developments in photographic science, announcing at the same time the inauguration of a 'Film and Photo' rubric in *Sovetskoe kino* that would display frame stills from contemporary releases side by side with works of still photography.[72] Issued in the name of the editorial board, this manifesto was followed by the publication of works by Rodchenko, Zhemchuzhnyi (a theatre director who would subsequently move into documentary), Kaufman and several photographers based in Germany.[73] Further testimony to the intimate relationship between the two media is suggested by the fact that Grigorii Boltianskii, a documentary filmmaker and enthusiastic promoter of amateur filmmaking clubs, introduced the catalogue to the exhibition of Soviet photographs organized in 1928 to mark the tenth anniversary of the October Revolution.[74]

Within this broad alignment of interests, however, there emerged differences of emphasis in relation to the compositional mechanisms that these revolutionary art forms should adopt. The relative balance required between the desire for aesthetic experimentation and the necessity of communicating social and ideological content was one area of dispute, certainly within the field of still photography.[75] Elsewhere, interventions were made that stressed the specificities of the individual media concerned. In an otherwise welcoming response to Brik's initiative, Kaufman nevertheless drew attention to the crucial differences between the procedures of cinematography and photography. 'In the making of the photographic still', he declared, 'we are dealing with a particular, detached subject

– the photograph is a ready-made, completed thing, whereas the separate fragment of a film reel, as a thing in itself, has no existence.'[76] Kaufman's objection conformed to a wide-ranging insistence among Soviet filmmakers on the specificity of filmic material, one that had largely been shaped by the 'discovery' of montage. The more celebrated interventions in this regard were Kuleshov's experiments with image juxtaposition, creating what became known subsequently as the 'Kuleshov effect';[77] Eizenshtein's early essays on montage;[78] and Pudovkin's article on Louis Delluc's concept of *photogénie* (photogenicity).[79] These interventions stressed the semiotic relationships between image sequences – their juxtapositions, collisions and poetic and intellectual associations – rather than the intrinsic poetry of the individual film frame or fragment.

As Eizenshtein later observed, the concept of montage was very much part of the *Zeitgeist* during the 1920s and informed much of the debate about cinema.[80] It was not, however, the only theoretical framework within which the visual language of film and its specificities was approached. Parallel channels of enquiry emerged in the form of contributions which, albeit emanating from abroad, nevertheless sparked important and energetic debates. Delluc's essay on *photogénie*, for example, published in France in 1920 and translated into Russian in 1924, acted as a catalyst for several thoughtful considerations on the relationship between filmic form and visual aesthetics.[81] Pudovkin's response, while ostensibly presenting itself as a form of polemic, nevertheless inadvertently echoed many of the Frenchman's prejudices, in particular his preference for streamlined, geometric forms and the textures of the modern, industrial world.[82] This 'democratization' of the photogenic was welcomed by other commentators.[83] A more substantial critique was offered by Mur, a now largely forgotten director and critic, but nevertheless a knowledgeable observer of the mechanics of filmmaking, who took issue with Pudovkin and the 'extreme urbanism' of his aesthetic preferences.[84] In the process, he erected an entire theoretical edifice, according to which, by virtue of the chemical composition (silver bromide) of film stock, and the action of both natural and artificial light upon it, cinema involved a profound deformation or distortion of material reality as perceived by the human eye:

Photogénie *is the silver bromide's reception of the objects of the exterior world; it is the aesthetics of emulsion, its conception of beauty.* Photogénie *is the science of the peculiarities of the sensitivity of the film stock to different combinations of light rays.*[85]

For Mur, the world could not be divided into photogenic or non-photogenic objects because there was no such simple division: the aesthetic value of any object depended on how it was photographed and the choices made by the camera operator in terms of composition and lighting. Furthermore, Mur's quoting of Tisse to this effect in his 1929 article (they had collaborated together on *Teplaia kompaniia (Zhizn' besprizornykh)* (A Cosy Crowd (The Lives of Street Children, 1924)) suggests that this position may have been shared by camera operators.[86] In a second and no less important intervention, Mur identified the action of artificial light in the studio as the main distorting mechanism of cinema, and examined lighting techniques in relation to portraiture, the evolution of which he attributed solely to the camera operator. For him, 'the camera operator is an artist whose brush consists of the shaft of light rays produced by the projector. The palette of the camera operator is the several thousand amperes of light which can create in various gradations all the nuances of the spectrum.'[87]

As suggested by his later mini-biographies of practising cameramen, Mur was one of the few directors of the 1920s who understood the art of cinematography. His various articles and books published during the decade, which bear the traces of his first-hand experience of working in the U.S.A., from which he had returned only a few years earlier, offer some of the most reliable and informed disquisitions on the importance of camerawork, in particular in the sphere of lighting technique. In his most extensive treatment of this subject, he called for a form of 'lighting montage'.[88] Furthermore, he may also have been the inventor of the term *chut'-chut'*, which he employed in the context of slight adjustment of the camera: in his view, this could radically change the composition of the frame, and was where the great artistry of the camera operator resided.[89]

Increasingly, the creative importance of the camera operator was also beginning to be recognized abroad. As part of an address to the A.S.C., for example, having analysed the camerawork of Karl Freund on F. W. Murnau's *Der letzte Mann* (The Last Laugh, 1924), the future avant-garde director and film teacher Slavko Vorkapich announced that: 'The future belongs to this new type of artist: *the creative cinematographer*' (emphasis in the original).[90] In Germany, moreover, where this film had been released, a similar kind of momentum was building. In *Der sichtbare Mensch* (The Visible Man, 1924), the director and critic Béla Balázs offered a wide-ranging discussion of the different facets of contemporary cinema, among them the language of mime and gesture, the function of the close-up, different (national) visual styles, the role of landscape and the rhythmic function of montage.[91] Not only did Balázs argue that cinema was an independent art form, he also proposed that, thanks to the invention of the close-up (he asserted that the 'poetry of film lies in the close-up'), cinema was engaged in an act of estrangement that approximated to the procedures of Expressionist art.[92] Objects were wrapped in the veil of our everyday distractions, he suggested, and it was the artist's function to tear away that veil and render objects palpable in the same way a child perceives their essence; this was described in terms of revealing 'the hidden physiognomy of things'.[93] Furthermore, drawing upon the transcultural term for cinema – *lichtspeil* (light-play) in German is analogous to the Russian *svetotvorchestvo* – Balázs defined cinema as the 'play of light and shade'. In his view, these two elements were its core matter, just as colour was the basic material of painting and sound the essence of music. As he argued, what cannot be expressed by photographic means cannot be represented in film.[94]

Balázs's statement in *Der sichtbare Mensch* that 'the camera operator must be a conscious artist' would have far-reaching consequences in the Soviet Union.[95] His subsequent writings would confirm his belief in the centrality of photography and the importance of the camera operator's creative role. This is illustrated by his consideration of issues pertaining to film style in an essay specially commissioned for *Kino-zhurnal A.R.K.*, in which he argued that style was determined solely by photographic means;[96] and his lecture to the German Cameramen's Club, entitled 'Cinema Tradition and the Future of Film', in which he argued that the status of cinema as an art form depended on the creative input of the camera operator:

> A film becomes a work of art only when the photography, having ceased to function as mere reproduction, itself becomes the creative object ... when the camera operator, who is the de facto maker of the film, becomes its creator, the poet of its composition, a genuine film painter, for whom the acting and staging are simply a 'pretext' to which he responds, as a painter does towards a landscape ... As long as the operator is accorded secondary importance, then cinema will itself be regarded as inferior to the rest of the arts.[97]

Balázs's key argument, prompted by his viewing of the recently released *Bronenosets Potemkin*, lay in his insistence on the intrinsic poetry of the individual sequence irrespective of the montage edifice. As an example, he cited the sequence in *Bronenosets Potemkin* that shows the growing excitement of the inhabitants of Odessa on hearing of the mutiny, this leading in turn to the 'ecstatic hymn' created by scores of yachts as they speed with billowing sails to supply food to the sailors:

> In this light, winged flight of hundreds of billowing sails is revealed a picture of collective excitement, joy, love and hope that could not possibly be expressed by the face of even the greatest of actors. These shots, and these shots alone (rather than the idea contained within the plot), are filled to the brim with the most powerful lyricism, one of such strength, visuality and poetry that even poetry itself cannot compare.[98]

In answer to the rhetorical question that he himself posed at the end of his lecture (whether these images were the product of directorial intent or the independent intervention of the camera operator), he responded that it did not matter: either way, such cinematic art was possible only 'via the lens' and achieved only as a result of the process of shooting.[99]

Balázs's lecture did not go unchallenged in the Soviet Union. Within two weeks, and publishing in the very same gazette in which the Russian translation had appeared, no less an authority than Eizenshtein himself took violent issue with it, to the point where, rather maliciously, he wondered whether the audience to which the remarks had been addressed had not influenced their content (such was his irritation, it would appear, that his two articles devoted to the lecture both misspelt Balázs's name in Russian).[100] Rehearsing the arguments he had advanced in his earlier, but as yet unpublished, essay on the montage of film attractions, Eizenshtein argued that the Hungarian theoretician had 'forgotten the scissors': the essence of cinema, he insisted, lay not in the individual frames themselves, but in the relationships between them.[101] The 'individualized frame', in his view, was an antiquated concept that was rejected in Soviet filmmaking practice because it reflected a bourgeois tendency to identify the creative act with a single person, rather than through a process of collective decision-making. The collaborative approach in the Soviet Union – he playfully resorted to the pun *ko-operator* (co-operator) to emphasize his point – made a nonsense of Balázs's claim that, as paraphrased by him, but not entirely accurately, 'the alpha and omega of filmmaking is the operator'.[102] In his view, the current focus on the cameraman was a 'fad': yesterday it was the actor; tomorrow it would be the lighting technician.

The dismissive and slightly sarcastic nature of this response suggests that Balázs's lecture had touched a raw nerve for Eizenshtein. It was well known within the profession that he was sensitive to claims that the visual inventiveness of *Stachka* (Strike, 1924) was largely the result of Tisse's creative ingenuity.[103] It comes as little surprise therefore to learn that the theoretical gauntlet imperiously thrown down by Eizenshtein was promptly accepted by Boltianskii, a known admirer and professional associate of Tisse, who had worked with him on the documentary entitled *Kreml' v proshlom i v nastoiashchem* (The Kremlin – Past and Present, 1925).[104] In *Kul'tura kino-operatora* (The Culture of the Camera Operator), a pamphlet dedicated to Tisse's career up to the moment of writing, and thus the first essay dedicated to the work of a camera operator in the history of cinema, Boltianskii sought directly to challenge Eizenshtein's concept of montage. His main argument was that montage, understood as a 'definitive coupling and assembling into a unified whole', was present in various art forms, both visual and non-visual, and for this reason could not be defined as the sole, identifying feature of cinema.[105] Furthermore, he identified several different stages of assembly in the filmmaking process: the first, during which the director draws up a scenario on the basis of his ideas; the shooting stage, during which the sequences are shot in such a way that their dynamism and expressivity permit a creative, and not merely mechanical, assemblage of the whole; and the third stage, in which the photographed material is assembled on the basis of the first two stages. According to Boltianskii, Eizenshtein was referring in his article to this third stage only. The question remained, however, whether fragments of film could be adequately assembled if the second stage, which he defined as 'shooting montage' (*s'emochnyi montazh*), had not been carried out effectively.[106] By placing emphasis on the first and second stages of film production, in other words, those that required the active participation of the camera operator, Boltianskii was essentially redesignating the zones of creative initiative. He argued not only that it is the camera operator who 'gives life to the frame [and creates] the living fabric of the picture', and that therefore he must be involved at all stages of the production process, but also that the '"directorial" bent' of the camera operator is 'inevitable and important', and that he should be considered to all intents and purposes 'co-director' of any given film.[107] In passing, and in an obvious allusion to Eizenshtein's initial experiences with Tisse, Boltianskii noted the frequency with which camera operators teach 'inexperienced' directors how to do their jobs.[108]

Boltianskii's pamphlet is significant not because it constitutes an effective demolition of Eizenshtein's argument, but because it offers crucial evidence of the movement towards recognition of the camera operator as equal partner. A further contribution to this debate was witnessed shortly afterwards when the Formalist theoretician Boris Eikhenbaum invited Moskvin and Mikhailov to contribute a chapter to his planned volume on the poetics of cinema. Significantly, both men were acquainted with *Der sichtbare Mensch*. According to Gordanov, the pamphlet made an enormous impression on the younger generation of cameramen in Leningrad.[109] Moskvin's copy, which has been preserved, reveals that he underlined several words and phrases, including the all-important sentence about the cameraman needing to be 'a conscious artist'.[110] Furthermore, before writing his essay, he also accessed the Russian translation of Balázs's lecture to the German Cameramen's Club and marked certain passages.[111]

Proposing that filmmaking is ideally a collective activity between people who 'share the same tastes and interests', Moskvin and Mikhailov nevertheless placed particular responsibility on the director, camera operator and production artist for the creation of a film from the artistic point of view.[112] For these authors, the camera operator was the main person to give expressive shape to the dramatic ideas contained in what they called the director's scenario or 'shooting plan' (*montazhnyi list*). In their view, echoing Boltianskii, montage was 'the almost purely mechanical process of combining the separate pieces of material which have been shot strictly according to the shooting plan'.[113] They refer to the importance of establishing a lighting and shooting scenario alongside the director's scenario (this would later become known as the 'operator's scenario'); to a detailed knowledge of the montage construction of the film as a whole; and to the involvement in the preparatory work of other members of the team, including close collaboration with the production artist over the construction, furnishing and design of the interior décor.[114] For stylistic harmony to be achieved, they argue, the director must understand the creative importance of the camera operator; in the case of the latter, it was important to accept that the technical and artistic resources at his disposal should not be exploited as ends in themselves (what they term 'technique for technique's sake').[115] On the contrary, such resources should be '[blended] organically with other elements of the picture, in tempo, atmosphere and tone, in order maximally to engross the viewer in the action'.[116] In an explicit echo of Balázs's position, they refer to 'the application of those technical devices which help him [the cameraman] more clearly reveal and show the viewer the *inner significance of things* [my emphasis], which is partly hidden in everyday life, and their hidden features – the art of "seeing" a thing and of reproducing the shooting material in a unique form'.[117] In a further, direct echo of Balázs, they state that 'light and shade … are the main and indeed sole expressive material of cinematography'.[118] For this reason, the creative power of light makes it the cameraman's 'basic and most powerful weapon and tool'.[119]

This essay was by no means the final contribution to the debate on the creative position of the camera operator in the 1920s and early 1930s. A manifesto written by Mikhail Kalatozov, issued in the name of the cinema section of the Georgian branch of LEF, emphasizes the role of lighting and compositional dynamic in the structuring of the visual image.[120] Iurii Zheliabuzhskii's *Iskusstvo operatora* (The Art of the Operator), published four years later, combined a strident polemic with the view that the camera mechanically records reality with a detailed discussion of the impact of technology on filmmaking and the poetics of composition.[121] Finally, as the silent era drew to a close, Vladimir Nil'sen, a camera operator who had worked alongside Tisse on *Oktiabr'* (October, 1927) and shot a number of comedies with the director Grigorii Aleksandrov during the 1930s, produced a monograph on the theory of representation in cinema which was envisaged as a textbook for the camera operators' faculty at VGIK.[122] Both Zheliabuzhskii and Nil'sen state as a given that the camera operator is one of the most important members of the film-production team, and that this role is essentially a creative one.

The Camera Operator's *'Mode d'emploi'* and his Trademark 'Signature'

In view of the general emphasis on collective enterprise, it might seem redundant to seek evidence of the camera operator's trademark 'signature'. For many camera operators, nevertheless, it is axiomatic that different individuals bring different aesthetic preferences and ways of perceiving the world to their work. In an article published in the same year as the Eikhenbaum volume, for example, Moskvin stated his view that:

> It is my serious conviction that each frame should carry within itself elements of the entire film, of each scene and of each episode. Ideally, each individual frame should, on the one hand, hint at the whole, and yet simultaneously be as characteristic as the signed painting of a great master.[123]

One way of understanding this paradoxical remark is to underline the fact that, although the camera operator was in theory working within a collective according to an agreed set of principles, in practice he had a degree of independent initiative. For example, it was not uncommon for directors to be absent during shooting, leaving overall responsibility to their assistants; this was the result of time pressures or other factors, but reflected an implicit trust in the camera operator's ability to fulfil the necessary task without overt supervision. In the case of *Oktiabr'*, the massive scale of the project and tight shooting schedule required the necessary footage to be shot by two units working in parallel, Aleksandrov directing alongside Tisse, and Eizenshtein working with Nil'sen.[124] Some of the material was shot while Eizenshtein was cutting the film; moreover, the lighting arrangements for one of its most famous scenes, the arrival of Lenin at Finland Station, were devised entirely on Tisse's initiative. This was not an isolated incident in the history of the Soviet avant-garde. Pudovkin regularly left Doller and the relevant camera operator to shoot sequences on their own. One of the most celebrated sequences in his silent films – the experimental 'Birth of Life' sequence in *Prostoi sluchai* (A Simple Case, 1932), a film designed to illustrate in visual terms his theory of 'time close up' (*vremia krupnym planom*) – was shot by Grigorii Kabalov with only nominal assistance from Doller; according to Leyda, the success of these images persuaded Pudovkin to alter the screenplay so that they could be included.[125] On Kabalov's own admission, the rhythms of the projected musical accompaniment were playing in his mind when he photographed the footage, but no specific instructions had been issued in relation to the kind of footage required.[126]

Even when present at the point of filming, the directors of the avant-garde were nevertheless receptive to creative initiative. Some of the most famous sequences of the 1920s and early 1930s were the result of the cameraman's direct intervention. The use of a monocle lens to produce the soft-focus images in Dovzhenko's *Zemlia* (Earth, 1930), for example, was the result of Demuts'kyi's direct intervention.[127] By the same token, the use of smoke on the set for the cabaret sequences at the beginning of *Novyi Vavilon* (The New Babylon, 1929), a technique for emphasizing aerial perspective which later became standard Soviet filmmaking practice, was Moskvin's solution to the problem of creating the right atmosphere for the images of decadent Paris during the Second Empire.[128] There was also the possibility of a last-minute intervention, the slight but all-important adjustment after the director had checked a particular scene through the viewfinder and given the instruction to shoot. The poetic impact of the Dnieper sequence at the beginning of Dovzhenko's *Ivan*, for instance, was immeasurably enhanced by Demuts'kyi's last-minute switch of lenses from conventional to wide-angle.[129] The routine nature of this procedure on the part of camera operators is echoed by the newspaper correspondent Mikhail Rozenfel'd, who described Tisse's habit of calling out the numbers of his lenses to his assistants on the set of *Bezhin lug*, apparently without Eizenshtein's knowledge and acquiescence; and by Leyda, who has commented that 'th[e] exquisite choice of lenses is one of Tisse's contributions to the Eisenstein-Tisse partnership'.[130]

The idea of these 'slight adjustments' is a surprisingly persistent theme in the writings of directors about their cameramen. Eizenshtein's comment in relation to Tisse, cited earlier in this chapter, is echoed almost exactly by Kozintsev in relation to Moskvin:

> *The camera operator Moskvin is valuable to me because when I, either in collaboration with him, or on my own, compose the image-frame, Moskvin comes along, [he] takes a good look through the viewfinder, we have a further discussion about it, we alter the angle of view, and when the frame is finally fixed and I give the signal to start shooting, Moskvin suddenly shifts the camera by about one-eighth of a turn of the tripod handle to the right or left, up or down, and in doing so produces precisely what the composition lacked. This purely photographic adjustment gives the composition a finished expressivity that I myself was incapable of producing.*[131]

The seeming generosity of this remark does not conceal its inadequacy as an example of the cameraman's specific contribution, however. On the contrary, it is a woefully incomplete summary of a complex process that involves lighting preparations (an area more or less completely neglected by directors in their writings about their works), choices of lenses for creating the right degrees of tension and the adoption of colour filters for the right balance or distribution of tonalities. As a rule, in fact, cameramen during the 1920s resented the interference of directors in relation to the composition of the frame. Tisse, for example, was content to discuss the positioning of the camera with Aleksandrov when they were left by Eizenshtein to shoot the last remaining scenes for *Bronenosets Potemkin*, but he refused to allow him to frame the image.[132] A different scenario existed in the working relationship between Pudovkin and Golovnia, according to which the former, despite being familiar with the technicalities of cinematography, apparently took little interest in the placing of the camera or the lighting arrangements.[133]

Something of the (perhaps inevitable) rivalry between director and camera operator, the former often claiming the credit for the achievements of the latter, can be gauged by Golovnia's celebrated party joke, legendary among Soviet camera operators, and one that may have been prompted by the very circumstances that gave rise to the shooting of the Odessa mist episode:

> The camera is shooting. It is morning. The director, seeing how his camera operator has filmed a particular episode, exclaims with enthusiasm: 'Eddie, you're a genius!'
>
> At lunch, the director tells a group of people gathered around the table that he and Eddie have filmed a tremendous scene.
>
> In the evening, in the company of a small circle of admirers (both male and female), our director wearily lets drop that 'This morning, it would appear, I succeeded in producing something exceptional'.[134]

Even within an avowedly collective and democratic unit, the directorial ego could be easily wounded. Evidence for this can be found in Eizenshtein's irritated response to suggestions at meetings of the ARK that the success of *Stachka* was due in no small measure to the brilliance of Tisse's camerawork: to repudiate this suggestion, he pointed to the films Tisse had shot recently with other directors – Czesław Sabiński's *Starets Vasilii Griaznov* (The Elder Vasilii Griaznov, 1924) and Aleksandr Granovskii's *Evreiskoe schast'e* (Jewish Luck, 1925) – and pointed to their relative conservatism.[135] Any suggestion that the dramaturgy of these productions, or the lack of experimental drive on the part of the directors themselves, might have hampered Tisse's room for creative manoeuvre was, perhaps unsurprisingly, not countenanced by him. With equal logic, Eizenshtein might have drawn attention to the relatively orthodox camerawork on his own first foray into the medium of cinema, the two fragments that constitute *Dnevnik Glumova* (Glumov's Diary, 1923) and which were photographed by Frantsisson as part of Eizenshtein's eccentric staging of Aleksandr Ostrovskii's *Na vsiakogo mudretsa dovol'no prostoty* (Enough Simplicity for Every Wise Man) for the Proletkul't.

Eizenshtein's remarks in relation to Tisse might be said to tap into a deep-seated anxiety on the part of directors in relation to cameramen. This lies in their relative technical ignorance of the camera, the instrument without which the impulses of their creative imaginations are destined to remain latent, and the resulting impotence that many of them feel. In some senses, the 'split' between director and camera operator, one that took place historically when film narratives began to require professional actors, might be said to possess a semi-mythic dimension. It is essentially a modern reincarnation of the Eden myth, the sense that, at the dawn of cinema, there existed a 'paradise' in which disagreement and disunity were impossible because only one person, in the vast majority of cases a photographer or someone with a strong interest in photography, was responsible for the shooting of the material. In no other visual art form is the division between imaginative striving and technical means of execution present to quite the same extent. The desire to make whole again, to achieve the unity and understanding that has been partially lost, perhaps explains why certain cameramen, no doubt irritated by the restrictions of their role, seek to become directors. Soviet examples from the 1920s are Zheliabuzhskii, who both photographed and directed films during this period, and Kalatozov, who moved into direction in the early 1930s. It may also explain why, conversely, certain directors have decided to try to shoot their films single-handedly; this phenomenon is much rarer historically, but a salient example from the silent period would be Dimitri Kirsanoff, a Russian émigré living in France who both directed and photographed the avant-garde classic *Ménilmontant* in 1925. It also explains the kind of doppelgänger metaphors which, even within mainstream cinema, seek to describe the relationship between these two key protagonists. Thus, for example, Ivan Perestiani describes Aleksandr Digmelov, his cameraman on *Krasnye d'iavoliata* (The Little Red Devils, 1923), as his 'second creative "I"'.[136] Eizenshtein expressed the same sentiment, albeit more poetically, in relation to Tisse:

> *Does one discuss and fall into disagreement with the proof of one's own eye? No, one looks and sees.*
> *Does one tell one's own heart to 'beat with such and such a rhythm'? No, it beats of its own accord.*
> *Does one discuss the diapason of one's breathing with one's own lungs when one experiences agitation?*[137]

In view of the imbalance in technical expertise, at least at the initial stages of a career, it is unsurprising to learn how frequently the camera operator is mentioned as the first 'teacher' of the director. Late in life, for example, having cited the ancient proverb that 'Your father is not the person who gave birth to you, but the person who taught you Latin and Greek', Kuleshov declared himself a 'pupil' of Levitskii.[138] In the same way, the memoirs of Aleksandrov, who worked with Eizenshtein throughout the 1920s as one of his 'Mighty Five' assistants, explain that Tisse was 'Eizenshtein's first authentic teacher', someone whom the group as a whole regarded as an 'old, experienced professor' and whose influence even extended to choice of attire.[139] He might have added that Tisse possessed a dynamism and sense of purpose that Eizenshtein on occasion lacked. Maksim Shtraukh, another of the 'Mighty Five' assistants, noted that, prior to Tisse's arrival in Odessa, the director of *Bronenosets Potemkin* was disorientated by the task ahead of his unit and incapable of effective decision making:

> *I never suspected how much support Eizenshtein needs when at work. I've only recently become aware that he loses himself like a child. When at work, and when a decision needs to be taken in relation to that work, it's as if a few screws start to come loose, and trying to do something counter to what he wants, or persuading him, isn't worth the candle. He takes on this childish expression, tries to find support among those around him, and asks the same thing about twenty times over.... And if you don't encourage him, he falls into a great depression.*[140]

Tisse's late arrival galvanized the group into action; indeed, Shtraukh's letters to his wife are emphatic that without him the production would certainly have foundered. As he writes: 'Only now do we understand the meaning of the word camera operator: it means a great, great deal!'; and elsewhere: 'If it was not for Tisse, we would have had a disaster on our hands – that's a fact!'.[141]

The desire to restore lost harmony possibly explains why, as creative individuals, camera operators tend to gravitate towards directors who share their vision of the world. This vision is an integral part of their personality and often transcends the relationship with the director concerned. Furthermore, its idiosyncrasy is best illustrated at moments of crisis when the camera operator in question is forced to work with a director (or vice versa) whose approach is fundamentally different from his own. Soviet (and Western) cinema is littered with examples of this kind of tension, but two examples from the 1920s prove instructive. Eizenshtein's acrimonious conflict with Levitskii while working on *1905 god* (The Year 1905), the ambitious project that would later develop into *Bronenosets Potemkin*, was essentially an artistic one. Furthermore, their rancorous 'split' and Levitskii's formal removal from the project was regarded as a sufficiently ominous precedent that it provoked a boycott on the part of the camera operators employed at the First Factory of Goskino, one of the first instances of its kind in the history of cinema. As Eizenshtein later explained:

> The experience with Levitskii showed me that the 'modernity' of the living half of the camera lens [is a quality] of enormous importance.
>   It is difficult to make a revolutionary and contemporary thing when the operator in question has a philistine hostility towards and non-acceptance of cranes, wharves and steam trains; and when his ideal lies in cardboard cut-out Catholic churches.[142]

Dovzhenko's struggle with Boris Zavelev over the experimental sequences in *Zvenyhora* constituted a similar kind of battleground. Although Zavelev was open to progressive ideas (his career alongside Evgenii Bauer and Petr Chardynin at the Khanzhonkov studio before 1917 suggests this), he was apparently exasperated by the radicalism of certain directorial suggestions. As he complained to the head of the studio:

> Dovzhenko is undoubtedly an interesting person, but he has worked in cinema for only a short period of time. He doesn't understand the composition of the frame and montage. I want to teach him, but he is stubborn. And I am forced to do everything he wants.[143]

The stylistic eclecticism of *Zvenyhora* suggests that the tension between these two figures was not entirely resolved. In relation to one of the sequences, which shows a semi-mythical episode from the Varangian invasion and occupation of Kyivan Rus', it would appear that Zavelev's resistance must partly have borne fruit. According to Pavlo Nechesa, the VUFKU studio director, the camera operator initially refused Dovzhenko's request to shoot this section entirely out of focus for fear that it would 'discredit' him throughout the Soviet Union.[144] As is apparent in the finished version, however, a compromise was reached: the theatrical set, which provides the context for the action, is shot out of focus, but most of the action, if the occasional resort to multiple exposure is excluded, is relatively sharp and clear.[145]

The existence of these tensions between cinematographers and directors tends to support Dolinin's view that each camera operator has his own *'mode d'emploi'*, by which he meant not only a specific technical specialization, but also a set of aesthetic preferences and interests for which he had already established a reputation.[146] While in theory the professional camera operator should be perfectly adaptable, capable of working with whomsoever the studio assigns, in practice his aesthetic flexibility and preferred method of working are more strictly limited. Golovnia, for example, refused to work with Pudovkin on *Prostoi sluchai* because he was unhappy with Aleksandr Rzheshevskii's 'emotional' screenplay: he preferred the certainties of an 'iron script', the cinematic adaptation of which had been agreed in advance by the film unit collectively, to the principle of improvisation, which seemed to be encouraged by what was universally recognized as a highly poetic but vague script.[147]

The *mode d'emploi* of the camera operator could also result in his being offered specific commissions outside his permanent unit. Golovnia, for example, worked with two directors in the late 1920s who were not closely aligned with the avant-garde: Iakov Protazanov, with whom he photographed *Chelovek iz restorana* (The Man from the Restaurant, 1927); and Fedor Otsep, with whom he collaborated on *Zhivoi trup* (The Living Corpse, 1929), a screen adaptation of Lev Tolstoi's play which was jointly produced by Mezhrabpomfil'm and Prometeusfilm in Germany. Both films bear the imprint of Golovnia's idiosyncratic style; this can be demonstrated by comparing them with earlier films made by these directors with other cameramen. Furthermore, it is possible that this characteristic style was deliberately solicited. In the case of Protazanov, someone whose political position had become uncertain after his box-office blockbusters of the mid-1920s had been excoriated by the progressive intelligentsia, Golovnia's presence behind the camera assured a more cutting visual edge to a film with strongly political content. Golovnia later admitted that he had deliberately and naively incorporated some of his customary devices, in particular unconventional angles of shooting and low-level lighting for portraiture.[148] In the case of *Zhivoi trup*, Golovnia's approach supplied dynamism and expressive force to a project that could easily have fallen into the trap of excessive theatricality. It is possible that his expertise with the hand-held camera facilitated one of the most innovative sequences in the film, if not in Soviet silent cinema as a whole – the gypsy choir sequence – in which rapid montage is combined with hand-held shooting to exhilarating effect. Prior to this moment, Otsep had not been renowned for his experimental leanings. It is therefore legitimate to speculate on the degree to which this director might have wanted to carve a more radical reputation for himself by engaging a camera operator whose avant-garde credentials at this time were impeccable and universally lauded, both at home and abroad.

A further example of the way in which a cameraman's *mode d'emploi* could result in his engagement on a specific project is the production of *Ivan Groznyi*. Eizenshtein's invitation to Moskvin to shoot the interior sequences of this film was regarded as something of a scandal at the time because there was an accepted etiquette among camera operators as far as this kind of situation was concerned; it was certainly a source of rancour for Tisse, who had not apparently been told in advance that this was going to happen, although his loyalty was such that he never voiced his complaint publicly.[149] This extremely delicate situation resulted in the fact that both cinematographers were later credited, Moskvin with the vast majority of the interior sequences, and Tisse the exterior sequences. The 'split' with Tisse was apparently traumatic for Eizenshtein, and caused a bout of ill health, but the crisis arose from his recognition that his first-choice cameraman might not be able to deliver the psychological nuance that he required. As he wrote after completion of the film, Moskvin's great expertise lay in 'the subtlest tonal nuance, what I would call "lighting intonation"'.[150] It may also have been the case that, in his search for a more operatic style, one that would recall the achievements of German Expressionist film in the early 1920s, Eizenshtein sought inspiration from Moskvin precisely because of his work many years earlier on *Shinel'* (The Overcoat, 1926) and *SVD*, both of which were regarded at the time as having Expressionist leanings. In this respect, *Ivan Groznyi* becomes a fascinating experimental laboratory, a litmus test of the degree to which camera operators can assert their individuality within the straightjacket of a project, the author of which had established a worldwide reputation for consistency of vision. Despite the meticulous nature of Eizenshtein's preparations for the film, which involved a multiplicity of detailed sketches that were expected to form the basis of the finished shot, it is impossible to confuse Tisse's dramatic exterior photography with Moskvin's delicate interior portraiture. The differences are striking and only partly explained by the fact that the two men were working with different kinds of light, Moskvin accompanied by his customary battery of incandescent lamps (he was famous for his dislike of exterior work) and Tisse forced to struggle with the harsh and unyielding sunlight of the desert terrain outside Alma-Ata (now Almaty) in Kazakhstan (he was known as 'the photographer of sunlight').[151] The dislocation between these competing styles, their inevitable tension, must surely bring into question the generally accepted view of the director as unifying auteur.

The relationship between Eizenshtein's sketches and their manifestation on screen demonstrates the ways in which Moskvin translated, interpreted, steered and in some cases shifted the emphasis of the directorial design, while at the same time remaining loyal to the dramaturgy and symbolic architecture of the film as a whole. It also bears witness to the fact that, even in the case of a director who was extremely knowledgeable about the visual arts and a practising artist himself, the cameraman still had a crucial role to play in the realization of his ideas.

Further evidence for this argument can be found in *Que Viva Mexico!*, the grandiose project based on Eizenshtein's stay in Mexico between December 1930 and February 1932, and one that he was forced to abandon when his financial backer, the American writer Upton Sinclair, withdrew to avoid incurring further losses. The footage that has survived – some seventy-five thousand metres in total, now held in the Russian State Film Archive (Gosfil'mofond) and the Museum of the Moving Image in New York – is fascinating for the light it sheds on Tisse's particular way of seeing. Like *Ivan Groznyi*, it is an experimental laboratory that allows an exploration of Eizenshtein's visual response to Mexico, which took the form initially of sketches in pencil, and the representation of that same raw material through the lens of what Eizenshtein called Tisse's 'incomparable camera'.[152] In the case of *Que Viva Mexico!*, it is fortunate that the camera negative preserved in the archive is so complete. It contains all the footage shot during the expedition, and thus many of the sequences that would in the normal course of events be consigned to the cutting-room floor: a whole series of preliminary 'études' or sketches of primary and secondary characters, some of which may have been taken purely for casting purposes, and all the different takes in relation to the same scene, object or action. Those who have studied the materials in their entirety testify to the supreme value of these repeated takes insofar as they offer evidence of the 'slight adjustments' that Tisse brought to bear on the filmic material. Leyda, who was responsible for cataloguing the footage after it was initially deposited in New York, and endeavoured to reconstitute the order of shooting on the basis of the edge numbers along the sides of the film stock, has borne eloquent testimony to this process:

> Brought back to the order of shooting, it was possible to study the development of certain ideas in the very process of taking form, including the trials, the mistakes, even an occasional tomfoolery. Quite unexpectedly, there emerged from this experiment in reconstitution a cinematic equivalent of all the notes

and sketchbooks that a painter accumulates in his preparation of a large work
…. In these reconstituted rushes, we could see Tisse, especially in the ritual burial
of the prologue, trying his whole gamut of lens qualities in search of just those
degrees of tension that would gather imperceptibly though the final editing of
the passage. With the composition being materially altered, you can watch
from behind the camera as Tisse decides to increase the optical relation between
the head and feet of the 'corpse'. Or, even in developing a close-up of a head
(apparently limited by ordinary standards), Tisse, from take to take, gradually
changes what we see from the naturalistic head to a monumental and screen-
expanding piece of sculpture.[153]

The Russian film historian and director Oleg Kovalov, who produced his own version of the film on the basis of this unassembled footage, has also testified to the way in which, after the first take, Tisse would invariably undertake minute compositional adjustments in order to achieve the desired effect, with the 'shadow areas lying where they should and the objects within the frame organized more precisely'.[154] The existence of this material in an unfinished state, in other words, in the formal absence of montage, raises again the question of the degree of autonomy which the individual frame sequence enjoys in relation to the whole. Close study of the material that has been commercially released hitherto suggests that, while such sequences undoubtedly offer evidence for the presence of an overall poetic design, their expressive force lies as much outside that design as within; in other words, that their poetry is intrinsic, rather than extrinsic.

Comparison of Eizenshtein's drawings with the footage of *Que Viva Mexico!* demonstrates not kinship but rather the gulf that separates spontaneous artistic impulse from considered photographic realization. There are a variety of reasons for this, some of them inevitable in the sense that they reflect two different means of visual expression, others the product of Eizenshtein's particular *modus operandi*. In relation to the latter, it is notable that his sketches are essentially linear explorations concerned exclusively with shape and contour: they are flat in terms of perspective, evince no interest in the play of light and shade, and contain nothing in the way of texture or tonal relationship. As several commentators have suggested, they are expressions of pictorial ideas or symbols that Eizenshtein composed 'spontaneously' and 'very quickly so as not to disturb the subconscious elements'.[155] The sketches are important in the sense that they illustrate the 'variety of contradictions' which the director later identified as the symbolic keystone of his

Mexican vision. Nevertheless, it would not be accurate to describe them, as some have done, as 'visual notes' that inform the individual film sequences.[156] In some senses, the sketches and the footage are independent creative initiatives. The austerity of line that characterizes the former – Eizenshtein subsequently referred to his 'pure "mathematical" line', his tendency towards abstraction and the influence of native art traditions[157] – is in flagrant contrast to the tonal richness and sensuous textures of the filmic material. In particular, it might be noted that, while geometric construction certainly does inform some of Tisse's compositions, it is the presence of the frame (something completely absent in the sketches) and the unusual vantage point of the camera, combined with Tisse's frequent recourse to wide-angle lenses, which bring these lines into tension with one another and supply the necessary compositional complexity and dynamism. From this one should not conclude that Eizenshtein's visual contribution to the end product was nebulous, but rather that it is a dubious procedure on the basis of a given director's artistic sensitivities and drawings to conclude that he, and he alone, is responsible for a series of images imprinted on celluloid.

The Soviet Camera Operator and Technology

The gorgeousness of the footage intended for *Que Viva Mexico!* lies in stark contrast to the grotesque and in some cases savagely erotic and pornographic quality of some of Eizenshtein's 'secret drawings' while staying in Mexico. In many ways, the footage echoes the 'silvery tonalities' of Murnau and Robert J. Flaherty's *Tabu: A Story of the South Seas* (1931), which was underpinned by a similar, quasi-documentary principle. Such footage gives the lie to the notion that the Soviet avant-garde, because of its drive towards verisimilitude, was anti-aesthetic; or that, due to technological illiteracy, the films that emerged from the Soviet Union during this period were technically inferior to Western products.

Something of this myth is inadvertently indicated by the rapturous response to Tisse's camerawork on the part of a reviewer in *American Cinematographer* when sections of the footage were released in 1933, albeit unsatisfactorily (and in Eizenshtein's view, immorally) in the guise of Sol Lesser's *Thunder over Mexico*:

> It is the first time that he [Tisse] has enjoyed the tremendous advantage of
> really good film and laboratory work – and the results that he has achieved

should give him unquestioned rank as one of the great cinematographers of the
world. He had little to work with in "Thunder Over Mexico" – no sets, no interior
scenes, no artificial lighting equipment, none of the many aids to exterior
photography enjoyed by his American confreres; just an old deBrie [sic] camera,
hand-cranked, perforce; a few crude reflectors; some filters; a few hundred
thousand feet of Dupont negative; a first-class American laboratory; and one
of the few living directors who really understands the visual foundation of
cinema. With these ingredients, Tisse has achieved one of the most superbly
beautiful examples of exterior cinematography ever made.[158]

While this reviewer was certainly accurate in his assessment of Soviet laboratory
work – in the very same year Zheliabuzhskii described the properly printed
negative and positive as an exception rather than the rule[159] – the general
assumption on which his review was based is essentially false. The notion of the
talented Soviet cameraman overcoming insuperable odds in his battle with inferior
equipment and conditions is a romanticized varnishing of the truth. In the case of
the Mexican project, it was mistaken on several counts. Tisse took with him an
American Bell & Howell and a French DeVry camera, both of them modern and
sophisticated apparatuses.[160] During his stay in Hollywood, moreover, he also
apparently acquired some Taylor Hobson Cooke lenses, manufactured in the U.K.
and regarded as among the very best quality lenses available at the time.[161] From
the evidence available even before this, it would appear that Tisse possessed
many of the standard accessories of the European camera operator. Mur describes
Tisse arriving on set 'like a banker', with fourteen suitcases of equipment: these
contained forty-five ground-glass lenses of various speeds and focal lengths, as
well as an array of light filters, matte boxes, diffusion filters, disks made from
frosted and opaque glass, silk nets and strips of gauze.[162] It is known that Tisse
travelled abroad on various missions during the 1920s, among them consultations
with optical specialists in Berlin and trips to Paris in order to meet the manufacturers
of his Debrie camera. In a letter to Eizenshtein playfully signed 'Edvard Debrishka',
he referred to a number of improvements, including a method of binocular
inspection through the viewfinder, which he had devised himself and was hoping
to patent.[163] In view of this, it is hardly surprising to learn that Eizenshtein was
forced to rent a second car in order to transport Tisse's equipment while they
were travelling in Mexico; or that the equipment itself was insured for eight
thousand dollars, a significant sum of money at the time.[164]

If the U.S. perception of Tisse was inaccurate, it was also imprecise in relation to avant-garde camera operators generally. The Soviet film press reported regularly on technological developments in Europe and North America during the 1920s. In this sense, although the magazines and newspapers themselves were not aimed specifically at the camera-operating fraternity, unlike the journals of the German Cameramen's Club and the A.S.C., they did nevertheless contain a great deal of information useful to the profession as a whole. In the field of camera technology, for example, there appeared from around 1925 onwards a number of articles with illustrations offering detailed information for both professionals and amateurs on the technical features of recently manufactured cameras and their improvements in relation to existing models. Highlights in this regard include a lengthy article by Guido Seeber, first published in 1924 in the journal *Die Kinotechnik*, in which he surveys many of the models currently on the market, as well as the history of their development;[165] a description of the new Debrie-Parvo 'L' by Tisse;[166] discussions of cameras constructed according to new designs, for example those that featured revolving turrets for the rapid switching of lenses;[167] articles relating to the appearance of lightweight, portable models;[168] reports on cameras equipped with electric motors for hand-held filming;[169] developments in the manufacture of tripods;[170] and the latest projecting equipment for both amateurs and professionals.[171] Information on the latest developments in the sphere of optical science is similarly rich and detailed. This includes: lengthy discussions of recent developments in German optical science;[172] details of new and faster anastigmatic lenses that permitted shooting in low lighting conditions;[173] descriptions of non-anastigmatic lenses (for example monocle lenses), which were not corrected for focus but commercially manufactured to meet the demand for soft-focus cinematography;[174] the appearance of long-distance, so-called 'telephoto' lenses;[175] discussions of the softening effects of optical accessories, for example molar lenses, portrait lenses and diffusion disks;[176] and the effects of certain trick lenses.[177]

As far as lighting is concerned, as well as descriptions of the systems employed in German studios and the lighting arrangements preferred by German and U.S. camera operators, correspondents report on the different types of lighting units commercially available abroad and the advantages and disadvantages of different light sources (mercury-vapour lamps versus carbon-arc lights) and later, during the move to sound, the properties of incandescent tungsten-filament lamps.[178] Reports also appeared on a series of other developments with specific relevance to camera operators: the release of a 'rapid-speed' Agfa film stock in 1926;[179] the introduction of panchromatic film stock;[180] conditions in Soviet film-processing laboratories;[181] the machines and chemicals used for processing film stock;[182] the development of chemical processes for the restoration of old films;[183] the widespread use of colour filters;[184] recent developments in the sphere of special effects and trick cinematography (for example, the Schufftan process);[185] discussions of the technicalities and theoretical implications of dissolve shots;[186] the importance of the relationship between camera operators and both make-up artists and set designers in order to ensure that tonal values were not inadvertently perverted through ignorance of the properties of orthochromatic film stock;[187] discussions of the problem of correct exposure in unusual atmospheric conditions and recent attempts (both Soviet and non-Soviet) to aid camera operators working on exterior locations in different geographical zones by drawing up tables for exposure-meter readings;[188] and reports on foreign exhibitions with relevance to cinema and technology generally.[189]

The wealth of this material suggests that, if nothing else, the Soviet camera operator was certainly well informed about the latest technological developments in Europe and North America. Nevertheless, in view of the exorbitant prices involved (many are given in foreign currency) and the fact that for the most part these were not studio but private purchases, it is difficult to judge the extent to which technical knowledge in theory reflected actual acquisition in practice. Anecdotal evidence suggests that conditions in the immediate aftermath of the Revolution and Civil War were difficult and only began to improve from the mid-1920s onwards. It is well attested that shortages of film stock during the early years after the Revolution were so severe that camera operators were forced to shoot on positive rather than negative film stock.[190] For this same reason, directors like Kuleshov were forced to rehearse their études in the complete absence of the camera, hence his celebrated 'films without film'.[191] The legends associated with such feats of ingenuity were partly to blame for some of the notions that began to gain currency as the decade progressed, most notably Freund's suggestion that montage theory emerged as a direct result of such shortages.[192]

Without a doubt, the situation in relation to film stock reflected a wider malaise in the sphere of production and exhibition generally. The vast majority of 'electric theatres' were in a parlous state at the beginning of the decade. The studios, moreover, having been stripped of their equipment, costumes and props by their pre-revolutionary owners in the run-up to the nationalization decree of 1919, were in a state of near total ruin. Aleksandra Khokhlova, Kuleshov's partner and student at his acting workshops at the GTK, has given a stark description of the conditions that prevailed during the shooting of *Neobychainye prikliucheniia mistera Vesta v strane bol'shevikov* (The Extraordinary Adventures of Mr West in the Land of the Bolsheviks, 1924): there were no stage props, costumes or decorations – the latter had to be built from scratch by the actors – and lighting units were in short supply.[193] The poor quality of available lighting units would appear to have been a universal problem during these years. Mikhailov, who made his debut on Fridrikh Ermler's *Kat'ka bumazhnyi ranet* (Kat'ka's Reinette Apples, 1926), has borne eloquent testimony to the problems of flickering arcs caused by the inconstant supply of electricity and poor-quality carbons.[194] There was also a universal shortage of cameras. It is symptomatic of the general crisis that newsreel specialists were still using Pathé cameras for actuality work (these were extremely cumbersome and unsuited for rapid-response filming) and that Gordanov, who was given a permanent placement at Sevzapkino in 1927, was only granted use of a Debrie-Interview, a first-generation camera that had first appeared on the market in 1908 and was not in good condition.[195] In such circumstances, the private ownership of a camera became something of a status symbol. This perhaps explains the anecdotes about Levitskii's unwillingness to shoot from dangerous heights while working on *1905 god* in case his camera was inadvertently damaged;[196] and Mur's humorous description of the typical camera operator cherishing his camera as if it was the 'apple of his eye', but perfectly prepared to betray his current 'love', and bankrupt himself in the process, in pursuit of the latest (foreign) model.[197] Zheliabuzhskii, who had been put in charge of the restoration of laboratory facilities after the Revolution, was arguing as early as 1922 that more money needed to be invested in this important part of the production process.[198] Judging by accounts published later in the decade, however, conditions were slow to improve. In 1925, Gordanov was appalled at the levels of dirt and dust in the rooms designated for chemical processing at Sevzapkino; he was even more depressed to learn that these were considered relatively advanced by the standards of the day.[199] One year later, dissatisfaction with the prevailing conditions prompted one professional to appeal for urgent action in order to rectify the situation.[200]

Even during this early period, however, the inventiveness and dedication of the artists could circumvent these terrible restrictions. *Neobychainye prikliucheniia*, although made on a shoestring budget, rivalled if not outshone imported products in terms of technical quality; this can be witnessed by the version held in Gosfil'mofond, which is copied from the original Agfa negative. By the mid-1920s, moreover, earnings of foreign currency through export and the importing of foreign films raised sufficient capital to permit the gradual refurbishment of studios and the acquisition of the latest German lighting equipment.[201] The studios of Goskino, Sevzapkino, Sovkino and Mezhrabpom-Rus', the capital for which had been raised by The Workers' International Relief Fund, began to be fitted with Jupiter and Wienart arc lamps in various strengths and sizes, as well as mercury-vapour lamps.[202] A technical study of Soviet lighting equipment, published in 1927 by Evgenii Goldovskii, indicates that the systems that had been installed in these studios by the second half of the decade were as sophisticated as their European counterparts.[203] Although complaints about conditions were frequently voiced during this period, it is indicative of the general improvement that Golovnia could travel to Berlin in 1928 for the making of *Zhivoi trup* and find that conditions in the Prometheus studio differed little from those in Mezhrabpomfil'm.[204] From the mid-1920s onwards, moreover, studios began to supply their camera operators with decent foreign film stock, either Belgian-manufactured Gevaert or Agfa 'Speziale', a German product which, while it might have lacked the sensitivity of later emulsions, was nevertheless respectable. Camera operators also began to gain access to superior camera models, for example the Debrie-Parvo 'L' and 'Super-Parvo', which were the cameras of choice for the modern European professional. As can be gauged from *Chelovek s kinoapparatom*, where it is prominently displayed, the gleaming silver and compact design of the Debrie made it a highly photogenic object in its own right (Kozintsev described it as a 'miracle' compared to the Pathé models and referred to the pleasant whirring sound made by its crank handle).[205] A variety of other cameras became available during this period. The Bell & Howell, which arrived along with Tisse on the set of *Bronenosets Potemkin* and facilitated the filming of the Odessa Steps sequence, was highly prized.[206] From 1924 onwards, lightweight, portable cameras, such as the German Ica-Kinamo and French Debrie-Sept, although only available on a sporadic basis, begin to be used with increasing frequency. Reports suggest that Soviet camera operators also made use of a specially developed metal harness and straps in order to simulate hand-held footage with an ordinary studio camera removed from its tripod. This was an idea that had been pioneered by Freund for the shooting of the dream sequence in *Der letzte Mann*, and the mechanics of which had been published in *Die Filmtechnik*.[207] Production stills from the period show Moskvin and Golovnia using an identical contraption during the making of *Shinel'* and *Konets Sankt-Peterburga* respectively.[208]

As far as other accessories were concerned, their provenance was German, French or American, the availability depending either on the foreign currency earned by the studio or the individual camera operator's ability to travel abroad. At a time when the most important innovations pertained to the sphere of lens optics, it is interesting to discover that many Soviet camera operators possessed some of the latest lenses. References to them can be found in a wide variety of literature during this period. Novitskii, for example, mentions using a long-focus 'telephoto' (*teleob"ektiv*) lens to shoot the May-Day celebrations on Red Square in 1925.[209] Tisse refers to his acquisition of a 28mm (wide-angle) lens and a 'telephoto' lens (500mm and above) for the shooting of *Staroe i novoe* (*"General'naia liniia"*) (The Old and the New ("The General Line"), 1926–29).[210] Kuleshov mentions the appearance of super-fast Plasmat and wide-angled Tachar lenses; both were employed by Tisse for the 'low-key' sequences in *Oktiabr'*, but with varying, if not disappointing, results.[211] Doubtless thanks to NEP, camera operators in Leningrad could buy foreign lenses at the Sevzapkino photographic shop on Vladimirskii Prospekt: Gordanov mentions a 500mm Hypar-Goertz portrait lens and a Voightländer heliostigmatic lens being available towards the end of the 1920s.[212] In their article for *Poetika kino*, moreover, in the section dealing with soft-focus optics, Mikhailov and Moskvin refer to Goertz 'molar' lenses, Verito lenses, Kodak diffusion disks and monocle lenses with varying degrees of correction.[213] These, and a number of other accessories, are mentioned by Zheliabuzhskii in his 1932 monograph.[214] Furthermore, there was also the possibility of customization, with lenses individually ground by specialists working in the field of lens optics, or alternatively (and more rarely) by foreign specialists. Tisse, for example, refers to a portrait lens that was constructed for him by the optical specialist Professor Heltz during his stay in Berlin in 1927;[215] and Moskvin, in his article for *Sovetskii ekran*, mentions collaborating with the optical engineer N. N. Zababurin in order to produce a number of lenses and accessories that facilitated soft-focus cinematography.[216] Such was the interest in optical experimentation that there emerged a veritable cult of the lens, with suspicion rife that certain camera operators at the studio were keeping information on their 'unusual lenses' from colleagues.[217] The use of coloured filters was also widespread during the silent period and beyond, as Zheliabuzhskii's detailed discussion of their optical effects makes clear.[218]

Notes

1. 'Pis'mo N. F. Agadzhanova-Shutko k S. M. Eizenshteinu', dated 14 October 1925, in *Bronenosets Potemkin*, Shedevry sovetskogo kino series, ed. by N. Kleiman and K. Levina (Moscow: Iskusstvo, 1969), p. 79.

2. Letter from Maksim Shtraukh, one of Eizenshtein's 'Mighty Five' assistants, to his wife, Iudif' Glizer, dated 5 September 1925, in '"Bronenosets Potemkin": Fil'my-iubiliary', publ. by V. P. Korshunova and G. D. Endzina, *Iskusstvo kino*, 1986.1, 129–37 (p. 133).

3   'Dvenadtsat' apostolov', in Eizenshtein, *Izbrannye proizvedeniia*, I, 122–35 (p. 130) (first publ. in Sergei Eizenshtein, *Izbrannye stat'i* (Moscow: Iskusstvo, 1956), pp. 366–78).

4. Eizenshtein, 'Dvenadtsat' apostolov', p. 130.

5. The popular notion of the cameraman as someone who merely mechanically turns the crank-handle of the camera dates from the pre-revolutionary period. See Philip Cavendish, 'The Hand that Turns the Handle: Camera Operators and the Poetics of the Camera in Pre-Revolutionary Russian Film', *Slavonic and East European Review*, 82.2 (2004), 201–45.

6. '25 i 15', in Eizenshtein, *Izbrannye proizvedeniia*, V, 422–25 (first publ. in *Kino*, 1939.24, 2). Eizenshtein's recognition of this support in the early stages of his career was given in a letter to Tisse dated 29 May 1939. See 'Predsedateliu torzhestvennogo zasedaniia v chest' XXV-letiia tvorcheskoi deiatel'nosti E. Tisse', publ. by L. F. Gudieva, *Kinovedcheskie zapiski*, 32 (1996–97), 171–72 (p. 171).

7. Eizenshtein, '25 i 15', p. 423.

8. Ibid., p. 424.

9. Jay Leyda, 'Eisenstein and Tisse', in the supplementary materials which accompany the Criterion DVD release of *Ivan the Terrible* and *Alexander Nevsky* (see 'Special Materials'/*Bezhin lug*/Important Texts).

10. The A.S.C. grew out of the Cinema Camera Club, which had been formed as early as 1913. See H. Lyman Broening, '"How It All Happened": A Brief Review of the Beginnings of the American Society of Cinematographers', *American Cinematographer*, 2.20 (1921), 13.

11. Cited in Ol'ga Surkova, *Tarkovskii i ia: Dnevnik pionerki* (Moscow: ZebraE/Eksmo/Dekont+, 2002), p. 188.

12. Maiia Merkel', *V sto sorok solnts* (Moscow: Iskusstvo, 1968), p. 10.

13. Apart from the GTK, there was the Vysshii Institut Fotografii i Fototekhniki, which had been established in Petrograd in 1919; it was one of three schools or institutes which trained cadres for the film industry, the other two being the Institut Ekrannogo Iskusstva, which specialized in training actors, and the Shkola Kino-mekhanikov, which offered courses for future film-industry technicians. None of these institutes, however, offered specific training for camera operators. Judging from reports in the Petrograd film press, the Vysshii Institut Fotografii i Fototekhniki suffered from funding problems in its initial years and was temporarily closed in 1923. It was renamed the Vysshii Fototekhnicheskii Institut in the same year, after which it began to receive financial support from the Sevzapkino film studio. See Mikhail Kresin, 'Kinematografiia i Sevzapkino', *Vestnik fotografii i kinematografii*, 1923.2, 34–36; Professor N. E. Ermilov, 'Pechal'noe polozhenie russkoi foto-kino-literatury', ibid., pp. 43–46 (p. 43); Veniamin Vishnevskii, 'Kino-tekhnika i kino-iskusstvo', *Art-EKRAN*, 1923.2, 3–4; and Vl. Novoselov, 'Vysshii Foto-Kino-Institut', ibid., 1923.3, 8–9.

14. According to Bergan, Tisse was born Eduard Kazimirovich Nikolaitis. His father was Lithuanian and his mother of Swedish extraction. It has never been satisfactorily explained

why he adopted a different surname. See Ronald Bergan, *Sergei Eisenstein: A Life in Conflict* (Woodstock, NY: The Overlook Press/Peter Mayer, 1999), p. 90. For the biographical information which appears here and later in this paragraph, see E. Tisse, 'Stranitsy proshlogo', *Iskusstvo kino*, 1941.6, 48–50 (pp. 48–49).

15. Eduard Tisse, 'Tvorcheskaia biografiia' [1952], publ. by L. F. Gudieva, *Kinovedcheskie zapiski*, 32 (1996–97), 161–68 (pp. 161–65).

16. A. Antipenko, 'Moi Demutskii', *Iskusstvo kino*, 1972.9, 93–98; and Nikolai Ushakov, 'Tri operatora: Kniga 1930-goda', publ. by A. S. Deriabin and E. Ia. Margolit, trans. by E. A. Movchan, *Kinovedcheskie zapiski*, 56 (2002), 157–83 (pp. 161–67) (first publ. as *Try operatory* (Kiiv: Ukrteakinovydav, 1930)).

17. Ia. L. Butovskii, *Andrei Moskvin, kinooperator* (St Petersburg: Dmitrii Bulanin, 2000), pp. 9–11.

18. Ibid., pp. 14–15 & 25–27.

19. E. Gromov, *Kinooperator Anatolii Golovnia: Fil'my: Svidetel'stva: Razmyshleniia* (Moscow: Iskusstvo, 1980), pp. 6–11. On the revelations in Golovnia's unpublished diaries, which suggest that his arrival in Moscow followed desertion from the ranks of the Red Army, in which he was serving as an officer in the Cheka, see Orlando Figes, *The Whisperers: Private Life in Stalin's Russia* (London: Penguin, 2008), pp. 166–67.

20. Gromov, *Kinooperator Anatolii Golovnia*, p. 11.

21. Anatolii Golovnia, *Ekran – moia palitra* (Moscow: Biuro propagandy sovetskogo kinoiskusstva, 1971), p. 3.

22. Gromov, *Kinooperator Anatolii Golovnia*, pp. 12–25.

23. Viacheslav Gordanov, *Zapiski kinooperatora* (Leningrad: Iskusstvo, leningradskoe otdelenie, 1973), pp. 8–12.

24. Ibid., p. 83.

25. Eduard Tisse, '"Na tom my stoim"', publ. by G. Maslovskii, trans. by Naum Kleiman, *Iskusstvo kino*, 1979.2, 100–04 (p. 101) (first publ. in *Die Filmtechnik*, 1927.6).

26. Eduard Tisse, '" Na tom my stoim"', p. 101.

27. V. Pudovkin, 'Pervaia fil'ma', in *Mat'*, ed. by N. A. Glagoleva, Shedevry mirovogo kino series (Moscow: Iskusstvo, 1975), pp. 184–85 (p. 184) (first publ. in *Kino*, 1932.44, 2).

28. 'Kak my delali fil'mu "Konets Sankt-Peterburga"', in V. Pudovkin, *Sobranie sochinenii*, ed. by A. Golovnia and others, 3 vols (Moscow: Iskusstvo, 1974–76), II (1975), 56–58 (p. 57) (first publ. in *Konets Sankt-Peterburga* (Moscow: Teakinopechat', 1928)).

29. Cited in Butovskii, *Andrei Moskvin, kinooperator*, p. 194.

30. Cited in ibid., p. 136.

31. Iosif Shpinel', 'Tvorcheskoe edinstvo', in *Dovzhenko v vospominaniiakh sovremennikov*, ed. by Iu. I. Solntseva and L. I. Pazhitnova (Moscow: Iskusstvo, 1982), pp. 76–79 (p. 77).

32. *Sovetskii ekran*, 1926.15, 2 & 3. The context of the photograph of Novitskii is explained in L. M. [Leo Mur], 'S vintovkoi i kino-apparatom', *Sovetskii ekran*, 1929.8, 6–7.

33. V. Fefer, 'Operator khroniki', *Sovetskoe kino*, 1926.6, 14–15.

34. For an account of the expedition, see Georgii Blium, 'Zametki operatora', in 'Kak snimalsia "Velikii perelet"', *Kino-zhurnal A.R.K.*, 1926.1, 28–29 (p. 29).

35. Gromov, *Kinooperator Anatolii Golovnia*, p. 48.

36. Butovskii, *Andrei Moskvin, kinooperator*, p. 40.

37. Ibid., p. 79.

38. For a production still showing this moment, see George O. Liber, *Alexander Dovzhenko: A Life in Soviet Film* (London: BFI, 2002), p. 127.

39. Fefer, 'Operator khroniki', p. 15.

40. Ibid., pp. 14–15.

41. Ibid., p. 14.

42. Ibid., p. 15; and V. Fefer, '"Povedenie cheloveka" ("Mekhanika golovnogo mozga")', *Sovetskoe kino*, 1926.1, 10–12 (p. 11).

43. On the importance of camera operators during this period, see V. M. Korotkii, *Operatory i rezhissery russkogo igrovogo kino 1897–1921* (Moscow: NII kinoiskusstva, 2008), pp. 6–7; and Cavendish, 'The Hand that Turns the Handle'.

44. Reproduced in *Kino*, 1924.38, 2.

45. Leo Mur, 'Operator kinok', *Sovetskii ekran*, 1929.4, 10; 'Khudozhnik sveta', ibid., 1929.5, 10; 'Eduard Tisse', ibid., p. 12; 'Iz Parizha v Moskoviiu', ibid., 1929.7, 10; 'Veteran kino-khroniki', ibid., 1929.9, 10; and 'Uchenik svoego uchitelia', ibid., 1929.11, 10.

46. Oleg Frelikh, 'Stil' operatora', *Sovetskii ekran*, 1927.10, 6–7; and Mikhail Shneider, 'Litso k ob"ektivu', *Kino*, 1927.6, 3.

47. For example, A. Moskvin, 'O svoei rabote i o sebe', *Sovetskii ekran*, 1927.38, 10.

48. A. Stanke, 'Rabota kino-operatora v Germanii', *Kino-zhurnal A.R.K.*, 1926.3, 29; P. K. Novitskii, 'Russkie i inostrannye operatory (Iz vospominanii operatora)', *Kino-front*, 1926.1, 31–32; Nik[olai] Anoshchenko, 'Zametki operatora', ibid., 1928.2, 27; Mur, 'Eduard Tisse'; and Ernst Lubich [Ernst Lubitsch], 'Amerikanskie kinooperatory', *Sovetskii ekran*, 1926.27, 14.

49. Evidence of the international reputation of Soviet camera operators is suggested by a back cover of *Sovetskii ekran*. This features a hand-written greeting from Charles Rosher, the preferred camera operator of Mary Pickford, 'to all Russian operators'. It was sent to the editors by its recipient, Tisse. See *Sovetskii ekran*, 1926.40, 16.

50. See the report on this conference in G. Alina, 'Spory o besspornom voprose', *Kino*, 1933.21, 4.

51. *Karl Struss: Man with a Camera*, ed. with introduction by John and Susan Harvith (Ann Arbor, MI: Cranbrook Academy of Art, 1976).

52. Horak, *Making Images Move*, pp. 79–108 & 109–36.

53. For reproductions of these designs, see *Alexander Rodchenko: Photography, 1924–54*, ed. with introduction by Alexander Lavrentiev (Cologne: Könemann, 1995), pp. 53 & 58.

54. Ibid., pp. 50–51; and Pack, *Film Posters of the Russian Avant-Garde*, pp. 168 & 170–71.

55. *Alexander Rodchenko: Photography, 1924–54*, ed. by Lavrentiev, pp. 81, 85, 94, 104, & 125.

56. Ibid., p. 129.

57. Ibid., pp. 115, 116, 118, 124, 127, 134, & 170. Several works by Rodchenko not included in this monograph also appeared in *Sovetskoe kino*. They are: *Dom na Vozdvizhenke*, *Sovetskoe kino*, 1926.4–5, 23; *Dvor s 8-ogo etazha*, ibid., 1928.2, 21; and *Opyt s"emki bystro-idushchego cheloveka sverkhu*, ibid.

58. O. Brik, 'Chego ne vidit glaz', *Sovetskoe kino*, 1926.2, 22–23.

59. See *Psikhologiia*, in *Kino-fot*, 3 (1922), 11; and *Detektiv*, in ibid, p. 12.

60. For example, see K. Malevich, 'I likuiut liki na ekranakh (V poriadke diskussii)', *Kino-zhurnal A.R.K.*, 1925.10, 7–9; and idem, 'Khudozhnik i kino', ibid., 1926.2, 15–17.

61. For example, see T. S., 'Kino na Vsemirnoi Khudozhestvennoi Vystavke v Parizhe', *Kino-zhurnal A.R.K.*, 1925.9, 28; and N. Kaufman, 'Foto-kino vystavka v Shtutgardte', *Sovetskii ekran*, 1929.16, 10.

62. For example, 'Russkoe fotograficheskoe o-vo', *Kino*, 1923.1, 25–26; 'Tsikl lektsii o foto i kino', ibid., 1922.4, 29; 'Fotograficheskie obshchestva', *Vestnik fotografii i kinematografii*, 1923.1,

21–22; and B. P., 'Russkoe fotograficheskoe obshchestvo (pri Gosudarstvennoi Akademii Khudozhestvennykh Nauk)', *Kino-front*, 1926.9–10, 34–35.

63. For example, Liudvig Gil'berseimer, 'Dinamicheskaia zhivopis' (bespredmetnyi kinematograf)', *Kino-fot*, 1 (1922), 7; and K. Fel'dman, 'Razval frantsuzskogo "levogo avangarda"', *Sovetskii ekran*, 1928.24, 8.

64. On developments in the art of the Soviet film poster, see K. Malevich, 'O vyiaviteliakh', *Kino-zhurnal A.R.K.*, 1925.6–7, 6–8; O. M. Brik, 'Poslednii krik', *Sovetskii ekran*, 1926.7, 3–4; and D. Aranovich, 'Sovremennyi kinoplakat', ibid., 1927.28, 13–14.

65. For example, V. Agden, 'Kino-khudozhnik na Zapade i v S.S.S.R.', *Kino-zhurnal A.R.K.*, 1926.3, 16–18; and Klavdiia Lesnaia, 'Khudozhnik v kino', *Sovetskii ekran*, 1929.38, 11.

66. O. M. Brik, 'Kino v teatre Meierkhol'da', ibid., 1926.20, 6–7.

67. See the covers for issue numbers 4, 5–6 and 8 of *Kino-front* for 1926.

68. Aleksei Gan, 'Kinematograf i kinematografiia', *Kino-fot*, 1 (1922), 1.

69. Ippolit Sokolov, 'Skrizhal' veka', ibid., p. 3.

70. L. V. Kuleshov, 'Iskusstvo, sovremennaia zhizn' i kinematografiia', ibid., p. 2.

71. N. Tikhonov, 'Fotografiia', ibid., 2 (1922), 4.

72. O. M. Brik, 'Foto i kino', *Sovetskoe kino*, 1926.4–5, 23.

73. These appeared under the 'Foto i kino' rubric in issue nos. 6 (p. 11) and 8 (p. 15) for 1926; issue nos. 1 (p. 15), 2 (p. 25), 3 (p. 23), and 4 (p. 23) for 1927; and issue no. 2 (p. 21) for 1928.

74. G. M. Boltianskii, *Sovetskaia fotografiia za desiat' let* (Moscow: Izdanie komiteta vystavki, 1928).

75. On these debates, see Margarita Tupitsyn, *The Soviet Photograph: 1924–37* (New Haven, CT: Yale University Press, 1996), pp. 66–98 & 99–126.

76. Operator M. Kaufman, 'Foto i kino', *Sovetskoe kino*, 1926.6, 11.

77. L. Kuleshov and A. Khokhlova, *50 let v kino* (Moscow: Iskusstvo, 1975), pp. 39–40.

78. See 'Montazh attraktsionov', in Eizenshtein, *Izbrannye proizvedeniia*, II (1964), 269–73 (first publ. in *LEF*, 1923.3); and 'The Montage of Film Attractions' [1925], in S. M. Eisenstein, *Selected Works*, ed. and trans. by Richard Taylor, 4 vols (London: BFI, 1988–1995), I (*Writings, 1922–1934*), 39–58 (p. 39).

79. 'Fotogeniia', in Pudovkin, *Sobranie sochinenii*, I, 90–94 (first publ. in *Kino-zhurnal A.R.K.*, 1925.4–5).

80. Eizenshtein, 'Sredniaia iz trekh', p. 70. For the views of Sergei Tret'iakov on the importance of montage for still photography, see Tupitsyn, *The Soviet Photograph*, p. 67.

81. 'Photogénie', in Louis Delluc, *Ecrits cinématographiques : Le Cinéma et les cinéastes*, ed. by Pierre Lherminier, 3 vols ([Paris]: Cinémathèque Française, 1985–90), I, 34–77 (first publ. in Paris: Brunoff, 1920). The Russian version of Delluc's essay was published by Novye vekhi in Moscow. See L. Rozental''s review in *Kino-zhurnal A.R.K.*, 1925.4–5, 43.

82. Pudovkin's views on this subject are discussed at greater length in Chapter Three.

83. V. Pertsov, 'Mif o fotogenii', *Kino-front*, 1926.2–3, 4–7.

84. Leo Mur, 'Fotogeniia', *Kino-zhurnal A.R.K.*, 1925.6–7, 3–6 (p. 5).

85. Ibid., p. 4.

86. Mur, 'Eduard Tisse'.

87. Leo Mur, 'Verkhom na luche', *Kino-zhurnal A.R.K.*, 1926.3, 7–10 (p. 8).

88. Apart from the article cited in the previous note, see also Leo Mur, 'S"emki na nature i v atel'e', *Kino-front*, 1926.2–3, 2–7; and idem, *Fabrika serykh tenei* (Moscow-Leningrad: Kinopechat', 1927).

89. Leo Mur, 'Operator: Ocherk iz serii "rabotniki kino"', *Kino*, 1925.4, 3.

90. Slavko Vorkapich, 'Motion and the Art of Cinematography', American Cinematographer, 7.9 (1926), 15, 16, & 17 (p. 17).

91. Two translations of Der sichtbare Mensch in Russian appeared almost simultaneously in 1925, although they differ slightly in title and content. The first, entitled Vidimyi chelovek: Ocherki dramaturgii fil'my, was published in Moscow by the Vserossiiskii Proletkul't publishing house with a foreword by V. Bliumenfel'd; the second, entitled Kul'tura kino, was published by the Leningrad State Publishing House (Lengiz) with a foreword by Adrian Piotrovskii. I shall cite the Moscow edition as reprinted in Bela Balash [Béla Balázs], 'Vidimyi chelovek', trans. by K. I. Shutko, Kinovedcheskie zapiski, 25 (1995), 61–121.

92. Ibid., pp. 82–84.

93. Ibid., pp. 88–89.

94. Ibid., p. 107.

95. Ibid.

96. 'Stil'naia fil'ma, stil' fil'my i stil' voobshche (Stat'ia Bela Balasha)', Kino-zhurnal A.R.K., 1926.2, 13–14.

97. This lecture was first published in the June 1926 issue of Die Filmtechnik. I shall cite from the (abridged) Russian translation. See Bela Balash, 'O budushchem fil'my', Kino, 1926.27, 3.

98. Ibid.

99. Ibid.

100. 'Bela zabyvaet nozhnitsy', in Eizenshtein, Izbrannye proizvedeniia, II, 274–79 (p. 275) (first publ. as 'O pozitsii Bela Ballasha [sic]', Kino, 1926.29, 3, and 'Bella [sic] zabyvaet nozhnitsy', ibid., 1926.32, 3).

101. Eizenshtein, 'Bela zabyvaet nozhnitsy', p. 277.

102. Ibid., pp. 274 & 276.

103. For further discussion, see p. 34 of the present chapter.

104. Tisse, 'Tvorcheskaia biografiia', p. 165.

105. G. Boltianskii, Kul'tura kino-operatora: Opyt issledovaniia, osnovannyi na rabotakh E. K. Tisse (Moscow-Leningrad: Kinopechat', 1927), pp. 56–57.

106. Ibid., pp. 57–59.

107. Ibid., pp. 62 & 73–74.

108. See note in ibid., p. 74.

109. Gordanov, Zapiski kinooperatora, p. 62.

110. Butovskii, Andrei Moskvin, kinooperator, pp. 86–87. See also Evgenii Mikhailov, 'Vospominaniia ob A. N. Moskvine', in Kinooperator Andrei Moskvin: Ocherk zhizni i tvorchestva: Vospominaniia tovarishchei, ed. with introduction by F. G. Gukasian (Leningrad: Iskusstvo, leningradskoe otdelenie, 1971), pp. 154–63 (p. 156).

111. Butovskii, Andrei Moskvin, kinooperator, p. 89.

112. E. Mikhailov and A. Moskvin, 'Rol' kino-operatora v sozdanii fil'my', in Poetika kino, ed. by B. M. Eikhenbaum, foreword by K. Shutko (Leningrad: Kinopechat', 1927); repr. [Berkeley, CA]: Berkeley Slavic Specialities, 1984), pp. 171–91 (pp. 173–74).

113. Ibid., p. 176.

114. Ibid., pp. 176, 177, 178, & 185.

115. Ibid., p. 175.

116. Ibid.

117. Ibid., p. 181.

118. Ibid.

119. Ibid., p. 183.
120. Tat'iana Nikol'skaia, 'Gruzinskie futuristy v kino (ranniaia stat'ia M. Kalatozishvili)', in *Ot slov k telu: Sbornik statei k 60-letiiu Iuriia Tsiv'iana*, ed. by Aleksandr Lavrov, Aleksandr Ospovat and Roman Timenchik (Moscow: Novoe literaturnoe obozrenie, 2010), pp. 238–42 (pp. 240–42).
121. Iurii Zheliabuzhskii, *Iskusstvo operatora* (Moscow: Gosudarstvennoe izdatel'stvo legkoi promyshlennosti, 1932).
122. Vladimir Nilsen, *The Cinema as a Graphic Art (On the Theory of Representation in the Cinema)*, appreciation by S. M. Eisenstein, trans. by Stephen Garry ([London]: Newnes Limited, 1937).
123. Moskvin, 'O svoei rabote i o sebe'.
124. G. V. Aleksandrov, *Epokha i kino* (Moscow: Politizdat, 1976), p. 96.
125. Jay Leyda, *Kino: A History of the Russian and Soviet Film*, 3rd edn (Princeton, NJ: Princeton University Press, 1983), p. 295.
126. G. Kabalov, 'Glazami operatora', *Iskusstvo kino*, 1983.2, 95–100 (pp. 99–100).
127. Antipenko, 'Moi Demutskii', p. 96.
128. Butovskii, *Andrei Moskvin, kinooperator*, pp. 98–99.
129. L. Kokhno, 'Poeziia truda', in *Dovzhenko v vospominaniiakh sovremennikov*, ed. by Solntseva and Pazhitnova, pp. 79–85 (p. 81).
130. Mikh. Rozenfel'd, 'Zolotoi potok', in *Kinovedcheskie zapiski*, 84 (2007), 219–22 (pp. 221–22) (first publ. in *Komsomol'skaia pravda*, 16 July 1935); and Leyda, *Kino: A History of the Russian and Soviet Film*, p. 331.
131. Cited in Butovskii, *Andrei Moskvin, kinooperator*, p. 137.
132. Aleksandrov's letter to Eizenshtein dated 27 November 1925, in *Brononosets Potemkin*, ed. by Kleiman and Levina, p. 83.
133. Gromov, *Kinooperator Anatolii Golovnia*, p. 51.
134. Cited in ibid., p. 116.
135. S. M. Eizenshtein, 'Tezisy k vystupleniiu na diskussii v ARKe' [1926], publ. by N. I. Kleiman, *Kino i zritel'*, 2 (1985), 31–37 (p. 31).
136. Ivan Perestiani, *75 let zhizni v iskusstve* (Moscow: Iskusstvo, 1962), p. 312.
137. Eizenshtein, '25 i 15', p. 424.
138. 'Vystuplenie na iubileinom vechere A. A. Levitskogo' (22 December 1960), in *Lev Kuleshov, Sobranie sochinenii*, ed. by R. N. Iurenev and others, 3 vols (Moscow: Iskusstvo, 1987–88), II (*Vospominaniia: Rezhissura: Dramaturgiia*), 1988, 413–16 (p. 414).
139. Aleksandrov, *Epokha i kino*, p. 42.
140. Shtraukh's letter to his wife dated 14 September 1925, in '"Bronenosets Potemkin": Fil'my-iubiliary', p. 134.
141. Shtraukh's letters to his wife dated 25 September and 11 October 1925, in ibid., pp. 134 & 136.
142. Eizenshtein, 'Tezisy k vystupleniiu na diskussii v ARKe', p. 32.
143. Cited (and translated) by Liber, *Alexander Dovzhenko*, p. 87.
144. Cited (and translated) in ibid., pp. 87–88.
145. For a detailed analysis of this sequence, see Chapter Five.
146. Cited in Butovski, *Andrei Moskvin, kinooperator*, pp. 188–89.
147. Gromov, *Kinooperator Anatolii Golovnia*, pp. 95–97.
148. Cited in Mikhail Arlazorov, *Protazanov*, Zhizn' v iskusstve series (Moscow: Iskusstvo, 1973), p. 174.
149. Butovskii, *Andrei Moskvin, kinooperator*, pp. 186–88. A slightly different account of this decision, one that stresses its traumatic impact on Tisse, is given in the recollections of his daughter, a

former student at VGIK. See Eleonora Tissé, 'Some Notes on the Work of the Cameraman in "Ivan the Terrible": The Visual Construction of the Film Image Form', in *Eisenstein Revisited: A Collection of Essays*, ed. by Lars Kleberg and Håkan Lövgren (Stockholm: Almquist & Wiksell International, 1987), pp. 133–44.

150. Cited in Butovski, *Andrei Moskvin, kinooperator*, p. 200.

151. Tissé, 'Some Notes on the Work of the Cameraman in "Ivan the Terrible"', p. 136.

152. '(Pri vstrechi moei s Meksikoi…)' [1946–47], in Eizenshtein, *Izbrannye proizvedeniia*, I, 442–45 (p. 442).

153. Leyda, 'Eisenstein and Tisse', p. 12.

154. O. Kovalov, 'Opticheskaia fantaziia no. 5', *Iskusstvo kino*, 1998.7, 35–42 (p. 37).

155. Eizenshtein's manner of working has been described by the painter Jean Charlot as 'close to an automatic writing type of drawing'. Cited in Marie Seton, *Sergei M. Eisenstein: A Biography*, revised edn (London: Dennis Dobson, 1978), p. 216.

156. *Mexico According to Eisenstein*, ed. with introduction by Inga Karetnikova in collaboration with Leon Steinmetz (Albuquerque: University of New Mexico Press, 1991), p. 17.

157. 'Kak ia uchilsia risovat' – Glava ob urokakh tantsa' [1946], in Eizenshtein, *Izbrannye proizvedeniia*, I, 257–72 (p. 265) (first publ. in *Kul'tura i zhizn'*, 1957.6).

158. Anon, 'Photography of the Month: "Thunder over Mexico"', *American Cinematographer*, 16.3 (1933), 92–93.

159. Zheliabuzhskii, *Iskusstvo operatora*, p. 206.

160. Julian 'Bud' Lesser, 'Tisse's Unfinished Treasure: *Que Viva Mexico*', *American Cinematographer*, 72.7 (1991), 34–40 (p. 37).

161. Ibid., p. 35.

162. Mur, 'Eduard Tisse'.

163. Tisse's letter to Eizenshtein dated 5 March 1927, in 'Eduard Tisse: "Rabotali my s nagruzkoi 100%"', publ. by G. R. Maslovskii, *Kinovedcheskie zapiski*, 8 (1990), 97–117 (p. 99).

164. Lesser, 'Tisse's Unfinished Treasure', p. 38. According to Salt, a Bell & Howell cost $3,500, and a Debrie-Parvo $1,500, at this time. See Barry Salt, *Film Style and Technology: History and Analysis*, 2nd (expanded) edn (London: Starword, 1992), p. 157.

165. Gvido Zeeber [Guido Seeber], 'Novoe v kino-s"emochnoi apparature', *Kino-zhurnal A.R.K.*, 1925.9, 15–17.

166. Eduard Tisse, 'Novaia model' kino-s"emochnogo apparata', *Kino-front*, 1926.4–5, 15.

167. Avladga, 'Kino-s"emochnyi apparat "Ekler"', *Kino-front*, 1926.9–10, 20; A. Gal'perin, 'Kino-s"emochnyi apparat "Mitshel'"', ibid., 1927.1, 16–20; Nik[olai] Anoshchenko, 'Novinki kino-s"emochnoi apparatury', ibid., 1927.2, 16–18; and A. Gal'perin, 'Perechen' chastei kino-s"emochnogo apparata "Mitshel'"', ibid., p. 18.

168. N. Tikhonov, 'Novosti zapadnoi kino-tekhniki', *Kino-zhurnal A.R.K.*, 1925.1, 8–9; P. Pavlov, 'Novosti kino-s"emochnoi apparatury', ibid., 1926.1, 15–16; A. Gal'perin, '120-metrovoi s"emochnyi apparat "Amata" firmy "Inzh. Linkhof Miunkhen"', *Kino-front*, 1926.2–3, 14; A. G., 'Novosti kino-liubitel'skoi apparatury', ibid., 1926.1, 16–17; A. Gal'perin, 'Novinki liubitel'skoi kinos"emochnoi apparatury', ibid., 1927.3, 22–23; N. A-ko, 'Novinki kinotekhniki: Novosti liubitel'skoi apparatury,' *Sovetskii ekran*, 1929.31, 12.

169. 'Avtomaticheskaia kino-kamera', ibid., 1926.8, 15.

170. N. A-ko, 'Novyi shtativ dlia s"emochnykh kamer', ibid., 1929.29, 12.

171. P. P. Pavlov, 'Novosti proektsionnoi apparatury' [two parts], *Kino-front*, 1926.1, 10–12, and 1926.2–3, 12–13.

172. See, for example, Fr. Villi Frerk, 'Sovremennoe sostoianie germanskoi fotograficheskoi optiki', *Foto-kino*, 1923.2–3, 22–24.
173. Ibid. See also 'Novyi ob"ektiv "Plasmat"', *Vestnik fotografii i kinematografii*, 1923.1, 23; and P., 'Usovershenstvovannyi ob"ektiv', *Sovetskii ekran*, 1925.7, 10. An advertisement for this lens appears in issue number 6 of *Sovetskoe kino* for 1926.
174. Frerk, 'Sovremennoe sostoianie germanskoi fotograficheskoi optiki', p. 24; and P. Novitskii, 'Saft-fokus', *Kino-front*, 1927.5, 22–23.
175. Frerk, 'Sovremennoe sostoianie germanskoi fotograficheskoi optiki', p. 24.
176. Nik[olai] Anoshchenko, 'Khudozhestvennaia kino-s"emka s dobavochnymi linzami', *Kino-front*, 1927.7–8, 18–23; and Novitskii, 'Saft-fokus', pp. 22–23.
177. See, for example, Nik[olai] Anoshchenko, 'Triuki troinoi prizmy', *Sovetskii ekran*, 1929.43, 10.
178. For examples, see Ar. Ialovyi, 'Trekhfaznye dugovye lampy', *Kino-zhurnal A.R.K.*, 1923.3, 29; P. Radetskii, 'Perenosnaia dugovaia lampa "Atom" dlia kino-s"emki', *Kino-nedelia*, 1924.29, 6; Nik[olai] Rakushev, 'Osveshchenie v kino-atel'e', *Kino-zhurnal A.R.K.*, 1925.6–7, 20–22; M. Bliumberg, 'Osveshchenie kino-atel'e', ibid., 1925.11–12, 17–18; Nikolai Anoshchenko, 'Shtaakenskii gigant', *Kino-front*, 1926.1, 24–26 (p. 25); N. Iudin, 'Amerikanskoe osveshchenie v kino', ibid., pp. 12–13; Nikolai Anoshchenko, 'Germanskaia kinematografiia nashikh dnei', ibid., 1926.2–3, 35–36; Stanke, 'Rabota kino-operatora v Germanii'; V. Nel'son, 'Voprosy osvetitel'noi tekhniki', *Kino-front*, 1928.2, 28–29; N. Anoshchenko, 'Prozhektora s poluvattnymi lampami', *Sovetskii ekran*, 1929.29, 12; and E. Goldovskii, 'O primenenii poluvattnykh lamp pri s"emke v kinoatel'e', *Kino i kul'tura*, 1929.3, 34–44.
179. On the super-sensitive Agfa film stock, see Karl Freind [Karl Freund], 'Revoliutsiia v kino-s"emkakh', *Sovetskii ekran*, 1927.31, 4; and V. Sol'skii, 'V polose perevorotov', *Kino*, 1927.36, 3. For the Soviet Union's consumption of Agfa film stock, see Vl. Erofeev, 'Proizvodstvo plenki', *Sovetskoe kino*, 1925.4–5, 63–67 (p. 66).
180. Iu. Fogel'man, 'Pankhromaticheskaia plenka', *Kino i kul'tura*, 1929.3, 45–48.
181. Iu. A. Zheliabuzhskii, '"Za grosh – piatak"', *Kino*, 1922.2, 17.
182. G. Knoke, 'Protsess obrashcheniia kino-negativov v pozitivy', *Kino-zhurnal A.R.K.*, 1925.4–5, 33; A. and L. Lium'er [Auguste and Louis Lumière] and A. Zeivetts, 'Usilenie negativov okrashivaniem', *Kino-front*, 1926.4–5, 16; Tolchan, 'O negativnoi plenke i negative', ibid., p. 19; and N. Spiridovskii, 'O novykh sposobakh okrashivaniia pozitiva', ibid., 1926.9–10, 18.
183. A. Gal'perin, 'Vosstanovlenie pozitiva', ibid., 1927.2, 20–22.
184. G. Kabalov, 'Tsvetochuvstvitel'nost' kino-plenki', ibid., 1927.1, 20.
185. A. Gal'perin, 'Novoe o patente Shiuftana', ibid., 1927.3, 24–25; idem, 'Stsenarii tekhnicheskogo triuka', ibid., 1927.5, 19–22; and Nik[olai] Anoshchenko, 'Kombinirovannye kadry', *Sovetskii ekran*, 1929.42, 12.
186. A. Anoshchenko-Anod., 'O naplyvakh', *Kino-zhurnal A.R.K.*, 1925.1, 20.
187. A. Grinberg, 'Tekhnika pavil'onnoi s"emki', ibid., 1926.3, 13–14.
188. '"Standartizuite svet"', *Kino-front*, 1926.2–3, 8–9; and Nik[olai] Anoshchenko, 'Pochemu na iuge severnye operatory inogda delaiut... nedoderzhki', ibid., 1928.2, 27–28.
189. '"Kino i ego tekhnika"', *Kino-zhurnal A.R.K.*, 1925.1, 32.
190. '"VGIK: Tvorcheskii vecher, posviashchennyi t. Tisse E. K." 20 fevralia 1940g (Stenograficheskii otchet)', publ. by L. F. Gudieva, *Kinovedcheskie zapiski*, 32 (1996–97), 172–79 (p. 175).
191. 'Fil'my bez plenki', in L. V. Kuleshov, *Stat'i: Materialy*, ed. by A. S. Khokhlova, introduction by E. Gromov, Kinematograficheskoe nasledie series (Moscow: Iskusstvo, 1979), pp. 131–46.
192. Freund, 'Just What Is "Montage"?', *American Cinematographer*, 15.4 (1934), 204 & 210.

193. Kuleshov and Khokhlova, 50 let v kino, pp. 87–88.
194. Mikhailov, 'Vospominaniia ob A. N. Moskvine', pp. 157–58.
195. Gordanov, Zapiski kinooperatora, p. 43.
196. Aleksandrov, Epokha i kino, p. 52.
197. Mur, Fabrika serykh tenei, p. 78.
198. Zheliabuzhskii, '"Za grosh – piatak"', p. 17.
199. Gordanov, Zapiski kinooperatora, p. 15.
200. V. Shneiderov, 'Bor'ba za kachestvo sovetskoi foto-kino produktsii', Kino-front, 1926.4–5, 32.
201. Vance Kepley, Jr, 'The origins of Soviet cinema: a study in industry development', in Inside the Film Factory: New Approaches to Russian and Soviet Cinema, ed. by Richard Taylor and Ian Christie (London: Routledge, 1991), pp. 60–79.
202. Ia. Korn, 'Tekhnicheskoe oborudovanie 1-i Goskino-fabriki', Kino-zhurnal A.R.K., 1925.9, 14.
203. E. Goldovskii, Osveshchenie kino-atel'e (Moscow: Kinopechat', 1927).
204. Golovnia, Ekran – moia palitra, pp. 19–20.
205. Grigorii Kozintsev, 'Andrei Moskvin [glava iz knigi]', in Kinooperator Andrei Moskvin, ed. by Gukasian, pp. 119–33 (p. 132).
206. Tisse's possession of this camera is mentioned in Shtraukh's letter to his wife dated 26 September 1925. He refers to the camera's use of three different lenses, including one which he calls a 'telephoto lens' (teleob"ektiv). See '"Bronenosets Potemkin": Fil'my-iubiliary', p. 136. Production stills show Tisse filming parts of the Odessa Steps sequence with this camera. See Richard Taylor, The Battleship Potemkin, KINOfiles Film Companion 1 (London: I. B. Tauris, 2000), p. 5.
207. Seeber, 'Die taumelnde Kamera', Die Filmtechnik, 1925.5, 92–93; and Von Ingenieur Friess, 'Neues uber Aufnahmetechnik', ibid., 1925.12, 260–61.
208. For this information, and the production stills in question, see Butovskii, Andrei Moskvin, kinooperator, pp. 62–63; and Sovetskoe kino, 1927.8–9, 27.
209. 'Operator-rezhisser (Iz besedy s P. K. Novitskim)', Sovetskii ekran, 1925.8, 3.
210. '"VGIK: Tvorcheskii vecher, posviashchennyi t. Tisse E. K."', p. 177.
211. Tisse's letter to Eizenshtein (date unknown), in 'Eduard Tisse: "Rabotali my s nagruzkoi 100%"', pp. 104–06 (p. 105). See also 'Iskusstvo kino', in Lev Kuleshov, Sobranie sochinenii, I (Teoriia: Kritika: Pedagogika), 161–225 (pp. 224 & 225) (first publ. Moscow-Leningrad: Tea-kino-pechat', 1929).
212. Gordanov, Zapiski kinooperatora, pp. 67–69.
213. Mikhailov and Moskvin, 'Rol' kino-operatora v sozdanii fil'my', p. 189.
214. Zheliabuzhskii, Iskusstvo operatora, pp. 60–75.
215. Tisse's letter to Eizenshtein dated 5 March 1927, in 'Eduard Tisse: "Rabotali my s nagruzkoi 100%"', pp. 99–100 (p. 99).
216. Moskvin, 'O svoei rabote i o sebe'.
217. Gordanov, Zapiski kinooperatora, p. 67.
218. Zheliabuzhskii, Iskusstvo operatora, pp. 76–77.

CHAPTER TWO

Eduard Tisse and Sergei Eizenshtein

The screen speaks for itself of how indebted I am to you for what we have managed to achieve during the fifteen years of our collaboration.[1]

You ask where my eye finishes and Tisse's eye begins? Here there is such a degree of intrusion in the composition of the frame on my part, and such an intrusion in the understanding of the directorial task on Tisse's part, that during the course of our eleven-year partnership you will find it impossible to tell where the one begins and other ends. The 'split' [razrezka] is invisible to the naked eye.[2]

Introduction

Eizenshtein and Tisse were introduced in the spring of 1923 by Boris Mikhin, the director of the first factory of Goskino.[3] The director's shooting scenario for *Stachka*, which was originally planned as a cooperative venture between Goskino and the Proletkul't, had already been drawn up on the basis of a libretto by the prose writer and dramatist Valer'ian Pletnev. Mikhin had proposed Tisse as camera operator on the grounds that the studio wanted someone with experience to help Eizenshtein negotiate the difficult transition from theatre to film direction.[4] Having been given a copy of the scenario, Tisse corrected a number of 'unprofessional' technical expressions.[5] He was subsequently invited to attend a performance of *Na vsiakogo mudretsa dovol'no prostoty*, which Eizenshtein was staging at the Morozov mansion for the Proletkul't. On that particular evening, so legend has it, the metal support for a tightrope which had been stretched above the auditorium for several of the production's 'attractions' collapsed close to where Tisse was sitting; he himself was uninjured and unperturbed, despite the fact that the chair next to him had been smashed to pieces (Aleksandrov, who was balancing on the tightrope at the time, later attributed Tisse's sangfroid to his years filming newsreels on various military fronts during the First World War and Civil War).[6] The first days of filming *Stachka* suggested that the nervousness on the part of the Goskino management was not misplaced. According to Mikhin, Eizenshtein and his team of youthful assistants had 'not the slightest idea about cinema'.[7] This prompted his decision to monitor the production extremely closely; indeed, if not for a written guarantee given by Mikhin and co-signed by Tisse, Eizenshtein would have been removed from the production altogether after the first few days.[8] The director generously acknowledged this fact in a letter sent to the organizer of an event held at VGIK on 29 May 1939 to celebrate Tisse's twenty-five years as a camera operator.[9] Clearly with this anniversary in mind, Eizenshtein also arranged for the publication of an essay, entitled '25 i 15' ('25 and 15'), in which he attempted to explain the basis of their creative partnership.[10] Along with Kozintsev's 1935 article on Moskvin, this essay constitutes one of the earliest directorial statements on the importance of the camera operator in the history of Soviet cinema.[11]

Despite Eizenshtein's generosity in these statements, they shed little light on Tisse's specific qualities as a cameraman, their working partnership or the artistic principles on which it was based; as Eizenshtein rather coyly admits towards the end of his essay, having intended ostensibly to celebrate the skills and talents of his professional colleague, he had inadvertently ended up writing mostly about himself.[12] In the public sphere, as evidenced by this essay, the emphasis lay on a mutual understanding that was so instinctive that it did not apparently require explicit communication. In the private sphere, there was clearly a degree of familiarity between the two men, despite the fact that, in their conversation and written communications, they employed the formal mode of address (the informal mode, in Eizenshtein's view, would have been a 'parody' of their 'inner compatibility').[13] The extent of this intimacy can be gauged by a playfully obscene cartoon, hitherto unpublished, but preserved in the Eizenshtein archives at RGALI, which the director sent to Tisse on 15 November 1927 (Fig. 3).[14] Entitled 'Budushchee vperedi' ('The Future Lies Ahead'), it shows Tisse standing behind a Debrie camera with his large, erect penis penetrating the apparatus via the viewfinder and reemerging through the lens aperture. Beneath this sketch Eizenshtein has penned the words 'Le grand pisdagiste Tissé [sic]', literally 'The Great Outdoors Fuckographer, Tisse', the neologism in question deriving from the combination of pizda, a vulgar term in Russian for 'vagina', and the French term paysagiste, meaning 'a painter of landscapes'.[15] Its shock value aside, this cartoon is a rare document. It is one of the very few Eizenshtein sketches during the course of his career that caricature friends or acquaintances; one of the very few drawings that date from 1923 to 1930, a period when Eizenshtein is conventionally assumed to have been inactive in terms of sketching; and lastly, as a 'secret drawing', one that for reasons of obscenity could not be published in the Soviet Union, the sketch is the earliest surviving example of that explicit body of work which is usually associated with the 1930s and 1940s.[16] The fact that Eizenshtein felt he could entrust Tisse with the possession of this potentially dangerous item speaks volumes about their relationship.

The artistic compatibility of these two men, however, poses a conundrum for those interested in Tisse as an independent creative artist. Although his status as a pioneer is assured in writings about the theory and practice of Soviet cinematography, he is a neglected figure as far as Eizenshtein studies and general surveys of Soviet cinema are concerned. Bearing in mind Eizenshtein's international reputation, both at the time and since, it is perhaps unsurprising that his photographic alter ego should have remained quite so deeply in the shadows. Eizenshtein's undeniable enthusiasm and invention, his intellectual sophistication and wide-ranging knowledge of the arts, and the fact that he was himself a practising artist have given rise to an understandable bias in the critical writing dedicated to his works. Even Leyda, who as a photographer and filmmaker was sympathetic to the cause of the camera operator, characterizes the relationship with Tisse in terms of the 'artist-logician' meeting the 'artist-craftsman'.[17]

Eizenshtein is undoubtedly one of the major theoreticians of film, yet Tisse's roles in their relationship were many and varied. As acknowledged by Aleksandrov, Tisse was the master and Eizenshtein his apprentice during the initial stages of their partnership: the 'old, experienced professor' initiated the director into the secrets of the motion-picture camera and patiently explained its possibilities to him.[18] Other commentators who had the opportunity of observing their partnership at close quarters confirm that it was essentially one of equals. Leyda, for example, has observed that 'they were both inventors and problem solvers, who approached difficulties with relish'.[19] Tisse's creative initiative is corroborated by anecdotes indicating that it was he who insisted on filming the Odessa port when it was shrouded in fog;[20] and that it was his decision to use searchlights for the shooting of the Finland Station sequence in *Oktiabr'*.[21] It is important to emphasize that Tisse could also boast a background in the visual arts and was himself a theoretician, albeit not one of Eizenshtein's originality and intellectual calibre. His lecture to the German Cameramen's Club, cited in Chapter One, established in embryonic form the theoretical basis for the promotion of the creative role of the camera operator; these ideas were developed more profoundly in an article co-written with Nil'sen in June 1933, two months after the groundbreaking Moscow conference of camera operators, which offered a brief gloss on the aesthetic history of cinema.[22] Although not as active as Golovnia in the field of pedagogical literature, Tisse did nevertheless publish numerous articles on film-related subjects during his lengthy career. He was a seminal figure in the establishment of the camera operators' faculty at the GTK, teaching there uninterruptedly for forty years, and was familiar with film industries abroad, courtesy of his travels to Europe and North America.[23] As well as being a camera operator, he was also a landscape photographer whose études were occasionally published in the film press of the 1920s.[24]

Tisse's career as a cameraman independent of Eizenshtein is sufficiently extensive to permit study of his compositional methods and aesthetic preferences in a wide variety of different contexts. These works consist of documentaries that he himself edited; partnerships with other Soviet directors as cinematographer; and feature-length films that he himself directed and photographed. It is important to appreciate that, despite Tisse's public stipulation that the camera operator should be involved at all stages of a feature-film production, the reality of working within Eizenshtein's unit was characterized by significant time pressures, numerous practical impediments and the tendency of the director to improvise after the shooting scenario had ostensibly been completed. In the case of *Bronenosets Potemkin*, for example, Tisse's relatively late arrival in Odessa because he was travelling abroad meant that he was not involved in the creation of this scenario (or rather, it was hastily revised after his arrival). In addition, the need to edit the material in time for the studio deadline meant that several sequences were photographed by Tisse alongside Aleksandrov, among them the very final sequence of the film.[25] Tisse was also absent for part of the drafting of the scenario for *Oktiabr'*.[26] As indicated in the previous chapter, the tight shooting schedule between April and July 1927 meant that the unit had to be split in two for the shooting of several, smaller-scale episodes.[27] Although familiarity with the project was not the issue here, a number of these episodes and some reshoots of earlier material deemed unsatisfactory were filmed while Eizenshtein was editing footage in Moscow.[28] As frequently stressed by Tisse himself, acute time pressures frequently affected the quality of the finished product.[29] It is also important to bear in mind that censorship and other interventions interfered with the production process to the extent that some projects remained incomplete and the artistic integrity of others was compromised. Political interference in the making of *Staroe i novoe* delayed the release of the film by nearly three years. *Que Viva Mexico!*, as noted in the previous chapter, was never finished due to the withdrawal of financial backing. The production of *Bezhin lug* was halted after seven months due to political interference and exists now solely in the form of one thousand frame stills which Eizenshtein, perhaps fearing intervention, had ordered his editors to preserve.[30] *Bol'shoi ferganskii kanal* (The Great Ferghana Canal, 1939), fragments from which were later presented as anonymous newsreel footage, is the ghost of a much more ambitious project, a full-length feature on the modernization of Uzbekistan.[31] The fact that Tisse's heritage has survived in so many different guises poses formidable challenges. At the same time, the consistency of his vision as represented by this amorphous heritage, and the fact that it very much bears his individual stamp, raises important questions about the autonomy of the individual film frame in relation to the larger montage context.

It is impossible to discuss the visual language of Eizenshtein's films without some reference to the director's shifting concept of montage as it evolved during the 1920s. For Eizenshtein, clearly aware of Ivan Pavlov's research in the sphere of reflexology (the direction of this research and his experiments were illustrated in Pudovkin and Golovnia's *Mekhanika golovnogo mozga*), filmic material was primarily an agitational, ideological tool. The first formulation of his theory conceptualized his stage adaptation of Ostrovskii's play as a 'montage of attractions'; in other words, a series of aggressive moments 'precisely calculated' to produce an emotional or psychological effect on the audience.[32] This idea was later applied to cinema, which was treated as a vehicle for exerting a 'series of calculated pressures on the psyche'.[33] At the heart of his theory lay the insistence on montage as a site of conflict rather than conflict resolution. In the essays of the late 1920s, the term 'intellectual montage' is employed to describe the method of juxtaposing seemingly unrelated frames by means of montage in such a way as to communicate an idea or concept.[34] Towards the end of this decade, Eizenshtein became interested in the latent montage potential within the individual film fragment itself, this giving rise to some detailed examinations of compositional dynamic. In 'Za kadrom' ('Beyond the Shot'), for example, he defined the individual shot as a 'montage-cell' that contains potentially explosive collisions (graphic, spatial and volumetric) within its own temporal limits. These embryonic impulses are described as exploding 'like the internal combustion engine';[35] even the image-frame itself is viewed as a potential site of conflict.[36] In 'Chetvertoe izmerenie v kino' ('The Fourth Dimension of Cinema'), this idea is refined through recourse to musical analogy. Here the 'explosions' of the individual 'montage-cell' are analysed in terms of physiological vibrations that can be triggered by a wide variety of technical means, for example lighting adjustment and optical distortion.[37] The process of montage is discussed in terms of 'dominants', with the individual sequences producing 'overtones' and 'undertones'.[38] Eizenshtein identifies four basic montage procedures – metric, rhythmic, tonal and overtonal. As an example of 'tonal' montage, he offers the emotional resonance of the Odessa mist sequence, with its 'scarcely perceptible ripple on the water, the slight bobbing of vessels at anchor, the slowly swirling mist, the seagulls landing slowly on the water'.[39] In an essay first published in 1934, '"E!": O chistote kinoiazyka' ('"E!": On the Purity of Film Language'), Eizenshtein offered a more detailed and concrete example of compositional dynamics from within *Bronenosets Potemkin*; this further illustrates his interest in the principle of conflict both within and between individual shots.[40]

While these essays may not be entirely convincing accounts of the actual production process – Aumont, for example, has argued that they 'provide rationalist ballast for what the filmic practice has achieved through the extemporaneous or the impulsive' – they do nevertheless demonstrate Eizenshtein's sensitivity in relation to compositional dynamics.[41] In broad terms, while confessing that he did not possess much in the way of a lyrical sensibility, his evolution during the 1920s may be characterized in terms of a progression away from semantic and intellectual content towards a greater interest in the compositional dynamics of the individual film frame and its aesthetic texture and fabric. It is symptomatic of this shift that, by the time *Oktiabr'* was being made, in the context of Aleksandr Kerenskii's ascent of the Jordan staircase in the Winter Palace, a sequence Eizenshtein advanced as an example of intellectual montage (the repeated shots of the ascent coupled with ironic intertitles were intended to satirize Kerenskii's vainglorious pursuit of power), he could express concerns in a letter to Aleksandrov, while editing the material in Moscow, that the marbled grandeur and opulence of the staircase had not been effectively communicated (he complains that it looks as if it has been made out of 'papier-mâché').[42] In the same letter, moreover, he also complains that the moving beams of light from projectors that illuminate the scenes showing Lenin's speech at Finland Station are an impediment to clarity of vision.[43] The fact that Eizenshtein was knowledgeable about painting and contemporary trends in the sphere of the visual arts is doubtless also significant. His stage and costume designs of the early 1920s are clearly influenced by Cubo-Futurist experiments.[44] His first essay on montage refers to Rodchenko's early photo-illustrations and sketches by George Grosz.[45] In 'The Dramaturgy of Film

Form', which was written for the 1929 Stuttgart 'Film and Photo' exhibition, he refers to abstract paintings by Malevich, Cubist sculptures by Oleksandr Arkhypenko, Suprematist paintings by Léger, 'kinetic' paintings by the Italian Futurist Giacomo Bella, and the 'fabulous mobility' of lithographs by Honoré Daumier and paintings by Henri Toulouse-Lautrec.[46] Eizenshtein's impressive knowledge of painting (he refers specifically to recent visits to museums while travelling around Europe) informs his discussion of aspect ratio in his 1931 essay 'The Dynamic Square'; here he considers the dimensions of paintings from the pre-Impressionist and Impressionist eras, medieval miniatures, Hokusai's *One Hundred Views of Mount Fuji*, the paintings of Edgar Degas and Japanese roll pictures, both horizontal and vertical.[47] It is well known that certain sequences in *Que Viva Mexico!* were influenced by contemporary Mexican artists working in the neo-primitive style, as well as various ethnographic artefacts, for example the statues of pre-Columbian (Aztec) gods which had been preserved in the National Museum in Mexico City.[48] It is symptomatic of this interest that Eizenshtein later compared the procedures of two of these artists, Diego Rivera and José Clemente Orozco, in his unfinished essay 'The Prometheus of Mexican Painting' (1935).[49] The decade of the 1930s witnessed Eizenshtein exploring the compositional dynamics of the 'golden section' in relation to Vasilii Surikov's *Boiarynia Morozova* (The Boyar's Wife, Morozova).[50] In an essay worthy of an art historian, he later analysed in microscopic detail Valentin Serov's portrait of the theatre actress M. N. Ermolova and Il'ia Repin's portrait of Tolstoi.[51] In the late 1930s and early-to-mid 1940s, moreover, he became interested in the challenges posed by the advent of colour and gave detailed consideration to how this technology might usefully be applied to cinema.[52]

This expertise and interest notwithstanding, with the exception of *Que Viva Mexico!*, the ethnographic and painterly sources of which have been extensively commented upon, the relationship between the works and artists cited in these essays and the visual language of Eizenshtein's films remains to be explored. It should be pointed out that many of the references to contemporary trends are prompted by a desire to expose kinetic tendencies in related art forms and the montage principles latent within them. By the same token, some of the essays are abstract speculations with little or no application to the actual practices of filmmaking. Eizenshtein's discussion of aspect ratio in 'The Dynamic Square', for example, falls squarely into this category; so, too, does his discussion of Surikov's painting, which turns out on closer inspection to be an analysis of the dramatic structure of *Bronenosets Potemkin,* rather than its visual poetics. The same caveats should be applied to Eizenshtein's drawings. Relatively few of these constitute preparatory work for the visual realization of cinematic material, or offer evidence of a particular set of aesthetic inclinations or a particular and individual approach to the depiction of concrete 'reality'. In their vast majority, they are either the visual expressions of intellectual ideas, or, where 'secret', the exploration of private fantasies and deep-seated, highly personal anxieties.[53]

When Eizenshtein talked in 1926 about his artistic principles in terms of the rejection of 'intuitive creativity' in favour of the 'rational constructive composition of effective elements', and described his early films as a 'purely mathematical affair' that was akin to designing 'a utilitarian steel works', he was consciously referring to concepts that had been developed by artists who belonged to the Constructivist movement (although his allegiance was informal for most of the decade, it was nevertheless formally 'ratified' by his signing of the manifesto issued by the so-called October Group in 1928).[54] For Gan, one of the founder members of the movement, cinematography was one of the three spheres of design activity (the others being architecture and graphic design) where the methods of Constructivism had been successfully implemented and their practical impact felt most keenly.[55] The interest in Eizenshtein as a 'Constructivist artist' has certainly produced one of the most illuminating studies of his approach to visual material in recent times.[56] The concept of the artist as an 'engineer'; the work of art as something 'manufactured'; the idea of montage as a mechanical form of assembly (the term here assuming the nuance of the factory assembly line); the promotion of the utilitarian function of art; and the adherence to the imperative of 'social command' all belong to the lexicon of early Constructivist manifestos.[57] Viewed from this perspective, Eizenshtein's films are analogous to the 'limited design tasks' which early Constructivist artists set themselves, these giving rise in due course to a range of practical initiatives which included graphic design, exhibition design and typography, and experiments in the spheres of photo-montage and still photography.[58] The settings of Eizenshtein's films within urban and proletarian environments, the interest they display in modern technology, the care and attention with which the films render the material textures of this technology, and the experimental approach to intertitles offer further evidence of his allegiance to models and practices that were pioneered by Constructivists. Even the move away from the studio interior and the shift towards the illusion of documentary realism, echoes of which can be found in Sergei Tret'iakov's designation of Eizenshtein as a 'plenarist' (from the French, plein air, meaning painters who prefer to work outdoors), might be viewed as analogous to the Constructivist rejection of the classical painter's atelier.[59] This tendency is manifested not only in Eizenshtein's directorial methods, but also in the compositional strategies of his films. The linear emphasis, the careful manipulation and choreographing of human movement within the frame to accentuate graphic imperatives, the laconicism and absence of decorativeness, the degree of expressivity, and the manipulation of tone in order to produce blocks of colour and extreme tonal contrasts offer powerful evidence of an essentially Constructivist inclination. This was recognized by Tisse, for example, who spoke of the plakatnost' (film-poster quality) of Stachka.[60] It is confirmed, moreover, by the ease with which frame stills from Bronenosets Potemkin were incorporated into poster designs by Constructivist artists themselves.[61]

The Constructivist model, however, while certainly productive, is not in itself sufficient to explain the compositional fabric of Eizenshtein's films. This is because there are too many instances where the individual shot or sequence deviates radically from Constructivist norms. Against the principle of laconicism, one might juxtapose those frequent instances where there is a saturation of pictorial information. Against the principle of clarity, one might oppose the impressionistic tendency, i.e., the interest in capturing flickering movement, the occasional resort to 'sentimental' soft-focus, and the adoption of a 'frenzied' hand-held camera, which ruptures the canon of a fixed viewpoint. Against the principle of realism, one might point to the tendency towards caricature, exaggeration and the grotesque by means of wide-angle lenses. Most importantly, as is the case with Rodchenko's photographs in the 1920s, the Constructivist model is inadequate for the study of lighting practices and the ways in which objects, textures and spaces are modelled by means of natural and artificial sources of illumination. It cannot account for the interest in dynamic lighting effects, or the lyrical treatment of natural landscape, or the use of ornament where it has a conceptual role to play as part of the dramaturgy. Neither does it explain images that seek to communicate a particular mood or atmosphere, or which aim to shock the spectator, such as the scene in the abattoir in Stachka, the locus classicus of the montage procedure as initially conceptualized by Eizenshtein.

A more productive and flexible model is required to take into account the variety of cinematographic methods adopted by Eizenshtein in collaboration with Tisse and their promotion as solutions to the very specific challenges posed by the dramaturgy of the libretto or screenplay. The revolutionary content of these libretti and the avant-garde ferment in the related visual arts no doubt determined the experimental nature of these solutions and their subversion of pre-revolutionary norms. Like Rodchenko, with whose photographic works during the 1920s their films bear close comparison, Eizenshtein and Tisse were essentially engaged in a project to 'discover the visible world'. Part of this process involved a new approach to the concept of photogenicity. Rather than ignore or repudiate the problem of aestheticism, they instead promoted new concepts of the beautiful that apply as much to the urban and rural topographies that feature in their films as to the landscape of the human face. Tisse's desire in *Staroe i novoe* to challenge the traditional disdain for rural areas on the grounds that they were allegedly 'unphotogenic' is symptomatic of this commitment.[62] What emerges is a new landscape, and a new photographic means of communicating this landscape.

Baptism of Fire: Documentary Newsreel and the Beginnings of Soviet Cinema

The degree of training that Tisse enjoyed in relation to the visual arts generally before he became a camera operator is unclear from his autobiographical statements. The courses he attended at the photography and painting studio of Professor Grenzinger in Liepája took place in the evenings, which suggests they were primarily a hobby.[63] Although Grenzinger himself gave lectures on art history for three months of the year at the Academy of Arts in Munich, a hotbed of Secessionist tendencies at the turn of the century, surviving photographs and paintings that bear the company logo suggest a commercial operation that specialized in conventional landscape views of the city and portraits of its inhabitants.[64]

Like those of other camera operators working in Russia, it would appear that Tisse's career proper started in the sphere of photography.[65] In his memoirs of these early beginnings, Tisse emphasizes his photographic studies, his rapid acquisition of the necessary skills as an apprentice, Grenzinger's purchase of a Pathé motion-picture camera, his study of the mechanics of this camera, and his first moving pictures in the summer of 1913. Typically for the time, these conformed to the genre of 'landscape scene'. As the sole person in charge of this camera, Tisse was responsible for filming, chemical processing, editing and the production of intertitles. Furthermore, such was the commercial success of his early shorts that the camera was given to him by Grenzinger as a present. With this camera, quite by chance, Tisse captured the outbreak of the First World War, in other words, the opening salvos of the German naval assault on Liepája. The same camera accompanied him on his various peregrinations during the war itself: his move to Riga with his parents to escape the German assault; his drafting into the imperial army; and his four years at the front as a camera operator attached to the 834th Preobrazhenskii Regiment. The Pathé camera was still in his possession when the overthrow of the monarchy in February 1917 forced the disbanding of the regiment and his demobilization to Moscow. This was followed by his application for work with the newly established Moscow Cinema Committee, and a number of assignments that consisted largely of shooting documentary or newsreel footage with an agitational imperative.[66] The next three years witnessed his shooting of newsreel material relating to important public events; the work of agit-trains during the Civil War; the military activities of the Red Army along the western, southern and eastern fronts; and images of the famine and typhoid epidemic that swept through the Lower Volga region in 1921.[67] During these same years, Tisse shot a number of educational documentaries, either in collaboration with directors or independently, and a number of agitprop features, including the first example of the genre, *Signal* (The Signal, 1918), which he photographed alongside the director Aleksandr Arkatov.[68] Remarkably, from 1918 to the spring of 1923, when he was introduced to Eizenshtein, Tisse could boast participation in the making of nearly fifty films in different genres. Twenty of these were longer than three reels in length; and half of these twenty were photographed and edited by him.[69]

So little of the wartime footage has survived, and such are the difficulties of attribution, that it is difficult to draw firm conclusions about the impact of these formative years on Tisse's development as a camera operator.[70] Quite clearly, it is necessary to draw a distinction between his approach to his material before and after the October Revolution. The footage Tisse shot during the First World War, for example, was invariably sent by his regiment to the film department of the Skobelev Committee; there it was censored and edited, and combined with material from other sources, before being released for propaganda purposes.[71] While a reasonable quantity of war-time footage has survived, the problem of authorship, as has been recognized by RGAKFD, is insuperable.[72] This can be gauged by a recent monograph which has published stills from such footage, the vast majority unattributed unless the product of an official commission.[73] The same applies to the war material Shub included in *Padenie dinastii Romanovykh* (The Fall of the Romanov Dynasty, 1927), the compilation of which is notorious because, among other things, in selecting the material for inclusion Shub made it virtually impossible to catalogue it properly.

Issues of specific authorship aside, however, some general points can be made about the imperatives of shooting newsreel chronicles during this war. Tisse belonged to a large contingent of camera operators, some Russian, some foreign, but nearly all of them employed by private companies, who were attached to tsarist army divisions and were active along various military fronts. Their recollections describe the war as a 'baptism of fire' and emphasize the qualities of fortitude, athleticism, patience and bravery. Novitskii, for example, an experienced camera operator with whom Tisse became acquainted in the Latvian city of Kreitsburg (now Krustpils), and from whom, on his own admission, he gained invaluable advice, drew a distinction between Russian and German cameramen: the former, he claimed, were prepared to risk their lives in order to capture images from the battlefield, whereas the latter generally steered clear of the action (they apparently fixed their Ernemann cameras to armoured vehicles and operated them mechanically with battery-powered motors without bothering to look through the viewfinders).[74] Novitskii himself developed an armour-plated shield to protect his camera from enemy fire, this allowing him to shoot the realities of trench warfare at relatively close quarters.[75] Tisse, moreover, experienced the dangers of such filming when he entered Dvinsk in advance of his division and was nearly executed by the Germans for espionage.[76]

The challenges of shooting effective footage in the arena of war were universally acknowledged at the time. As Mur pointed out a few years later, the mechanics of modern combat were not in themselves intrinsically photogenic. Only the presence of heavy artillery (smoke, he claims, being the mainstay of much wartime footage) was potentially effective on screen, but there was a drawback in the sense that such explosions could create so much fog that visibility was seriously impaired. In such circumstances, he argued, the best material was shot by operators who were daring, fearless and able to respond to events quickly.[77] Tisse himself managed to record his regiment being attacked by planes equipped with machine guns.[78] During the course of the war, moreover, as he himself indicates, what began purely as a mechanical operation to record the 'facts' of war was transformed into a search for 'interesting subjects [and] interesting frames'.[79] One of the very few stills to have survived from his newsreel footage of this period displays a characteristic laconicism and strongly linear emphasis: a line of soldiers in semi-silhouette moves towards the camera across an empty terrain, with only a single windmill and lone tree visible on the horizon against the background of a cloudless sky.[80]

The events of the February and October Revolutions undeniably added fresh impetus to the creative endeavours of those Russian camera operators who decided to stay in Russia and work for the new Soviet government. For Tisse, who described the enthusiasm with which crowds flocked to watch newsreels that concerned their daily lives, the origins of Soviet cinema lay precisely in the agitational footage produced during the Civil War.[81] His view is confirmed by Boltianskii, a member of the Petrograd Cinema Committee and a tireless advocate of documentary film, who argued that it was the *engagé* position of the camera operator and his ability to communicate that sense of commitment which was the crucial difference between early Soviet newsreels and their tsarist-era precursors.[82] For the filmmakers themselves, the element of political agitation required a more organized and planned approach to their material. Tisse spoke of the need to record that which was 'most important [and] typical', an approach which, in part, was conditioned by shortages of negative film stock and gave rise to a high degree of selectivity (like others, he experimented with positive film stock for some of his work).[83] Furthermore, the camera operator was now frequently in charge of his material and thus responsible for its coherence as an edited whole.[84] It is unclear whether these skills were acquired independently or via the directors with whom they were sometimes assigned engagements. Kuleshov, for example, who worked with several camera operators during the Civil War, has claimed that few appreciated the significance of montage and the possibility of deliberately organizing the material by introducing close-ups and expressive shots; specifically, he refers to his 'endless disputes' with Tisse, with whom he directed three agit-films on the Eastern Front in 1919, and who dismissed such manipulations as 'impermissible' and 'illiterate'.[85] Without being able to compare their respective films during this period, the truth of the matter is difficult to ascertain.[86] Certainly, Tisse's inventiveness is not open to question. Kuleshov himself remarks on Tisse's 'miracles of documentary agility' and recalls an incident, possibly the first instance of its kind in the history of cinema, when Tisse responded to unexpected artillery fire by removing his Eclair camera from its tripod and recording the attack.[87] A later example of inventiveness was noticed by Eizenshtein himself. The sequence in question was a tracking-shot in Tisse's 1923 documentary on the Nadezhdinskii factory in the Urals (entitled *Ot stali do rel's* (From Steel to Rails), it was the result of a special expedition organized by Goskino).[88] According to Aleksandrov, having watched the footage in a state of 'rapture', Eizenshtein later enquired about the technical execution of a sequence that involved the camera travelling the entire length of a conveyor belt carrying iron ore above the floor of the workshop, and seemingly on the verge of disappearing into a burning furnace.[89] Tisse explained that it was an unorthodox trick shot that had been achieved by splicing together two separate segments of film, one shot with a 50mm lens, and the other with a 75mm lens.[90]

Stachka: Documentary Authenticity Meets Theatrical Eccentricity

By the time Eizenshtein made this enquiry, he was a well established figure within the Proletkul't theatre movement. He had been appointed chief set designer in July 1921 by Valentin Smyshlaev and had produced a number of costume and set designs, most notably for Smyshlaev's theatre adaptation of Jack London's 'The Mexican', which was staged in 1921, as well as for a number of productions that were never realized.[91] Attendance at the GVYRM under the tutelage of Vsevolod Meierkhol'd and twice-weekly lectures in theatre and art history at VKhUTEMAS in 1921 and 1922 were sufficient to facilitate Eizenshtein's move into theatre direction, a long-harboured ambition which he achieved courtesy of the commission to stage Ostrovskii's classic as part of the centenary celebrations of the dramatist's birth. A recently published reconstruction of the performance shows it to be an energetic piece of agitprop that fizzed with invention and drew very much on the vogue for circus-style attractions.[92] Among these attractions were two fragments of film that Eizenshtein arranged to have projected onto a screen at different intervals during the play's epilogue. A third fragment of film, which consisted of a 'director's farewell' and showed Eizenshtein bowing to the camera in front of a production poster, was screened right at the end of the performance as the actors were taking their bows, and was accompanied by fire-crackers being let off under the seats of the audience. These fragments are usually referred to by the title *Dnevnik Glumova*, although for reasons which I have explained elsewhere this title is highly misleading.[93]

In 'Montazh attraktsionov' ('The Montage of Attractions'), his first essay on the subject of montage, Eizenshtein described two of the fragments as parodies of the detective and comedy genres; this article and a short essay that he co-authored in 1922 with Sergei Iutkevich, an artist and set designer who had become a key figure in FEKS, suggest that his film interests at this stage lay in popular genres, in particular the works of Charlie Chaplin.[94] This is confirmed by his later writings, which discuss the two fragments of *Dnevnik Glumova* in the context of the stunt-filled adventure thrillers of Harry Piel, an actor and director known at the time as the 'German Douglas Fairbanks', and the *Mysteries of New York*, an American murder-mystery series starring Pearl White.[95] In '25 i 15', Eizenshtein seems to relish the stark contrast between his fascination for American comedies – he mentions a number of foreign film stars who were household names in Russia before the Revolution – and Tisse's more serious preoccupations during the early years of the First World War.[96]

The parodying of these genres in *Dnevnik Glumova* doubtless explains the rather conventional camerawork in all three fragments; indeed, two of Eizenshtein's left-wing associates, Gan and Shub, criticized the footage for its lack of 'cinematic' qualities.[97] Levshin's retrospective account of the filming of *Dnevnik Glumova* suggests a degree of nervousness on Eizenshtein's part in relation to the 'magical' apparatus of the camera: he recalls the director's disappointment, after eventually summoning up the courage to place his eye against the viewfinder, on discovering that the image was projected upside down.[98] As other memoirs from the period attest, however, Eizenshtein was keen to educate himself about filmmaking generally. This explains his attendance at classes in Kuleshov's workshop at the GTK, his private conversations with Kuleshov specifically on the subject of montage, and his invitation to Kuleshov to give lectures to the Proletkul't in March 1923.[99] It also explains his experiments with Aleksandrov in the editors' suite at Goskino, where Shub was reediting foreign films in order to make them palatable for domestic consumption. Aleksandrov has suggested that by repositioning or removing certain scenes, as well as by altering existing intertitles or inserting new ones and on one occasion even combining two entirely different films into a single entity, it was possible to reveal themes that were either non-existent or only latent within the original material.[100] This is confirmed by Eizenshtein, who claimed that the method of *peremontazhka* (re-editing) allowed him to reverse completely the meaning of a climactic scene in Dimitri Buchowetzki's *Danton* (1921).[101] Whether these experiments were entirely successful is difficult to judge. Some commentators found the replacement intertitles intrusive and patronizing, and complained that the removal or repositioning of crucial sequences often rendered the action and meaning incoherent.[102] These experiments nevertheless appear to have confirmed for Eizenshtein the validity of the 'Kuleshov effect' and thus supplied the foundation for his own theory of montage.

Although it is customary to analyse *Stachka* from the point of view of Eizenshtein's embryonic theory of montage, there has been less emphasis on the film as a series of 'attractions' which depend specifically on the technical possibilities of the camera. The significance of this film for the future of Soviet cinematography actually lies less in the semantic potential of montage collision and the accumulation of associations than in the investigation into the camera's potential to produce striking and expressive images. These take a multiplicity of different forms in the film itself. Some are based on the principle of juxtaposition (for example the 'Grand Guignol' abattoir sequence); others manifestly are not (for example the hosing of the demonstrators by firemen). A broad understanding of the concept of the 'attraction' would include the many set-piece and choreographed sequences, the visual gags involving the police spies and the 'King' of the hobos, and the whole paraphernalia of trick photography which, while it may have its origins in the pre-revolutionary era, is given a radically new dimension by virtue of the comic and agitational context. The category of 'attraction' would also include the compositional and lighting strategies in the film. As Kuleshov observed, it was not the montage collisions of *Stachka* that were its most striking characteristic, but rather the radical approach in terms of composition. As he writes:

> He is a director of the single shot, always pleasing to the eye and expressive, less of montage and the human being in movement ... . It is enough to recall the hosing episode in Strike, the infinite savouring of these photogenic sequences, to become totally convinced of the director's good 'eye', of his particular fondness for the plastic construction of the shot.[103]

In microcosmic form, this set-piece sequence, with the jet sprays of water striking the surfaces of bodies to produce a dazzling splintering of the image, also demonstrates the influence of experimental trends in contemporary art, in particular, Cubo-Futurism and Rayonism, which were themselves influenced by cinema (Fig. 4).[104]

From the point of view of its cinematography, *Stachka* is a veritable powder keg of inventive ideas. It employs a panoply of devices that are full of audacity and push to the limit the boundaries of cinematic invention: extreme close-ups, shots that involve the camera being removed from its tripod, the adoption of unconventional angles of vision, the 'Dutch tilt', 'washing' (allowing the main subject to move out of focus) and a range of trick photography, as well as diagonal and vertical wipes and eccentrically shaped irises. It is a modernist experiment that demonstrates acute awareness of the ways in which objects and space can be modelled expressively within the frame. *Stachka* activates the full height, breadth and depth of the cinematic image and adopts a number of compositional principles that break radically with convention: decentralization, the truncation of the body by the frame periphery and exploration of the permeability of the frame by means of objects falling or protruding into it. These devices endow the film with an extraordinary visual energy. Despite its overall pathos, *Stachka* borders on the playful and self-referential, revealing at regular intervals the potential illusionism of cinema, with its conjuring tricks and apparently magical transformations. In some respects, *Stachka* is a love letter to the technical possibilities of the moving-picture camera: it returns film to its origins as fairground attraction and forces the audience to re-experience it as a technological marvel. No better illustration of this procedure can be given than the sequence near the beginning which shows the boot of a factory foreman stepping into a puddle, a scene presented in reverse, and seemingly with the camera upside down. The possibility that this might be an editing error should not be excluded. The more likely scenario, however, is that Eizenshtein opted on the editing table to turn the footage upside down and in so doing reverse its motion.

One of the defining characteristics of *Stachka* from the visual point of view is its predilection for frame-within-frame constructions. These occur at regular intervals and are intriguing in the sense that they are potentially self-referential, reminding the viewer not only of the presence of the frame boundary, but also of the ways in which the space within the frame has been organized pictorially. Within the first few minutes, for example, the viewer encounters an image of shadowy figures and objects cast against a huge glass wall on a factory floor which has been organized vertically and horizontally into a grid pattern (Fig. 5). The scene in question belongs to a series early in the film that seeks to evoke the conspiratorial nature of the strike agitation. The presence of this grid, however, draws attention to the way in which the shot has been composed: the division of the frame into six rectangular zones; the arrangement of lines, contours and visual patterns within those zones; and the human activity taking place within each zone, all of which is presented within a single plane, the glass wall functioning almost as a semi-opaque canvas. As the film progresses, this exercise in spatial dissection is repeated with variations. Shortly afterwards, for example, there is a scene in the director's office which is photographed through the panes of a door. The image gives the impression of being masked along the left-hand side of the frame. In addition, the respective figures (the manager and foreman on the left and the director on the right) are compartmentalized by means of the glass squares within the door. This split-screen effect is echoed later in the trick shots with the police-style photographs. On the first occasion, the viewer is presented with four photographs of police spies that suddenly come to life. The screen is divided into four rectangular frames, each one active in the pictorial sense. Furthermore, the visual joke relies not only on the fact that the figures in question unfreeze, this humorously marking the distinction between cinema and still photography, but also that one of the spies hangs his bowler hat nonchalantly on a hook outside the frame, thus revealing the 'frame' to be an optical illusion. The second example, which involves two photographs of a wanted strike leader (his face is presented in profile and from an axial position), works in a similar way: not only does he also come to life, but he disappears from view by apparently walking into himself, a gloriously surreal visual joke.

Although such shots are clearly intended as 'attractions', they belong to a series of frame-within-frame compositions which dissect the screen into separate zones of activity. In their most primitive forms, these compositions involve the use of vignettes to mask parts of the screen, for example creating the 'widescreen' effect of the four women accompanying the accordion player towards the end of Part One. Elsewhere, natural objects are used to frame the action. In the scene of the four shareholders in Part Three, for example, which is shot from an axial position and realized so cleverly that it is initially unclear whether the camera is filming into a mirror, the action is framed by high columns and steps. In Part Six, a female inhabitant of the tenement blocks is framed by the legs and underbelly of a soldier's horse; a striking worker lies wounded, if not actually dead, in a doorway while troops on horseback continue their chase of his fellow strikers in the background; and as women in the tenement blocks desperately climb ladders to escape these same troops, it is the side of a building, reduced to a black, rectangular mass by means of exposure, which limits the zone of their movement. As variations on such devices, the square-shaped and rectangular irises that frequently, and rather unusually, focus the spectator's attention on a particular part of the screen should also be emphasized. The same result is achieved by means of rhomboid and diamond-shaped irises which, while not reminiscent of the film frame proper, nevertheless frame the action for brief moments. The most interesting of these frames follows an inventive and self-referential double exposure that combines an image of a police spy taking a photograph of a wanted strike leader with the actual image seen by the camera and then printed in a darkroom (the image here is also framed, this time by means of an iris). The shapes of these irises are further echoed in shots that frame human portraits by means of rhomboid-like shapes: the window that frames the dwarf who introduces the police spy to the 'king' of the hobos; and the shot of the king's reflection in a mirror.

If these sequences emphasize screen dimension and form a nexus of images in which simultaneous action occurs on a single plane, *Stachka* is also noteworthy for its staging in depth, in particular its incorporation of simultaneous action on several planes receding into the depth of the frame. Some of these compositions, for example those in which parts of human bodies or natural objects are brought close to the camera, were facilitated by Tisse's use of a 35mm lens, something which, while it did not possess the distorting capacity of the wide-angle lens proper (28mm and below), allowed him to increase the depth of field in conditions of strong sunlight. Relatively straightforward versions of this kind of staging are found in the opening sequences, but these become more complex as the film progresses and reach their climax during the storming of the tenement blocks sequence in Part Six. During the agitational sequences in Part One, for example, the viewer is presented in the foreground with the back of the factory foreman's body (shoulders and head), while in the background workers are visible, perched on scaffolding. This compositional device is echoed in the chase sequences (a police agent tries to spy on two of the striking workers as they walk around town), which involve an astonishing number of shots in which architectural structures, most characteristically the walls of the Kremlin, but also various arcades, are exploited to supply depth to the frame. In the 'Liquidation' chapter, there is a whole series of such compositions: the initial dispersal sequence, in which a small crowd is positioned in front of the camera, while in the medium background the legs of Cossack horses are visible; the scene that shows a young child walking between the legs of these same horses; the shots of two children playing on a tenement walkway; the shot of workers trying to escape towards the camera; and the distressing moment in which a Cossack rider lifts one of the children and drops him or her from a walkway. In general, the tenement sequence is an orgy of simultaneous action, the position and angle of the camera exploiting the architecture of the building, namely, the railings and spanning walkways, to divide the frame into diagonal sections, each one activated in order to indicate the scale and brutality of the pacification (Fig. 6).

Set-piece scenes like the storming of the tenement blocks are revealing about the potential power of cinematography. If they are visually arresting, it is less the result of their position within a larger montage sequence than that of their compositional dynamism. The editing of these sequences, still very much indebted to D. W. Griffith, lends dramatic tension and rhythm to the whole. But the individual images themselves have been manipulated in such a way as to maximize what Eizenshtein described later as the effect of 'extreme expressivity'.[105]

One device for achieving this effect lies in the positioning of the camera at extremely high or low angles, not necessarily to communicate a subjective point of view. This technique, known as foreshortening, signals a major subversion of accepted convention at the time. As far as the Soviet Union was concerned, the device of foreshortening was associated primarily with photographers grouped around LEF, in particular Rodchenko, who expressed his profound disdain for the conventional view, or what he later dubbed 'photography from the belly button'.[106] *Stachka* is one of the first films in world cinema to explore radically and systematically the effects of foreshortening. This is undertaken not merely to supply unexpected points of view, in other words, as part of a modernist project to defamiliarize the spectator, but also as a means of enhancing the sense of linear perspective. In their more extreme variants, for example in the tenement block sequence, these camera positions strongly accentuate the essential drama of the action. It is noticeable that Eizenshtein and Tisse resort to such compositions at moments of greatest tension, for example just before the body of the child is thrown over the railings during the 'Liquidation' sequence. This scene is preceded by a vertical panning shot which involves the camera being initially positioned on the ground and then gradually tilted upwards to reveal the upper walkways of the block. Here, the effect of foreshortening is shown in the process of realization: the angular lines of the walkways gradually become steeper to accentuate the full height of the block, and thus, by extension, the distance of the child's fall. A similarly dramatic juxtaposition, but one conveyed by means of two separate shots, involves the camera being positioned axially in relation to the blocks and then moved slightly closer and upwards: here the lines formed by the railings on both sides of the screen angle steeply downwards into the middle of the frame.

The entire tenement sequence consists of a myriad of linear constructions, with the lines of the building and the shadows cast by railings combining to form dramatic intersecting and diagonal patterns. This interest in geometric form is a consistent feature of *Stachka* and is anticipated during the earlier hosing sequences when jets of water produce strongly graphic and textured patterns. In the close-ups of the fleeing workers, water strikes their faces and bodies and explodes into glittering sprays, which, like frenzied brushstrokes, erase the contours of the human forms. At several intervals this water creates a semi-transparent curtain between the camera lens and the object, at moments verging on abstraction. The use of *contre-jour* in this context is also extremely expressive. When one of the strike leaders is pushed by two streams of water into a hole from which he is captured later by the firemen, the jets create brilliantly white clouds which are juxtaposed against the black masses of nearby buildings. A similar operation is witnessed for the scene in which another demonstrating worker, moving unsteadily between buildings, is caught in the crossfire of two jets, one of them aimed directly at the camera by a fireman framed in the background. Photographing into the sun here creates a silhouette of the body that is sharply contrasted with the white flashes produced by the water.

Eizenshtein later rejected the deliberate calculation of such scenes. In his view, they were simply 'a technical analysis of the combination of bodies and rushing water', and he compared them with the Odessa Steps sequence in *Bronenosets Potemkin*, where there were 'real' bullets and 'dead bodies'.[107] Yet if the expressive effect was disproportionate to the actual danger faced by the victims – here, in essence, lay the charge of formalism that would fatally cripple the avant-garde at the end of the 1920s – these images blazed a trail towards the establishment of what would later become known as 'poetic cinema'.

Evreiskoe schast'e: Documentary Authenticity Meets the Poetics of Nostalgia

In the absence of detailed information about the relevant decision-making processes, it is difficult to assess Tisse's specific contribution to the visual ingenuity of *Stachka*.

Within the ARK, it would appear, there were voices that spoke of Tisse having 'co-created' the film; this provoked a sharp riposte from Eizenshtein, who invoked the cinematography on *Starets Vasilii Griaznov*, an anti-religious drama shot in 1924, as evidence of an outdated and conservative tendency.[108] The rancorous debate was recalled in hindsight by Eizenshtein in a speech that he was planning to deliver at the ARK discussion of *Bronenosets Potemkin* in January 1926: here, he wanted to point to *Evreiskoe schast'e* in further support of his argument.[109]

Doubtless part of the defensiveness displayed in this planned speech reflected a genuine concern with the issue of authorship, one that had been played out publicly in the pages of the film press, but which had revolved primarily around the authorial rights that Pletnev and the Proletkul't were claiming in relation to *Stachka*; according to Kleiman, Eizenshtein's appeal for his authorial rights to be recognized because of the ways in which he, as director, had given filmic expression to Pletnev's libretto was one of the first declarations of its kind in the history of cinema.[110] The relative lack of charity in Eizenshtein's planned remarks about Tisse (the course of the debate within the ARK prevented him from delivering them in their entirety) is not necessarily the issue here; they were, in any case, balanced by his acceptance that, having shown 'fraternal solidarity' by ignoring the camera operators' boycott of *1905 god* at Goskino and cutting short his trip abroad, Tisse had rescued *Bronenosets Potemkin* from disaster (Eizenshtein described his arrival in Odessa as the first 'sunny day' of the production).[111] More important is the fact that, in relation to *Evreiskoe schast'e*, Eizenshtein's planned comments were wide of the mark and suggest a lack of analytical sophistication. Not only is the camerawork on *Evreiskoe schast'e* unorthodox for a film that aspires to the genre of comedy, but it also constitutes a very obvious bridge between the compositional methods adopted in *Stachka* and those that would be utilized in due course in *Bronenosets Potemkin*. The fact that they pertain to a work Tisse shot with a different director – one, moreover, with no prior experience of cinema – is powerful evidence, indeed crucial evidence, of his trademark 'signature' at this relatively early stage in his career.

The importance of *Evreiskoe schast'e* as the first example of Yiddish cinema in the Soviet Union has tended to detract from detailed analysis of its camerawork. The screenplay was based on several pre-revolutionary stories by the popular Jewish writer Sholom Aleichem, and the production boasted the participation of a number of prominent Jewish artists: the director, Granovskii, who had been a founding member and director of the Moscow State Jewish Theatre (GOSET);[112] Solomon Mikhoels, the actor playing the role of the main protagonist, Menachem Mendel, who was affiliated to GOSET; Isaak Babel', the writer whose *Konarmiia* (Red Cavalry) and *Odesskie rasskazy* (Odessa Tales) would be published shortly after the release of *Evreiskoe schast'e*, and who composed the intertitles; and Natan Al'tman, the artist renowned for his Cubo-Futurist portraits of Anna Akhmatova, who was responsible for the production design.

The film has been interpreted as a pointed critique of the conditions that prevailed in the *shtetls* of tsarist Russia, but one nevertheless characterized by a gentle humour and a 'preservationist spirit'.[113] The plot consists of a series of humorous episodes that chart the attempts of the main protagonist, Menachem Mendel, to escape a life of poverty in his home town of Berdichev. Having failed in his attempts to sell life insurance to a wealthy Jewish magnate, Kimbak, Menachem Mendel joins forces with a young friend, Zalman, to try and acquire a fortune by other means (the latter loves the daughter, Beila, of the same magnate, but has been told in no uncertain terms that he is not wealthy enough to become her husband). The adventures of these two men take them initially to Odessa, where they try their hand at selling clothes at a local market. They rent a room in a bed and breakfast owned by a local *shadkhen* (matchmaker) called Itzik, find themselves arrested by a policeman for not having a licence to trade, bribe this policeman (and his immediate superior) in order to escape a jail sentence, tout for insurance business by trying to make the acquaintance of mourners at a passing funeral, and then, quite by chance, acquire Itzik's list of eligible brides. On his way home to Berdichev by train, Menachem Mendel falls asleep and dreams of exporting Jewish brides to America on an industrial scale. This slightly surreal vision begins with him meeting a potential client on the famous Odessa Steps and introducing her to Baron Hirsch, the director of an American marital agency. Our hero promises to supply the baron with hordes of eligible brides from Berdichev; these are then shown being transported to the city in goods wagons, after which they are hoisted onto the decks of a steamship and set sail. Such is Menachem Mendel's excitement at the thought of having 'saved' the Jewish bachelors of America that he ascends a lighthouse in the harbour to watch the ship depart, energetically rings the lighthouse bell and joyfully leaps into the sea below. By dint of another chance acquaintance, this time with a genuine *shadkhen*, Usher, from Iarmolinsk, whom he meets on the train after waking from his slumber, and with whom he tries to arrange the marriage of Beila, the plot takes an even more farcical twist. The wedding preparations are organized and the two 'parties' in the company of their respective families and matchmakers arrive at the chosen venue, only to discover that the 'parties' in question are both women. In the absence of any other suitable partner at the venue, a humiliated and desperate Kimbak allows Zalman, now gainfully employed as Menachem Mendel's assistant, to marry his daughter.

As a comedy set in the provinces, despite the differences in milieu and chronological setting, *Evreiskoe schast'e* is analogous to Protazanov's *Zakroishchik iz Torzhka* (The Tailor from Torzhok), which was released in the same month and with which it was compared by a number of reviewers. As they noted, both films presented themselves as critiques of pre-revolutionary life (or, in the case of *Zakroishchik iz Torzhka*, the vestiges of unreconstructed mentalities which had survived into the post-revolutionary epoch), and both enlisted the talents of actors specializing in eccentric comedy to play the roles of the hapless heroes.[114]

One of the crucial differences between the two productions, however, lies in their respective camerawork. In the case of *Evreiskoe schast'e*, this endeavours to create an impression of ethnographic authenticity which is entirely absent from *Zakroishchik iz Torzhka*. The scenes in Berdichev and Odessa are clearly filmed on location; the interiors, even where the presence of sets may be suspected, aspire to a high degree of verisimilitude; and the lighting of these interiors, with the adoption of rarely more than two directed sources at any given time, one of them invariably a 'natural' light source (a window to the rear), strives for an unassuming, modest and uncomplicated effect, rather like the design of the interior itself. For a comedy of manners, even a Soviet comedy of manners, this approach was innovative and clearly reflected Granovskii's desire to evoke the period in question with maximum fidelity. As a result of this strategy, the attention given to period detail throughout the film is impressive. This includes the various signs for Jewish shops in Odessa, written in pre-revolutionary orthography; the interior of Itzik's bed and breakfast, with its customary tap to facilitate the ritual washing of hands; and the dramatic treatment of the wedding ceremony itself, with its careful delineation of costumes, ritual gestures and actions, the presence of a jester and band of musicians, and the ritual dancing on tables. This material is presented in painstaking detail, very often at the expense of plot momentum.

At the same time, Tisse's cinematography incorporates within this quasi-documentary impulse a powerful lyricism redolent of a certain nostalgia. This is perhaps understandable because the Jewish communities that formed the pre-revolutionary *shtetls*, thanks to the atrocities perpetrated by occupying White forces and Polish armies fighting for independence during the Civil War, had either been murdered in large numbers or forcibly dispersed (Tisse's time spent with Budennyi's Red Cavalry meant that he may well have experienced this phenomenon at first hand).[115] The landscapes of Berdichev and Odessa are charmingly evoked by Tisse, to the extent that, on occasion, the images assume the character of picture-postcard scenes: tree-lined boulevards stretch endlessly into the distance; rivers flow lazily within their generous banks; houses on stilts populate the steep banks that lead down to these rivers; little 'barges' facilitate the crossing of stretches of water; golden cupolas of Orthodox churches gleam in the distance; lime-daubed apple trees populate the orchards; and neglected, leaning wooden palisades mark the boundaries of ramshackle and impoverished dwellings. For many of these landscape scenes Tisse employs the framing device of the iris. Indeed at times, such as the moment when Zalman and Beila rush to be reunited after the former's return from Odessa, the iris is narrowed to such an extent that the resulting image (a view of the couple sitting on a bench with the river stretching beyond them) is reminiscent of pre-revolutionary still photography. In much the same way, Tisse exploits to the maximum the varieties of southern sunlight, filming at different times of the day and incorporating natural light-effects, for example shadows, which are deployed for compositional purposes, in order to heighten the lyricism of certain scenes. A good illustration of this procedure is the scene in the early part of the film in which Zalman and Beila enjoy a secret rendezvous at the back of Kimbak's house: this shows them moving towards each other blindly, not entirely sure of the other's exact whereabouts, because they are separated by the vertical line of an exterior chimney. Tisse splashes the dark shadows of leaves exquisitely across the whitewashed wall of this building as if the scene were an Impressionist painting, their momentary quivering due to a slight breeze appearing to communicate the lovers' palpitating hearts.

Despite the fact that analogous procedures had been exploited by Tisse in *Stachka* for the lyrical scenes that show the early days of the strike in a seemingly blissful rural setting, one may speculate that it was precisely this kind of pictorial decorativeness that Eizenshtein found so anachronistic in relation to *Evreiskoe schast'e*. It confirms Frelikh's view of Tisse as the camera operator whose most natural milieu was landscape.[116] Furthermore, it lends weight to Aleksandrov's observation that Tisse possessed the unique capacity 'to communicate the air, the spatial depth and the atmosphere of the action', a characteristic that he had detected as early as *Serp i molot* (Hammer and Sickle, 1921).[117] This lyrical sensibility was doubtless anathema to Eizenshtein; on his own admission, he cared little for lyrical sensibilities and had very little appreciation of poetry.[118] By contrast, Tisse emerges on the basis of *Evreiskoe schast'e* as a genuine poet of the provinces, a landscape artist who displays an extraordinary sensitivity to the contours, textures and colours of the natural world. To some extent, *Evreiskoe schast'e* explains the intrusion of lyrical impulses in his later work, in particular those films that he directed himself prior to the advent of Socialist Realism, but also those made with Eizenshtein where the landscape required a response that was intensely exhilarating. Dramaturgical necessity to some extent explains and justifies these impulses, but it does not explain the particular visual forms that these impulses assume.

If this tendency is conservative or, as Frelikh suggests, 'classical', the camerawork in *Evreiskoe schast'e* nevertheless has features that are unorthodox for their time and, as indicated earlier, strongly reminiscent of *Stachka*. The conscious endeavour to enhance the perception of spatial depth within the frame is one such compositional technique. For general landscape views, for example the very first scene of *Evreiskoe schast'e*, which shows children standing by a tree in the foreground, a river flowing slowly in the medium background and buildings huddled together in the distance, Tisse ensures that the frame consists of multiple planes that are all active in the pictorial sense. Although such scenes are more carefully composed than the standard postcard, they are nevertheless conventional as far as artistic photography is concerned. A striking variation on this approach involves the positioning of unimportant figures in the medium background and sometimes, more radically, in the depths of the frame. The moment when Menachem Mendel scolds a group of children who have been playing war games among the local ruins is structured so that he is positioned in the foreground, the children stand in the medium foreground, and in the background there is the wall of a ruin that stretches into the far distance, leading the eye towards a figure who is completely unimportant from the dramatic point of view. It is surprising how often random figures or mobile objects appear in the background of Tisse's compositions; their function, it would appear, is solely to add pictorial dynamism to the frame.

A variation on this technique lies in compositions where Tisse deliberately exploits objects to enhance the spatial depth of the frame. A straightforward example consists of the serried ranks of poplar trees, presented from an axial position, which line the road that brings the guests to the wedding in the film's final episode. A more radical type of composition, one that has analogies to compositions in *Stachka*, occurs during the dream sequence and involves the positioning of the camera right next to the ship's hull for the moment when Baron Hirsch, Menachem Mendel, the ship's captain and the female client descend a staircase from the ship's deck to the quayside in order to inspect the assembled brides: the metallic plates of the ship's hull, and the ropes stretched across them, anchor the right-hand side of the frame all the way into the foreground, which is out of focus. A parallel technique involves positioning the camera so that objects cut into the frame from below, often at an angle, to create diagonal patterns that accentuate the impression of spatial depth. Various objects, for example palisades, benches, staircases and, sometimes, shadows, are deployed solely for this purpose. One such moment occurs when the Odessa policeman, having arrested Zalman for not possessing a trading licence, marches him off to the police station and encounters Menachem Mendel on the way (the angle of a bench and the intruding wall of a nearby house supply the necessary perspective); another is the moment when Menachem Mendel and his female client climb the steps leading to the lighthouse, the camera positioned high above them and casting its gaze downwards at an extreme angle as they climb. A further strategy involves composing the frame so that silhouetted objects, for example trees, are positioned on either side of the frame, but at receding intervals, for action that takes place in the depth of the frame.

Evreiskoe schast'e is full of roads, lanes, pavements and paths that stretch into the distance, very often with a dark 'curtain' of foliage, or the leaning trunks of trees, in the foreground to establish a sense of deep perspective. Another feature of the mise en scène in *Evreiskoe schast'e* arranges for figures to move towards the camera from a long distance away, or vice versa. Numerous examples could be furnished, but the most instructive is the moment when Menachem Mendel meets his client on the Odessa Steps: the camera is positioned at the bottom of the steps and looks upwards, as the former moves from the background into the medium plane and the latter moves from the foreground, with the steps functioning not only as part of a graphic design, but also as markers of the distance travelled in each case. Highly inventive variations on this staging device can be witnessed elsewhere, for example those instances where a character combines movement towards the camera with a traverse across the frame, such as the flight of Itzik from his wife, which follows his horizontal movement along a path beside a river or pond, but which subsequently involves a sharp turn as the path brings him in a loop towards the camera; and the very final scene of the film, which shows the figure of Menachem Mendel standing next to a tree, both of them silhouetted against the rays of the setting sun, after which he moves laterally across the frame, essentially into an empty space, but also, as the viewer realizes after only a few seconds, towards the camera. On two occasions Tisse permits characters to approach the camera and exit via the bottom edge of the frame; and on both occasions, which occur at the end of the wedding scene, the character in question (Menachem Mendel) moves out of focus.

As well as this persistent interest in spatial depth, Tisse also demonstrates an acute awareness of the lateral space of the frame and a systematic penchant for *décadrage*, or decentering. The principle of *décadrage* motivates the compositional arrangements for the scene in which Menachem Mendel walks with a potential client along a riverbank in Odessa in stifling heat: both figures hug the extreme right-hand side of the frame, while the centre and left-hand side consist of a picturesque view of a river punctuated by silhouetted tree trunks and foliage. A direct echo of this composition can be found at the moment when Beila, having learned of Zalman's return to Berdichev, emerges from the door of a house located along one side of a boulevard and runs along the right-hand side of the frame to meet him. A particularly innovative example, because it involves the division of the frame into active zones and a staging in depth, is the scene during Menachem Mendel's dream which shows brides disembarking from a train. The frame here, courtesy of the wagon and its open doors, is organized laterally: brides walk from left to right in front of the wagon in the foreground; a small group of brides peers out of the wagon through the doors, also in the foreground; and beneath the undercarriage of the wagon, thanks to the low position of the camera, a line of brides is shown in the background snaking its way to the embarkation point. Less innovative, but certainly unorthodox, compositions include the shot of Zalman as he moves along the white wall of the rear of Kimbak's house; the moment when Iosele, the maid who acts as a go-between for Zalman and Beila, tries to pass on a message from a cook who is participating in the intrigue; and the moment which uses the veranda of Itzik's bed and breakfast as a graphic dividing line that separates the action on the first floor from that which takes place in the basement (an anonymous figure passes through a door in the lower left-hand corner of the image and exits the frame).

In view of this degree of invention, which is highly experimental in relation to the genre of the film, it is worth scrutinizing in detail Tisse's handling of the port scenes in Odessa. In many respects, the anatomy of this port is communicated to the viewer in ways that anticipate the camerawork on *Bronenosets Potemkin*, despite the very different dramaturgical contexts. Geometric arrangement and linear emphasis, combined with extreme camera angles, inform the compositional approach to the dream sequence in *Evreiskoe schast'e* no less than the mutiny sequence in the later and more famous work. Tisse arranges multiple planes of action and uses the linear patterns created by decking and other objects to create diagonal constructions. A good illustration of this tendency is the shot from a high angle that depicts brides being hoisted aboard the ship by means of a cargo lift. Three planes of action are present here: the ship's crew standing by the railings;

the brides in the lift; and a group of brides on the quayside waiting to be lifted aboard. Furthermore, the lines of the railings, the ship's deck and the planks of the quayside, as well as the sides of the lift, create a striking set of diagonal patterns. An analogous, albeit more complicated arrangement, because the effect brings lines into conflict, shows various brides as they walk along the deck: the benches on which other passengers are seated and the ship's deck produce lines in one direction, while a counterweight exists in the form of bars and the shadows formed by these bars, as well as the shadows of the brides and a large funnel positioned to the right of the frame. As in *Bronenosets Potemkin*, Tisse exploits the ship's architecture for compositional purposes. The masts, cables and wires create geometric patterns for the scene in which one of the brides, a 'special consignment', is hoisted high above the deck, and also for the scene in which the ship's captain gives the command to depart, where the funnels with steam escaping from them are photographed *contre-jour* in order to emphasize contour rather than surface texture. Tisse offers forward-looking views towards the ship's prow, populated by clusters of brides, with the ship's structures intruding into the depth of the frame. There is also an additional, angled view upward that shows a sailor in the crow's nest looking out to sea, the mast, rigging, cables, chains and curved railing supplying a simple, linear poetry. The geometry of human form is also exploited in *Evreiskoe schast'e* to the extent that the brides, who are dressed in white and lined up en masse alongside railings, ascending staircases or being winched aboard, have their equivalent in the serried ranks of sailors in uniform who crowd the sides of the destroyer in *Bronenosets Potemkin*. Even the round shape of the iris for these scenes, which would normally be viewed as little more than a mainstream framing device, acquires a geometric resonance.

A Visual 'Minefield': The Reenactment of 'History' in *Bronenosets Potemkin*

In the third of five feuilletons that appeared in *Gamburgskii schet* (The Hamburg Reckoning), a collection of essays, articles and reminiscences published in 1928, the Formalist theoretician Viktor Shklovskii drew attention to the inclusion of the Odessa Steps in *Evreiskoe schast'e* and compared Granovskii's conventional exploitation of its architecture and spatial dynamics with Eizenshtein's significantly more complex treatment in *Bronenosets Potemkin*; as he comments, 'the steps are the same, the camera operator is the same, but the goods are different!'.[119] There may have been an ulterior purpose behind this observation in the sense that Shklovskii had been involved in an ungentlemanly spat with Tisse shortly after the release of *Evreiskoe schast'e*. In a brief exchange of letters published in *Kino* and euphemistically entitled 'An Exchange between Friends', the critic had complained that the film was 'badly shot', to which Tisse responded, somewhat tartly, that his learned comrade was insufficiently versed in the mechanics of filmmaking to realize that the problem lay with the laboratory technicians who had developed the negative and printed copies for distribution. (Tisse had abandoned the film at the post-production phase in order to join Eizenshtein's unit for the shooting of *Bronenosets Potemkin*, and thus had forfeited his usual control of these procedures). Shklovskii nevertheless stuck to his position: not only did he assert that there were 'mistakes' in the film that could not be blamed on the laboratory, he added, rather confusingly, that there were no close-ups in the film, 'perhaps because they could not be distinguished from the others'.[120]

Shklovskii's assertion of the importance of the director is unquestionably accurate in the general sense. In the case of *Bronenosets Potemkin*, however, it is testimony less to Eizenshtein's creative initiative, although this was undoubtedly crucial, than to the demands of dramaturgy. The 'goods' in question, brides for sale to Jewish bachelors on the one hand, and a mutiny of sailors which leads to the massacre of innocent civilians on the other, speak volumes about the gulf between the two films in terms of their respective dramatic ambitions. In *Evreiskoe schast'e*, the Odessa Steps function modestly as a metaphor for social advancement. They belong to a series of ascending structures in the film which culminates in the steps to the lighthouse, this constituting the highest point in the film from the architectural point of view, but also, albeit in the form of a wish-fulfilment fantasy, the moment of Menachem Mendel's greatest entrepreneurial triumph. Such a metaphor does not require a complex or particularly dynamic visual coding. By contrast, the massacre which took place on or at the foot of the Odessa Steps on 14 June 1905 (Old Style), whether historically accurate in its cinematic realization or not, is the emotional and dramatic pivot around which the whole of *Bronenosets Potemkin* revolves; as Aleksandrov has made clear, it was precisely Shtraukh's chance discovery of a visual depiction of this event by an alleged eyewitness (a correspondent working for a French magazine) that prompted the abandonment of the screenplay originally commissioned by the first factory of Goskino, Agadzhanova-Shutko's *1905 god*, and the exclusive focus on the events in Odessa triggered by the murder of a sailor on the *Potemkin* battleship.[121] For Eizenshtein, the mutiny on the ship and the murder of the citizens who had rallied to its cause were a microcosm of the revolution and the very epitome of its pathos; in his own words, whereas *Stachka* was a 'treatise based on the principle of abstraction and logical technicism', *Bronenosets Potemkin* was a 'hymn' and a 'tragedy in five acts'.[122]

Reconstruction of the creative process that gave rise to the montage treatment of this sequence suggests that its cinematographic realization was subject to continual adjustment and had not been agreed in its entirety by the time shooting commenced on 22 September 1925. The extent of Tisse's involvement in this process is not entirely clear. He arrived in Odessa on 19 September – in other words, only three days before shooting proper began on the basis of a director's scenario – but sources suggest that the final weekend before the shoot witnessed some detailed preparations in which he was involved.[123] He himself talked subsequently about having inspected the steps on several occasions with Eizenshtein in different lighting conditions.[124] This seems partially confirmed by Shtraukh's letters to his wife, in which he refers to detailed discussions with Tisse about camera positions and 'perspectives' which continued long into the night on 21 September;[125] and his recollections of the production, published many years later, in which he describes Eizenshtein and Tisse energetically running up and down the steps and devising 'ever more inventive ways' of filming them.[126] Shtraukh's letters written during the making of the film make clear that it was not merely rehearsals for the crowd scenes that began on 22 September.[127] Nevertheless, the working diary that he kept at the same time shows that there were adjustments to the initial scenario that led to delays in the shooting schedule.[128] Furthermore, a later letter to his wife, dated 30 September, refers to it having taken seven days to shoot the Odessa Steps sequence in its entirety, with two days lost to poor weather.[129] In view of this, Tisse's claim shortly after the film's release that shooting proper began only on 28 September would seem a little dubious, although it is possible that very little material was shot during the earlier rehearsals.[130]

As outlined in Shtraukh's working diary, the director's scenario for 22 September envisaged three basic perspectives – from above, from below and from the sides – with the cameras at the top and bottom of the steps positioned on high platforms.[131] Some of the shots from the top of the steps, for example those from an elevated perspective looking downwards towards the harbour (these were filmed 'through' the statue of the Duc de Richelieu, which is located at the very top of the staircase), had already been planned, although the manipulation of spatial depth was doubtless enhanced by the use of a Bell & Howell camera that

Tisse had recently purchased, which boasted a rotating turret with four lenses, one of them long-distance.[132] Also envisaged was the use of tracking-shots to convey the downward momentum of the crowd and the pursuing soldiers, as well as the descent and ascent of the mother and son (after the son is shot and falls to the ground, the mother climbs back up the steps carrying his body in order to confront the soldiers).[133] These shots were something of an innovation at the time, not because they were tracking-shots per se (Tisse himself had engineered two lateral tracking-shots for the train sequence in *Evreiskoe schast'e*), but because they were not taking place on flat terrain and were thus difficult to execute from a technical point of view. Overcoming this challenge involved the construction of wooden rails along one side of the steps, and the lowering and elevation of a small truck by means of ropes in which Tisse, Eizenshtein and one of their assistants were positioned.[134] The scenario at this stage did not, however, include several of the sequences that would subsequently attain iconic status, for example the shooting of the teacher in the pince-nez. Neither were tracking-shots envisaged for the sequence in which a perambulator with a baby trundles with increasing momentum down the steps before overturning, perhaps the most dramatic sequence in the entire film. In order to track this rapid descent, with the camera at times filming at close quarters, the truck containing the film crew was released by the rope-holders and allowed to speed downwards, with assistants positioned at the bottom of the steps in order to catch the camera as the crew jumped off.[135]

Eizenshtein's dynamic editing of the Odessa Steps sequence depends very much on the tracking movement of the camera. The impact of the sequence as a whole depends on the rhythms established by means of editing cuts, but also by the movement taking place within the frame and the movement and speed of the camera itself. Perhaps deliberately in view of the ubiquity of sea imagery in the film, the sequence in its totality conjures associations with the motion of water, its downward momentum represented by the fleeing citizens and the regular footfalls of the regimented soldiers. Within this downward flow there are impediments that produce 'eddies' at various stages of the staircase; these show either the bodies of the fallen victims or the mini-dramas that revolve around specific individuals, for example the teacher, the student, the mother with the perambulator and the mother with the wounded child, several of whom have been introduced to the spectator in the sequence that directly precedes the massacre. The repeated shifts in camera angle and perspective and the stylistic juxtaposition between the chaotic movements of the crowd, which create the impression of a documentary-style spontaneity, and the regimented, staccato-like movement of the soldiers belong to this perception of intra-frame rhythm. A further compositional tension is supplied by the manipulation of light via the placement of mirrors at strategic intervals along the steps, a device for reflecting light back towards the photographed subject which had certainly been employed in the sphere of photography, but which, according to Tisse, was an innovation in relation to a Soviet film production.[136] The presence of mirrors is clearly detectable in the scene that shows the mother carrying her son back up the steps to confront the soldiers: here, a large rectangle of light has been positioned directly in front of her which frames her shadow and projects its elongated contour towards their serried ranks. Because the sun for the most part is directly behind the soldiers during the sequence, the reflected light of the mirrors acts as a counterweight to the downward direction of the soldiers' shadows, and thus to some extent becomes associated dramaturgically with the idea of resistance to the violent tide of events. Mirrors are employed throughout the massacre sequence from the very moment shots are fired and the crowd begins to flee, and their presence can be detected for long-shots, as well as close-ups of people who have taken refuge behind the stones.

The Odessa Steps sequence is more than just the key dramatic episode in *Bronenosets Potemkin*. Because it was the first sequence to be filmed, it contains in microcosmic form several of the compositional devices that characterize the film as a whole. For Tisse, the film represented 'the culmination of a whole series of creative strivings and experiments which began in the period of my work in documentary'.[137] His main purpose, as evidenced by this retrospective essay, was the achievement of a stylistic unity which sought to move beyond the poster-like qualities of *Stachka* in favour of a greater realism and with more emphasis on what he described as 'living textures'. This unity consists of discrete episodes which, because they reflect the demands of dramaturgy, inevitably strike different notes in terms of their mood and atmosphere. Nevertheless, like a musical composition, they have certain motifs in common. Thus the Odessa Steps sequence, with its diagonal patterns, illustrated most strikingly by the bayonets aimed sharply downwards and the shadows of the soldiers that stretch along the steps, is anticipated by the geometric handling of the execution sequence on board the battleship prior to Vakulenchuk's murder. Similarly, the application of *contre-jour* for the evening sequence that shows the return of his body to shore aboard a motor-launch at the end of Part Two establishes the funereal mood which is continued by the celebrated morning mist sequence at the beginning of Part

Three. In turn, this mood is echoed by the series of lyrical images, also filmed *contre-jour*, which mark the beginning of the 'anxious night' sequence in Part Five. Within these sequences, there are further visual echoes, for example the smoke from a crane on the wharf which drifts in front of the sun during the mist sequence in Part Three, or the smoke from the funnel of the battleship which passes in front of the sun as it speeds towards its encounter with the squadron in Part Five. Further echoes can be found in the images of silhouetted vessels which move slowly in front of the sun, and occasionally in front of each other, that feature in all of the above-mentioned sequences. The principle of musical reprise also applies to the scenes that take place aboard ship, the quasi-documentary images of the sailors going about their daily duties in Part One anticipating the portrayal of the ship's mechanical operations in Part Five. Another compositional device that links separate episodes is the filming of numerous scenes aboard floating vessels, the very slight, bobbing movement of the camera suggesting participation in the action, rather than mere observation. This device informs the evening sequence which shows the body of Vakulenchuk being returned to shore; the mist sequence; the scenes that depict yachts sailing out to meet the mutinous sailors with supplies of food; and the shots of waving soldiers standing on deck as the danger of being attacked by the squadron recedes. The presence of an 'emotional' camera is suggested by the resort to soft-focus for the 'Port in Mourning' sequence, just after the scenes of the harbour shrouded in mist. The logic of Tisse's camerawork, which rigorously adhered to dramaturgic requirements, and its seeming lack of artifice, prompted a chastened Shklovskii to remark that 'Tisse films as a person should breathe'.[138] The universal praise with which his cinematography was received can be gauged by Mur's remark, uttered apprehensively at the ARK discussion of the film, presumably for fear of offending the director, that Tisse should actually be given greater credit than Eizenshtein 'because there are whole sequences of shots which only reach the viewer because they have been so beautifully shot'.[139]

Many of the compositional strategies in *Bronenosets Potemkin* have their origins in Tisse's previous work on *Stachka* and *Evreiskoe schast'e*. These include the preference for staging in depth, witnessed most radically in the shots of the guns from an axial position (these inspired Rodchenko's poster design, which accompanied the release of the film in the Soviet Union);[140] multiple planes of action, for example the scenes of agitational activity in Part One, which take place on deck after the complaints about the unacceptable quality of the meat; and the division of the frame into active zones, a technique employed most forcefully for the scenes in which the citizens of Odessa stream towards the port to pay their respects to the dead Vakulenchuk. Tisse's interest in lighting effects, in particular the effect of filtered light, is a feature that *Bronenosets Potemkin* also shares with his earlier work. The scene in Kimbak's garden in the final third of *Evreiskoe schast'e*, for example, with its slanting strips of light falling onto a tablecloth courtesy of the slatted structure of a gazebo, is analogous to the polka-dot effect of light filtering through the metal walkways of the battleship, most notably in the scene outside the ship's kitchen which shows the cook saluting Giliarovskii. The documentary-style footage of the ship in parts one and five, with its express interest in material texture, has a precedent in the factory material that features in the opening scenes of *Stachka*. The extreme close-ups of the doctor with his pince-nez have their precursor in the portraits of the police spy. The frame-within-frame compositions, discussed earlier in relation to *Stachka*, are also present in *Bronenosets Potemkin*, for example for the scene in which the officer with responsibility for the watch and Smirnov, the ship's doctor, walk through a door onto the deck; the image shot through the porthole of the ship's food store as canned food is distributed; and the shots that look out towards the harbour through the triangular aperture of Vakulenchuk's tent. The removal of the tripod during the Odessa Steps sequence was also anticipated in *Stachka* in the scene of a tramp stuck in his oak barrel, and the sequence that shows the drunken point of view of a provocateur as she sets fire to the interior of a drink store. Even the compromising of the 'fourth wall' of the camera by allowing figures at key moments to approach the lens and move out of focus was anticipated in *Evreiskoe schast'e*, albeit without the extreme emotion that motivates its deployment in the later film.

At the same time, there are certain scenes that take place on board the armoured carrier in *Bronenosets Potemkin* which represent a significant development in Tisse's approach to composition. The metal structures of the ship, for example, which reflect and bounce light in several directions, are treated as a rich source of photogenic material. Tisse's exploitation of this material is witnessed in his attempts to render the ship's material textures and their tonal properties, but also in the geometric structure of individual compositions that seek to communicate the ship's architecture. Thus, for example, on two occasions Tisse films from directly beneath a grille, an unconventional angle of vision which, by placing a visual barrier between camera and action, accentuates the clandestine nature of the discussions (Fig. 7). In a similar way, Tisse exploits the shadows produced by some of the ship's structural features, most importantly its railings and walkways, for compositional purposes, these adding layers of complexity to the visual rendering of the ship's spatial geography. In a radical break with convention, these shadows are permitted to eclipse partially the human face at crucial, dramatic moments, the most striking example being the medium close-up of Vakulenchuk when he complains to the ship's doctor about the quality of the meat: the narrow bar that runs vertically down his face endows the footage with the quality of the non-choreographed, and thus spontaneous.

The capacity of the ship's structures to reflect light to some extent also justifies the adoption of mirrors: the effects of these are apparent in several scenes, and would otherwise strike the viewer as incongruous and unmotivated. The presence of reflected light is apparent in many of the scenes in Part One. These include close-ups (for example the portrait of Giliarovskii just before he issues the command to fire (Fig. 8)); medium-shots (for example the scene that observes the officer of the watch and the ship's doctor, having rejected the sailors' complaints about the meat, as they move through a doorway); and some of the scenes at the prow of the ship (for example the row of cadets who line up to execute the complaining sailors, the mirror effect palpable on the lower half of their bodies).

In relation to some of the portraits on deck, the mirrors de facto become a secondary source of illumination that can be potentially manipulated for the purposes of 'sculpting with light'; to some extent, paradoxically, they replicate the conditions that more usually pertain to a studio interior. This tendency can be witnessed in the close-up of the officer in charge of the watch whose face is lit from diametrically opposed angles. This method of cross-lighting represents a continuation of Tisse's general policy in relation to portrait lighting in the interiors of *Stachka* and *Evreiskoe schast'e*; in fact, contrary to his subsequent claims, it would appear that he applied the device of reflection (*podsvetka* in Russian) on exterior shots as well, for example the scene in *Evreiskoe schast'e* which shows the female client as she sits in a café overlooking the Odessa harbour. A further echo of studio methods lies in the procedure adopted for the lighting of the priest (a role not played by Eizenshtein, as legend has it, but by a gardener from a local orchard), who gives his sanction to the execution of the sailors: here, a mirror has been placed directly in front of him at a low angle to replicate the sinister effects associated with the portrayal of negative characters in German Expressionist film.[141] This method is artificial and compromises the conceit of verisimilitude. To some extent, moreover, the deployment of mirrors transforms the vessel into something akin to a floating stage, and thus 'theatricalizes' an open-air space in a manner not far removed in principle from Eizenshtein's production of *Protivogazy* (Gas Masks).[142] In reality, the unit was not actually filming the *Potemkin* battleship; indeed, neither was it shooting in the open seas, where the mutiny took place historically. Because the original ship had either been decommissioned or sunk by Whites during the Civil War, Eizenshtein was forced to film aboard *Potemkin*'s 'double', the *Twelve Apostles*, the upper half of which was artificially remodelled on the basis of plans still held in the admiralty in order to simulate the appearance of its historical twin. Furthermore, because the *Twelve Apostles* was carrying dangerous explosives (mines), it was moored in the harbour and simply pointed seawards at a ninety-degree angle from the quayside in order to give the illusion of the open sea.[143] Recognition of the artifice involved in recreating the conditions of the mutiny may possibly have suggested, at a subconscious level, the idea of treating the ship as if it were an open-air set, rather than a natural, exterior location. In this context, it is worth noting that the technique of bouncing light off studio walls or screens positioned off-camera was standard North American practice during the 1920s and had been reported upon in the Soviet film press at the time.[144]

All the World's (Not) a Stage: The Reenactment of 'History' in *Oktiabr'*

From the conceptual point of view, *Oktiabr'* is undoubtedly the most ambitious and intellectual of Eizenshtein and Tisse's films together. In essence, it is a cinematic re-creation of the Bolshevik seizure of power in October 1917, one commissioned as part of the celebrations planned for the tenth anniversary of this event and scheduled to be screened at a special evening dedicated to the Revolution on 7 November 1927 in the Bolshoi Theatre.[145] As was universally acknowledged at the time, it is essentially a revolutionary pageant that placed before an audience in cinematic form the historical event that had already been reconstructed theatrically by Nikolai Evreinov.[146] This spectacle, which involved around three thousand participants and was staged in the environs of the Winter Palace in November 1920, offered early evidence of the avant-garde principle of subverting bourgeois convention by removing theatre from the confines of the closed stage and into the open air. A similar principle explained the participation of progressive theatre directors in the staging of popular festivals, for example the

May-Day parades, which were regarded as visual spectacles, as well as vehicles for political agitation.[147]

The initial formulation of the project was drafted by Eizenshtein and Aleksandrov in January and February 1927. This scenario underwent several alterations as a result of negotiations with the Party's Anniversary Committee, and was only agreed upon in a definitive form in early March.[148] A letter from Tisse to Eizenshtein during this month suggests that he had been involved in the preliminary discussions about the project, and for this reason had been despatched to Germany to check the quality of certain lenses that would be required for the filming of events which, historically speaking, took place in the evening, at night or in the early hours of the morning.[149] The technical difficulties involved in the production, in particular the lighting requirements for the exterior sequences, have since become the stuff of legend. An unprecedented number of projector arcs were deployed for the scenes depicting the seizure of power; moreover, these projectors necessitated a supply of electricity that far exceeded normal requirements and famously caused blackouts in other parts of Leningrad while filming was taking place.[150] Apart from the purely technical challenges, it became increasingly clear during the process of filming that the time allocated for shooting (four months, from April to July) was insufficient; as indicated earlier, this required the splitting of the unit into two teams.[151] A letter from Eizenshtein to Aleksandrov at the end of July indicates his unhappiness in relation to some of the material that had been shot prior to his departure for Moscow to begin the process of editing; the reshooting of this material, along with the shooting of episodes which still needed to be filmed, was undertaken by Aleksandrov, Tisse and Nil'sen in unison during August and the better part of September.[152] Further challenges lay ahead with the editing once the material was processed. A full version of the film was not ready by the time of the 7 November screening; indeed, only some of the longer fragments were shown, these including the storming of the Winter Palace. Subsequently, Eizenshtein was advised to alter the montage concept, re-edit some of the fragments and shorten the film's overall length.[153]

Critical discussion of *Oktiabr'* hitherto has tended to focus either on the film's presentation of historical 'facts' or on its function as a vehicle for Eizenshtein's concept of 'intellectual montage'.[154] These aspects were highlighted in the initial critical response to the film in the Soviet Union.[155] The original concept for *Oktiabr'*, however, despite its commitment to documentary fidelity (genuine documents are shown as part of the depiction of events leading up to the seizure of power), was based less on an interest in producing a historically accurate version of events and more on the vibrant impressions that had formed in the minds of Eizenshtein and Aleksandrov after their reconnaissance of the venue which lay at the geographical epicentre of the Bolshevik insurrection, namely, the Winter Palace, with its dual function as former residence of the deposed royal family and as a museum for the collections of valuable artworks which had been assembled in the Hermitage. As the letter from Eizenshtein to Aleksandrov makes clear, their encounter with the opulence of the private rooms formerly inhabited by Tsar Nicholas II and Tsarina Aleksandra Fedorovna, with their architect-designed interior décor, antique furniture, luxurious furnishings and collections of gifts and artworks, many of them exotic and bizarre, reminded them of the famous department store in Moscow, Muir and Merrilees, a store in which 'anything can be bought' (the 'unbelievably rich cinematic material' in the palace was noted by Eizenshtein in a private journal entry dated 13 April).[156] According to this concept, the Winter Palace would be presented as a quasi-Parisian shopping mall, a grandiose embodiment of the bourgeois fetish for cultural artefacts which they planned to treat in a 'grotesque-satirical fashion'.[157] On the basis of an unpublished director's scenario, Tsiv'ian has drawn attention to the ways in which Eizenshtein sought to portray the Revolution not merely as a series of events that culminated eventually in a military assault on an inert and politically repressive structure, but also as a symbolic challenge to an entire aesthetic edifice.[158] Although Eizenshtein subsequently came under pressure to modify this concept, the presentation of art treasures from the private rooms of the royal couple and the Hermitage collections (including those, such as Rodin's *L'Eternel printemps* (Eternal Spring, c.1884), which were acquired only after the Revolution) is ubiquitous, which suggests that they remained central to his overall vision. As Shklovskii observed nearly fifty years later, the storming of the Winter Palace represented not so much the overthrow of a 'king' as that of a 'kingdom of objects' (a contention that reversed, or at least moderated, his view, committed to print only one year after the film's release, that 'Eizenshtein lost his way in the thousands of rooms of the Winter Palace much as did those who were laying siege to it').[159]

The visual treatment of these objects will be commented upon in due course, but it is important to emphasize at this stage that *Oktiabr'* constitutes a photographic study not merely of interior objects, but also of exterior objects; namely, those that constitute the architectural landscape and cultural heritage of St Petersburg. To some extent, these objects have a pragmatic function as part of the mapping process which is introduced for the scenes that immediately precede the seizure of power. This seeks to establish in minute detail the geographical terrain of the assault, and consists of four maps that the Military-Revolutionary Committee unfurls in order to formulate its plan of action. Pencils are shown ringing strategically important objects, the inner circle restricted to the immediate environs of the Winter Palace, and the outer circles embracing areas slightly further afield: the stretch of the Neva river bordered by the Admiralty Embankment; the eastern tip of Vasil'evskii Island (known as the Strelka); the Peter and Paul Fortress, from which the initial bombardment was directed; and the Hermitage Bridge, which lies to the east of the palace.

This mapping process, however, while undeniably orientating the viewer geographically in relation to the ensuing action, does not explain the persistence with which heritage sites are presented in the film well before the military assault itself commences; these are emphasized compositionally even in scenes for which, from a purely dramaturgical perspective, their visible presence is superfluous. A selective list of examples would include the following: shots of the 3,500-year-old sphinxes, imported from Egypt in 1832 and reputed to be cast in the image of King Amenhotep III, which are located in front of the Academy of Arts building on the University Embankment (they appear in the scene in which a Bolshevik demonstrator is beaten to death as part of the 'July Days' repression); the statue of General Aleksandr Suvorov, which is presented in the foreground, and slightly out of focus, for the long-shots of demonstrators marching over the Troitskii Bridge at the beginning of the 'July Days' episode; the limestone sculptures representing the sea-god Poseidon and the goddesses of seafaring commerce, which are located at the base of the Rostral Columns on the Strelka (these feature in the scenes showing Bolshevik detachments assume their positions in readiness for the assault on the Winter Palace); the two griffins that adorn Bank Bridge (these figure in the sequence that shows the elderly citizens of the Committee for the Salvation of the Country and the Revolution attempting to cross the Griboedov Canal in order to support the Provisional Government); the several Atlas caryatids that support the portico entrance to the New Hermitage (these are portrayed repeatedly, initially in the scenes that show Junkers assembling to defend the palace, and later as the assault proper begins); the sculptures and caryatids positioned along the roof of the Winter Palace (these are intercut with images of the all-woman Death Brigade); the spherical ball that lies on the Strelka embankment not far from the Rostral Columns (this is twice depicted in silhouetted form as part of the waiting sequence on the eve of the military assault); the sculptures of lions located along the Admiralty Embankment not far from the Winter Palace (these are also photographed in silhouetted form during the waiting sequence); the angel at the top of the Alexandrine Column in Palace Square (four different shots of this sculpture from different angles are inserted as a prelude to the final assault); and the gates that open into Palace Square from the Hermitage, located opposite the more famous Arch of the General Staff, which feature in the scene that shows Kerenskii's flight by chauffeur-driven car and the later sequences that show the assault proper (their ornate ironwork, designed in 1885 by the architect N. A. Gornostaev in the style of Rastrelli, one of the celebrated architects of the Winter Palace, is highlighted on several occasions by means of *contre-jour*).

These examples are sufficiently numerous to suggest that they belong to the wider nexus of images which consists of objects and art treasures located within the Winter Palace. They imply that, much in the manner of the concentric circles drawn around the palace in the map sequences to mark the terrain of the assault, this building is envisaged as both a seat of power and a cultural epicentre, the influence of which radiates outwards. The idea at the heart of this nexus, as the opening scene of the destruction of the monument to Alexander III makes clear (a scene that is historically inaccurate in the sense that the monument was removed from its position in front of the Cathedral of Christ the Saviour only in the summer of 1918), is that of violent dethronement. A related idea, clearly expressed in the scenario discovered by Tsiv'ian, lies in the concept of petrification; in other words, the landmark and heritage sites symbolize the paralysis of the Provisional Government and its inability to counter the dynamism of Bolshevik-inspired revolutionaries.[160]

Eizenshtein's assault on the cultural products of a supposedly civilized world, both ancient and modern, and his dethroning of them as sacred objects of veneration possess a dual dimension. On one level, in the moments leading up to the assault, their status as art is mockingly subverted when they are pressed into more mundane service: the crooked arm of one sculpture becomes the resting place for an empty bottle of wine; and the bust of the Greek philosopher Socrates becomes the home for an astrakhan hat. On a second level, the sacred power of these objects is undermined by virtue of the unorthodox ways in which they are represented cinematographically; as Tret'iakov astutely observed at the time, *Oktiabr'* represents the 'storming of an aesthetic' as much as the 'storming of a citadel'.[161] Through its treatment of art objects and heritage sites, *Oktiabr'* challenges the aesthetic values associated with classicism and neoclassicism, for example the preference for symmetry, proportion, clarity of form and smoothness of texture, but also the decorative ornamentation associated with the Baroque and Gothic periods. A good example of Baroque architecture is the cathedral situated within the Peter and Paul Fortress, interior shots of which show an Orthodox bishop performing a service to celebrate the overthrow of the Romanov dynasty;[162] a useful example of the neo-Gothic style is the design of Tsar Nicholas's library, which features in the scenes showing Kerenskii's assumption of power.[163] In place of these styles, *Oktiabr'* proposes a photographic modernism which privileges *décadrage*, truncation, diagonal construction, manipulation of depth of field, unexpected angles of vision, extreme close-ups (with their capacity for a degree of graphic distortion), a flickering, impaired style of vision, extreme degrees of tonal contrast occasioned by the use of powerful arcs on exteriors, and in general a rather crude expressivity occasioned by the rough textures of the skin and 'non-classical' profiles of the *typage* selected for the roles of soldiers, sailors and workers.

Eizenshtein's sensitivity to the visual aesthetic of *Oktiabr'* is amply illustrated by the detail of his letter to Aleksandrov while editing in Moscow. Significantly, apart from his remonstrations in relation to scenes that he felt lacked visual clarity, or that he argued were 'pretentious' in their manner of presentation (the use of the word *pestriatina* – which in Russian refers to a 'colourful' or 'flashy' quality – suggests he may have been alluding to Tisse's use of mobile arc lights for the Finland Station sequence), there is a general reproach that, compared to the rushes of *Staroe i novoe*, much of which had been shot by the time *Oktiabr'* went into production, the photography and lighting were guilty on occasion of a Levitskii-style 'academicism'.[164] In Eizenshtein's lexicon, prompted by the parting of the ways over the footage shot for *1905 god*, also in Leningrad, this was shorthand for a cinematographic approach which he regarded as insufficiently modern. It is not clear to which sequences he was referring specifically in his letter. It is undeniable, nevertheless, that some of the objects in the Winter Palace are photographed as if they are museum exhibits; in other words, in a manner that would not appear out of place in an exhibition catalogue or, as illustrated by the current Hermitage website, a virtual museum tour. The treatment of the statuettes of Napoleon (presumably the realization of Lenin's essay, written in Razliv, which drew comparisons between Kerenskii's dictatorial ambitions and his illustrious

French predecessor); the religious and pagan artefacts shown as part of the Kornilov coup sequence, each one a figurative or symbolic representation, in reverse chronology, of the historical evolution of belief systems; and some of the imperial gifts, for example the celebrated peacock clock, which was the work of the British inventor James Cox and was purchased by Prince Potemkin as a gift to Empress Catherine the Great in 1781 (it is perhaps the most potent symbol in the film of majesty, power and aristocratic display), are filmed for the most part from an axial position with the object centred in the frame and lit against a dark background. The fact that the lighting, which is invariably from the sides and slightly behind the object in question, is not typical of the diffuse conditions that usually pertain in a museum does not alter the 'academic' quality of these images, although it might be argued that, in a montage context which stresses cultural conservatism, such a quality might not necessarily be regarded as inappropriate.

This is manifestly not the case in relation to other interior objects, which have been photographed according to a different set of compositional principles. One of the most important techniques is truncation, a device that involves objects being arranged in such a way that the edges of the frame, both horizontal and vertical, compromise their integrity as complete entities. This approach is adopted for the close-ups of crockery (the stacks of plates and two rows of porcelain gravy boats); the two medals shown in close-up as part of the Kornilov coup sequence; the toy soldiers in a glass cabinet; the two sets of crystal wine glasses; the rows of empty chairs and glasses of tea associated with the futile deliberations of the Provisional Government; and the medium close-ups of the tsarina's chamber pot. In many of these images the objects in question have been positioned diagonally in relation to the camera and recede at angles into the depths of the frame. The principle of diagonal construction is illustrated most forcefully in the scene in which, shortly after his ascent to power and occupancy of the state rooms, Kerenskii opens the side of a chess board in order to extract a glass stopper that completes an ornate, four-piece decanter; here, the lines of the board function as a graphic representation of the compositional method employed.

The penchant for *décadrage* is another tendency that informs the shots of these interior objects. This is witnessed most strikingly in the image of the tsar in a document which he himself has signed.[165] In this composition, the head of the tsar is positioned at the bottom of the frame and partially truncated; in addition, the crucial words of the inscription lie in the top left-hand corner of the frame. Even when the document is shown in its totality, the face and torso are still decentred. Elsewhere, coupled with a lighting arrangement that illuminates only the left-hand side of the frame, the principle of *décadrage* informs the image of a chandelier that shakes as the assault on the Winter Palace begins in earnest (the shapes of the glass beads suggest that this might be one of the twenty-eight chandeliers, designed by Andrei Stakenschneider in the mid-nineteenth century, which hang in the Pavilion Hall). This ornament has been photographed out of focus, presumably from the gallery that forms part of the hall, to the point where the image is almost abstract. In these shots, while the aesthetic quality of the objects in terms of their forms and textures has been communicated effectively by means of lighting, their method of presentation from the visual point of view is unconventional.

In the absence of specific information that would establish the authorship of these compositions, it is difficult to judge whether the stylistic disparities between the two different sets of images – the museum-style exhibits on the one hand, and the decentred, diagonal constructions on the other – are the result of different aesthetic inclinations on the part of the camera operators filming the material. At present, it is known only that Nil'sen was responsible for the shots of the peacock clock, and thus also presumably the shots of the owl that forms part of this mechanical invention and is shown at a later juncture;[166] and that Tisse photographed the 'icon' of the tsar and tsarina receiving divine blessing, which is shown briefly as part of the assault sequence in the tsarina's bedroom.[167] In his letters to Eizenshtein, Tisse mentions the filming of gods, clocks, figurines, and 'busts' of Napoleon (not statuettes), as well as a number of other palace objects, such as teapots, knives, forks and a small fridge, but few of these objects appear in the final edit of the film.[168]

This uncertainty notwithstanding, it is noticeable that the principles that govern the more radical compositions of the interior objects have been applied in relation to some of the other shots of the royal apartments, the various halls in the Winter Palace, and some of the heritage sites. Many of these bear the hallmarks of Tisse's earlier compositional style. *Décadrage*, for example, is evident in the visual treatment of the sequence in which Bolshevik agitators, having gained entry into the palace via the cellars, move surreptitiously along the circular gallery of Auguste de Montferrand's Rotunda. More radical forms of *décadrage* are encountered during the 'July Days' episode. Prior to the frenzied and fatal attack by bourgeois onlookers, for example, a demonstrator moves down the steps of the University Embankment towards the Neva: here, the scene is composed so that the face of the agitator is pushed towards the extreme right-hand edge of the frame, while the left-hand side is dominated by the umbrella that later becomes the instrument of his death. A similar arrangement informs the shots of the large granite balls, sculpted by Samson Sukhanov in the early nineteenth century, and located along the lower part of the Strelka embankment, which offer views towards the Peter and Paul Fortress. These images, photographed in the early evening from different distances, or very possibly using different lenses, position the key architectural features on either side of the frame: in the first, the spherical ball dominates to the extent that it is truncated by the top of the frame (the cathedral is positioned in the distance, to the extreme left); in the second, the ball is much smaller, but still positioned off-centre, and the focus now is the evening cloudscape that dominates the upper section of the frame. This tendency to activate the peripheries of the frame with significant information is further witnessed in the scenes in which members of the female Death Brigade are shown in the royal billiard room. Here the frame is dissected unevenly by the billiard cues, which stand vertically, but at a slight angle, and slightly out of focus: to the left a woman from the brigade is shown wrapping her feet in cloth; on the right, assorted billiard balls lie neglected on the floor. A variation on this device is the positioning of culturally significant monuments or statues at the extreme right-hand margins of the frame. A shot of the stock market during the 'July Days' demonstration, for example, shows a fragment of the statue of the 'Neva' goddess at the base of a Rostral Column. This is echoed by the long-shot of the Palace Bridge at the moment when the horse and carriage hang suspended from the top of one of its raised sections, which positions a sculpture from the roof of the Winter Palace on the extreme right-hand edge of the frame; and the medium-shot of the Bank Bridge at the moment when Mayor Shreider and his elderly supporters try to cross, which adopts the same technique in relation to one of the golden-winged griffins that adorns the bridge. All these objects are deliberately positioned so that they lie beyond the depth of field.

If the landmark monuments, sculptures and buildings act as embodiments of the idea of the static, the celebration of kinetic energy in *Oktiabr'* clearly poses a challenge to the cultural heritage of pre-revolutionary St Petersburg. This celebration is the visual and aesthetic equivalent of the Bolshevik seizure of power, an act of boldness and courage which trumps the inertia of toothless political opponents. Ironically, the only act of kinetic impulse on the part of these opponents is the act of surrender – in other words, Kerenskii's flight by car – but even during these moments his latent association with the static is accentuated by the shots of the flag-waving statuette fixed to the car's bonnet. The perception of kinetic energy in *Oktiabr'* is achieved partly by the careful choreographing of action within the frame (flurried shapes of soldiers and sailors running across Palace Square), and partly by montage rhythm, for example the machine-gun and *lezginka* (Cossack dance) sequences; at moments like these, images flash on the screen too rapidly for the human eye to register and make sense of them. The impressionistic effect is enhanced through deliberate manipulation of the depth of field and its compression to such an extent that crucial objects and actions lie beyond the field of focus. A useful demonstration of this tendency can be found in the Finland Station sequence, where a combination of arc lights (presumably searchlights) roving over the heads of the crowd from above, smoke drifting across the frame and rippling flags close to the camera lens for the shots depicting Lenin standing atop an armoured carrier produces a powerful, flickering sensation. It might be argued that Eizenshtein's criticism of this sequence for its *pestriatina* is misplaced in the sense that it captures the mood of the crowd and communicates the sense of agitation and excitement. More importantly, in terms of the frenzied atmosphere, the handling of the scene from the compositional point of view supplies an important visual bridge with the sequence showing the 'July Days' demonstrators which follows immediately afterwards (this is launched with views of rippling flags carried aloft at such close proximity to the camera that it is almost impossible to decipher their slogans). Although this approach, at Eizenshtein's insistence and with a self-evident lack of continuity, was abandoned for the medium-shots of Lenin (these were reshot later in front of the Leningradkino studio), the film as a whole consists of a series of moments where extreme close-ups, coupled with rapid movement within the frame, give rise to the sacrifice of distinct picture information in favour of rapid impressions of energetic movement.

Although loss of focus in *Oktiabr'* is not always deliberate – there is evidence from Tisse's letters to Eizenshtein to suggest that the fast-speed Tachar and Plasmat lenses acquired in Germany may have been faulty – the play with visibility is clearly part of the film's overall aesthetic design.[169] The revolutionary subject and epic scale of the production render inexact the musical term 'nocturne' to describe this aesthetic. Nevertheless, much of the film's action takes place in the evening or at night, and the visual handling of the material in terms of mood and atmosphere, with its frequent recourse to silhouette, echoes the scenes of nervous anticipation as the sailors await possible reprisals in Part Five of *Bronenosets*

Potemkin: the silhouetted shapes of human figures and objects and the shots of glinting light along the surface of the water are common to both. A similar argument can be made in relation to the diffuse images of Razliv, Lenin's refuge after the repressions of 4 July, which, perhaps logically in view of the funereal atmosphere that the respective dramaturgies share, evoke the atmospheric conditions of the Odessa mist sequence. The careful capturing of the sun's reflection in the surface of the water, the silhouetted shapes of reeds and trees and the lack of focus display a powerfully lyrical impulse that approaches the poetics of Pictorialism. These scenes serve as a useful reminder of Tisse's strengths as a *paysagiste*. Furthermore, insofar as the Winter Palace lies geographically in the vicinity of water – it is a 'ship of state', as it were, lying anchored at the shores of the Neva – the landscape of which it forms a crucial part is not in principle different from the *Potemkin* battleship and urban landscape of Odessa. Subconscious recognition of the analogies may partly explain the symbolic function of bridges in *Oktiabr'*, one apparently triggered by a view of the Palace Bridge from the state rooms of the Hermitage while Eizenshtein was filming the interiors.[170] They are presented as modern architectural features that span the Neva and mark the division between imperial and working-class Petersburg. At the same time, they are also engineered, metal structures, each with its own hydraulic system (some are raised vertically, and others revolve horizontally, in order to allow the passage of ships), which are treated as aesthetic objects in their own right, much like the guns on the *Potemkin* battleship.

Staroe i novoe ("General'naia liniia"): The Many Faces of Marfa Lapkina

According to an interview given by Eizenshtein to the film magazine *Kino-front* on 4 March 1927, by the time the draft scenario for *Oktiabr'* had been completed he and his team had shot around nineteen thousand metres of film stock out of a planned total of around twenty-five thousand for *General'naia liniia*; indeed, if not for the commission of *Oktiabr'*, he claims, the crew would have been in a position to release the film in mid-February 1927, despite adverse weather conditions that had severely limited the number of days filming between July and December the previous year.[171] Footage had been shot in a variety of different locations, some of them thousands of kilometres from Moscow: the Mugan Steppe, an area south of Baku along the border with Iran, famous for its cotton fields and mechanized forms of transport; large-scale collective farms, cooperatives and specialist breeding farms outside Moscow; the 'Harold' American commune, which specialized in machinery relating to harvest collection; the Bronnitsa Meadows, situated along the Moscow River on the road to Riazan, which provided the location for the harvest and scything sequences; the village of Mnevniki, which featured in the 'approaching storm' scenes; and the Konstantinovo State Breeding Farm in the province of Riazan, which provided the model buildings and cowsheds equipped with state-of-the-art American machinery.[172]

The unforeseen interruption of *General'naia liniia* by the production of *Oktiabr'* delayed the release of the film by nearly three years; by the time the collective was in a position to resume the project, the Party line on agriculture had shifted and a different ideological emphasis and new title (*Staroe i novoe*) were required. The extent to which these interventions altered the conceptual framework of the film is not entirely clear.[173] Eizenshtein reported that the original title of the film derived from the 'General Line' announced at the Fourteenth Party Congress in relation to agriculture;[174] this has been confirmed by Aleksandrov, who reveals that the origins of the project lay in a 'social commission' proposed personally by Kirill Shutko on behalf of the Party's Central Committee which would demonstrate the need to modernize and collectivize the Soviet countryside.[175] The acceptance of this commission involved a thorough and time-consuming fact-finding mission: reading newspaper reports on the state of the countryside; conducting interviews at research institutes specializing in agricultural matters; and reconnaissance missions to villages and cooperatives outside Moscow in search of likely candidates for *typage*.[176] According to Aleksandrov, the structure of the film at this stage consisted of six parts. The first episode was planned to show the benefits of cooperation among impoverished peasants. The second consisted of the religious procession, drought and cream-separator sequences, which were intended to dramatize the peasants' rejection of religion and embrace of new technology. The third part consisted of Marfa Lapkina's dream of a utopian future, the acquisition of a bull for the expansion of the collective, and the now-famous nuptials sequence. The fourth episode was designed to show the benefits of mechanization, the collective scything interrupted by the arrival of a tractor equipped with cutting blades. The fifth part was intended to satirize bureaucratic obstruction. And the sixth part, entitled 'Fordzosha' in recognition of the fact that the Soviet Union at this time imported its tractors from the U.S.A. (the Fordson being a typical product of the period), would show a tractor pulling along scores of rickety old carts as a demonstration of the power of modern technology to transform the countryside.[177] This scenario fell victim to three unforeseen circumstances: as already indicated, the first was the invitation to produce *Oktiabr'*; the second was a resolution of the Fifteenth Party Congress in December 1927, which called for acceleration of investment in the countryside and the mechanization of agricultural life;[178] and the third, which took place in the early months of 1929, only weeks before the planned release date of the film on 8 March, was the inauguration of the first Five-Year Plan, with its policy of rapid industrialization and forced, rather than voluntary, collectivization.[179] The second two interventions required the filming of further material that would show the degree to which the utopian vision entertained by Lapkina had become a reality. Nevertheless, apart from revision of scenes charting the blossoming romance between Lapkina and the tractor driver, the inclusion of scenes that showed futuristic buildings designed by Andrei Burov, a Constructivist architect, and the sections that depicted the blast furnaces of the Dzerzhinskii metallurgical factory in Kamenskoe, the surviving prints of *Staroe i novoe* suggest that these interventions did not fundamentally alter the conceptual framework of the original.[180] The fact that other treatments of the subject had appeared in the interim (Tret'iakov hinted at this problem when he defended the film from accusations of 'theft, misappropriation and embezzlement') explains why, when *Staroe i novoe* was eventually released in November 1929, it was regarded as outdated.[181] Ironically, Eizenshtein had been unable to prevent the 'new' being perceived as the 'old'.

In an article published in advance of the March 1927 release date, Eizenshtein claimed that his forthcoming film would be devoid of the 'trumpet fanfare of formal "discoveries"' and 'head-spinning attractions' of his previous works.[182] This is a curious claim in the light of the complex series of multiple exposures that illustrate Lapkina's dream; the shots that involve a hand-held camera attached to a scythe (it would be difficult to claim that these were not 'head-spinning'); and the dazzling light effects that occur during the cream-separator sequence, one which, as a study of the kinetic beauty of a mechanical object, can be compared to the poetry of Léger and Murphy's *Ballet mécanique* and indeed a number of avant-garde shorts that poeticize the interaction of mechanical movement and light-play, for example the nearly contemporaneous *Ein Lichtspiel: Schwarz-weiß-grau* (Light Spill: Black-White-Grey, 1929) by Moholy-Nagy.[183] Many years later, Eizenshtein drew attention to the pathos of this sequence, the montage of images geared towards creating a sense of anticipation and gradually increasing tension that erupts finally into ecstasy as the separator begins to produce cream. Such was the expressive power of the images (he describes them as a 'firework display of unceasing splashes') that he decided to have the shots of the spurting fountains of milk hand-tinted in different colours, thus contributing a further layer of sensory stimulation.[184] As he points out, the conceptual framework of this sequence was planned in terms of a montage collision with the drought episode that immediately preceded it. This collision occurs on the level of semantics, via the intertitle *'obman'* (deceit), which links both episodes formally, and on the level of metaphor, through the juxtaposition of two kinds of emotional ecstasy, one antiquated and fruitless (religion), the other progressive and fruitful (the separator).

This sequence notwithstanding, the montage structure of *Staroe i novoe* goes beyond the principle of collision or tension between sequences which prior to this point had formed the basis of Eizenshtein's theory of montage. Eizenshtein himself drew attention to this shift in 'Chetvertoe izmerenie v kino'. Drawing on his study of the formal devices of Kabuki theatre and the terminology of acoustics, he speaks in this essay about the 'sign' of the shot as the product of a range of secondary physiological stimuli or vibrations which occur within the frame, the montage potential described in terms of the relationship between a 'dominant' and a series of resonating 'overtones' and 'undertones'.[185] One of the examples he gives is the delayed harvest episode, the 'tonal' effects of which were achieved through variations in the quality of light, the shifting registers of which gradually herald the eruption of an approaching storm.

Working with natural light, perhaps unsurprisingly in view of the importance of the sun in agricultural rituals and the symbolism of fertility and abundance that runs throughout the film, was certainly an important element in the visual poetics of *Staroe i novoe*; indeed, Eizenshtein argued that the sun was his 'main protagonist'.[186] By this, he presumably meant that it was the search for the sun that forced the collective to move continually southwards, initially to Rostov-on-Don, and then to the Mugan Steppe, in order to maximize available light for shooting purposes. Furthermore, this search motivated the deployment of mirrors, which create the illusion of light and heat although the filming was actually taking place in the (relatively) cold Russian autumn.[187] As Tisse reported during the initial phases of filming, lack of certainty about weather conditions meant that for some scenes multiple cameras were employed as a security measure in case retakes turned out to be impossible.[188] The importance of light conditions prompted him to take photographs at different times of the day and to keep a meticulous record of intervals.[189] For the first time in his working practice, moreover, he employed large shades on exterior locations in order to manipulate tonal balance in the different planes of depth within the frame. For the drought sequence, for example, shades were positioned to avoid the high levels of contrast that normally pertain when the sun is overhead: reflectors covered in tin and aluminium foil were positioned in front of these subjects in order to illuminate the eyes with a softer light; and the effect of *contre-jour* was produced by means of the reflected light obtained from mirrors positioned above and behind them.[190] The articles on *General'naia liniia* written by Tisse at the time confirm that the dynamics of tonal relationship was one of his most fundamental preoccupations during the making of the film.[191]

One of the starting points for Eizenshtein's discussion of visual stimulus was the U.S. concept of 'sex appeal', the dominant 'sign' of which is created by a range of subsidiary stimuli: costume (material texture), type of illumination (lighting method) and physiognomy (gender, class, nationality and ethnicity).[192] In view of his own preference for *typage* – in other words, the selection of non-professionals on the basis of social origin, physiognomy and physical mannerism – this reference to 'sex appeal' might be regarded as ironic. As Shtraukh pointed out in relation to *Staroe i novoe*, the selection of *typage* was an art form in its own right, a process full of frustrations but also immensely rewarding. As well as the practical impediments involved, for example the nervousness of peasants in relation to the camera (for some rural communities it was regarded as a magical apparatus that could see through clothing), the recruitment process involved encounters with an array of people with individual life stories, each one a reflection of recent history and social conditions in the Soviet Union.[193] No other avant-garde unit in the 1920s selected untrained actors for important roles to quite the same extent. The result is a document of unparalleled wealth, a tapestry of skin textures, bone structures and facial characteristics, the vast majority of them deriving from the still relatively impoverished sectors of Soviet society. The richness of this landscape was recognized in the film press as early as the time that *Stachka* was released, a film saluted for its multiplicity of faces which 'sharply and deeply etch [themselves] on the memory'.[194] For Tret'iakov, *typage* was a deliberate challenge to the glamour conventions of mainstream cinema and even the international avant-garde; in his view, the choice of Lapkina for the main role in *Staroe i novoe* was a deliberate 'sacrilege, a blasphemy, a deviation from the usual cinematographic beauties of the chocolate-box variety'.[195] It is symptomatic of the difficulty of finding the right person for the role that the search for this character took several months and at one stage involved interviews with professional actresses, but ultimately only Lapkina, a worker at the Konstantinovo *kolkhoz* who performed her duties with a baby in tow, was deemed to possess the right qualities.[196] Although she is not the 'heroine' of *Staroe i novoe* in the conventional sense, the variety of portraits in the film's final sequence, which capture her at the different stages of her personal odyssey from impoverished peasant to emancipated tractor driver, establish her as the incarnation of rapid social change, modernization and gender emancipation. These images have been composed with such care and tenderness that they must count as among the most human portraits produced during the Eizenshtein–Tisse partnership of the silent era.

The challenges posed by the portrayal of the non-professional actor's face gave rise to solutions which, from the point of view of studio convention, both within the Soviet Union and abroad, were unorthodox. By and large, Tisse preferred to work according to a relatively straightforward system of lighting which involved directed sources striking the face from the sides and slightly from the rear. There are minor variations in terms of the angles of the rays and the strength of the illumination, but only relatively weak, diffuse sources provide the necessary fill-light from the front.[197] In North American cinematography this was known as 'core lighting' or 'double-cross back lighting', but it was a marginal practice that appears to have been confined to the work of a single cameraman, John Seitz.[198] Tisse's adoption of this lighting approach was clearly prompted by the challenges of *typage*. Rather than the nuance of the trained theatre actor's psychological and emotional response, with its shades of expression, its slight and subtle movement of the muscles, and the faint intimation of emotional turmoil, this method sought to convey the expressive force of powerful reactions and an impression of naturalism. 'Core lighting' tends to move the focus of attention away from the eyes as the main medium of expression towards the contours and textures of the face, giving a strong sense of muscular definition and depth. It relies a great deal less on tonal nuance, and a great deal more on expressive contrast.

The requirements of dramaturgy aside, Tisse's method was also prompted by the search for a new aesthetic, one that would privilege the value of lived experience, the lines indelibly imprinted on the face indicative of this experience. Nil'sen would later criticize 'bourgeois' cinema for its non-dramaturgical, 'waxwork' portraiture. He argued that the star system produced actors who were nearly always modelled in the same way, irrespective of the roles they were playing;

as he noted (correctly), the most successful Hollywood actresses by the end of the 1920s enjoyed their own personal cameramen whom they trusted to present them in the most flattering light possible, and whom they insisted the studios hire as part of their own contracts.[199]

Tisse's portraiture is no less manufactured than his U.S. or European counterparts, but the aesthetic priorities are different. In essence, we witness the birth of a new architecture and aesthetics of the human face. His portraits are celebrations of 'imperfection': taut, weathered skin, sagging folds of flesh, heavy bags under the eyes, wrinkles, lines and furrows, flared nostrils, low brows, high foreheads, sweaty, unkempt hair and beards, and stubble – in other words, an entire gamut of 'non-classical' protuberance. In his handling of light, moreover, both natural and artificial, Tisse's close-ups are more varied than avant-garde portraiture in the realm of still photography. The majority of Rodchenko's studies of his 'inner circle' during the 1920s and early 1930s, for example, tend to be modelled with natural light only, and for this reason look relatively flat and unsculpted. There are exceptions that prove the general rule. The 1927 portrait of Nikolai Aseev shows several small lamps on a bookshelf behind the poet's body which give rise to a *contre-jour* effect; his 1928 study of Stepanova uses low-level lighting from a realistic source to produce an expressive and highly poetic effect; and his celebrated 1928 portrait of Tret'iakov is almost a classic close-up from the silver screen.[200] For the most part, however, where artificial light sources feature in Rodchenko's portraiture during the 1920s, they tend to function as part of the interior décor rather than as instruments for modelling.

Tisse's sculpting of the non-professional actor's face evolves over time. His starting point lies in the desire to create the impression of spontaneity through use of natural light, this being very possibly a vestige of his background in documentary. This method acquires a greater expressive force with the passage of time so that, by the time of *Staroe i novoe*, his portraits have become more experimental in terms of composition, lighting, optical treatment and camera angle. Brownlow has commented on the 'incandescent intensity' of Tisse's portraiture, but his early work, as illustrated by *Stachka*, is characterized by a reliance on natural lighting, or at least the illusion of natural lighting.[201] This can be demonstrated by reference to the portraits of the police spies, who are initially presented to the viewer in the form of photographs kept in the files of the security apparatus. Both the photographs and subsequent moving images rely on single sources of light striking the figure in question from one side, usually at head-height; these arrangements are then replicated for the close-ups of the animals into which they are metamorphosed by means of dissolves. The vast majority of portraits in exterior locations in *Stachka* tend to follow this pattern; depending on the position of the sun (and the headgear worn), there is occasionally partial or even total shadow across the face. This is also the method adopted for the interiors filmed on location, for example the factory in the opening sequences, where strong sunlight is shown streaming through large panes of glass. By contrast, the interiors filmed within the studio, for example the office of the factory manager, the palatial home of the shareholder or the bureau of the police chief, adopt a core lighting procedure with some illumination from above. This device is encountered for the dual portraits of the factory manager and his assistant as they report the trouble brewing on the factory floor, and also for the medium close-ups of the figures who telephone each other in a state of alarm: the corpulent factory owner, the shareholder and the chief of police. The most emphatic demonstration of this technique is the portrait of Strongin, the worker accused of theft, who eventually hangs himself. At the moment he enters the office to report the theft of his micrometer, core lighting accentuates his knitted brows, his aquiline nose, the flared curves of his nostrils and his blazing eyes, even though parts of these eyes lie in shadow. The predominant emotion here is pent-up, uncontrollable anger.

This portrait of Strongin is analogous to several close-ups in *Bronenosets Potemkin* where anger is the primary emotion; these suggest that the procedures with regard to lighting positions used within the studio, thanks to the availability of mirrors, began to be replicated in exterior locations. The first is the scene in which a young sailor, having noticed the inscription on a plate he is washing ('Give us this day our daily bread'), smashes it on the floor in disgust; the force of this portrait lies not so much in the expression in his eyes, which are partly shrouded, as in the muscular definition of his jaw. An echo of this approach can be found in the portrait of the crowd member who reacts angrily to the attempt to stir up anti-Jewish sentiment during the Vakulenchuk mourning sequence; his is an unremarkable face by any standards, but it is contorted into an expression of incandescent rage which offers a sharp contrast to the soft-focus portraits of the onlookers prior to this moment. Core lighting on interiors and exteriors manifests itself on several occasions during *Oktiabr'* as well. The portraits of the frenzied citizens who participate in the brutal beating of a Bolshevik demonstrator during the 'July Days' sequence reveal the use of mirrors to create subtle but nevertheless unmistakeable cross-lighting effects (Fig. 9). These medium close-ups, with their hint of the grotesque, have their precursors in the earlier shots of the figures celebrating the overthrow of the Romanov dynasty in the film's opening sequences (Fig. 10). The most expressive close-ups involving core lighting can be found among the portraits of the Cossack Savage Division; these are classic examples of *typage* in the sense that the types in question were drawn from Caucasian shoe-shiners working in Leningrad at the time (Fig. 11).[202]

The images of Marfa Lapkina in the concluding section of *Staroe i novoe* are different in terms of their poetic valence, but they are no lesser textbook illustrations of the different effects of lighting, choice of lens and camera angle on the portrayal of the human face. The fact that some of the shots in the series have been taken directly from earlier sequences in the film suggests that the modelling must have been carefully considered in advance. In its entirety, the series shows Marfa in the grip of various emotions: the anguish of physical struggle; her determination to improve her circumstances and persuade sceptical peasants to join the cooperative; her distress at the theft of the cooperative's takings; her joy at the moment when the separator produces cream; and her sense of achievement once a tractor has been acquired. The structure of the sequence involves a repeated cut-back to the image of Marfa behind the wheel of the vehicle; in essence, therefore, the series invites an explicit process of comparison. Within the general method of core lighting, there are variations in the degree of harshness or softness of the light; adjustments in the height and position of reflectors; different intensities of light falling onto the face from the front; attempts to narrow or broaden the face depending on the emotional context; greater or less emphasis on the wrinkles under the eyes and the furrows of her brow; occasional reliance on overhead sunlight only; greater or less insistence on the smoothness and tonality of the skin; and variations in the illumination of the eyes. It is worth noting that Marfa's trajectory involves not only the acquisition of self-confidence, but also the discovery of the independent, sensual self. The two initial images in fact reveal the two different faces of the contemporary Marfa. The first consists of her portrait in nominally 'masculine' attire, but beneath this concealment, after she has removed her goggles and pilot's helmet, the discreet presence of make-up and her hair pulled into a bun are revealed. The second, which does not belong to the chronology of the film proper, and follows immediately afterwards, shows her without the modern 'uniform': a strand of hair casually flops over her face, there is no make-up, and the image has been composed with the help of an iris and with very slight soft-focus. This glamorizing technique, like the 'happy ending' of the film, is subversive: the image appears to be stating that the Russian peasant woman, with her 'button nose', as Tret'iakov describes it, deserves her place in cinema just like any other.[203]

The many faces of Lapkina in this sequence are the realization of a conceptual idea – the idea of transformation – which has been established during the separator sequence, except that here the viewer is presented with several figures, not merely one. The artifice of this sequence lies mainly in the fact that the light-spots that splash across the faces of these observers are unmotivated in terms of the functioning of the machine itself; as Eizenshtein subsequently acknowledged, the effects were produced by means of splintered mirror parts stuck to a spinning sphere.[204] Neither are the lighting arrangements for the sequence motivated by the locale in which the action is taking place; this can be gauged by the number of units reflected in the metal surface of the separator when it is unveiled by the agronomist.[205] Furthermore, the portraiture is artificial in the sense that the arrangements for the general shots of the group as they watch the experiment are not replicated for the subsequent close-ups.

Within this scene, there are two general shifts in lighting accent: the initial stage of curiosity blended with scepticism; and the stage of revelation and excitement as the separator works its technological magic. This shift is registered by the dazzling play of light-spots across the faces, but also by the generally lighter tone of the skin, the variations in (diffuse) light coming from the front and the softer quality of the light coming from the sides. During the first stage, the emphasis is placed on physical variety: each portrait is handled differently and emphasizes the particular qualities of the faces and their range of expression. These are not random machinations: the same faces, assuming that the observers have not changed their position, are subjected to subtly varying lighting arrangements. Thus the sceptical woman initially filmed from a low angle as she looks across her shoulder, her head inclined slightly backwards, but with a fair degree of illumination from the front, is plunged into darkness a few seconds later; this time her head looks slightly downwards towards the camera, the lighting from the front has been reduced and the area around her mouth and nose lies in shadow. A similar procedure has been adopted for the portrait of the old man. In the first shot, his head inclines to the left, a directed light source from the front illuminates his beard and a lighting unit to his left has been positioned in front of him and casts light upwards from a forty-five degree angle; in the second, his head is slightly tilted backwards, the lighting unit to his left has been moved slightly behind his shoulder, and most of his face, with the exception of the eyes, lies in shadow. Further variations in compositional strategy can be found in the treatment of the peasant with the beard, who is presented in four separate shots. The first two are variations on the same view (a close-up is followed by a medium close-up, but the pose is identical) and involve lighting units at diametrically opposed angles: the first produces a *contre-jour* effect across the back of his head and shoulders; the second directs light from a low angle in front of him, but slightly to his left. The third is the most extraordinary portrait in the film – two lighting units, positioned in front of him, but to the sides, direct beams of light towards his face, leaving his eyes virtually as sockets, with dark curves of shadow just beneath them, while a third unit, positioned behind him to his right, produces a *contre-jour* effect (Fig. 12). This arrangement highlights his sallow cheeks and high cheekbones, both of which were previously undetectable, as well as the grey flecks in his beard, and is repeated with slightly less expressiveness moments later. For the close-up of another of the female observers, the lighting arrangements have been modified to accentuate the softness of her skin and the roundness of her face (Fig. 13). All these portraits, it should be noted, are linked in terms of their modelling to the final image of the drought sequence, the portrait of a male worshipper, who stares suspiciously from beneath his eyebrows, his face sweating and the muscles on his neck quivering, and who stands as the embodiment of growing religious doubt.

Epilogue: A Landscape of Tears

Eizenshtein, Aleksandrov and Tisse left the Soviet Union on 19 August 1929 at the invitation of Stalin, ostensibly to learn more about the introduction of sound technology abroad. Their peregrinations in Europe, which took them to several countries and included participation in the Congress of Independent Filmmakers in La Sarraz, Switzerland, as well as numerous encounters with a host of progressive artistic and journalistic figures, have been well documented.[206]

In contrast to this relative abundance of biographical material, comparatively little is known about the three films with which they were associated before their departure for the United States. The first, *Giftgas* (Poison Gas, 1929), was the screen adaptation of a play by the left-wing journalist and painter Peter Martin Lampel (it was released by Levfilm, one of two studios based in Berlin with links to Mezhrabpomfil'm).[207] The second, entitled *Frauennot-Frauenglück* (Misery and

Fortune of Women, 1930), was a documentary drama which sought to expose the health risks of illegal abortion in Germany. The third, entitled *Romance sentimentale* (A Sentimental Romance, 1930) and released by Sequana Films, was bankrolled by a wealthy Russian émigré jeweller, Léonhard Rosenthal, who was the owner of the Maison de Perles in Paris and supported the film largely as a vehicle for his girlfriend, Mara Gris, a singer and actress who had aspirations to become a film star.[208] The extent of the involvement of Eizenshtein, Aleksandrov and Tisse either as a team or individually in the genesis and realization of these projects is still not entirely clear. It is possible that Eizenshtein offered some advice towards the end of the filming of *Giftgas*, but in general his participation was minimal (he was forced to deny rumours that he had been actively involved in the production).[209] Tisse later claimed to have been engaged as 'chief operator' on the film, although it is difficult to see how this could have been the case bearing in mind the shooting schedule (the camerawork is usually credited to Akos Farkas).[210] As for *Frauennot-Frauenglück*, it is now generally accepted that this was both directed and filmed by Tisse, with Eizenshtein acting as consultant and editor: a letter from Tisse which dates from December 1929 reveals that it was still being shot while Eizenshtein was in London.[211] Two versions of this film apparently exist: a shorter, silent version with Russian intertitles, and a longer, sonorized version, which includes scenes later filmed by a Swiss camera crew.[212] In relation to *Romance sentimentale*, the issue of authorship is vexed. Eizenshtein always maintained that his involvement was minimal, and that it was a piece of 'hack work' undertaken in order to pay for their planned voyage to the U.S. at the invitation of Paramount studios.[213] Recently published archival sources and the memoirs of others working at the Billancourt studios at the time, however, suggest that he was more directly involved in the realization of this project than he subsequently cared to admit. The surrealist filmmaker Luis Buñuel, for example, remembers Eizenshtein directing the swan sequences in the studios and has scoffed at his later attempts to distance himself from the project.[214] Furthermore, a letter from Eizenshtein to Pera Atasheva at this time gives an enthusiastic and detailed account of the editing of the soundtrack, albeit in relation to the experimental opening section, rather than the 'sentimental' second section (this exploits the words and music of a pseudo-gypsy romance by the Russian émigré composer Aleksei Arkhangel'skii).[215] The uncertainty over authorship is aggravated by claims that Aleksandrov and Tisse were responsible for the exterior sequences (Bergan claims that the two men drove around Brittany and Provence in search of locations, but gives no source for this information);[216]

and the fact that Tisse, in a creative biography compiled several years after Eizenshtein's death, and thus at a time when the latter's association with the project could no longer be a cause for embarrassment, nevertheless attributed the direction to Aleksandrov.[217]

From the point of view of Tisse's cinematography, the uncertainties over the degree of Eizenshtein's involvement in these projects are irrelevant. The same might be said for the view that treats these works as purely commercial ventures rather than genuinely artistic endeavours. Whatever their status, and whatever the degree of collaboration involved, the films constitute a revealing and interesting epilogue to Tisse's camerawork during the silent era. Although the projects are very different in terms of their conceptual framework, and the montage context complicates the status of certain sequences, they are nevertheless linked by their formal originality and lyrical intensity. Their most important shared feature lies in the treatment of landscape, which bears the strong imprint of Tisse's earlier work. Towards the end of the first narrative strand in *Frauennot-Frauenglück*, for example, there is a montage interlude that consists exclusively of evening landscapes and links the scenes showing the distress caused to a working-class family by the unwanted prospect of a fifth child with those that dramatize the fatal consequences of a backstreet abortion. The sequence in question contains eight compositions in total: a shot of willow or birch branches silhouetted against the sun; a sunset framed by tree trunks and branches; two shots of an illuminated street lamp against a background of church spires; two reflections of the sun in a body of water (in the second, the area of the frame above the horizon line is completely black); a shot of an urban embankment that looks across a body of water towards low-lying hills; a landscape of urban buildings barely illuminated by street lamps in the evening gloom; and shots of moving trams with church steeples in the background.

These scenes may be compared with the sequence of images that marks the shift between the tumultuous movement and explosive soundscape which characterize the beginning of *Romance sentimentale* and the static interiors which lead eventually to Gris singing a song in her sumptuous mansion. These images are static and possess an air of relative tranquillity. They are launched with an image of a silhouetted branch ranging diagonally across the frame. This is followed by a darkish cloudscape; the silhouettes of tree branches flickering gently against a setting sun; the branches of a silhouetted tree quivering in a strong breeze; the reflections of indistinct shapes in the surface of a body of water (these later assume the solidity of a row of poplar trees); a series of studies of trees standing next to a body of water in which the reflections of other trees can also be glimpsed; and a double exposure involving two different cloudscapes, one of which has been filmed by a horizontal panning action of the camera. A further sequence of images, which interrupts the first lines of the song but is accompanied by a reprise of the musical accompaniment, echoes these earlier motifs: shots of bare branches against a setting sun; a silhouetted clump of reeds situated by a body of water; silhouetted branches placed against the background of dark-grey tree trunks enveloped in mist; three variations on this same composition, but with only a single branch visible in the foreground; and three almost abstract images of light dancing on water, very possibly the product of raindrops, with only the darkened lines of flora framing the edges.

The persistent resort to *contre-jour* in these compositions, very often with the sun visible within the frame, the penchant for starkly silhouetted shapes and outlines, the interest in cloud formation, the semi-abstract play of light on the surfaces of water, the gentle flickering of the image, the manipulation of tone and the deliberate play with depth of field belong to a highly individual and recognizable body of work. In many respects, they are the direct descendants of the Odessa mist sequence in *Bronenosets Potemkin* and the Razliv sequence in *Oktiabr'*. The sentimental mood further links these sequences: the harbour shrouded in mist heralds the period of mourning for Vakulenchuk's death; the shots of Razliv seek to communicate the sombre atmosphere of mourning which has been prompted by the crushing of the 'July Days' demonstrations; the montage interlude in *Frauennot-Frauenglück* succeeds portraits of the family members which have been composed for the most part in sentimental soft-focus; and the sequences in *Romance sentimentale* are suffused with the melancholic sentiments of a song that expresses yearning for a passionate love that is now lost.

There is a significant difference, however, between the second sequence in *Romance sentimentale* and the earlier sets of images: the considerably higher degree of diffusion or soft-focus. Such is the level of diffusion, in all likelihood the product of uncorrected lenses or disks, that the images approach the poetics of Pictorialism, a movement in photography in the early part of the twentieth century which was directly influenced by the aesthetics of French Impressionism. This movement could boast a significant following in Russia before the Revolution, and was still practised in the Soviet Union during the 1920s.[218] Interestingly, in view of the film's foreign setting, the choice of subject (the depiction of poplars along the side of a pond, albeit in the absence of colour, and in autumnal rather than summer conditions), has a solid French pedigree, namely, Monet's 1891 studies of poplars along the banks of the River Epte, near his home in Giverny. In terms of compositional handling, moreover, there are striking similarities between Tisse's images and certain Pictorialist works from the early part of the century, for example Eduard Steichen's *Moonlight: The Pond* (1906), which shows a range of poplars with trunks and foliage reflected in water, and *The Flatiron – Evening* (1906), which positions the darkened silhouette of a single branch in the foreground while the grey shape of the Flatiron building looms hazily in the background.[219] Like their Impressionist and Pictorialist precursors, Tisse's compositions in *Romance sentimentale* involve a delicate tracery and are characterized by an elusiveness reminiscent of the pencil or charcoal sketch. Certainly, they represent an evolution of the principles that informed his earlier compositions in soft-focus. Albeit not within the sphere of landscape, the extent of the development can be gauged by comparing the respective treatment of sculptures by Rodin in *Oktiabr'* and *Romance sentimentale*: the lighting schemes for the most part are similar, and the two sculptures in question, *Le Baiser* (The Kiss, 1889) and *L'Eternel printemps*, involve an almost identical positioning of bodies, but the level of diffusion in the latter renders the sculpture an impressionistic haze of barely perceptible outlines and textures. Indeed, the embracing figures are sensualized and eroticized to a much greater extent than in *Oktiabr'*, where the intent lies in gentle irony (a woman soldier serving in the Death Brigade stares curiously at the attitude of the lovers, this prompting the decision to abandon her military duties and reengage with the dictates of 'feminine' life-giving, as opposed to 'masculine' life-denying).

The possibility of irony is not entirely absent in *Romance sentimentale*. Those familiar with Eizenshtein's formidably anti-bourgeois reputation, and thus puzzled by the visual hyperbole and sentimental poetry of the second section, were forced to conclude that the film must have been conceived as a parody of émigré melancholy. The scenes of the song's performance are so *haut bourgeois* that they approach the level of the absurd: an aristocratically attired woman playing a grand piano; a sumptuous interior filled with antique objects (period furniture, ornate chandeliers, gleaming grandfather clocks and wall clocks, and polished parquet floor); the arrival of a hunting dog; images of white swans floating in a pond; and portraits of the *chanteuse* herself seated at a white piano that has been positioned in a meadow of blooming wild flowers. It might be deemed noteworthy that none of these images features in the actual song itself. From this perspective, the montage sequence that links the two sections might be regarded as existing within stylistic quotation marks, suggesting that they constitute a psychologized landscape that reflects the preoccupations of a melancholic but extraordinarily privileged (and not particularly talented) person. It is worth conjecturing that Tisse adopted soft-focus precisely as a parodic strategy because it was a technique associated with the overly glamourized cinematography of mainstream cinema. Furthermore, there is more than a hint of the citational in the sense that the levels of diffusion for both interiors and exteriors evoke the atmospheric inserts and *paysage* interludes of French directors heavily influenced by the poetics of Impressionism, for example in *La Chute de la maison Usher* (The Fall of the House of Usher, 1928), Jean Epstein and Buñuel's surreal exercise in Gothic excess, and also, perhaps even more pertinently, because the director was himself a Russian émigré, Kirsanoff's *Brumes d'automne* (The Mists of Autumn, 1928), a twelve-minute 'cinegraphic poem' (in fact, one of the very first experiments with sound in France) which mourns the passing of an amorous relationship, features a melancholic score (specially composed by Paul Devred), makes extensive use of soft-focus for its rain-soaked atmospheric inserts, and, as the title makes clear, takes place during the same season as *Romance sentimentale*.

The problem with the idea of parody, however, lies in the fact that Tisse's images are too strikingly original from the compositional point of view to be considered banal or ironic. This was recognized by one of the early reviewers of *Romance sentimentale*, the émigré philosopher, poet and musicologist Boris Shletser, who commented that 'the photography is excellent: ... all the autumnal visions [are] new and unusually fresh [*ostry*] and expressive'.[220] It is important in this context to emphasize that the film was conceived as a radical form of experiment which attempted to exploit sound technology in innovative ways that were only just beginning to be explored within the avant-garde. The nearest equivalent in Europe, Walter Ruttmann's *In der Nacht: Eine musikalische Bildphantasie* (In the Night: A Musical Picture Fantasy), which combined shots of natural landscapes with images of the concert pianist Nina Hamson performing Robert Schumann's famous piece for piano, was not released until 1931. As such, *Romance sentimentale* might be regarded as a renewed articulation of the interest in the relationship between film and musical forms which had featured in debates about cinema in the Soviet Union and elsewhere during the 1920s, as well as in Eizenshtein's very own essays.[221] Approached from this perspective, the images of landscapes, while their sound accompaniment establishes a different mood and atmosphere, are in principle little different from the scenes of the opening section, which are radically inventive for their time, even within the context of the Soviet avant-garde. The daring use of the hand-held camera for the images of overhead foliage, clearly taken from a moving vehicle; the pounding of waves on the shore, much more forceful than the opening images of *Bronenosets Potemkin*; and the scenes of trees collapsing to the ground, rather than representing the antithesis of what follows, clearly seek to communicate the tumultuous passion that lies at the heart of the song. The fact that these are quintessentially cinematic moments, their expressive force relying on the movement within and outside the frame, whereas the landscapes that introduce the second section embrace the condition of photography and painting, does not negate the experimental impulse that links them.

The manifest disjunction between the banality of the music and the experimental nature of the imagery creates a stylistic tension which is ultimately unresolvable. The problem of the montage interlude is further enhanced by the fact that, in terms of their compositional handling, the images are autonomous in relation to their acoustic context. Whether they are removed from their sound accompaniment or not, and whether they are exhibited as independent fragments or within a larger sequence, the impact on the viewer is nevertheless striking. Not only do they offer further confirmation of Tisse's particular way of perceiving the world, but they problematize Eizenshtein's conviction, asserted throughout the 1920s, that the cinematic image has no intrinsic meaning beyond its specific montage context. Like the scenes of the Odessa harbour, photographed on the morning of 25 September 1925, they produce the same impressions irrespective of the larger sequence to which they belong.

Notes

1. Eizenshtein, 'Predsedateliu torzhestvennogo zasedaniia v chest' XXV-letiia tvorcheskoi deiatel'nosti E. Tisse', p. 171.
2. Eizenshtein, cited in Leonid V. Kosmatov, 'Sovershenstvuia khudozhestvennuiu formu...', *Iskusstvo kino*, 1957.12, 23–26 (p. 23).
3. Boris Mikhin, 'Pervoe znakomstvo', in *Eizenshtein v vospominaniiakh sovremennikov*, ed. by R. N. Iurenev (Moscow: Iskusstvo, 1974), pp. 168–74 (p. 169).
4. Ibid.
5. Eizenshtein, '25 i 15', p. 423.
6. Aleksandrov, *Epokha i kino*, p. 41; Eizenshtein, '25 i 15', p. 423; and Mikhin, 'Pervoe znakomstvo', p. 169.
7. Ibid., p. 171.

8. Ibid.
9. Eizenshtein, 'Predsedateliu torzhestvennogo zasedaniia v chest' XXV-letiia tvorcheskoi deiatel'nosti E. Tisse'. The letter is dated 29 May 1939.
10. The essay was published on 23 May 1939. See *Kino*, 1939.24, 2.
11. Grigorii Kozintsev, 'Andrei Moskvin', *Sovetskoe kino*, 1935.11, 35–43.
12. Eizenshtein, '25 i 15', p. 425.
13. Ibid., pp. 423 & 424.
14. RGALI, fond 123, opis' 2, ed. khr. 1210.
15. The objects of the camera's interest, stalks of rye depicted in the shape of vulvas, would seem to confirm the *double entendre*.
16. S. M. Eisenstein, *Dessins secrets*, texts by Jean-Claude Marcadé and Galia Ackerman (Paris: Editions de Seuil, 1999); and Joan Neuberger, 'Strange Circus: Eisenstein's Sex Drawings', *Studies in Russian and Soviet Cinema*, 6.1 (2012), 5–52. On the different phases of Eizenshtein's production of drawings, see François Albera, 'Eisenstein: The Graphic Question', in *Eisenstein at Ninety*, ed. by Ian Christie and David Elliott (Oxford: Museum of Modern Art, 1988), pp. 119–27.
17. Leyda, *Kino: A History of the Russian and Soviet Film*, p. 182.
18. Aleksandrov, *Epokha i kino*, p. 42.
19. Cited in David Stirk and Elena Pinto Simon, 'Jay Leyda and *Bezhin Meadow*', in *Eisenstein Rediscovered*, ed. by Ian Christie and Richard Taylor (London: Routledge, 1993), pp. 41–52 (p. 49).
20. Interview with Maksim Shtraukh, cited in Norman Swallow, *Eisenstein: A Documentary Portrait* (London: George Allen & Unwin, 1976), p. 51.
21. A. D. Golovnia, *Masterstvo kinooperatora* (Moscow: Iskusstvo, 1965), p. 12.
22. V. Nil'sen and E. Tisse, 'O tvorchestve kinooperatora', *Sovetskoe kino*, 1933.7, 58–65.
23. E. Tisse, 'Budushchie mastera', *Kino*, 1940.1, 1. On his study of filmmaking practices in North America, see his report to the 1933 conference of Moscow camera operators, excerpts from which are cited in Nilsen, *The Cinema as a Graphic Art*, pp. 182–83.
24. See, for example, the two études which accompany N. Sh., 'O fotogenii', *Sovetskii ekran*, 1925.6, 8–9.
25. Aleksandrov, *Epokha i kino*, pp. 72–74.
26. Tisse's letters to Eizenshtein dated 5 and 9 March 1927, in 'Eduard Tisse: "Rabotali my s nagruzkoi 100%"', pp. 99–100 & 101–02.
27. Aleksandrov, *Epokha i kino*, p. 96.
28. Tisse sent two letters to Eizenshtein which detailed the material shot so far. One of them is dated 27 September; the other has no date, but judging from the contents it probably predates this letter by a week or so. See 'Eduard Tisse: "Rabotali my s nagruzkoi 100%"', pp. 102–04 & 104–06.
29. Eduard Tisse, 'Tekhnika s"emki "Bronenostsa Potemkina"', *Kino-zhurnal A.R.K.*, 1926.2, 10–11 (p. 10); idem, 'S"emki "Oktiabria"', *Sovetskii ekran*, 1927.46, 4; and idem, '"General'naia liniia"', ibid., 1926.50, 10.
30. Bergan, *Sergei Eisenstein*, pp. 285–86.
31. Oksana Bulgakowa, *Sergei Eisenstein: A Biography*, trans. by Anne Dwyer (Berlin: Potemkin Press, 2001), pp. 201–03. See also 'Fil'm o ferganskom kanale', in Eizenshtein, *Izbrannye proizvedeniia*, I, 187–88 (first publ. in *Pravda*, 13 August 1939).
32. Eizenshtein, 'Montazh attraktsionov', p. 270.
33. Eisenstein, 'The Montage of Film Attractions', p. 39.

34. 'The Dramaturgy of Film Form (The Dialectical Approach to Film Form)' [1929], in Eisenstein, *Selected Works*, I, 161–80 (p. 179) (first publ. (and translated) in Sergei Eisenstein, *Film Form: Essays in Film Theory*, ed. and trans. by Jay Leyda (New York: Harcourt, Brace & World, 1948), pp. 45–63).

35. 'Za kadrom', in Eizenshtein, *Izbrannye proizvedeniia*, II, 283–96 (pp. 290–91) (first publ. as the afterword to N. Kaufman, *Iaponskoe kino* (Moscow: Tea-kino-pechat', 1929), pp. 72–92).

36. Eizenshtein, 'Za kadrom', p. 293.

37. 'Chetvertoe izmerenie v kino', in Eizenshtein, *Izbrannye proizvedeniia*, II, 45–59 (pp. 53–56) (first publ. [first half only] as 'Kino chetyrekh izmerenii' in *Kino*, 1929.34, 4).

38. Eizenshtein, 'Chetvertoe izmerenie v kino', pp. 47–48.

39. Ibid., p. 54.

40. '"E!": O chistote kinoiazyka', in Eizenshtein, *Izbrannye proizvedeniia*, II, 81–92 (pp. 87–91) (first publ. in *Sovetskoe kino*, 1934.5, 25–31).

41. Jacques Aumont, *Montage Eisenstein*, Theories of Representation and Difference series, ed. by Teresa de Lauretis, trans. by Lee Hildreth, Constance Panely and Andrew Ross (London: BFI, 1987), p. 25.

42. Eizenstein's letter to Aleksandrov dated 7 August 1927, cited in Aleksandrov, *Epokha i kino*, p. 102.

43. Ibid., p. 96.

44. Albera, 'Eisenstein: The Graphic Question', p. 123.

45. Eizenshtein, 'Montazh attraktsionov', p. 271.

46. Eisenstein, 'The Dramaturgy of Film Form', pp. 162 & 165.

47. 'The Dynamic Square', in Eisenstein, *Selected Writings*, I, 206–18 (pp. 211 & 212) (first publ. in *Close Up*, 8.1 (1931), 3–16, and 8.2 (1931), 91–94).

48. Masha Salazkina, *In Excess: Sergei Eisenstein's Mexico* (Chicago, IL: University of Chicago Press, 2009), pp. 21–53 & 54–90.

49 Sergei Eisenstein, 'The Prometheus of Mexican Painting', in *Mexico According to Eisenstein*, ed. by Karetnikova, pp. 159–67.

50. 'O stroenii veshchei', in Eizenshtein, *Izbrannye proizvedeniia*, III (1964), 37–71 (pp. 56–60) (first publ. in *Iskusstvo kino*, 1939.6, 7–20).

51. '[Montazh] (1937)', in Eizenshtein, *Izbrannye proizvedeniia*, II, 329–484 (pp. 376–92).

52. See 'Tsvetnoe kino' [1948], in ibid., III, 579–88 (first publ. in S. M. Eizenshtein, *Izbrannye stat'i* (Moscow: Iskusstvo, 1956), pp. 311–20). See also 'Pervoe pis'mo o tsvete' [1946] and 'Iz neokonchennogo issledovaniia o tsvete' [1946–47], in Eizenshtein, *Izbrannye proizvedeniia*, III, 487–91 & 500–67, respectively.

53. David Elliott, 'Taking a Line for a Walk', in *Eisenstein at Ninety*, ed. by Christie and Elliott, pp. 19–40 (p. 31).

54. 'Eisenstein on Eisenstein, the Director of "Potemkin"', in Eisenstein, *Selected Works*, I, 74–76 (first publ. in *Berlin Tageblatt*, 7 June 1926). The October Group was established by the German communist Alfred Kurella and its members included a number of artists who had been formerly associated with the Constructivist movement in the Soviet Union. See Albera, *Eisenstein et le constructivisme russe*, pp. 140–48.

55. Aleksei Gan, 'Chto takoe konstruktivizm' [1928], cited in Lodder, *Russian Constructivism*, p. 182.

56. Albera, *Eisenstein et le constructivisme russe*.

57. Ibid., pp. 113–48, 149–68, & 169–94.

58. Lodder, *Russian Constructivism*, pp. 181–204.

59. Albera, *Eisenstein et le constructivisme russe*, p. 126.

60. Eduard Tisse, 'Kak snimalsia "Bronenosets Potemkin"' [1945], in *Bronenosets Potemkin*, ed. by Kleiman and Levina, pp. 292–95 (p. 293).

61. Pack, *Film Posters of the Russian Avant-Garde*, pp. 168–71.

62. Eduard Tisse, 'Na s"emkakh "General'noi"', *Sovetskii ekran*, 1929.5, 13.

63. Tisse, 'Stranitsy proshlogo', p. 38.

64. See the examples featured on <http://www.libava.ru> (accessed 4 September 2011).

65. Novitskii, 'Russkie i inostrannye operatory (Iz vospominanii operatora)'.

66. Tisse, 'Stranitsy proshlogo', p. 50.

67. This footage was included in Pudovkin's *Golod... golod... golod...*, an agit-feature filmed for export in order to raise awareness of the tragedy internationally. See Tisse, 'Tvorcheskaia biografiia', pp. 162–63.

68. Ibid., pp. 162 & 164.

69. Ibid., pp. 162–65.

70. Eduard Tisse, 'Na frontakh grazhdanskoi voiny: Vospominaniia operatora-boitsa', *Kino*, 1933.10, 2.

71. Tisse, 'Stranitsy proshlogo', p. 49.

72. <http://www.pbs.org/redfiles/rao/archives/rgakfd/ textind6.html> (accessed 14 June 2011).

73. *Rossiia v kinokadre, 1896–1916*, ed. by V. N. Batalin and others (Moscow: ROSSPEN, 2007).

74. 'Kino na voine (Iz lichnykh vospominanii operatora P. K. Novitskogo)', *Sovetskii ekran*, 1925.6, 4. On Tisse's acquaintance with Novitskii, see 'Doklad E. K. Tisse na seminare operatorov kinostudii "Mosfil'm" 27 aprelia 1956 goda', *Iskusstvo kino*, 1979.2, 104–13 (p. 104).

75. L. M. [Leo Mur], 'S vintovkoi i kino-apparatom', p. 7.

76. Tisse, 'Na frontakh grazhdanskoi voiny'.

77. L. M. [Leo Mur], 'S vintovkoi i kino-apparatom', p. 7.

78. Tisse, 'Stranitsy proshlogo', p. 49.

79. 'Doklad E. K. Tisse na seminare operatorov kinostudii "Mosfil'm" 27 aprelia 1956 goda', p. 104.

80. The frame still in question is only available via the internet. See the illustrations which accompany A. Simonov's essay on Tisse in *Desiat' operatorskikh biografii*, ed. by M. Goldovskaia (Moscow: Iskusstvo, 1975) <http://www.photographerslib.ru> (accessed 25 November 2011).

81. Eduard Tisse, 'Nezabyvaemye gody', *Iskusstvo kino*, 1940.1–2, 83–84 (p. 83).

82. G. Boltianskii, 'Kino-khronika i kino-agitka', *Kino*, 1922.3, 18–20.

83. Tisse, '"Na tom my stoim"', p. 102. See also '"VGIK: Tvorcheskii vecher, posviashchennyi t. Tisse E. K."', pp. 174 & 175.

84. 'Doklad E. K. Tisse na seminare operatorov kinostudii "Mosfil'm" 27 aprelia 1956 goda', p. 105.

85. L. Kuleshov, 'Pochemu plokho sniali voinu', *Sovetskii ekran*, 1928.30, 5; and also idem, 'Nashi pervye opyty', *Sovetskoe kino*, 1936.11–12, 126–37 (p. 126).

86. It is perhaps worth noting that nothing of these 'disputes' was recorded in Kuleshov's notebooks at the time. See 'Kinokhronika: Fil'm "Na krasnom fronte"', in Kuleshov, *Stat'i: Materialy*, pp. 60–65.

87. Kuleshov, 'Nashi pervye opyty', p. 11.

88. Evgenii Ivanov-Barkov, 'Ural'skaia promyshlennost' na fil'me', *Kino*, 1922.3, 23–24.

89. Aleksandrov, *Epokha i kino*, p. 41.

90. '"VGIK: Tvorcheskii vecher, posviashchennyi t. Tisse E. K."', p. 175.

91. On Eizenshtein's theatrical activities during this period, see R. Iurenev, *Sergei Eizenshtein: Zamysly: Fil'my: Metod (Chast' pervaia: 1898–1929)* (Moscow: Iskusstvo, 1985), pp. 35–56.

92. '"Mudrets" S. M. Eizenshteina: Opyt slovesnoi rekonstruktsii spektaklia', publ. by N. Kleiman, *Kinovedcheskie zapiski*, 39 (1998), 54–110.

93. Philip Cavendish, 'From "Lost" to "Found": The "Rediscovery" of Sergei Eizenshtein's *Dnevnik Glumova* and its Avant-Garde Context', http://www.kinokultura.com/2013/issue41.shtml.

94. Sergei Eisenstein and Sergei Iutkevich, 'The Eighth Art: On Expressionism, America and, of course, Chaplin', in Eisenstein, *Selected Works*, I, 29–32 (first publ. in *Ekho*, 7 November 1922).

95. Eizenshtein, '[Montazh] (1937)', p. 454.

96. Eizenshtein, '25 i 15', p. 422.

97. See his diary entry for 12 December 1923, in 'Teatral'nye tetradi S. M. Eizenshteina' [1919–24], publ. by M. K. Ivanova and V. V. Ivanov, *Mnemozina: Istoricheskii al'manakh*, ed. by V. V. Ivanov, II (Moscow: Editorial URSS, 2000), 190–279 (p. 255).

98. Aleksandr Levshin, 'Na repetitsiiakh "Mudretsa"', in *Eizenshtein v vospominaniiakh sovremennikov*, ed. by Iurenev, pp. 136–50 (p. 148).

99. Kuleshov and Khokhlova, *50 let v kino*, p. 81. See also Aleksandrov, *Epokha i kino*, p. 33.

100. Ibid., pp. 35–36.

101. Eizenshtein, 'Sredniaia iz trekh', p. 70.

102. V. Pertsov, 'Mest' zarezannykh kadrov (Zagranichnaia kartina na sovetskom ekrane)', *Sovetskoe kino*, 1926.2, 16–17.

103. 'Volia: Uporstvo: Glaz', in Kuleshov, *Sobranie sochinenii*, I, 111–13 (p. 112) (first publ. in *Eizenshtein: Bronenosets Potemkin* (Moscow: Kinopechat', 1926)).

104. Harte, *Fast Forward*, pp. 101–28.

105. Eizenshtein, '25 i 15', p. 424.

106. Rodchenko, 'Puti sovremennoi fotografii', cited in A. N. Lavrentiev, 'The Photo Eye/Das Photo-Auge/L'Oeil de l'appareil', in *Alexander Rodchenko: Photography, 1924–1954*, ed. by Lavrentiev, pp. 10–37 (p. 21).

107. Sergei Eizenshtein, 'Konstantsa (Kuda ukhodit "Bronenosets Potemkin")' [1926], in *Bronenosets Potemkin*, ed. by Kleiman and Levina, pp. 290–92 (p. 291).

108. Eizenshtein, 'Tezisy k vystupleniiu na diskussii v ARKe', p. 31.

109. Ibid.

110. Ibid., pp. 34–35, n3. For the dispute between Eizenshtein and Pletnev, see Sergei Eizenshtein, 'Beseda s rezhiss. S. M. Eizenshteinom', *Kino-nedelia*, 1925.4, 17; and V. Pletnev, 'Otkrytoe pis'mo v redaktsiiu zhurnala "Kino-nedelia"', ibid., 1925.6, 9.

111. Eizenshtein, 'Tezisy k vystupleniiu na diskussii v ARKe', p. 32.

112. J. Hoberman, 'A face to the *shtetl*: Soviet Yiddish cinema, 1924–36', in *Inside the Film Factory*, ed. by Taylor and Christie, pp. 124–50 (pp. 125–26).

113. Ibid., p. 127.

114. Khr. Khersonskii, 'Komicheskaia i komediia', *Kino-zhurnal A.R.K.*, 1925.11–12, 27–28.

115. The pogroms which accompanied the fighting, and the responses of the Jewish inhabitants to them, feature prominently in *Konarmiia*, Babel''s graphic account of the military campaign conducted against the Poles by Budennyi's Red Cavalry, and also in Vasilii Grossman's 'V gorode Berdicheve' (1934), a short story adapted for the screen many years later in the form of Aleksandr Askol'dov's *Komissar* (1967).

116. Frelikh, 'Stil' operatora', pp. 6–7.

117. Aleksandrov, *Epokha i kino*, p. 32.

118. Eizenshtein, 'Konstantsa (Kuda ukhodit "Bronenosets Potemkin")', p. 291.

119. Viktor Shklovskii, 'Piat' fel'etonov ob Eizenshteine', in *Bronenosets Potemkin*, ed. by Kleiman and Levina, pp. 296–98 (p. 297) (first publ. in *Gamburgskii schet* (Leningrad: Izdatel'stvo pisatelei v Leningrade, 1928)).

120. Eduard Tisse, 'Perepiska druzei', *Kino*, 1926.5, 6. See also Viktor Shklovskii, 'Gore ot shpagi', ibid., 1925.40, 3.

121. Aleksandrov, *Epokha i kino*, p. 56.

122. Eizenshtein, 'Konstantsa (Kuda ukhodit "Bronenosets Potemkin")', p. 291.

123. Shtraukh's letters to his wife dated 15 September and 22 September 1925, in '"Bronenosets Potemkin": Fil'my-iubiliary', p. 134.

124. '"VGIK: Tvorcheskii vecher, posviashchennyi t. Tisse E. K."', pp. 175–76.

125. Shtraukh's letter to his wife dated 22 September 1925, in '"Bronenosets Potemkin": Fil'my-iubiliary', p. 134.

126. M. Shtraukh, 'Vstrechi', *Iskusstvo kino*, 1940.1–2, 89–91 (p. 91).

127. Shtraukh's letter to his wife dated 22 September 1925, in '"Bronenosets Potemkin": Fil'my-iubiliary', p. 134.

128. M. Shtraukh, 'Iz s"emochnogo dnevnika M. M. Shtraukha' [1925], in *Bronenosets Potemkin*, ed. by Kleiman and Levina, p. 67.

129. Shtraukh's letter to his wife dated 30 September, in '"Bronenosets Potemkin": Fil'my-iubiliary', p. 135.

130. Tisse, 'Tekhnika s"emki "Bronenostsa Potemkina"', p. 10.

131. 'Iz s"emochnogo dnevnika M. M. Shtraukha'.

132. On Tisse's acquisition of the Bell & Howell, see Shtraukh's letter to his wife dated 26 September 1925, in '"Bronenosets Potemkin": Fil'my-iubiliary', p. 135.

133. The term 'apparat v dvizhenii', which presumably refers to a tracking camera, rather than a hand-held camera, is employed in relation to four shots in total. See 'Iz s"emochnogo dnevnika M. M. Shtraukha'.

134. Tisse, 'Tekhnika s"emki "Bronenostsa Potemkina"', p. 11.

135. Ibid.

136. Tisse made this claim at least three times. See ibid., p. 10; Tisse, 'Kak snimalsia "Bronenosets Potemkin"', p. 294; and 'Doklad E. K. Tisse na seminare operatorov kinostudii "Mosfil'm" 27 aprelia 1956 goda', p. 104. For the use of mirrors on exteriors in still photography, see Beaumont Newhall, *The History of Photography from 1839 to the Present*, revised and enlarged edn (New York: The Museum of Modern Art, 1982), p. 48.

137. Tisse, 'Kak snimalsia "Bronenosets Potemkin"', p. 293.

138. Viktor Shklovskii, 'Eizenshtein', *Kino-zhurnal A.R.K.*, 1926.2, 5–6 (p. 6).

139. 'Diskussiia o kartine "Bronenosets Potemkin" v ARK (7 ianvaria 1926 goda)', in *Bronenosets Potemkin*, ed. by Kleiman and Levina, pp. 198–200 (p. 200).

140. Pack, *Film Posters of the Russian Avant-Garde*, p. 168.

141. Philip Cavendish, *Soviet Mainstream Cinematography: The Silent Era*, 3rd edn (London: UCL Arts and Humanities Publications, 2010), pp. 52–53.

142. 'Dva cherepa Aleksandra Makedonskogo', in Eizenshtein, *Izbrannye proizvedeniia*, II, 280–82 (p. 281) (first publ. in *Novyi zritel'*, 1926.35, 10).

143. Eizenshtein, 'Dvenadtsat' apostolov', p. 125.

144. Iudin, 'Amerikanskoe osveshchenie v kino'.

145. Yuri Tsivian [Iurii Tsiv'ian], 'Eisenstein and Russian Symbolist Culture: An Unknown Script of *October*', in *Eisenstein Rediscovered*, ed. by Christie and Taylor, pp. 79–109 (p. 80).

146. Richard Taylor, *October*, BFI Film Classics series (London: BFI, 2002), pp. 8–11.

147. James von Geldern, *Bolshevik Festivals 1917–1920* (Berkeley: University of California Press, 1993), pp. 134–74.

148. Taylor, *October*, p. 12.
149. See his letter dated 5 March 1927, in 'Eduard Tisse: "Rabotali my s nagruzkoi 100%"', pp. 99–100.
150. Tisse, 'S"emki "Oktiabria"'.
151. Aleksandrov, *Epokha i kino*, p. 96.
152. Ibid., pp. 96–103. See also 'Eduard Tisse: "Rabotali my s nagruzkoi 100%"', pp. 102–04 & 104–06.
153. Tsivian, 'Eisenstein and Russian Symbolist Culture', p. 80.
154. For example, David Bordwell, *The Cinema of Eisenstein* (Cambridge, MA: Harvard University Press, 1993), pp. 79–96; and James Goodwin, *Eisenstein, Cinema, and History* (Urbana: University of Illinois Press, 1993), pp. 79–92.
155. For example, see 'RING LEFA: "Odinnadtsatyi" Vertova; "Oktiabr'" Eizenshteina', in Osip Brik, 'Kinopublitsistika 20-kh godov', publ. by A. V. Valiuzhenich, *Kinovedcheskie zapiski*, 69 (2004), 274–332 (pp. 326–32) (first publ. in *Novyi LEF*, 1928.4).
156. Cited in Bulgakowa, *Sergei Eisenstein*, p. 74. See also Aleksandrov, *Epokha i kino*, p. 96.
157. Ibid.
158. Tsivian, 'Eisenstein and Russian Symbolist Culture'.
159. Viktor Shklovskii, *Eizenshtein* (Moscow: Iskusstvo, 1973), p. 153; and idem, 'O zakonakh stroeniia fil'my S. Eizenshteina' [Part 2], *Sovetskii ekran*, 1928.7, 7.
160. Tsivian, 'Eisenstein and Russian Symbolist Culture', p. 81.
161. S. Tret'iakov, 'Kino k iubileiu' [1927], cited (and translated) in Katerina Clark, *Petersburg: Crucible of Revolution* (Cambridge, MA: Harvard University Press, 1995), p. 238.
162. Tisse's letter to Eizenshtein dated 27 September 1927, in 'Eduard Tisse: "Rabotali my s nagruzkoi 100%"', p. 102.
163. *Ermitazh: Istoriia stroitel'stva i arkhitektura zdanii*, ed. by B. B. Piotrovskii (Leningrad: Stroiizdat, leningradskoe otdelenie, 1989), pp. 305–12.
164. Cited in Aleksandrov, *Epokha i kino*, pp. 96 & 98.
165. Tsivian, 'Eisenstein and Russian Symbolist Culture', p. 98.
166. Aleksandrov, *Epokha i kino*, p. 102.
167. Ibid., p. 103.
168. Tisse's letter to Eizenshtein dated 27 September, in 'Eduard Tisse: "Rabotali my s nagruzkoi 100%"', p. 103.
169. Tisse's letter to Eizenshtein (undated), in ibid., p. 105.
170. 'Books on the Road' [1946], in Eisenstein, *Selected Works*, IV (*Beyond the Stars: The Memoirs of Sergei Eizenshtein*), trans. by William Powell, 390–402 (p. 396).
171. V. F., 'General'naia liniia (Beseda s S. M. Eizenshteinom)', *Kino-front*, 1927.4, 29–30 (p. 29). Eizenshtein makes similar claims in '"General'naia liniia" (Beseda s S. M. Eizenshteinom)', *Kino*, 1927.11, 3.
172. Sergei Eizenshtein, 'O "General'noi linii" (Beseda s S. Eizenshteinom i G. Aleksandrovym)', *Kino*, 1929.5, 2.
173. For the differing views, see Ian Christie's introduction ('Rediscovering Eisenstein') in *Eisenstein Rediscovered*, ed. by Christie and Taylor, pp. 1–30 (pp. 6–7).
174. V. F., 'General'naia liniia (Beseda s S. M. Eizenshteinom)', *Kino*, 1926.2, 1.
175. Aleksandrov, *Epokha i kino*, p. 79.
176. V. F., 'General'naia liniia (Beseda s S. M. Eizenshteinom)' (*Kino*).
177. Aleksandrov, *Epokha i kino*, pp. 82–85.
178. Ibid., p. 106.
179. Boris Shumiatskii, *Kinematografiia millionov*, cited in Bulgakowa, *Sergei Eisenstein*, p. 86.

180. Aleksandrov, *Epokha i kino*, pp. 107–08. For a revealing report on the unedited material which had been completed by December 1926, see "'General'naia liniia'", in Sergei Tret'iakov, 'Izbrannye teksty 20-kh godov', *Kinovedcheskie zapiski*, 34 (1997), 6–19 (pp. 10–12) (first publ. in *Prozhektor*, 1927.6). For a comparison between this unedited material and the version that was ready for release on 8 March 1929 (what he dubs 'General'naia liniia nr. 2'), see 'Perevoploshchenie odnoi fil'my', in Tret'iakov, 'Izbrannye teksty 20-kh godov', pp. 16–19 (first publ. in *Literaturnaia gazeta*, 1 July 1929). For the surviving prints of *Staroe i novoe*, see Myriam Tsikounas, 'Eisenstein and the Theory of "Models"; or, How to Distract the Spectator's Attention', in *Eisenstein Rediscovered*, ed. by Christie and Taylor, pp. 189–99 (p. 189n3).

181. Tret'iakov, 'Perevoploshchenie odnoi fil'my', p. 17. See also Khris. Khersonskii, "'Staroe i novoe'", *Kino*, 1929.41, 5.

182. S. Eizenshtein and Gr. Aleksandrov, 'Eksperiment, poniatnyi millionam', in Eizenshtein, *Izbrannye proizvedeniia*, I, 144–47 (p. 145) (first publ. in *Sovetskii ekran*, 1929.6, 6–7).

183. For the centrality of the sequence, which existed in the very earliest drafts of the screenplay, see Anne Nesbet, *Savage Junctures: Sergei Eisenstein and the Shape of Thinking* (London: I. B. Tauris, 2003), pp. 99–103.

184. 'Pafos' [1946–47], in Eizenshtein, *Izbrannye proizvedeniia*, III, 37–233 (p. 77).

185. Eizenshtein, 'Chetvertoe izmerenie v kino', pp. 46–47.

186. Eizenshtein and Aleksandrov, 'Eksperiment, poniatnyi millionam', p. 144.

187. Ibid.

188. Eduard Tisse, "'General'naia liniia'".

189. 'Doklad E. K. Tisse na seminare operatorov kinostudii "Mosfil'm" 27 aprelia 1956 goda', p. 111.

190. Ibid., pp. 111–12.

191. Eduard Tisse, "'General'naia liniia'", *Sovetskii ekran*, 1927.36, 12.

192. Eizenshtein, 'Chetvertoe izmerenie v kino', p. 47.

193. M. Shtraukh, 'V poiskakh akterov "General'noi" (Iz zapisok assistenta)', *Sovetskii ekran*, 1928.7, 4–5.

194. A. I., 'Litso "Stachki"', *Sovetskii ekran*, 1925.7, 7–8.

195. Tret'iakov, "'General'naia liniia'", p. 12.

196. P. Attasheva, 'Geroi "General'noi"', *Sovetskii ekran*, 1929.6, 8.

197. For Tisse's use of *skreshchenie* (literally, 'crossing'), see Golovnia, *Masterstvo kinooperatora*, p. 113.

198. Salt, *Film Style and Technology*, p. 154.

199. Nilsen, *The Cinema as a Graphic Art*, pp. 176–80.

200. *Alexander Rodchenko: Photography, 1924–1954*, ed. by Lavrentiev, pp. 93, 95, & 96.

201. Cited in Lesser, 'Tisse's Unfinished Treasure', p. 36.

202. Aleksandrov, *Epokha i kino*, p. 100.

203. Tret'iakov, "'General'naia liniia'", p. 12.

204. Eizenshtein, 'Pafos', p. 84.

205. Eizenshtein, 'Za kadrom', p. 149.

206. Bulgakowa, *Sergei Eisenstein*, pp. 94–107.

207. This film was scripted by Natan Zarkhi, directed by Mikhail Dubson (a lawyer turned filmmaker), and starred Vera Baranovskaia, the actress famous for her roles in Pudovkin's *Mat'* and *Konets Sankt-Peterburga*, who had recently emigrated to Germany. Tisse gives an incorrect title for this film and misspells Dubson's name in his creative biography. See Tisse, 'Tvorcheskaia biografiia', p. 166.

208. Bulgakowa, *Sergei Eisenstein*, p. 103.
209. Ibid., pp. 99–100.
210. Tisse, 'Tvorcheskaia biografiia', p. 166.
211. See Tisse's letter to Eizenshtein dated 11 December 1929, in 'Eduard Tisse: "Rabotali my s nagruzkoi 100%"', p. 100.
212. Tisse, 'Tvorcheskaia biografiia', p. 166. Also Valerii Bosenko, 'Staryi "Sentimental'nyi romans"', *Kinovedcheskie zapiski*, 54 (2001), 285–94 (p. 286).
213. Ibid.
214. Cited in ibid.
215. Cited in Bulgakowa, *Sergei Eisenstein*, p. 103.
216. Bergan, *Sergei Eisenstein*, p. 172.
217. Tisse, 'Tvorcheskaia biografiia', p. 166.
218. Elena Barkhatova, 'Pictorialism: Photography as Art', in *Photography in Russia*, ed. by David Elliott (London: Thames and Hudson, 1992), pp. 51–60.
219. Alfred Stieglitz, *Camera Work: A Pictorial Guide*, ed. by Marianne Fulton Margolis (New York: Dover Publications/International Museum of Photography, George Eastman House, 1978), pp. 38 & 39.
220. Boris Shletser, '"Sentimental'nyi romans"', publ. by Rashit Iangirov, *Kinovedcheskie zapiski*, 54 (2001), 297–98 (p. 298) (first publ. in *Poslednie novosti*, 4 July 1930).
221. Pudovkin's interest in this relationship will be discussed further in the next chapter.

CHAPTER THREE

Anatolii Golovnia and Vsevolod Pudovkin

Without you it is difficult and awkward, but the important thing is I don't feel relaxed and uninhibited. Z is a very nice person, a very painstaking and competent camera operator, but he has his own set of artistic beliefs which, at the end of the day, are alien to me, and he is not open to new ideas.

We both try to take each other's views into account, but what emerges is only friendship, not love. I hold back, and he holds back. I make concessions, and he makes concessions, but the sense of real excitement, of a genuine pushing against boundaries and a precise meeting of minds, is lacking.

So I am finding work difficult at the moment, perhaps even impossible. I live with the conviction that we will again be together. Our collaborations are based on such a close mutual understanding of each other, and (most importantly) on such a belief in each other, that of course it is impossible to replicate this with anyone else. I will always feel this sense of inhibition.[1]

We first learned to express our feelings visually, and to make them understood.[2]

Introduction

The sentiments expressed in the first epigraph above are contained in a letter written by Pudovkin to Golovnia during the early stages of the Second World War, when the former was working in Alma-Ata, the capital of the Kazakh Soviet Socialist Republic, having been evacuated from Moscow, and the latter was based in the Georgian capital of Tbilisi, having been assigned a project with the director Vladimir Petrov. Golovnia cites the fragment in an article written many years later in which he describes Pudovkin's search for a contemporary hero who would reflect the challenges and achievements of the grand revolutionary epoch in which they were living. This subject, which apparently first suggested itself in 1928, preoccupied Pudovkin for much of the next decade, and prompted consideration of a number of projects, among them a celebration of the life of Valerii Chkalov, the pilot and Hero of the Soviet Union who completed a number of record-breaking flights before his tragic death in 1938, and a film based on the war reportage of Konstantin

Simonov, the journalist, writer, playwright and poet whose despatches from various military fronts later gained him several state prizes. As Golovnia tacitly acknowledges, the films based on the lives of national heroes that he and Pudovkin made in the 1940s and early 1950s, nearly all of them historical rather than contemporary figures, were poor substitutes for the original impulse. The article hints at the considerable difficulties that Pudovkin experienced in finding suitable material during the restrictive era of Socialist Realism. Its initial paragraphs, however, seek to establish a different and not entirely related point; namely, the problems which arise when a film director works alongside a cameraman with whom he is unfamiliar, and with whom he shares little from the artistic point of view. Pudovkin's observation that the person in question, his identity (Boris Volchek) disguised by the editors of *Iskusstvo kino* for reasons of discretion, already possessed his own set of convictions, and that their collaboration lacked the necessary excitement and intuitive understanding, speaks eloquently about the need for a creative alliance that goes beyond the purely formal or professional.[3]

This letter serves as a useful reminder of something that is frequently neglected in Pudovkin studies; namely, the enormous debt that the director owed to Golovnia as his cameraman. For many, it might come as a surprise to learn that these two men worked side by side for nearly thirty years in a relationship that began in the mid-1920s and ended only with Pudovkin's death in 1953. During this period, they become close friends and allies whose creative affinity, apart from a brief moment of tension at the end of the 1920s, and their enforced separation as a result of the Second World War, never faltered. It is a moving testimony to the solidity of this friendship that Golovnia opted to abandon his professional career altogether after Pudovkin died.[4]

Unlike other partnerships within the avant-garde, their working practices were characterized by a great degree of independence for the camera operator. Not only was Golovnia actively involved in the generation of ideas and the writing of screenplays, but he was also regularly given permission to shoot scenes unsupervised. According to Golovnia himself, Pudovkin was not particularly prescriptive about how individual scenes should be shot:

> [Pudovkin] *never noticed how the camera operator arranged the lights or made his choice of camera angle; he only told him* what *should be in the frame. On finishing his rehearsals, Pudovkin would stretch out his hand towards the cameraman and give the signal to start shooting.*[5]

Golovnia explains this relative lack of interest in terms of Pudovkin's intense focus on acting technique. His rehearsals are described as a form of 'co-participation' in which the director performs alongside the actors and creates the appropriate conditions for the 'unmediated discharging of emotion'.[6] In the conditions of creative tension which emerged, reflecting the nervous energy of the director himself, the role of the camera operator was to be attentive and precise, ready at a moment's notice to capture the authentic gesture which might be produced spontaneously, and potentially without repetition. This method, which Golovnia describes in terms of an 'ever-ready camera', was pioneered during the filming of *Mekhanika golovnogo mozga*, an educational documentary about the scientific experiments being pursued by Ivan Pavlov in the field of the nervous system at the Leningrad Institute of Experimental Medicine.[7]

Although Pudovkin's reception in the Soviet Union and abroad has been subject to considerable fluctuation over the last ninety years, he is still regarded as an important early theorist of cinema and acting methodology.[8] It might be argued that Golovnia was his cinematographic alter ego, one of the leading theorists of camera operation in the Soviet Union and someone who has done more to explain the creative dimension of his craft than any other practitioner in the field either before or since. Although his international reputation was far less impressive than his partner's, Golovnia was nevertheless revered within the profession; until his death in 1982, he was the living antithesis of the maxim that cameramen by their very nature are taciturn, their talent lying in the ability to communicate in images rather than in words. From 1936, when he became involved in the teaching of camera operation at VGIK, Golovnia produced a wide-ranging series of textbooks and writings which became required reading for aspiring Soviet cameramen. Although there were other practising camera operators who were invited to give lectures at VGIK, it was Golovnia who modernized teaching methods and created the pedagogical framework within which students acquired the necessary training before embarking on careers in the Soviet film industry.[9] It is symptomatic of his status within the avant-garde that he was invited to perform the role of the camera operator in *Stekliannyi glaz* (The Glass Eye, 1928), a groundbreaking documentary by Lilia Brik and Vitalii Zhemchuzhnyi which sought to explain the technical functions of the camera. As already mentioned in Chapter One, at certain junctures during the 1920s Golovnia was also commissioned to work on mainstream commercial projects. These films offer a useful illustration of the degree to which Golovnia's 'signature' was able to transcend genre limitations and the personalities of the directors concerned. While increasingly conservative with the passage of time, he nevertheless cautiously welcomed the 'new wave' that emerged in the Soviet Union during the 1950s and 1960s.[10]

Examination of Golovnia's partnership with Pudovkin is important in the sense that it corrects some of the misconceptions that have arisen about this director's silent-era works. Kepley Jr has recently referred to his contradictory and ambiguous status; on the one hand a director identified as belonging to the avant-garde, and on the other an 'aesthetic conservative' and 'resident classicist among the practitioners of modernist montage'.[11] It is certainly the case that Pudovkin's approach to montage was less radical than Eizenshtein's, but montage is not the sole criterion for innovation during this period. From a generic and stylistic point of view, Pudovkin's films during the 1920s and early 1930s were consistently experimental. *Shakhmatnaia goriachka* blazed a new trail with its blend of (comic) staged and non-staged material. *Konets Sankt-Peterburga*, with its unorthodox dramatic structure and extended montage collisions, has long been recognized as one of the pioneering examples of what the Soviet film historian Nikolai Iezuitov has described as the 'lyrical epopeia'; in other words, a film seeking to dramatize and poeticize epic (revolutionary) events through the prism of private experience.[12] *Potomok Chingis-Khana* (The Descendent of Genghis-Khan/Storm over Asia, 1928) represented a marked shift towards the 'literature of fact', a radical tendency expounded most vociferously by progressive intellectuals grouped around LEF – in particular, Brik, Shklovskii and Tret'iakov – which privileged documentary 'fact' over fabricated literary or feature-film 'fiction'.[13] *Prostoi sluchai*, although a critical failure, was based on an experimental screenplay by the same dramatist who later adapted Ivan Turgenev's 'Bezhin lug' for Eizenshtein's ill-fated film of the same title. *Dezertir* (The Deserter, 1933), with its asynchronous approach to sound recording and editing, certainly deserves its reputation alongside Vertov's *Entuziazm: Symfoniia Donbasy* (Entuziazm: Simfoniia Donbassa, Enthusiasm: Symphony of the Donbas, 1931) as a formidable avant-garde experiment with sound. The conventionality of Pudovkin's statements on directing, the methodology of the actor and the art of screenplay writing has tended to distract from his more innovative writings, for example his essay on photogenicity, which advances some interesting ideas about modernist aesthetics and compositional rhythm in cinema. Very few of the studies of his works published hitherto either in Russian or English offer a detailed investigation of the visual language of his films.

As will be demonstrated, although both Pudovkin and Golovnia started their careers under the moderate influence of Kuleshov and his cameraman Levitskii, with the passage of time they developed their own idiosyncratic approach to visual material and moved in directions far more radical than their mentors could have anticipated. Although Golovnia would establish a reputation for severity and formal restraint, it would be erroneous to describe his camerawork and lighting techniques as in any sense aesthetically conservative.

Beginnings: The Meeting of Minds

Like other longstanding collaborations within the avant-garde, Golovnia's partnership with Pudovkin was the product of circumstance. Although Golovnia mentions seeing a photograph of Pudovkin performing a stunt on *Neobychainye prikliucheniia,* and then seeing him released from hospital after he was injured, they did not become formally acquainted until *Luch smerti* (The Death Ray, 1925), Kuleshov's third full-length feature.[14] Pudovkin wrote the screenplay for this film and played one of the main protagonists; Golovnia was engaged as second camera operator under the guidance of Levitskii, who had been working with Kuleshov since 1921.[15] In the summer of 1925, after deciding not to return to his studies, Golovnia was invited by the management of Mezhrabpom-Rus' to shoot *Kirpichiki* (Little Bricks), which was jointly directed by Leonid Obolenskii, an actor with the Kuleshov collective, and Mikhail Doller, who would later become Pudovkin's main directorial assistant. Just before the shooting of this film, only fragments of which remain, Golovnia was invited by Pudovkin to make *Mekhanika golovnogo mozga.* Because of the difficulties of bringing this project to fruition, they decided in the interim to make a short comedy based on the mania for chess that was sweeping the country as a result of the International Chess Tournament in Moscow. Entitled *Shakhmatnaia goriachka,* this was released in the early part of 1926.

Although he was clearly the more senior and experienced of the two men, Pudovkin's entry into the nascent Soviet film industry was by no means conventional. His 1955 autobiographical statement emphasizes his life-long interest in music, literature and painting, but his formal education after gymnasium consisted of a degree in chemistry at Moscow University which was interrupted by the outbreak of war.[16] He returned to Russia when hostilities had been concluded, and decided to join the acting and directing section of the GTK, apparently prompted by his enthusiasm for Griffith's *Intolerance: Love's Struggle Throughout the Ages* (1916). His two chief mentors at the GTK, Vladimir Gardin and Kuleshov, had both started their careers before the October Revolution. Gardin had joined the studio of Thiemann and Reinhardt in 1912 and directed many screen adaptations of literary classics as part of the studio's 'Golden Series'. Kuleshov was a trained artist and set designer who had been employed at the Khanzhonkov studio from 1916 onwards and had worked on several films by Bauer before directing his first independent work, *Proekt inzhenera Praita* (The Project of Engineer Prait), in 1918. While attending his courses at the GTK, Pudovkin was involved in a number of stage and film initiatives. Along with other students on his course, he acted in *Zheleznaia piata* (The Iron Heel, 1919), an adaptation of a novel by Jack London, which was staged at the Theatre of Revolutionary Satire by Ol'ga Preobrazhenskaia (it was the first stage production after 1918 to incorporate the screening of filmed material). Pudovkin was subsequently assigned an acting role on the agitprop feature *Serp i molot*, another GTK production, and also worked as assistant director. In the same year (1921), he wrote and directed *Golod... golod... golod...* (Hunger... Hunger... Hunger...), one of the first agitprop films in the Soviet Union to incorporate genuine actuality footage. In 1923, he collaborated with Gardin on a screen adaptation of Anatolii Lunacharskii's play *Slesar' i kantsler* (The Locksmith and the Chancellor). In 1924, after having worked in Kuleshov's atelier, he was cast as the criminal hoaxer Zhban in Kuleshov's *Neobychainye prikliucheniia*.

Although Gardin was one of the moving spirits behind the establishment of the GTK, it was Kuleshov's experimental acting and directing workshop, initially affiliated to the GTK but from 1923 onwards existing independently, which proved to be more decisive in relation to the formation of Pudovkin's views on cinema.[17] Although there were differences in emphasis in relation to acting methods, the crucial role ascribed to montage was something that emerged from several experiments at the GTK which Kuleshov had instigated and conducted, apparently with Pudovkin's knowledge and participation. The most important of these, many years later dubbed the 'Kuleshov effect', consisted of splicing three 'neutral' portraits of the actor Ivan Mozzhukhin from genuine pre-revolutionary films with random footage that had been sourced from other material; the experiment was designed to show how viewers adjusted their perceptions of the actor's expression depending on the sequences with which it was juxtaposed. Whatever the true circumstances of this experiment – Pudovkin gave the first detailed account in a lecture to Ivor Montagu's

London Film Society in 1929, but this was not properly corroborated by Kuleshov until some forty-five years later (his earlier account, given in his 1929 book publication *Iskusstvo kino* (The Art of Cinema), differs in certain key respects)[18] – this discovery, while hardly scientific, nevertheless shaped their thinking. In *Kinorezhisser i kinomaterial* (The Film Director and Film Material), which was published as a brochure in 1926, Pudovkin argued that no material or human object acquires a 'screen life' without juxtaposition with a related set of images as part of a dramatic design. As he writes in the preface to the German edition:

> *I maintain that each object, photographed from a particular point and shown on a screen, is a lifeless object, even if it moves in front of the camera … . Only when an object is positioned among other objects, when it becomes part of a synthesis of different visual images, does it acquire a screen life.*[19]

According to this theory, filmic reality and actual reality are related but different perceptual categories, and the link between them arbitrary. In Pudovkin's formulation, the role of the camera is to force the audience to view actual reality through the eyes of the director; as such, the process of image-making de facto consists of a form of estrangement. As he writes in an oft-quoted statement: 'To show a thing as everyone else sees it is to achieve nothing.'[20] He describes the camera as an 'active observer' which ceaselessly interrogates reality and seeks to penetrate beyond the surface of things.[21] While the camera can be placed in any position in relation to the reality depicted on screen, its position should never be selected at random, but rather should be determined by the desire either to show the screen object in the most expressive form possible or to communicate the mood and atmosphere of the scene in question.[22] As an example, Pudovkin mentions the adoption of soft-focus in Griffith's *Broken Blossoms* (1919), an innovation which he argues is a valid mechanism for communicating an emotionally subjective viewpoint (what he describes as viewing as if 'through tears').[23] By the same token, lighting should not be employed merely to 'fix' the image on film, but rather to accentuate the emotional and psychological state of the actor.[24]

Although the appreciation of montage in this essay accords with the general principles articulated by Kuleshov, there are various aspects of Pudovkin's theory that deviate from these principles and merit closer scrutiny insofar as they are relevant to the issue of image construction. The process of montage, identified primarily as a method for manipulating the emotional, psychological and intellectual response of the audience, is also perceived as a regulating mechanism with which to control the rhythmic flow of images. This applies not only to the montage architecture of the whole, but also to the composition of the individual frames. In 'Fotogeniia' ('Photogenicity'), for example, a brief essay published in 1925 which constituted one of several responses in the Soviet film press to the theoretical treatise by Delluc, the intervention of montage is described as a series of visual 'blows' or 'accents' which have their equivalents in musical beats.[25] Pudovkin's conceptualization of these 'accents' applied not only to the audience's perception of the impact of the editing cut, but also to the organization of physical material within the space of the individual film frame and the movement of this material in space and time. In the case of objects in motion, for example, Pudovkin maintained that there was a rhythmic dimension to that movement which had to be carefully assessed and calibrated. Even in cases where such material was static, however, the visual composition in spatial and plastic terms contained its own interior 'accents'; as he explained:

> Corners, the abrupt twisting of lines which block the contours of a visible object, are perceived as accents; all lines in a single direction which possess a perceptible length are analogous to temporal periods, in other words, what I call intervals. The same can be said of successions of tonal values, which determine the colouring of an object or its chiaroscuro form.
>
> The static rhythm of various degrees of complexity is characteristic of all spatial forms. Beholding a long colonnade, we form the impression of a distinct rhythm. In a dark forest, this rhythm is extraordinarily confused and complex, almost chaotic.[26]

The interest expressed here in the relationship between compositional dynamic and musical form is unusual for its time: not only does it radically extend his initial investigation in 'Vremia v kinematografe' ('Time in the Cinematograph'), it also to some extent anticipates Eizenshtein's 'Chetvertoe izmerenie v kino'.[27] As Pudovkin elaborated (in 'Fotogeniia'), with the average sequence lasting around nine seconds, it is crucial that visual material strives for the maximum possible simplicity and clarity. From this, he derived his conviction that photogenicity – a term he defined in terms of what was effective on screen – lay in material that was visually distinctive and produced an immediate impression on the viewer:

Everything that is simple, clear and distinct in its spatio-rhythmical construction, every movement that is clearly and simply organized in space and time, will undeniably be photogenic, because it genuinely reflects the principal character of film.[28]

Pudovkin follows this statement with a list of objects deemed intrinsically photogenic: cities, city streets (Western), railway bridges, steam trains, motor cars and machines.[29] In the same breath, he refers to the 'rhythmically clear, square forms of urban dwellings', the 'rectilinear geometry of streets' and the 'symmetrical forms' of 'mathematically engineered constructions'.[30]

Despite the polemical tone of this article, in seeking to subvert the link between the photogenic and the conventionally beautiful Pudovkin was in fact advocating rather than challenging Delluc's point of view. Unlike his Soviet counterpart, Delluc did not privilege montage as the defining feature of film per se. Nevertheless, his treatise is concerned to reclaim the concept of the photogenic from its popular understanding (or, as he argued, debasement). Cinematic images are most impressive, he asserts, when they offer a simple and distinct impression, not when they strive for 'artistic' or 'tasteful' effects.[31] Indeed, his provocative opening passage describes actuality footage as creating a far stronger impression in the minds of the public than the feature-film material that usually followed.[32] In its place, he proposed a modern, streamlined aesthetic which privileged the simple and clear rather than the ornate or decorative. He regarded the telephone, locomotive, ocean liner, aeroplane and railway line as inherently photogenic by virtue of their geometric structures.[33] Like Pudovkin, who accepted soft-focus as part of the necessary armoury of the modern cinematographer, Delluc criticized the modern fetish for the anastigmatic lens on the grounds that lack of sharp focus accorded more to the faculties of the human eye.[34] He criticized the vogue for chiaroscuro, low-key lighting and *contre-jour*, but on the grounds that their exploitation was frequently unjustified from a dramaturgical point of view.[35] Also like Pudovkin, he observed that lighting should possess a dramatic rationale and should not be exploited solely for the purpose of supplying 'beautiful pictures'.[36] He argued that French cinema suffered from a fetishization of period furniture, the ornate qualities of which lacked the necessary 'sobriety'.[37] He also regarded certain kinds of textual material and costume as intrinsically photogenic.[38] Finally, anticipating Pudovkin's interest in the rhythmic dimension of film material, Delluc was sensitive to the importance of 'cadence'.[39]

As several commentators pointed out at the time, neither Delluc's nor Pudovkin's essay actually constitutes an objective investigation into the phenomenon of the photogenic; rather, they represent a series of subjective artistic preferences which echo the contemporary vogue for the geometric and modern. Neither author appeared alert to the possibility that photogenic potential depends ultimately on compositional procedure, lighting technique, and optical and chemical manipulation, rather than any intrinsic quality that a given object itself may possess. This point was forcibly made by Mur in the very next issue of the journal in which 'Fotogeniia' had been published. He not only rejected the specific arguments put forward by Delluc and Pudovkin, but offered a theoretical basis for the specificity of cinema which, while echoing earlier responses to the advent of photography eighty years earlier, nevertheless deserves much wider recognition than it has enjoyed hitherto.[40]

According to Mur, apart from the two-dimensional nature of screen reality and the fact that cinematic images are presented across a colour spectrum from extreme black to extreme white (this he calls the first 'arbitrary' principle of cinema), the singularity of cinema lies in the action of light upon the emulsion of the film stock and the differences that exist between reality as recorded on this film stock and the perception of that same reality when beheld by the human eye. The chemical composition of the emulsion means that, whether the source of illumination is natural or artificial, certain rays of the spectrum (the shorter rays at the ultraviolet end, with actinic properties) act more powerfully on the silver bromide salts than the rays at the red-yellow end of the spectrum, with the result that, to use his words, material reality is 'deformed'.[41] From the point of view of optical and chemical science, screen reality consists not of a series of three-dimensional objects perceived by the human eye, but rather of a series of two-dimensional surfaces that reflect light and act upon the emulsion in order to produce an image. From the point of view of this 'aesthetics of emulsion', as he describes it, every object is potentially photogenic. Furthermore, in a polemic specifically against Pudovkin, whose aesthetic preferences he deemed overtly 'urbanist', Mur took issue with the notion that only that which is simple and effective forms a distinctive photographic impression. What is photogenic for one person may not be photogenic for another, he argues; it is thus largely a question of taste, which is formed by a complex series of cultural, social and psychological mechanisms or prejudices. To the question 'What looks good on screen?', his answer was: 'Everything that has been well photographed.'[42]

Pudovkin's 'urbanist' orientation, while clearly representing something of an artistic manifesto, is not of course unique in the context of the 1920s. Like those of other avant-garde directors, his approach to the visual material of modernity represented a radical departure from the decorative excess of Russian cinema during the pre-revolutionary period. This was characterized by highly artistic and tasteful camerawork that was chiefly designed to produce aesthetically pleasing images as part of an approach that sought to establish cinema as a legitimate art form, and not simply an 'attraction' to excite the masses. The renewal of perception intrinsic to the interest in the material textures and geometric forms of the modern urban landscape was very much part of the 1920s *Zeitgeist*. The idea of the camera as an agent of poetic enquiry, a mechanical *flâneur* that records reality from a series of unconventional perspectives, echoed a number of theoretical speculations on the nature of cinema during the 1920s. To some extent, Pudovkin's approach replicates Vertov's idea of the 'ciné-perception of the world', which he had advanced in a manifesto published in 1923.[43] It also echoes some of the ideas put forward by Balázs in *Der sichtbare Mensch*.[44] Balázs's repudiation of cinema's status as a 'corrupted, deformed and cheap theatrical surrogate', his assertion that the close-up was the defining feature of modern cinematic practice because it forced the viewer to examine the surrounding world in minute detail, and his argument that the film artist should tear away 'the veil ... of conventional and abstract understandings' which concealed everyday objects in order to reveal their 'hidden expressivity' are propositions that are very much in accord with this *Zeitgeist*.[45]

Pudovkin's embrace of modernity and new forms of visual expression distanced him from Kuleshov, who, while progressive in many other respects, nevertheless rejected many of the experimental tendencies currently in vogue, for example dismissing the aesthetics of Impressionism and Cubo-Futurism and arguing that avant-garde photographers and camera operators had little understanding of light.[46] This final point, while inaccurate in relation to the avant-garde generally, was manifestly erroneous as far as Golovnia was concerned, if only because he had learnt the rudiments of his craft at the hands of Kuleshov's very own camera operator. In subsequent years, Golovnia would pay handsome tribute to Levitskii's importance both for him and for other camera operators of his generation in the spheres of lighting technique and compositional strategy.[47] This is doubtless something of a paradox in view of Levitskii's pre-revolutionary vintage, but indicates the complex relationship between avant-garde and mainstream cinema at this point in time.

A graduate of the Iuon and Dudin studio for painters and sculptors in Moscow, Levitskii had worked as a photographer in the spheres of newsreel and studio portraiture before joining the Moscow branch of Pathé Frères in 1911. One year later, he moved to the studio of Thiemann and Reinhardt, where he was assigned responsibility for the camerawork on a number of films which constituted the so-called 'Golden Series'. After opting to stay in Russia after the Revolution, he worked for the Moscow Cinema Committee and shot several newsreel chronicles during the immediate post-revolutionary period.[48] He was, nevertheless, regarded with a degree of suspicion within avant-garde circles. This was based on his known distrust of radical tendencies in art and his split with Eizenshtein over *1905 god*.[49] This suspicion notwithstanding, Levitskii was a leading authority on camera operation during a time when bona fide professionals were in desperately short supply. Furthermore, he was responsible for several innovations in the sphere of lighting which were eagerly studied by his disciples, this giving rise to his status as 'godfather' of Soviet cinematography and, as another contemporary director explained rather grandly, 'the Velázquez of our screens'.[50]

In his discussion of the formative influences on Soviet cinematography, alongside a number of camera operators who specialized in newsreel photography, Golovnia draws attention to the singularity of Levitskii: he was the first Russian photographer-turned-camera operator to repudiate the conventions of the atelier; to reject the practice of high levels of overall illumination within the studio; and to make light an instrument for creative exploration in relation to portraiture.[51] As far as the latter was concerned, Golovnia cites the influence of Rembrandt; in his view, Levitskii's work incorporates the same directed beams of light, the same tonal nuance in the shadow areas, the same presence of large masses of shadow and the same modelling of light in order to render volume, texture and tone.[52] Golovnia confesses that his own approach to portraiture in the early years of his career was similarly influenced. As he makes clear in his discussion of *Mat'*, the realism of the literary source required a lighting approach that would accentuate the sphere of emotional and psychological revelation:

> To understand and depict this we studied Rembrandt: we studied not only the way light operates in his paintings, but also the ways in which he deployed chiaroscuro, his ability with the subtlest of nuances in the handling of light and shade to communicate volume and texture, and to reveal the form of the object.

We were captivated by Rembrandt's ability to introduce light into his painterly narrative, into the theme of his painting.

The second thing we learned from Rembrandt was his painterly way of perceiving his human subjects. Rembrandt knew how to locate and communicate the individual essence of his subjects. He searched for the original and characteristic feature; he was able to locate in each person his hidden image, often concealed by clothing, social position and the daily reality of his life.[53]

The same essay also shows that dramaturgical imperative gave rise to solutions that did not always accord with the principles of simplicity, precision and maximum expressiveness as advocated in Pudovkin's various writings. Golovnia compares the 'stiff severity of straight lines', 'bureaucratic monumentality' and 'blunt symmetry' of the court sequence in *Mat'*, which was apparently modelled on the courtroom scene in Tolstoi's *Voskresenie* (Resurrection, 1902), and shot for the most part from an axial position, with its dramaturgical 'antipode', the tavern sequence at the very beginning of the film, with its visual 'formlessness' and attempt to communicate the 'dirty and crude' atmosphere of the reactionary milieu associated with it.[54] Here, he explains, the composition of the frame was characterized by interrupted lines, lack of balance and blocked beams of light.[55] Furthermore, the adoption of low-level and flat lighting for the harmonica players in the same sequence was intended to create a mask-like effect. These are not human beings, it is implied, and therefore the camera is not interested in penetrating beyond their surface reality.[56]

Golovnia's account of the camerawork in *Mat'* constitutes the most detailed explanation of the visual construction of a film in the silent era, not just in the Soviet Union, but anywhere in the world. He describes early Soviet cinema as a time of tentative exploration when the potential value of different compositional devices and lighting techniques was only just beginning to be investigated. One aspect of his work which is not mentioned in this essay, but which becomes important in subsequent years, is the adoption of quasi-documentary techniques to communicate an impression of verisimilitude. If, as Iutkevich has contended, the realism of Pudovkin's films was removed from the sphere of naturalism by virtue of an aesthetic sensibility that sought to remove everything extraneous to the frame, there are nevertheless resemblances between some of Golovnia's compositions and actuality footage of the period.[57] This can be illustrated by comparing, for example, the portraits of foundry workers in the Lebedev factory in *Konets Sankt-Peterburga* with Kaufman's close-ups of workers in *Shestaia chast' mira* (it is unsurprising to learn that both were filmed on the site of the Putilov armaments factory in Leningrad). Similar parallels can be found between documentary footage dating from the pre-revolutionary period, for example the shots of brokers outside the St Petersburg Stock Exchange in *Padenie dinastii Romanovykh*, and Golovnia's shots of similarly attired brokers milling around busily on the same steps in *Konets Sankt-Peterburga*. One of the shots (a mass view of bowler hats from the rear) is so similar that it would appear to have been closely modelled on the earlier documentary footage.

Mekhanika golovnogo mozga and *Shakhmatnaia goriachka*: Between Staged and Non-Staged

Before Sargeant's recent monograph on Pudovkin, little critical attention had been given to *Mekhanika golovnogo mozga* and *Shakhmatnaia goriachka*; this was largely on the grounds that they were perceived to be apprentice pieces or études which represented a short-lived phase in Pudovkin's filmmaking practice.[58] In terms of their visual aesthetic, however, and in particular in their treatment of documentary material, these films merit scrutiny because of the adoption of certain principles which, here displayed in embryonic form, characterize the mature work of Pudovkin and Golovnia together later in the decade.

The link between the two works lies primarily in their approach to actuality footage and their tendency to manufacture the reality depicted on screen. In relation to *Mekhanika golovnogo mozga*, Pudovkin pointed out the necessary deceit involved in filming several experiments and presenting them to the viewer as if they were a single event.[59] He also drew attention to the difficulties of capturing life 'unawares', along the lines proposed by the Ciné-Eye group, in a documentary on the human and animal response to stimuli which required reactions to specific events to be artificially provoked.[60] For his part, Golovnia later objected to the use of the word 'documentary' in relation to the film, pointing out that he and Pudovkin had carefully selected their locations and installed their own lighting equipment in the laboratories and colonies in which the filming took place; as he indicates, among other obstacles, the reaction of the animals to the glare of arcs posed a significant problem in relation to capturing their responses.[61] The footage was composed with a view to eventual assembly and aimed for a particular visual texture that would be echoed from section to section, this giving rise to a certain aesthetic quality in relation to the material. In Golovnia's view, while this was certainly authentic, or at least semi-authentic, it was also clearly something of a construct.[62]

The tendency to isolate the subjects of the scientific experiments (animals and human beings) by means of arcs against darkened backgrounds, coupled with the decision to frame the images by means of an iris with varying degrees of narrowness, was an aesthetic associated more with feature film than documentary; in its most primitive variant, it can be witnessed in the opening shots of the crocodile in its indoor tank. More artistically, it resurfaces in the images of the mother awaiting the birth of her child as she lies on a hospital bed, a sequence that one academic participant in the project hailed as a unique moment in the history of documentary film.[63] In this instance, the camera is positioned at body level by the side of the bed, with the iris focussing attention on the head and upper torso, and the woman's pillow. As the labour pains begin, the iris closes and opens several times to mark the different stages of the woman's labour and the increasing tempo of her contractions. A single studio arc has been placed at a relatively low angle in relation to the subject and only picks out the details of the woman's face as she looks towards the camera, this producing a pleasing chiaroscuro effect. In an allusion to the modes of photographic reproduction in the previous century, the first shots of Pavlov at his desk reading a book are framed by an elliptical, not circular, vignette.

At times, this artificial manipulation gives rise to an impression that is presumably unintended. As the experiments, distressing enough in relation to animals (the surgical removal of certain parts of the brain to demonstrate the malfunctioning of the nervous system), move into the human domain, the isolation of the subject either by lighting or by iris produces a degree of pathos. This approach is signalled early in the film by the shots of a monkey that has lost the use of its right paw due to brain surgery. Golovnia's deployment of low-level lighting from right and left against a dark background, the truncation of the animal's shadow by the edge of the frame, the isolation of the subject and the absence of any decorative detail have the effect of accentuating the animal's suffering, potentially evoking pity rather than fascination on the part of the viewer. The decision to show only the hands of the scientists as they provoke reactions and offer inducements also tends to dehumanize the experimental subject. In a later sequence, which shows the same monkey being offered an orange with a pair of tongs poked through the bars of its cage, rather surprisingly, the camera is positioned inside the cage looking outwards; this unusual point of view, apart from its artifice, places the viewer in the position of the animal and, perhaps unwittingly, encourages him/her to confront the effect of the experiment on its helpless subject. In another, later sequence, the analogy presumably intended, food is offered to a young man suffering from a neurological disability which means that he lacks the power of differentiation. One shot, framed by the iris, shows an anonymous hand gradually entering the frame holding a piece of bread; another shows the same hand offering a bunch of flowers, which are then eaten by the patient in question. Even allowing for the modern distaste in relation to experiments of this kind, it would not be correct to describe the mise en scène here as an example of a neutrally enquiring or scientific camera. The use of truncation (the removal of a part of the body from the space of the frame) in the composition of certain shots might be identified metaphorically as a form of surgical excision in its own right. Insofar as the film itself constitutes a form of stimulus – in other words, a set of images that acts to stimulate a response on the part of the viewer – *Mekhanika golovnogo mozga* might be regarded as something of a *mise en abîme*.

Shakhmatnaia goriachka opens with material that also purports to be actuality footage; namely, the international chess tournament that took place in Moscow from 10 November to 8 December 1925 and constituted the first state-sponsored tournament of its kind. The very first image, shown as part of the opening credits, consists of the Cuban grandmaster and reigning champion, José Raul Capablanca, standing by an exterior wall and glancing nervously towards the camera. The conceit of documentary material is reinforced in the sequences that follow. The viewer is introduced to other grandmasters participating in the tournament; what would appear to be a number of genuine locations (a chess shop and a pharmacy); and 'found' material on the streets outside (publicity posters). Photographs taken at the time when the tournament was staged (in the 'Fountain Hall' of the Second House of Soviets, formerly the Hotel Metropol) confirm the authenticity of the main interior: the tables on which the grandmasters are playing, the ornate chairs on which they are seated, the clocks, chess boards and pieces, the large chess board hanging in the background to show the audience the individual moves, and the general décor are all identical.[64] Furthermore, rather than the scenes in question being staged specifically for the camera, the movements and gestures of the grandmasters themselves have a natural air about them, as if they are being filmed 'unawares'.

As the film progresses, however, its authenticity as documentary fact is open to doubt. Unlike the lighting arrangements that existed in the House of Soviets at the time – judging from the same photographs, these appear to consist of incandescent light bulbs positioned in lamps hanging from the ceiling and attached to the walls – it is clear that arcs have been imported and positioned on the floor in order to illuminate the action.[65] The restriction of the lighting to a small area in which the chess players are seated and the use of the iris for framing purposes further confirm the staged nature of this spectacle. There are strong indications that the shots which show the audience's reactions to the matches supposedly being played in front of them have been produced in a studio rather than on location. This can be gauged again by the lighting arrangements, which show rays of light striking the members of the audience from floor positions directly in front of them (the reflections that appear in the glasses of certain participants confirm this hypothesis). Similar arrangements have been adopted for the shots of the competing grandmasters. Not only are there highlights along the chairs, which suggest the presence of studio arcs, but the directed quality of the lights' beams is revealed when one of the players exhales smoke from a cigarette. The use of directed light and the framing of the action by means of the iris to a great extent explain the seamless stylistic match between the 'non-staged' and 'staged' sequences in the rest of the film. When the camera moves into the domestic realm – the apartments of the main protagonists and the locales of the chess shop and pharmacy – it might be speculated on the basis of the earlier lighting arrangements that these are sets rather than genuine locations. Indeed, the positioning of the lights in these sequences is highly reminiscent of Levitskii's work for Kuleshov: the same tonal balance, the same positioning of arcs to the sides and slightly to the front of the actors, and at times the same restricted zones of illumination can all be detected. This suggests that, like *Mekhanika golovnogo mozga*, the film is a construct that plays with the illusion of documentary.

Mat': From 'Document' to 'Emotional Sincerity' and 'Inner State of Mind'

As several commentators have observed, apart from its generic playfulness and ironic attitude toward obsessive modes of behaviour, *Shakhmatnaia goriachka* essentially constitutes a tribute to the acting techniques of the Kuleshov collective; these were based on the concept of the 'model actor' (*naturshchik*) and are handsomely illustrated by the mimes and gestures of Vladimir Fogel' in the role of the main protagonist.[66] Subsequently, in his effort to meet the challenges posed by the studio's proposed screen adaptation of Maksim Gor'kii's *Mat'*, Pudovkin developed an entirely different methodology of the actor, which emphasized the quality of 'emotional sincerity' and the study of 'inner states of mind', giving rise to the employment of trained actors from the theatre to play the roles of the main protagonists.[67] As the director himself recognized at the time, working with actors trained according to different schools of acting posed a number of challenges.[68] While Golovnia regarded this shift as a refinement of the 'model actor' approach, rather than its outright repudiation, he nevertheless drew attention to the ways in which the evolution in the psychology of the main character (the mother) needed to be signalled by means of camera angle and lighting.[69]

The production of *Mat'*, which took place during the early part of 1926, marked a significant shift towards more serious dramatic territory and demanded a more sophisticated consideration of visual aesthetics. The overall conception of the film was characterized by a powerfully prosaic quality that sought to continue the documentary-style conceit of the first works produced by Pudovkin and Golovnia. In the historiography of Soviet film, albeit according to an overly crude schema, *Mat'* is reliably positioned as the epitome of realist cinema. In some respects, despite the significant alterations to the source text in Zarkhi's screenplay, its treatment of the 'coming to conscious' paradigm is an important forerunner of Socialist Realism.[70] Lunacharskii, the People's Commissar for Enlightenment, paid handsome tribute to the production's impression of authenticity when he commented that 'practically one hundred per cent of the film is shot in such a way that it seems as if, by some stroke of magic, the cameraman has ingeniously managed to photograph reality itself'.[71] It was recognized nevertheless that within this broadly realistic framework there was a lyrical and highly poetic dimension to the imagery which gave rise to a complex formal dynamic. For Shklovskii, the intrusion of these formal elements transformed *Mat'* into a 'centaur'; in other words, a stylistic hybrid in which the prosaic impulses established at the beginning were gradually superseded by a highly poetic lyricism as the film reached its dramatic conclusion.[72] Pudovkin's interest in the manipulation of montage as a form of musical orchestration doubtless explains the inclusion of *paysage* interludes and the repetition of images and motifs at carefully calibrated intervals. The tension between lyrical impulse and documentary imperative, which is characterized by a tendency towards pictorial austerity and economy of expression, is never entirely resolved. Something of this paradox is captured by Gromov's observation that the cinematography on *Mat'* is 'severe and laconic', and yet at the same time 'complex, capacious and emotional'.[73]

Pudovkin's desire for realistic volume and emotional plenitude is best illustrated by Golovnia's handling of the portraiture for the mother, Pelageia Vlasova, the key figure as far as the dramaturgy of the film is concerned insofar as she is transformed from a wretched and fearful conformist in the opening sequences of the film into a determined and powerful embodiment of revolutionary conviction by the end. Two images that have subsequently become icons of Soviet cinema illustrate this transformation most forcefully: the opening scene, a point-of-view and angled shot downwards from the perspective of her drunk husband; and the image of her clutching a red flag just prior to being trampled to death by mounted Cossack soldiers, this portrait having been photographed from a diametrically opposed viewpoint in natural and relatively diffuse daylight. The shift is achieved by a number of subtle modulations in camera angle and application of light, and the possible adoption of different lenses, which cause the skin tone and texture, as well as the viewer's appreciation of volume and contour, to vary gradually as the film progresses. As a general principle, it should be noted that narrowness of physiognomy is reserved for the diminished figure at the beginning of the film, the oppressive circumstances of the mother seeming to shrink or squeeze her face along the vertical axis, whereas greater amplitude is emphasized towards the end. In relation to the opening sequences, the sculpting by means of light places particular emphasis on the mother's suffering eyes, the bags under those eyes, the (at times) severe line of her eyebrows, the wrinkles along her forehead, and her slightly sagging cheeks (Fig. 14). This approach remains consistent throughout the first half of the film until her son's arrest, but at key moments, when the mother is gripped by powerful emotions, the sources of light are intensified and their position in relation to the actor is altered to produce a more expressive effect. These moments occur during the scenes in which the mother pleads, first with her husband and then with her son, in both cases falling to the floor and clasping their respective knees. For both scenes a single arc light has been placed in a low position and directs light across and at a slightly raised angle in order to capture the desperate contortions of the mother's face. A similar technique can be witnessed for her outraged outburst in court after her son has been sentenced to prison: here, through use of a low-angled source positioned to the actor's left, her features are transformed into a skeletal scream of pain and anger (Fig. 15). By the time of the jail sequence, during which the mother slips her son a message that announces a planned breakout by his comrades, the portraiture subtly irons out the creases and wrinkles of her face, and affords her a human dignity that was so signally lacking at earlier intervals; this is the product of a light source that strikes her face directly from the front. By the time of the demonstration, where the mother is seen marching forward and confidently clasping the red flag, the diffuse light – a curious inconsistency in view of the bright, early spring sunlight that has prevailed for the scenes of the breakout and demonstration (Fig. 16) – results in a further smoothing of her features. This is the most celebrated image of the film, and the point at which the visual aesthetic moves deliberately into the sphere of two-dimensional *plakatnost'*. Just before this moment, however, Golovnia composes a much more interesting portrait; this is the first time, in fact, that the viewer has been presented with the mother's profile. Working within a relatively narrow tonal range, Golovnia succeeds in combining a strongly graphic emphasis (the lines of her profile) with a subtle application of chiaroscuro to highlight the texture of the skin and the structure of the bones. Unlike the more iconic image, which borders on the unreal, this portrait shows a determined and beautiful human face with the quality of a classical sculpture.

Golovnia's psychologized portraiture of the mother, played by the established theatre actress Vera Baranovskaia, constitutes one of the first studies of its kind in silent-era Soviet cinema. Even Levitskii, who had pioneered this kind of approach in his pre-revolutionary work, had not produced such variety in his commissions prior to 1926. In relation to Baranovskaia, the portraiture was so unflattering, and so starkly at odds with her public image and foregrounding as an actress both on stage and in film (her screen debut took place in 1916), that she was almost unrecognizable. As if keen to draw attention to the incongruity, the editors of *Sovetskii ekran* positioned a theatre still showing her in period costume for a production of Edward Sheldon's *Romance* (1913) at the Bol'shoi Dramaticheskii Teatr in Kharkiv alongside a frame still from the early part of *Mat'*.[74] Although lighting is largely responsible for this evolution, it is also worth emphasizing the novelty of camera angle. An eyewitness account of the making of the film recalls the experimental nature of Golovnia's camera angles in relation to portraiture. According to the author, Golovnia was the first Soviet camera operator to use a tripod with adjustable, ultra-short legs in order to lower the position of the camera almost to the floor, a position described as 'the frog'.[75]

In relation to the film's other protagonists, because their characters for the most part are stable in dramatic terms, the lighting and compositional strategies are less prone to radical development. Nevertheless, even in these cases Golovnia sought to modify established conventions and pioneer new methods of approach. This is particularly evident in his use of low-angle lighting, a technique which, because of its capacity to deform the human face (especially if the spotlight in question has been positioned directly in front of the actor), had become associated by the middle of the 1920s with the idea of the grotesque, sinister and villainous.[76] Something akin to this approach can be witnessed in Golovnia's arrangement for the father at the beginning of the film when he stands drunkenly on the threshold of the family home, just before the brutal assault on his wife: here the arc strikes the actor's face at a low angle from the left, with the effect, as Golovnia explains, of rendering his features 'indefinite' and 'broken' (Fig. 17).[77] Elsewhere, Golovnia placed gauze over the lights to soften the harsh glare and thus lessen the potential for distortion. This can be illustrated by the scene in which the tearful mother betrays her son by pointing to the place where he has hidden a revolver from the arresting authorities.[78] A further refinement of this technique can be detected in relation to the arresting colonel. As can be gauged from the establishing shot, which shows the mise en scène in its entirety, two directed sources have been employed for the lighting of the stage, one coming from the left, and one from the right, but at some distance from the actor. The intensity of the light has also been slightly softened, with the result that the officer's face appears relatively flat. Coupled with the lower angle of the camera, this leads to the viewer's attention being drawn to the officer's narrowed eyes, which communicate his degree of suspiciousness (the weapon has not yet been located), and the sharp strokes of his moustache, eyelashes and peaked cap (Fig. 18).

Another example of inventiveness in relation to established methods of studio lighting is Golovnia's approach to *contre-jour*. As numerous sources for the period have attested, backlighting by means of arcs positioned on floor stands to the rear of the set, or hung from railings in the upper reaches of the set, was a standard technique for cloaking the human subject with a rim of light, either for the straightforward purpose of glamour or to render the subject distinct from the décor.[79] In *Mat'*, however, the adoption of this method is subjected to subtle variation. For the portrait of the mother in court, for example, Golovnia applies a harsh, almost explosive *contre-jour* as a dramatic weapon to emphasize violence of feeling. Likewise, in the same sequence, *contre-jour* is applied ingeniously in relation to the presiding figure of the judge. The medium close-up in question involves shadowless illumination from the front, which gives a clear view of his severe expression, and strong lighting from behind, which hits his bald head at such an angle that a little gleam of light is visible just on the top (Fig. 19). The effect is akin to a halo, presumably intended to emphasize the God-like authority that the judge enjoys, his decisions capable of determining individual destinies.

If dramaturgical considerations influence Golovnia's approach to portrait lighting, they are also implicit in his treatment of landscape. According to Golovnia himself, *paysage* was approached as a form of musical accompaniment:

> Paysage *here was something akin to a poetic phrase or image. The camera operator's treatment of* paysage *was based on its dramaturgical importance and role within the film. It was a landscape of sensations, rather than of nature: the frames were selected on the basis of the absence of any material concreteness which would distract the attention of the viewer. In a whole series of sequences the landscape shots constitute a form of musical accompaniment which amplifies the emotional perception of scenes which lie outside the narrative proper, but alongside which they have been inserted.*[80]

Golovnia's statement divorces the 'landscape of sensation' in *Mat'* from the insertion of *paysage* fragments in contemporary European films of the period. Often described as 'atmospheric inserts', these sequences afforded enterprising camera operators the opportunity to experiment with recent aesthetic trends in the spheres of photography and painting, but were often included without dramaturgical rationale.[81] In *Mat'*, by contrast, the viewer is presented with a series of lyrical interludes which, while initially opaque in terms of their purpose, nevertheless acquire important symbolic values as the film progresses. These interludes consist of a number of different landscapes, many of them evoking a sense of tranquillity and harmony. The very first image of the film, for example, is a peaceful, evening cloudscape. This is followed shortly afterwards by a series of atmospheric inserts, the first and most celebrated of which is the view of a river shrouded in mist, the early morning sun partially eclipsed by silhouetted trees. The same location features later in the film, but this time the vision of pastoral idyll has been augmented by the inclusion of a peasant farmer and his horse, which is drinking quietly from the river. Pudovkin's retrospective account of the moment of shooting, which speaks of the tremendous emotional significance of the scene for him personally, clarifies the intended analogy between dawn in nature and the dawning of radical political consciousness.[82] As the film progresses, however, the inserts become endowed with a more explicit dramatic import: the onset of spring, the blossoming of shrubs and trees, and the momentum of thawing blocks of ice carried along a provincial river are juxtaposed by means of montage with Pavel's thoughts of freedom while in prison, his desire to escape from his prison cell, and his joy on receiving news that his colleagues are planning a breakout. Like the river itself, these brief fragments swell into a broader rhythmic flow that gathers momentum and moves in a crescendo towards the climax of the film, which shows the procession of a crowd of Bolshevik demonstrators and their brutal dispersal and killing at the hands of mounted soldiers. Rhythmically, the flow of ice towards and past the camera is calibrated precisely so that it becomes associated with the streaming movement of the demonstrators; in turn, the images of these same ice-blocks crashing against the stanchions of an iron bridge become a visual metaphor for the clashes between the demonstrators and the determined barrage of soldiers that faces them. It should be stressed that the compositional approach for these sequences ensures that they avoid direct imitation of Griffith's *Way Down East* (1920).[83] In Griffith's film, the ice floes function solely as a thrilling means of escape. In *Mat'*, by contrast, the multiplicity of camera viewpoints in relation to the ice floes, and their proximity in relation to the camera lens, including, at times, close-ups directly from above, imbue the images with an unsteadiness that anticipates the flurried shapes and rapidly shifting perspectives of the suppression sequence. At one point Golovnia even places the camera at ground level so that the lens is splashed with mud and water by charging hooves, one of the rare instances in the 1920s where the agency of the camera is explicitly revealed to the viewer.[84] This image constitutes an ironic reversal of the earlier morning tranquillity of the river – the quietly drinking horse has now been transformed into a rampaging agent of destruction. A similar procedure is adopted for the image of the red flag that flutters in the wind after the demonstration has been dispersed: through the material of this flag, in a moment of symbolic closure, there appears a cloud in the sky which recalls the film's opening shot.

Within this series of interludes there is a sub-category, the three sequences that involve a combination of dissolve or superimposition with various types of panning movement of the camera, which deserves particular mention because of the stylistic innovations involved. The sequences in question are the images of the factory and the adjoining tenement blocks that function as a prelude to the call for strike action; the shots of the courts of justice, which establish the locale for

Pavel's trial; and the shots of the Moscow Kremlin with which the film concludes. In essence, with the exception of the final sequence, these images might be regarded as unprecedented variations on the standard establishing shot. Multiple exposure itself was not a particularly avant-garde device at this time, although it had been combined with slow shutter speeds in the early experiments of Italian Futurist photographers, a procedure imitated by Rodchenko for several of his portraits taken in 1924, and it had been endowed with a futuristic veneer in relation to landscape by virtue of having been incorporated by Protazanov and Zheliabuzhskii in their 'vision' of New York as seen through an intergalactic telescope in *Aelita* (Aelita, Queen of Mars, 1924).[85] In *Mat'*, it is the combination of multiple exposure and simultaneous vertical and horizontal panning movements of the camera that elevates these sequences into the category of artistic vision. This vision draws upon the aesthetics of Cubo-Futurism, with its use of simultaneous shifts in perspective (what in Russian Futurist poetry was known as *sdvig*), and also Constructivism, with its interest in linear arrangement and geometric design.[86] The images of the factory are characterized by a slow, hypnotic dance of geometric shapes which consist of metal structures, electric cables, telegraph wires, chimneys and tenement buildings; to a degree, the blurring of the images caused by the movement and the double exposure verges on the abstract. Although less abstract, the courts sequence and the final shots of the Kremlin are no less graphic in design. In relation to the latter, it is worth noting that Golovnia shoots for the most part *contre-jour*, and in so doing emphasizes structure and form at the expense of material texture; indeed, the manipulation of the scale and dimension of the overlapping images creates something akin to a photo-collage effect. In one frame, the principle of contiguity triumphs over the principle of superimposition by virtue of the introduction of discrete zones within the frame: the centre of the frame is dominated vertically by the grand silhouette of the Moscow Kremlin's Spasskaia Tower; other towers, photographed from distances further away, anchor the margins of the frame. Although this final collage does not conform straightforwardly to Pudovkin's idea of montage as a series of visual 'accents' or 'blows', its kinetic energy offers an instructive illustration of the singularity of cinema in the context of the silent era.

Pudovkin and Golovnia's interest in geometric relationships within the frame can be demonstrated by other compositions that borrow or study precursor works in the realms of painting and photography in order to explore the possibility of structural tension through the introduction of kinetic material. The scene in the second half of *Mat'*, for example, that shows prisoners undertaking their allotted exercise just prior to the breakout is a good illustration of this phenomenon. As Iutkevich has pointed out, the source for this composition was either Van Gogh's *Prisoners Exercising* (1890) or a lithograph by Gustave Doré, entitled *Newgate – Exercise Yard* (1872), on which the Van Gogh was ostensibly modelled.[87] Golovnia's visual treatment of this subject, although it also adopts *contre-jour*, nevertheless begins with a radical form of *décadrage* that is absent in the precursor works: the centre of the frame is void, and the compositional structure is organized primarily along diagonals. These are formed by the shapes of two silhouetted guards standing at the bottom left-hand and top right-hand corners of the frame, and the shadows of a building which intrude into the frame from the right. Structural tension is introduced in the form of prisoners who enter the top right-hand corner of the frame and move towards the camera, gradually assuming the shape of a circle. Unlike the composition of the precursor works, the angle of vision is adjusted so that the prisoners in the foreground do not block those in the background. Furthermore, a third guard is deliberately positioned in the centre of the frame at the apex of the shadow intruding from the right. This compositional arrangement has semantic implications that subvert the precursor models. In Van Gogh and Doré's works, the prisoners are presented as depressed and debilitated ghosts; the sense of enclosure, and thus of the futility of escape, is accentuated not only by the shape of the circle, but also by the prison walls, which stretch vertically beyond the upper limits of the frame and create a sense of oppression and claustrophobia. In *Mat'*, by contrast, the space to the rear of the image is open, and it is the prisoners, after they have arrived and stopped moving, who enclose a single guard. The hint at the potential for liberation is duly realized when the circle is broken and the attack on the guards begins.

Other compositions in *Mat'* betray the influence of recent developments in the spheres of photography and cinematography. One of the images of the prison-escape sequence, for example, is modelled directly on Rodchenko's *Pozharnaia lesnitsa* (The Fire-Escape, 1925), from the *Dom na Miasnitskoi* (The House on Miasnitskaia) series, with its unusual perspective from beneath a ladder looking upwards at an extreme angle.[88] This sequence also borrows from Tisse's handling of the tenement-block scenes in *Stachka* and his tendency to exploit the structure of the building in order to split the screen into discrete zones of action. In the case of *Mat'*, the expressivity of the images has been augmented by the introduction of lighting effects that consist of beams of sunlight streaming onto the walkways through the windows of the cells, an indication that the cells in question have recently been vacated. Elsewhere, the use of shadow play for the scene in which the father clambers onto a stool in order to steal money from behind the grandfather clock is reminiscent of Murnau's *Nosferatu, eine Symphonie des Grauens* (Nosferatu, a Symphony of Horrors, 1922), the *locus classicus* of this device in Expressionist cinema. A similar influence may also be detected in Golovnia's resort to manual focus adjustment for a point-of-view shot as his wife watches the same incident through bleary eyes. Boltianskii's brief article on recent developments in cinematography, which appeared one year after the release of *Mat'*, commented specifically on the use of optical distortion to imply subjective perception; in this case, it reflects the fact that Pelageia has only begun to regain her sight after a severe beating.[89]

First Commercial Break: *Chelovek iz restorana*

The variety of stylistic devices on display in *Mat'* did not go unnoticed in the film press. While the film itself was applauded both on the national and international stage, it was an article devoted to the new generation of Soviet camera operators, published in early 1927 by the actor-director Oleg Frelikh, which was the most perceptive in relation to Golovnia.[90] Here Frelikh describes Golovnia as the most 'restless' and 'probing' cameraman of his generation, and his creative endeavours are compared to a laboratory in which a series of experiments is being conducted:

> In his work there is nothing of the smoothness of the honest hack or the impeccable quality of an emerging master. Errors are piled on top of achievements. When you watch the work of Golovnia, it is as if you have found yourself in a large laboratory in which a whole host of simultaneous experiments are being carried out. Some are brilliantly successfully, others you don't even have time to inspect before they have fizzled out. He achieves a quality of richness by a variety of different means; the style of his work is not consistent, and here one wonders whether this is due to the absence of style or some form of eclecticism.[91]

Bearing in mind the origins of the Pudovkin–Golovnia partnership in the laboratories of the Leningrad Institute of Experimental Medicine, the metaphor of the laboratory may not have been entirely coincidental.

Before there was time to pursue these investigations further in the form of *Konets Sankt-Peterburga*, the initial plans for which were being formulated in early 1927, Golovnia found himself distracted by work on *Chelovek iz restorana*, a mainstream commission from the studio of Mezhrabpom-Rus' which was put into production in February (the shooting took place in April and lasted for two months). Because this invitation was the result of a particular set of circumstances – namely, a fire on the premises which had destroyed much of the studio, including many of the sets for films currently in production, around half of the lighting equipment and part of the processing laboratory – it was not one that Golovnia felt he could refuse. The choice of *Chelovek iz restorana* as the basis for the screenplay, a novel published in 1911 by the neo-realist writer Ivan Shmelev, was entirely dictated by the precarious circumstances of the studio at this time. The calamitous financial situation meant that the studio required an instant commercial success at the box office in order to restore its income stream. Furthermore, the fact that the narrative action of the novel took place for the most part in a restaurant was convenient in the sense that the fire had forced the studio to decamp temporarily to the Iar restaurant, a grand establishment on the main highway to Leningrad which was very much associated with the opulence (and decadence) of the pre-revolutionary epoch. For Protazanov personally, there may have been poignancy in the fact that he was returning to a location where, alongside Levitskii, he had filmed the scene of Bagration's banquet at the English Club for his screen adaptation of *Voina i mir* (War and Peace, 1915) for the studio of Thiemann and Reinhardt. The decision to shift the chronology of Shmelev's novel from the revolutionary years of 1905–1906 to the wartime years of 1915–1916 meant that he was obviously in a good position to evoke the atmosphere of the restaurant as he had experienced it personally at that time.[92]

With its dramatization of the sufferings of the 'little man', a waiter who witnesses the decadence of the military, political and merchant élite which frequents the restaurant while at the same time seeking to come to terms with the death of his son at the Front, the screenplay of *Chelovek iz restorana* possessed some obvious cinematic precursors. Zheliabuzhskii's *Kollezhskii registrator* (The Collegiate Assessor, 1925), for example, a screen adaptation of Aleksandr Pushkin's masterful tale of faux-sentimentalism, 'Stantsionnyi smotritel'' ('The Stationmaster', 1830), had starred the same theatre actor, Ivan Moskvin, whom Protazanov had initially approached to play the role of the main protagonist in *Chelovek iz restorana*.[93] Another film that had drawn on a similar literary tradition, albeit far more experimental in its approach to the challenge of literary adaptation, was the FEKS version of Nikolai Gogol''s 'Shinel'' ('The Overcoat', 1842), which had been released in 1926. Apart from these relatively recent precursors, there were also the screen adaptations of the Shmelev novel itself, four in total, which had appeared in the pre-revolutionary era.[94] The decision to shift the action to the years of the First World War and introduce a more politically correct ending (Skorokhodov, the waiter, acquires class consciousness and successfully challenges his privileged tormentors) was doubtless prompted by the need to distance the film from these pre-revolutionary adaptations. Apart from the issue of personal availability, it may also have explained the decision to approach Golovnia as a potential cameraman. Doubtless as a result of his commercial success, Protazanov was at this time the object of derision on the part of left-wing critics, who regarded him as a director insufficiently 'Soviet' in outlook. During a discussion about the future of Sovkino which took place shortly after the release of *Chelovek iz restorana*, for example, Vladimir Maiakovskii rudely gave voice to this charge by dismissing the 'hundred-year-old aesthetic vulgarity' of his films and observing that they 'have nothing to do with our Soviet reality'; rather acidly, he added that 'even before there was cinema there was Protazanov with his ****' (the stenographer who recorded the views expressed at the meeting, doubtless on grounds of public decency, declined to record the actual word used).[95] By contrast, Golovnia was a camera operator who, thanks to his work on *Mat'*, had established a reputation for a more cutting-edge visual style.

Chelovek iz restorana announces itself forcefully after the opening credit title as a product that differs significantly from Protazanov's earlier works. There is a brio and unbridled energy about the opening sequence which derives initially from the exclamation mark in the intertitle: 'Za gorod!' ('Let's head out of town!'). This verbal invitation, full of breathless excitement, heralds an extended and ambitious set-piece sequence, a series of tracking-shots as the camera weaves its way to the restaurant by means of a horse and carriage along the main highway towards the outskirts of the city. Motor-car traffic moves dangerously between horse-drawn carriages, and the camera casts its gaze leftwards and rightwards as it is overtaken by other vehicles, and upwards as it passes beneath bridges. The rapidly shifting points of view, the jagged rhythm of the editing cuts, the speed with which the vehicles heave into and out of view and the occasional lapse in sharp focus imbue the sequence with a spontaneous and improvised feel; such is the lack of smoothness that it might indeed be regarded as a simulation of inebriation itself.

Moments later, as the camera arrives at the restaurant, its name illuminated by neon lights, the film reverts to the more sober montage patterns associated with the pre-revolutionary era. The spectator is introduced to the spatial topography of the interior and the identities of the key protagonists, who are paraded in front of the camera in a series of relatively static axial shots. The viewer is doubtless struck by the conventional nature of this operation. The lack of overall illumination for the restaurant scenes, however, is unusual for the period and gives rise to the impression of a quasi-documentary style. As Golovnia himself later pointed out, this was not a deliberate experiment, but rather the product of *force majeure*:

> We shot in a manner which exists to the present day, in a documentary fashion in genuine interiors. We shot in this way not because we were looking for innovations, but because we had to. The shooting was difficult. For a locale of this kind there was insufficient light, although the scenes which we were shooting were crucial and fairly imposing. We had to illuminate the restaurant in such a way that it looked like a genuine location. After all, it was not simply a set.[96]

The lighting of the interiors in *Chelovek iz restorana* feels impoverished, and hardly accords with the illumination employed historically. Pre-revolutionary photographs of the lar restaurant's interior, as might be expected, show extensive overhead and side lighting, but, as witnessed in relation to the House of Soviets in *Shakhmatnaia goriachka*, this took the form of incandescent lighting, which was low in actinicity, and therefore useless as far as orthochromatic film was concerned. As Levitskii's memoirs make clear, the same problem of lighting the restaurant with arc lights was encountered during the shooting of *Voina i mir* a decade or so previously, the particular challenge lying with the massive amperage required for such a huge locale.[97]

This lack of overall illumination for the interior sequences did not, however, affect Golovnia's approach to portraiture in *Chelovek iz restorana*. It is here, despite some minor differences (for example, the overtly theatrical application of make-up, which is typical of Protazanov productions), that the greatest continuities with *Mat'* can be found. Although the trajectory of the narrative required less in the way of nuanced psychological shift, such shifts do nevertheless occur and can be gauged in the first instance by scrutinizing the lighting applied to the main protagonist, who was played by the established theatre actor Mikhail Chekhov. The opening portrait of Skorokhodov, for example, uses arc lights positioned to the sides and slightly behind the actor for the purposes of rendering volume and texture, with diffuse or softened sources coming from the front. A series of subtle modulations of this arrangement can be detected in later sequences where emotional turmoil is the crucial ingredient. The first moment occurs when Skorokhodov receives a telegram informing him of his son's death at the Front: here the light source has been moved to a higher angle and strikes the actor's face slightly from behind, producing a shadow along the front of his face. This arrangement is reprised at two identical moments later in the film. The first occurs when Skorokhodov is asked by the lascivious industrialist Karasev to deliver a bouquet of flowers to his own daughter Natal'ia, who is employed as a violinist in the restaurant's chamber ensemble; the second occurs when Skorokhodov receives a letter from the local gymnasium informing him that this same daughter has been expelled for non-attendance of classes. On both occasions, although the reaction shots are brief, there is a significant 'clouding' along the front of the face which indicates the extent of the character's distress.

Further parallels with the lighting and compositional strategies in *Mat'* can be found in Golovnia's portraits of unambiguously negative characters. The various studies of Karasev, played by the established theatre actor Mikhail Narokov, who would play an equally unappetizing role (the landowning father) in Otsep's *Zemlia v plenu* (The Captive Earth, 1927), exploit camera angle and lighting to produce powerfully expressive images of decadence, moral turpitude and unbridled sexual appetite. Publicity photographs from the decade and Forestier's studies of Narokov in *Zemlia v plenu*, which is also set in the pre-revolutionary period, give little hint of the rapacious alligator that lies concealed beneath the actor's facial exterior. The first meaningful portrait after the introductory cameos shows him distractedly munching the petals of a flower as he watches Skorokhodov's daughter seated among the ensemble. The positioning of light sources to the side of, and slightly behind, the actor produces an unflattering study of protuberance. The application of chiaroscuro accentuates the unappealing fleshiness of the face, the bulbous, impressive nose, the sagging cheeks, the double chin and the flabby neck, which spills over the sharply drawn collar of his tuxedo. Due to the actor's determined expression and the camera angle, which reprises the portrait of the arresting officer in *Mat'*, this mound of flesh is nevertheless punctuated by a series of sharply etched lines consisting of eyebrows, narrow eyes, sloping lines of the nose and cheeks and a thin mouth. During the crucial scene later in the film in which Karasev approaches Natal'ia with the intent of rape, the portrait becomes even more expressive. The camera has been moved into an axial position, but is now slightly elevated, so that it is looking downwards towards the actor's face, while the lighting from the left has been lowered so that it is striking him at a low angle. The foreshortening and new position of the arc produce a narrower face with gimlet eyes just visible beneath the eyebrows. Seconds later, a second portrait as Karasev stands with a cigar raised to his lips maintains the low-angle lighting from the left, but at a slightly reduced level of intensity; apart from their evil glint, his eyes are now shrouded in darkness. Furthermore, the proximity of the cigar to his mouth in this shot, coupled with the earlier, distracted munching of the flowers, reinforces the semantic equation between consumption of food and sexual appetite.

Many years later, Golovnia spoke of his naivety in importing the techniques of low-angle lighting and unorthodox angles into Protazanov's mise en scène.[98] This is a curious statement in view of the portraiture for Karasev, since the compositional approach is clearly justified from the dramaturgical point of view. The association of these techniques with the concept of the sinister is something of a visual leitmotif in *Chelovek iz restorana*. Furthermore, they are on display again a few minutes after the above-mentioned portraits when Karasev wrestles with Natal'ia in order to force her physical submission. Low-angle lighting, striking the actors from right and left and reflected in the metal surface of a nearby samovar, and the slightly higher camera angle, produce a compositional tension that seeks to communicate the disturbing nature of the violation.

Golovnia's most surprising departure from the strictly dramaturgical approach of *Mat'* lies in the soft-focus photography that is adopted for several of the portraits of Vera Malinovskaia in the role of Natal'ia. Diffusion, of course, was associated in the 1920s with glamour photography, and was a well established aestheticizing device in mainstream cinema, even in the Soviet Union. Malinovskaia, a former ballerina who had studied under Preobrazhenskaia and was a relative newcomer to the screen (her debut took place in Aleksandr Anoshchenko's *Vsem na radost'* (To Everyone for Luck, 1924)), had already been the recipient of the soft-focus treatment courtesy of Zheliabuzhskii, who had cast and photographed her in the role of the stationmaster's daughter, Dun'ia, in *Kollezhskii registrator*. The glamour treatment here was to some extent justified on the grounds that the precocious flirtatiousness of her character attracts the attentions of travellers and leads in due course to her 'abduction' by an officer in the Hussars. Nevertheless, the poetics of soft-focus are also justified by the sentimental context. As in *Broken Blossoms*, the diffusion of the portraiture often projects the point of view of a beholding subject, in this case a doting father whose loss of his daughter eventually causes him to drink himself to death.

The combination of glamour and sentiment, perhaps even prompted by the example of *Kollezhskii registrator*, may explain Golovnia's approach in *Chelovek iz restorana*. In his retrospective account of the production, he recalls Malinovskaia's 'amazingly beautiful blue Russian eyes' and his determination to bring them out by resorting to yellow filters because the Agfa 'Speziale' film stock would otherwise have rendered them white.[99] Diffusion is not universally applied throughout the sequences in which Malinovskaia appears, however, which suggests a dramaturgical rationale. When the character is first introduced, as she lies asleep, her face is presented through a soft veil: the lighting, which strikes the face diagonally from both sides, accentuates the porcelain smoothness of her skin and endows the portrait with an impression of innocence and tranquillity. The subsequent editing cut and angle of vision, however, suggest the viewpoint of her father, who has just entered the bedroom. The second occasion on which Golovnia adopts soft-focus is the scene in which Natal'ia is shown playing the violin: three viewpoints are given here – two diametrically opposed profiles and an orthogonal position – and it is noteworthy that the father and mother are both present. The possibility of a subjective viewpoint is reinforced in a later scene in which the violin is played, this time as part of an audition for the ensemble, but again in the presence of the father. One further example occurs when Natal'ia takes her place in the ensemble on the first day. Again, although there are other men watching her performance, the cutaway immediately to the gaze of the father suggests his perspective.

Konets Sankt-Peterburga: The Poetics of Peripatetics

Several months before receiving the commission for *Chelovek iz restorana*, Golovnia had proposed a screenplay for a film entitled *Peterburg-Petrograd-Leningrad*, the three names in question referring to the recent changes in the city's nomenclature as a result of war and revolution. The newspaper *Kino* carried a 'conversation' between Pudovkin and Zarkhi in February 1927 which suggested that, while the project had been revised and its ambition (three centuries of the capital's history) significantly scaled back, it had reached an advanced stage of preparation.[100] Golovnia's account of the location-scouting process, in particular the view of the sculptures adorning the roof of the Winter Palace, the complacency and powerful symbolism of which he and Pudovkin planned to destroy through use of a hand-held camera (a production still of this moment has survived which shows Golovnia with his Debrie-Parvo 'L' strapped to his chest) hints at the importance of the city's architecture, landmark monuments and sculptural myths to the project.[101] In his conceptualization of the film, Golovnia was apparently inspired by a 1907 gouache by Valentin Serov; entitled *Petr*, although sometimes also given the title *Petr na postroike Peterburga* (Peter at the Building of Petersburg), it shows the tsar battling strong winds as he strides across the marsh on which the city is being erected, his entourage struggling to keep pace with him.[102] According to Valkenier, the intention of this painting, one of a series which Serov dedicated to Peter the Great, was to illustrate Petersburg's 'march through history' and the determination of the tsar to pursue his Westernizing vision irrespective of hostile conditions.[103] The execution, however, in particular the unusual angle of vision from slightly below the subject, produced a degree of perspectival distortion which, as Serov himself admitted, could be interpreted as the representation of something monstrous.[104] In view of Golovnia's camera positions, many of which adopt extreme angles of vision in relation to landmark monuments, it is conceivable that Serov's painting influenced not only the interest in sculptural forms, but also the ways in which those forms were visually rendered.

Even in its castrated form, Zarkhi and Golovnia's screenplay was marked by a degree of structural invention. Not only does *Konets Sankt-Peterburga* consist of two parallel narratives that have only two points of dramatic intersection, but it also includes several lengthy montage episodes and a number of Eizenshtein-style montage collisions. In terms of décor, lighting and general visual treatment, the narrative of the Bolshevik striker and his wife is strongly reminiscent of the scenes with the mother in *Mat'*: the sets are austere and Spartan, and, in a further echo, Baranovskaia was invited to play the role of the wife. Woven between the narrative of this couple and the story of a young peasant lad who arrives in the city searching for employment are various satellite landscapes or 'montage phases': the establishing shots of the city; the scenes of the stock exchange; the workshop floor of the armaments factory; the office of the factory director, Lebedev; the police station; the streets of the city as patriotic fervour takes hold after the declaration of war; the trenches and battlefields of the military front; and the uprising that sweeps the *ancien régime* from power. Shortly after the completion of the film, Pudovkin drew attention to the decisions that had informed the visual presentation of these various landscapes. He mentioned Golovnia's camera positions, some of which were so unconventional and extreme in terms of their angle of vision that journalists visiting the set during filming concluded that they must be a form of eccentricity (for example, see Fig. 20). He also described Golovnia's endeavour to convey not the 'external effect', but rather the 'inner essence' of the monuments and statues that had been selected as examples of Petersburg's architectural heritage.[105] If *Konets Sankt-Peterburga* is the most experimental of Pudovkin's silent-era films, it is primarily because of this search for new forms of expression and the audacity with which this search is executed.

Konets Sankt-Peterburga is much more interesting as an apocalyptic vision of a late-imperial city on the threshold of revolution than as a 'coming-to-consciousness' narrative. The presentation of St Petersburg in its capitalist and autocratic dimension is a probing portrait which engages energetically with the perception of the city as established in literature and the figurative arts during the previous two centuries – what is now commonly referred to as the St Petersburg 'myth'.[106] This 'myth' is rich in symbolic associations, its treatment ranging from eulogies to its classical perfection during the Enlightenment era to explorations of the ambiguities of the Romantic era (Pushkin's *Mednyi vsadnik* (The Bronze Horseman, 1834)) and of the anxieties of the Silver Age, with its portents of revolutionary turmoil and imminent destruction (Andrei Belyi's *Peterburg* (1916)). Like many of these precursors, *Konets Sankt-Peterburga* seeks to confront the material reality of the city: its spatial topography, architectural styles, monuments, textures, atmospherics, quality of light and colours – in other words, everything that makes it, in Golovnia's words, 'unique and individual'.[107] The film explores the city's cultural identity and demonstrates a particular interest in its equestrian statues, which function as geographical landmarks while at the same time serving as reminders of Russia's imperial past. The sculptural myth of Pushkin (*Mednyi vsadnik*) and the ekphrastic descriptions of monuments generally in Silver Age poetry are clearly important influences in this regard. It is testament to this intertextual dimension that, as in *Oktiabr'*, the storming of the Winter Palace in the final sequence is depicted as much in terms of architectural desecration as physical occupation, the remnants of ebbing authority represented symbolically by the sculptures that run along the roof of the building. These are physically dislodged, or perhaps it is better to say dethroned, as a result of naval bombardment prior to the *coup d'état* proper.

While undeniably an exploration of sculptural myth, *Konets Sankt-Peterburga* is simultaneously an exercise in estrangement. This is motivated dramaturgically by the fact that the first views of the city are presented as if through the eyes of a pair of peasant newcomers who arrive there in search of work. To all intents and purposes, this is a subversion of the *flâneur* tradition, one that forces the viewer into an awareness of the capital's multiple topographies: the classical, tourist-oriented centre, with its moats, picturesque canals, governmental buildings, monuments and wide expanses of river, is contrasted with the working-class tenement blocks and armaments factory, both of which are situated on the city's periphery. The result of these unusual perspectives, while certainly an extended disquisition on the relationship between monumentalizing authority and powerless citizen-subject, is a form of poetic renewal in the modernist tradition. The tendency towards defamiliarization is witnessed in the exploitation of the white nights, a phenomenon linked to the city's latitudinal position which features frequently as part of the Petersburg 'myth'. Golovnia has written about the idiosyncratic qualities of this 'twilight' zone, the moment 'when contours become uncertain, the space nebulous and the image loses its naturalistic quality'.[108] In particular, he mentions two watery reflections as illustrations of the 'transparency' of the Petersburg landscape: the statues on Lion Bridge reflected in the waters of the Griboedov Canal; and the New Holland Arch, built by the Frenchman Jean-Baptiste Vallin de la Mothe in 1765, as reflected in the waters of the Moika.[109] Several other scenes were filmed at moments when day was merging imperceptibly into night. A particularly remarkable example, because the light tones of the Neva prompt associations with underwater illumination, is the vision of the Winter Palace just before the first bombardment from the *Avrora*: here the palace has all the appearances of an ocean liner at anchor, its every window illuminated and casting pale gleams of light into the waters below (Fig. 21).

Konets Sankt-Peterburga opens in the provinces and follows two impoverished peasants as they make their way by train to the city. This is succeeded by an extended sequence that introduces historical St Petersburg in terms of its buildings and monuments. Many of these compositions will be repeated, some of them more than once, at later intervals. Included as part of this sequence are conventional landscapes, for example a panorama dominated by St Isaac's Cathedral, but also views of certain equestrian statues which place the viewer almost directly beneath the monument, and thus at a much closer proximity than would normally be possible bearing in mind its actual height. The key works in this regard are Etienne-Maurice Falconet's statue of Peter the Great (1766–1782), popularly known as 'The Bronze Horseman'; Paul Klodt's statue of Nicholas I

(1856–1859); and Paolo Trubetskoi's statue of Alexander III (1909). Golovnia derives enormous advantage from the availability of long-focus lenses in his depiction of these statues. Because he forces the viewer to engage intensely with the design of the sculptures through the rendering of their musculature, bulging veins and wrinkled skin, their power and solidity become palpable. The first image in this sequence is the monument by Trubetskoi, which was originally situated on Znamenskaia Square (renamed Ploshchad' vosstaniia (Uprising Square) after 1917). The rear view, which accentuates the solidity of the horse's haunches, appears to have been selected deliberately: this is a work renowned for its representation of brutality (even the sculptor himself described it as 'one brute sitting astride another'), so much so that not long after the Revolution the plinth was daubed with the mocking word *pugalo*, which means 'scarecrow' in Russian.[110] By placing the camera directly beneath the hooves in the two cases where the horses are rearing (Falconet's statue of Peter the Great and Klodt's statue of Nicholas I), Golovnia challenges the viewer to confront at close quarters the symbolic meaning of the statues as represented by the stances of rider and horse. This is important in the case of Falconet's statue of Peter, where the ambiguity of the stance, which gives rise to uncertainty as to whether the rider is holding the horse back from the abyss or driving it recklessly forward, is crucial to the symbolic meaning of Pushkin's narrative poem. Such images might be regarded as a form of polemic against the conventions not only of the tourist-style photograph or picture postcard, but also of the sketches, watercolours and engravings of the Silver Age, a period when the 'Northern capital' was experiencing a cultural renaissance.[111] Golovnia's compositions are a great deal more sinister and threatening than the watercolours by Alexandre Benois that were commissioned for a 1905 illustrated edition of *Mednyi vsadnik* (Nil'sen later juxtaposed the compositional mechanisms of these watercolours with a dynamic shot-by-shot film treatment of the poem in his monograph on cinema as a graphic art).[112] Golovnia's depiction of Falconet's statue might also be regarded as a form of radical polemic against Levitskii's nocturnal images of the same statue for *1905 god*; although never used by Eizenshtein, these shots had nevertheless been published as frame stills in the journal *Kino-zhurnal A.R.K.*[113]

The symbolic suggestiveness of this initial sequence is reprised with a retrospective justification in the scenes that show the peasant lad and his relation subsequently wandering through the spaces of classical St Petersburg. The direction of their journey is by no means logical. They begin at the Moscow railway station and end by crossing the Bol'sheokhtinskii Bridge (completed in 1911 and initially christened the Bridge of Emperor Peter the Great), which suggests that they have taken a circuitous route in order to visit famous landmark sites and thus engage with the city's symbolic meaning. What follows is a simulation of the tourist's gaze which not only shares their amazed point of view, but also positions them in relation to what they see. Thus initially, the young man is shown standing in a doorway and staring leftwards and upwards out of the frame, after which Pudovkin cuts to a view of the Trubetskoi monument. Significantly, this is the first time the autocrat's gaze is highlighted. The next image is a truncated view of the same statue which shows the legs of the horse in the foreground and the boy and his relation walking across the frame in the background. The shadow of the statue falls diagonally within the frame, reminding the walkers of its presence and reach. At the same time, a truncated reflection in the Varlaam granite of the plinth stretches towards the camera. This ingenious piece of compositional organization confronts the Lilliputian dimensions of the pedestrians with the monumentality of the statue.

This image is followed by a cut which takes the visitors to St Isaac's Cathedral, the quintessential embodiment of St Petersburg's imperial grandeur and architectural ambition. First, the ornate bronze door of Ivan Vitali's early-nineteenth century southern portico is shown; this is followed by a close-up of one of its many rose-granite columns. A series of gliding double exposures showing the same columns simulates the gaze of a head turning in admiration: the camera is positioned by the door and looking outwards, but then pans left and right in an echo of the choreographed movements for the courts-of-justice sequence in *Mat'*. Shifting position again, the camera now looks slowly up towards 'The Adoration of the Magi', a bas-relief which adorns the southern portico, and then moves further upwards still towards the golden dome and spire. The peasant couple are subsequently shown walking along the side of the square that faces the western portico, the camera now in a raised position behind the statue of St Bartholomew which stands on the roof. The upper torso of this figure is visible in the foreground, and the shadows of the bell tower and part of the drum of the main dome stretch out diagonally, as if to point the visitors in the right direction.

Subsequently, the viewer is presented with further views of the equestrian statue of Nicholas I and, for the first time, permitted to admire the sculpture in its entirety. This series of shots includes another unorthodox perspective, this time right beneath the horse's tail, which shows details of the four female figures carved at the top of the pedestal, and supposedly symbolizing Justice, Power, Faith and

Wisdom. A return to the equestrian statue of Alexander III is then juxtaposed by means of montage with a mounted gendarme who gives the couple permission to cross the metal structures of the Bol'sheokhtinskii Bridge. The request to cross this bridge implies that the tenement block to which they are seeking access is located in the Okhta district, a working-class area far removed from the imperial grandeur of the centre; this is confirmed when the lad is subsequently arrested for attacking Lebedev in his office and incarcerated in the Okhta police station, the plaque for which is shown within the frame. Ironically, the freedom the couple have enjoyed in relation to the tourist sites is radically curtailed as soon as they wish to enter an impoverished zone.

Insofar as these sequences offer a celebration of the grace and harmony of the city, albeit one that hints at the oppressiveness that lies beneath its granite surfaces, *Konets Sankt-Peterburga* follows the structural model of Pushkin's *Mednyi vsadnik*. The transition in this narrative poem from the classical perfection of the city's facades to the humble abode of its civil-servant hero, a prelude to the natural disaster of the flood and the vision of political persecution symbolized by Falconet's statue, is analogous to the shift from the monuments in the centre of the city to the tenement blocks and the Lebedev armaments factory at the peripheries. At this point, the tensions that characterize modern class relations intrude. The sequences that follow juxtapose the claustrophobic 'lower depths' of the factory floor with the hustle and bustle of activity outside the stock exchange on the Strelka. Several associations are proposed and accentuated by means of montage. A portrait of Lebedev talking on the telephone is juxtaposed with a close-up of Peter the Great's face as sculpted by Falconet. Moments later, a series of portraits of perspiring workers in the foundry pouring molten iron into moulds is succeeded by crowds of stockbrokers frenetically buying and selling armaments shares, some of them also perspiring. Both arenas play with the illusion of documentary-style authenticity. The scenes on the factory floor appear to have been illuminated using the light provided by furnaces, but the modelling is too carefully textured to have been undertaken in the absence of studio arcs. By the same token, while some of the shots of the exchange are similar to pre-revolutionary actuality footage, the illusion of verisimilitude in the subsequent portraits is undercut by compositional mechanisms which involve forms of truncation and the positioning of mirrors for the purposes of *podsvetka*.

Golovnia's treatment of portraiture in both arenas combines dramaturgic imperative with generalized iconography. The lower or higher angle of the camera in relation to the human subject is unjustified by point of view within the diegesis and reflects rather an authorial stance bent on ideological edification. For the scenes on the factory floor, for example, Golovnia applies light to create a hellish atmosphere of sweat, vapour and heat. This is accentuated by *contre-jour* shots of silhouetted factory chimneys, the smoke from which billows upwards and partially obscures the sun. In the scenes of the exchange, by contrast, portraits are presented which border on the grotesque: facial expression, skin texture, physiognomy and clothing produce an entirely different range of tonal values. In the factory, for example, the low-level lighting from the sides captures the beads of perspiration, the lean, toughened skin and the suffering expressions of the workers' eyes; in addition, the tone of the skin for the most part is dark grey. One of the most striking images in this sequence shows an older worker wearing goggles. He is glimpsed initially next to a furnace, but shortly afterwards his goggles have been raised to his forehead as, appalled and concerned, he reacts to the incident of the exhausted colleague struck to the ground by his foreman (Fig. 22). In the stock exchange, by contrast, the viewer's attention is drawn to bowler hats and straw boaters, tightly knotted ties, braided jackets, starched collars, the corpulence of cheek and double chin, and, in many cases, due to the relatively low angle of the camera, the narrow slits of eyes. There are indications that in some cases mirrors or some other reflecting surfaces have been employed for the purposes of modelling. Such an effect can be detected in the portrait of the broker with the pince-nez whose face is illuminated from a low angle, which is quite impossible by natural means, and the quality of the light that strikes the rim of his straw hat.[14] As a specific illustration of Golovnia's compositional idiosyncrasy, one may propose the close-up of the broker which, in many respects, anticipates Tisse's celebrated portrait of the kulak exploiter in *Staroe i novoe*: here the neck and chin are inflated, but not exaggerated, by means of a wide-angle lens, and thus the effect of caricature is avoided. A comparable example, far more radical in terms of lighting, can be found during the montage sequence which follows the overthrow of the tsar (initiated by the intertitle which exclaims 'Svoboda!' ('Freedom!')). This takes the form of a portrait of a male member of the audience which applauds as Kerenskii predicts a victorious conclusion to the war. The camera angle is extremely low and the lighting strikes both sides of the face, but not from the front, which leaves a strip of dark across the face and narrows its contours. The backward tilt of the head emphasizes the distorting mechanism of the lights, and the teeth are menacingly accentuated.

The compositional mechanisms employed for such portraits suggest a vision of the city which borders on Expressionist madness. This is reinforced by a number of visual tropes that present the city as a dehumanized and frenzied monster populated by crowds that respond mechanically and hysterically to patriotic impulses. Part of this vision is achieved by means of truncation. As a painterly procedure, truncation is usually identified with the works of Degas and Toulouse-Lautrec; specifically, the former's paintings of ballet dancers either training or dancing in the theatre, and the latter's scenes of performers and revellers at the Moulin Rouge.[115] In *Konets Sankt-Peterburga*, Golovnia radically extends this formal method for sequences in which barely controlled hysteria (the patriotic scenes) or the speculative frenzy of potential economic gain (armaments shares rise rapidly after the announcement of hostilities) is the dominating atmosphere. During the 'Motherland Calls' sequence, for example, there are several cases of metaphorical disfigurement that accentuate the ugliness of patriotic fervour. The generals and politicians are presented for the most part with only the lower halves of their bodies within the frame. Among the baying crowds on the streets, moreover, Golovnia's framing is so tight on occasion that the faces of cheering onlookers and the musicians in military bands are truncated either vertically or horizontally, sometimes with extraordinary radicalism (Fig. 23). The same method is adopted for the scenes of battle, although in such cases the compositional echoes are bleakly ironic: here the truncation of the dead bodies of soldiers implies physical mutilation. In these frames, for example the 'still lifes' that follow a German attack and the intertitle that states that 'both parties are satisfied', no heads are visible, only the lower halves of the torsos. In a further ironic echo of the earlier scenes, the bared teeth of the roaring crowds have been transformed into the gruesome rictuses of fallen soldiers. The final irony lies in the fact that, having been transferred from the realm of the living to that of the dead by imperial decree, these soldiers have become petrified monuments; their only difference from the autocrats who have ruled over the city since its founding is that they have not been placed on pedestals and thus are viewed from above, rather than from below.

Potomok Chingis-Khana: The 'Literature of Fact'

Although the action of *Potomok Chingis-Khana* takes place in a very different part of the world, namely the region near Lake Baikal which would soon become known as the Buriat-Mongol Soviet republic, it is the exploration of the poetics of place that links the film straightforwardly to *Konets Sankt-Peterburga*, the desire to convey the landscape of a specific region, the everyday life of its inhabitants, their modes of dress, their belief systems, customs and rituals, the architectonics of their dwellings and places of worship, and the atmosphere and quality of light as reflected in interior and exterior spaces. If the latter, as has been discussed above, is a work that operates within the cultural paradigm known as the 'myth' of St Petersburg, the former might be said to belong to the Orientalist strain in Russian culture, one that seeks to poeticize the 'exotic' and 'unfamiliar' East.[116]

Two decades after the film was made, Golovnia explained the task of shooting this material in the following way:

> *In order for people watching the film properly to understand and feel the authenticity of the unfolding drama ... we deemed it necessary for them to appreciate the limitless scope of the steppe, the grandeur of the surrounding mountains ..., the freedom of the wind, the distance and transparency of the horizon, and the lonely sound of the silver bells which hang from the unusual roofs of the Buddhist monasteries.*
>
> *As I have indicated above, every place has its own specific atmospheric nuance, its own quality of light, and the lengths and depths of its shadows.[117]*

The film is set in a region just north of the border with Outer Mongolia, which at the time of the narrative action was languishing under occupation as part of the Allied intervention in Siberia during the Civil War.[118] Several of the landscapes that constitute this region feature geographically in the film: the Borgoiskaia Steppe, which was predominantly home to herdsmen and trappers; the mountains surrounding the village of Tarbakhatai in the southern Altai region, where partisan activity was at its strongest during the Civil War; the interiors and exteriors of the monastery complex in Gusinoe Ozero; and the town of Verkhneudinsk (now Ulan-Ude), the regional capital and trading centre. Golovnia had been dispatched to the area on a reconnaissance mission in March 1928.[119] Many years later, he recalled the monotony of the steppe, its flatness compromised only by low-lying hills and the occasional ravine; the sense of isolation, with yurts dotted sporadically along the horizon; the dominating skies, with their occasional cloud; the violent winds that swept across the plain from Lake Baikal; and the grand vistas of the mountains near the village of Tarbakhatai, with their conifer forests stretching along peaks and hugging the bases of steep cliffs. He described the storm debris in the form of devastated tree trunks and dismembered branches, the density of light filtering down through the trees due to the absence of needles on the remaining branches, the transparency and thinness of the air near the mountain summits, and the darker tone of the sky at higher altitudes.[120] He also mentioned the shards of light in the monastery interiors and the rich, decorative detail of the costumes worn by masked dancers during the ceremony of Tsam, which he photographed on a special film stock, Kinochrome, in order to communicate the ornamental detail and wealth of tones.[121]

The conceit of ethnographic authenticity lies at the very heart of this film's visual poetics. The narrative was based on a screenplay by Brik which drew upon a curious anecdote that had been related to him by Ivan Novokshonov, a writer and journalist who had spent many years in the Far East and fought during the Civil War in Siberia (his own literary version of the anecdote would be written in 1933 but could not be published until after his death and his rehabilitation in 1966).[122] This told the story of how a partisan fighting for the Reds had been captured by the British and identified as a descendant of Genghis Khan on the basis of a Mongolian inscription sewn onto an amulet in his possession. Seeking to derive political advantage from this ancestry, of which the partisan himself was apparently unaware, the British Army designated him a puppet king in the hope of quelling the growing insurgency. The partisan decided to escape captivity, however, and at the time of writing was serving as the commander of a Red Army division.[123]

The quasi-documentary basis for the screenplay, buttressed by the fact that the amulet in question was claimed to be genuine and had been donated to the Irkutsk Ethnographic Museum, to a great extent determined the filmmakers' creative method.[124] The film was shot on location in May and June 1928 in the presence of an advisor, who gave detailed information on the way of life and customs of the local people.[125] Although several scenes purportedly taking place on location were shot in the studio after the crew's return, these scenes, which included some temple interiors and the encounter between a British military delegation and a newly reincarnated lama, were staged in order to simulate as accurately as possible the lighting conditions that had been experienced in the monastery in Gusinoe Ozero.[126] The opening sequence in the yurt of the main protagonist's family was apparently shot without any alteration to the original décor. The lighting effects, moreover, were achieved purely by natural means, a combination of sunlight and the yurt's authentic latticework and the circular opening in its roof.[127] The sequence set in the Verkhneudinsk bazaar included actuality scenes of Buriat Mongols performing genuine sword dances. Furthermore, Pudovkin inserted additional 'found material' in the form of the Tsam ceremony, a Buddhist ritual with ancient roots that was performed every year on 26 June in Gusinoe Ozero. This ceremony consists of masked figures performing symbolic dances and mimed gestures, and was not envisaged as part of the original screenplay. Because the unit was obliged to return home before the traditional date, it was performed especially for the cameras, but not adjusted or halted in any way.[128] In a continuation of his previous practice (the use of *typage* for several of the subsidiary characters in *Mat'* and the figure of the peasant lad in *Konets Sankt-Peterburga*), Pudovkin offered several roles to genuine Buriat-Mongol inhabitants of the region who were not professional actors. Furthermore, he invited Red partisans who had fought the British in the mountains during the Civil War to reenact their historical roles.[129] The conceit of authenticity also explains his decision to invite Valerii Inkizhinov, a trained theatre actor who had worked for eight years as a tutor in biomechanics with Meierkhol'd and was ethnically Mongol, to play the role of the main protagonist, the herdsman and trapper Bair. An interview with Inkizhinov after the crew had returned explains the rigorous training he had undertaken in order to divest himself of his Russian education and theatrical background, and thus to resurrect what he described as his 'inner Mongol'.[130] Apart from paying tribute to Pudovkin's exacting standards and his ability to grasp the uniquely individual skills of his actors, he spoke warmly of his relationship with Golovnia and the importance of the latter's camerawork in highlighting certain features of his work:

> *Golovnia's camera painted its severe Mongolian poem and led the character of Bair in a direction of which I was consciously aware. It is actually quite difficult to express in words the relationship between the actor and the camera operator. The method of filming which the camera operator has deliberately formulated determines not only the position of the body, or the angle at which the body is turned to the camera, but also the fundamental character of the actor's work.*
>
> *Golovnia's camera is a living object which is not indifferent to the object it is filming, but is active, searching and temperamental.*[131]

Although Pudovkin made clear before filming began that he did not wish the documentary sequences to be regarded as exotic background material, but rather as a means with which to express the emotional psychology and everyday life and customs of his protagonist, it is important to stress that 1920s Soviet cinema was characterized by a powerful interest in ethnographic material.[132] The pursuit of the 'exotic' and 'primitive' was a standard feature of early cinema generally and took the form either of ethnographic studies for scientific purposes or travel chronicles through regions and territories regarded as exotic from a metropolitan (European) perspective.

In the post-revolutionary period, however, this interest acquired a greater degree of momentum and a specifically agitational dimension thanks to the policy of *osvoenie* – in other words, the state's impulse to map territories geographically that had been insufficiently explored and to observe and catalogue their 'backward' inhabitants scientifically with a view to demonstrating the benefits of socialism. This phenomenon was reflected in the numerous expeditions undertaken by teams of documentary filmmakers from 1922 onwards to peripheral regions or republics of the Soviet Union and the regular reports supplied to the film press on the part of the camera operators involved.[133] The most ambitious illustration of this phenomenon was *Shestaia chast' mira*, a celebration of the Soviet Union's ethnic diversity which involved an entire team of chroniclers being dispatched to regional republics in order to record images of minority peoples recently 'liberated' from the yoke of capitalist imperialism; brief sequences of Buriat Mongols had featured in this documentary. Another important precursor is *Velikii perelet*, the documentary by Shneiderov and Blium which recorded their journey by plane from Moscow to China. This consisted of aerial footage of the flight, actuality footage of the places at which they stopped to refuel, and scenes of everyday life in Shanghai and other cities. Three of these stopovers took place in towns with Mongol populations: Verkhneudinsk; Alton-Bulak (a town on the Soviet-Mongol border); and Ulan Bator, the capital of the Mongolian People's Republic. The footage included images of a bronze statue of Buddha in a temple in Ulan Bator; scenes of everyday life in the same town; and examples of what Blium called 'national types'.[134] Furthermore, documentary material originating from the Buriat-Mongol region, although it is unclear when or indeed whether it was ever released, had been filmed one year before Pudovkin and Golovnia's expedition by the actor and filmmaker Mikhail Kastorin (the account of his journey suggests that he also managed to film the Tsam ceremony, on the traditional date).[135] The critical reception of *Potomok Chingis-Khana* in the Soviet Union may also to some extent have been conditioned by Flaherty's *Nanook of the North* (1922), which had appeared on Soviet screens for the first time only two months previously. This ethnographic documentary, having provoked controversy abroad because of its staging of certain sequences, nevertheless aroused tremendous interest among Soviet critics because of its filmmaking method. On discovering that Flaherty's familiarity with Inuit life was the product of thirteen months spent in their midst, one reviewer championed his method as a model for the educational documentary in the Soviet Union.[136]

In the light of the ethnographic conceit in *Potomok Chingis-Khana*, it is important to note Golovnia's involvement in a separate project which, although it was filmed after his return, was actually released beforehand and constituted a further demonstration of the widespread interest in documentary and ethnographic material at this time. The work in question, *Stekliannyi glaz*, was the brain-child of Lilia Brik, the wife of Osip, who, having been immortalized in several photo-montage compositions by Rodchenko, most famously the cover design and accompanying illustrations for Maiakovskii's *Pro eto* (About This, 1923) and the advertising poster *Knigi* (Books), which was commissioned by the Leningrad section of the State Publishing House in 1925, had recently started working in the film industry.[137] Golovnia's involvement in this 'film-within-a-film' was two-fold: he 'performed' the role of a camera operator and explained the functioning of his camera; he was also shown in the act of shooting a documentary, the material from which was later incorporated into the film itself. Two stills showing him at work were published while the film was in production: in the first, Golovnia is dismantling his camera in order to explain the functions of its individual components; in the second, he is photographed filming female students from the GTK as they perform physical education exercises on a small stage. In turn, he is being filmed by Konstantin Vents, who was second camera operator on *Potomok Chingis-Khana* and had photographed several of the publicity stills that appeared in the Soviet press both before and after its release.[138]

Although neglected in writings about Soviet cinema, and not complete in its surviving versions, *Stekliannyi glaz* is a fascinating film that has many points in common with *Potomok Chingis-Khana*. The most important connection, apart from the involvement of Golovnia, is the creative contribution of the Brik husband-and-wife team, both of whom were known for their commitment to the documentary principle. Despite his position as head of the literary (screenplay) section of Mezhrabpomfil'm, Brik had consistently championed the superiority of documentary fact over literary fiction during the 1920s. In an article on Shub's *Padenie dinastii Romanovykh*, for example, he pointed out that the material assembled to show the events that gave rise to the October Revolution was infinitely more authentic than any staged version could be, and was compiled at only a fraction of the cost. For Brik, the emergence of this work signalled the 'defeat' of the feature film and constituted unequivocal evidence in support of his view that shooting in the studio should now be abandoned altogether.[139]

Unlike Shub's compilation documentary, with which it otherwise possesses crucial similarities, *Stekliannyi glaz* not only constitutes a polemic against the artificiality of mainstream filmmaking, but also offers one of the most potent examples during the 1920s of the wealth and attractiveness of actuality material. It begins by demonstrating the technical properties of the camera and its capacity to enrich the perspective of the human eye. It then presents a typical feature-film sequence, which purports to take place on an exterior location (two lovers caught on a ship during a storm) but in fact has been staged in the studio, and shows how the illusion has been artificially created.[140] This Formalist 'revelation of the device' is followed by repetitions of the staple ingredients of mainstream cinema, for example dramatic kisses and violent murders, all of them culled from recent releases, which aim to show, despite the international origin of the sources, their banal quality. These sequences are subsequently compared to the camera's ability via documentary to convey the wonders of the modern world. The viewer is presented with recent discoveries in medical science, the awesome splendour of large-scale industrial processes, the incremental growth of plants, ethnographic material, images filmed from the top of the Eiffel Tower, an aerial perspective over Manhattan, the coronation of Nicholas II, and recent events in the history of post-revolutionary Russia and the world as captured by newsreel camera operators. The skill with which *Stekliannyi glaz* combines material that stretches across time, space and geographical location is a showcase illustration of the power of documentary. According to one reviewer, Nikolai Kaufman, *Stekliannyi glaz* was the first 'film-review' (*fil'm-obozrenie*).[141]

The presence of a dramaturgical framework does not necessarily distinguish *Potomok Chingis-Khana* from the kind of documentary material promoted by Brik and other intellectuals during the mid-to-late 1920s. In Brik's formulation, the scenario within the feature film was only a 'motivation' for the filmed material; by the same token, it was naïve in his view to think that documentary material could be assembled without what he called 'interior thematic links'.[142] His screenplay, because it was based on a genuine story (the 'literature of fact'), was doubtless conceived as a vehicle with which to bridge the gap between the staged and non-staged. There are similarities here with *Nanook of the North* in the sense that this film presented itself as genuine documentary material while at the same time contriving occasional moments of drama. The difference lies not only in the moments of drama per se, or the fact that the original anecdote of the screenplay took place in the past, and was therefore being restaged, but rather in the rich tapestry of visual motifs and ironic juxtapositions which is woven about this anecdote in *Potomok Chingis-Khana.*

A useful and very obvious example of deliberately manipulated visual choreography lies in the pattern of images relating to the presence of powerful winds; this is a feature of the landscape that is persistently insinuated in *Potomok Chingis-Khana* even when the wind itself is not actually present. This motif is absent in the screenplay, and would therefore appear to be the product of Golovnia and Pudovkin's response to the natural landscape during the period of location research. It is subtly introduced during the opening sequences and reaches its culmination in the film's finale, a poetic *tour-de-force* that exploits the natural phenomenon as a metaphor for revolutionary triumph (its power, like the tidal wave produced by a tsunami, sweeps everything before it in a God-like act of creative destruction). The establishing shots at the beginning of the film and some of the early sequences in the mountains are photographed at angles that show clouds briskly scudding across the horizon, the wind thus implicitly present. These initial impressions are reinforced by shots of the flag outside Bair's family yurt, which flutters agitatedly in the wind; the establishing shots of the Gusinoe Ozero monastery, which show little bells hanging from the roof and swinging briskly; and the footage of the Tsam ceremony, with its flags, pendants and other materials all flapping in the wind. Subsequent moments present trees that have been bent and twisted by this wind. Indeed, these trees are ubiquitous throughout the film and to some extent function as metaphors in their own right. This pattern of motifs includes the tree that is knocked down by a boulder during the initial hunt sequence (a hint at the devastation that will occur in the film's culminating moments); the solitary trees that populate the rocky outcrops in the episodes which show Bair joining the partisans; the images of storm damage during the struggle sequence high in the mountains; the tree, shot in soft-focus, which symbolizes the solidity of the partisan leader who dies from a bullet wound; the tree glimpsed in the background beyond the depth of field in the moments leading up to the execution of Bair; and the trees first bent and then uprooted by the ferocity of the storm in the closing sequences.

In the sense that this metaphorical storm sweeps away all the emblems of British authority, it is also the culmination of another imagistic nexus in the film, at the centre of which lies the importance of costume and uniform as accoutrements of power. The key sequence in this regard is the preparations for the Tsam ceremony, which adopts parallel montage procedures to juxtapose the dress codes and dressing rituals of spiritual and secular authority systems (in so doing, with deliberate irony, the film is engaged in the reverse procedure, an unmasking or deconstruction of these power mechanisms). As demonstrated by the introduction of Bair as archetypal Mongol herdsman, dress is treated initially as part of the film's ethnographic fabric. Subsequently, this fabric acquires a more complex set of associative layers as the formal and decorative procedures which underpin the ceremony on the part of the performers and those who intend to act as observers (the British general and his wife) are presented. Admittedly, these parallels are present in Brik's screenplay, but they are insisted upon by Pudovkin and Golovnia in much greater and more elaborate detail.[143] At the beginning of Part Four, for example, the audience is presented with an impressive array of ladies' shoes and a display of toiletries and perfumes in glass decanters positioned on a dressing table. These images are followed by close-ups of shaving foam applied to the general's cheeks and chin; the hair of his wife being blow-dried; close-ups of the general being shaved with a razor; military boots being assiduously polished; a uniform being carefully cleaned; the general's corpulent body standing in a wash basin; the soaping of his body as he washes; cream being applied to his wife's hands and arms; powder being applied to her neck and shoulders; an officer donning leather gloves; and two officers removing hairnets. This series of domestic interior scenes, which associates the display of power with affluence and hygiene, is interrupted by an intertitle which explains that 'There are ceremonies ... and rites ... among all races', after which the viewer is shown establishing shots of the monastery complex in Gusinoe Ozero and images of priests cleaning a giant statue of Buddha with a brush. The scene subsequently returns to the general and his wife. The wife is shown pulling on a pair of stockings; her corset is tightened; the general pulls on a pair of trousers and wraps a cummerbund around his stomach; and his wife is dressed in a gown. At this point another cut shows the analogous procedures undertaken by a Lamist priest in preparation for the ceremony. We are again returned to the general, who is tying his tie. This is followed by images of a priest donning an elaborate headdress; the wife's head being adorned with a diadem or tiara; medals being pinned to the general's uniform; rings being placed on the wife's fingers; and an expensive fox-fur wrap being placed around her shoulders and neck (Brik comments that the couple represent 'the finished products of European lustre').[144] Finally, during the ceremony itself, the jewellery worn by one of the masked dancers is compared to the necklace worn by the general's wife. Furthermore, the wife's fingering of these pearls during the ceremony is juxtaposed with the fingering of beads on the part of the Mongolian observers of the ceremony.

The elaborate nature of these procedures reflects the importance of dress and costume to the cult of power. This idea is further enhanced by the treatment of Bair after his capture by the British authorities: his recovery from execution and promotion to the office of high state are accompanied by a radical metamorphosis which sees his everyday clothing stripped away in favour of a Western dressing gown, a suit with waistcoat and tails, and patent leather shoes. The level of discomfort experienced by Bair in this new guise is functional, psychological and cultural. During the operation, he has been reduced to a state of nakedness, his body bearing the marks of oppression in the form of bullet wounds and horrific bruising. This is followed by the surgical wrapping of his body in bandages that cover his torso and head almost completely. As well as constituting an ironic echo of the earlier preparations by the general and his wife, these bandages severely restrict his movements. To all intents and purposes he is imprisoned within his own body and resembles a mummy or, in a further ironic commentary on the ceremonial preparations, a static idol. Only his eyes manage to communicate the level of anguish he is experiencing. As the intrigued reactions of three visitors subsequently confirm, he has become an exhibit in a museum to be displayed for the curiosity of tourists.

Bair's transformation from hunter to puppet king during the 'Ruler Recovers' sequence is an intriguing form of *mise en abîme* in the sense that it reverses the usual Orientalist procedure, according to which the exotic 'other' is romanticized. From the point of view of the British, Bair as a trapper is simply another 'native' who does not merit the interest of the colonial occupier. Now transformed into a nominal Westerner, however, he has become an object of fascination: from 'other', he has become a humiliated 'self'; from 'primitive' subject he has acquired the status of cosmopolitan 'ruler'. In carefully charting this process, Golovnia and Pudovkin explore further their interest in surfaces as sites for concealment. In his account of his preparations for the role, Inkizhinov emphasized the control required in relation to the movements of the face and body. He refers to the need to communicate the narrow horizon of movement during emotionally tense moments; the gradual accumulation of feeling leading to explosive outburst; and the restrained, modest smile (Pudovkin apparently referred to this as the 'hint' or 'thought' of a smile).[145] Such were the levels of control, that Eizenshtein was misled into thinking that Pudovkin had not permitted Inkizhinov to act at all.[146] Yet it is important to distinguish between the different types of mask. For the British and the Tsam dancers, the mask is part of a performance or ritual; for Bair, it is a natural expression of modesty and humility. During the encounter with the lama, the British officials seek to conceal anxiety about the security of their return journey by performing forced smiles. By contrast, the smiles and laughter to which Bair succumbs when he discovers to his surprise that the partisan whom he has rescued in the mountains is a woman are a reflection of spontaneous feeling. Furthermore, the fact that his response is encouraged by the partisans themselves bears early witness to his gradual acquisition of political consciousness.

Second Commercial Break: *Zhivoi trup*

Apart from *Stekliannyi glaz*, Golovnia's return to Moscow from the time spent in the Altai found him working on another commission from Mezhrabpomfil'm. This was not directed by Pudovkin, although he was very much part of the project in the sense that he was cast as the main protagonist. The production in question, Otsep's *Zhivoi trup*, was based on a play that Tolstoi had written in 1900 but which, because it drew on the proceedings of a genuine court case, the litigants in which were still alive, he did not allow to be published until after his death. Like *Chelovek iz restorana*, *Zhivoi trup* had also been adapted for the screen in the pre-revolutionary era. The first version was directed by Boris Chaikovskii for R. Perskii & Co.; it was released in September 1911, just before the stage première of the play and the actual publication of the text, and caused something of a scandal because the company had been denied the rights for public performance by the Tolstoi family.[147] The second version, released in early 1918, was directed by Sabiński for Kharitonov & Co., and starred Vera Kholodnaia in the role of Masha, the gypsy girlfriend of the main protagonist.[148] As indicated in Chapter One, Otsep's film was a coproduction with Prometeusfilm in Berlin; indeed, it was the second cooperative venture between these two studios, and one that was followed by several productions in the late 1920s and early 1930s, before the Nazi ascent to power brought such arrangements to a halt.

The oxymoronic title of Tolstoi's play ('The Living Corpse') is usually thought to derive from Paul's first epistle to Timothy (5:6), in which it is written that a widow who 'giveth herself to pleasure' (the context suggests remarrying after the death of a husband) is 'dead while she liveth'. Despite the fact that the play was conceived during a period when Tolstoi's concern with the moral predicaments caused by unhappy marriages gave rise to a number of compelling and controversial but ultimately didactic works, *Zhivoi trup* is a complex psychological drama that remains largely objective in its treatment of the key characters. The main protagonist, Fedor Protasov, is a man of probity who has nevertheless sunk into despair as a result of his deteriorating marriage, this manifesting itself in his tendency to drink and gamble, as well as his pursuit of a number of adulterous liaisons, or so the viewer is initially led to believe. Protasov believes that his wife, Liza, loves another man, a childhood friend called Viktor Karenin, who has remained a friend of the family. In the interests of releasing her from her marital obligations, Fedor decides to give Liza the freedom to pursue this relationship. However, the strongly religious convictions of Karenin and his mother force the couple to request that the marriage be legally annulled. This can only be achieved by bribing church officials, which Fedor refuses to do on grounds of conscience, or by committing suicide, which he rejects on the grounds of his growing attachment to Masha. Prompted by her pleading, he decides to simulate suicide by bathing in the Moscow river and leaving his clothes and a fake suicide note on its banks, after which he disappears and leads the life of a homeless vagrant. Coincidentally, the drowned body of another man is found in the vicinity shortly afterwards and is positively identified by Liza, who is too shocked to inspect the body closely. Convinced that her husband is dead, she marries Karenin, but is horrified one year later to be summoned to the prosecutor's office and charged with deliberately misleading the authorities. The humiliation of the trial, and recognition that a guilty verdict could result in their both being sentenced to Siberian imprisonment, prompts Fedor's genuine suicide by means of a revolver outside the court.

Although it is thought that the play's title refers to Fedor's wanderings incognito after his staged suicide – he is bodily alive but legally he does not exist – the allusion to Paul's epistle to Timothy, albeit with an ironic twist, suggests that the concerns of the play lie rather with the emotional volatility of Liza, a solid and decent woman who, it would appear, cannot cope with the idea of loving two men simultaneously. Tolstoi's interest in the complex emotional dynamic of the *ménage à trois* (although actually the play depicts something approaching a *ménage à quatre*) is explicitly revealed when Masha refers to the simulated suicide of Rakhmetov in Nikolai Chernyshevskii's *Chto delat'?* (What is to be Done?, 1863) as a possible solution to Fedor's dilemma. Bearing in mind his public views at the time, it is hardly likely that Tolstoi could have been advocating bigamy or open relationships within marriage; for this reason, it may be speculated that the real target of his play lies in the lack of communication between the protagonists, one that renders their motivations opaque and misguided. Thus Protasov, who is introduced to the audience by means of a series of shifting viewpoints, emerges as an intellectually honest man who nevertheless fails to investigate the causes of his marital distress and allows his moral distaste for society's norms to dictate his actions. It might be argued that the decision to allow Liza to pursue her relationship with Karenin, rather than being the product of a generosity of spirit, is motivated by the deepening bond that has developed between him and Masha, and his desire for the freedom of spirit (*volia*) that the gypsy community represents. The scene at the beginning of Act II, which shows Fedor listening drunkenly to a gypsy ensemble, suggests someone who has grown weary of polite society, has not found a meaningful role for himself within it, and for these reasons, rather like Aleko, the main protagonist in Pushkin's *Tsygany* (The Gypsies, 1824), has decided to abandon the 'civilized' world and embrace the uncertain status of the internal émigré. The fact that he is unable to do so (it is a chance confession of his identity that leads to the discovery of his whereabouts by the authorities) indicates that his will-power is insufficient.

Otsep's adaptation of *Zhivoi trup* is largely faithful to the literary source in terms of the overall dramatic framework, although it replaces the scene between Karenin and his mother, which articulates their religious opposition to the open relationship being proposed by Fedor, in favour of a scene that takes place in the offices of an Orthodox bishop, who explains the grounds on which Fedor may seek a divorce. It also introduces two scenes absent in the play, namely, the moments when Fedor approaches a group of men who specialize in staging compromising scenes with witnesses so that adultery can be claimed as the grounds for divorce. Despite the interest in triangular relationships at this time, witnessed in *Tret'ia Meshchanskaia* and *Vasha znakomaia*, not to mention the semi-public entanglement between the Briks (Osip and Lilia) and Maiakovskii, the lukewarm reception by certain reviewers suggests that the problem of divorce within a privileged, pre-revolutionary milieu lacked intrinsic interest for the Soviet viewer, who had in any case benefited from the reform of divorce laws courtesy of the Family Codes of 1918 and 1926. It was argued, for example, that this second joint venture between Mezhrabpomfil'm and Prometeusfilm was unhealthy in the sense that, like Grigorii Roshal''s *Salamandra* (The Salamander, 1928), the first product of this collaboration, it had resulted in a film that seemed directed more towards German audiences, where religious objections to divorce were still a pressing issue.[149] The 'self-satisfied' and 'middle-brow' style of the film, which one reviewer complained only 'tickled' the senses rather than 'provoking genuine thought', was an additional cause for complaint.[150] The 'posing' and 'archaic' acting styles of the non-Soviet actors – the Italian Maria Giacobini (Liza), the Austrian Gustav Diessl (Karenin) and the relatively unknown Viola Garden (Sasha, the sister of Liza) – invited a degree of mockery.[151] So, too, did Golovnia's camerawork, which was condemned as a 'sweet-wrapper' and a 'philistine *féerie* (enchanting story)'.[152]

Undeniably, these reviews are evidence of a more truculent trend in Soviet criticism, one which was broadly reflective of official cultural polices that were beginning to reject everything even obliquely related to *inostranshchina* (obsession with all things foreign) and the NEP in favour of a more obviously Sovietized and proletarian product; the supposedly 'formalist' tendencies of the avant-garde would also fall victim to this trend in due course.[153] With the benefit of hindsight, while no doubt broadly correct in terms of the commercial ambitions of *Zhivoi trup*, these criticisms seem misguided and, at times, myopic. Otsep, having scripted a number of blockbusters during the 1920s, was certainly a stalwart of the Mezhrabpomfil'm brand, if not one of its crucial pioneers, yet after his move into direction with *Miss-Mend* (Miss-Mend/The Adventures of Three Reporters, 1926), which he co-directed with Boris Barnet, he had shifted into a more sophisticated territory. This is evident in *Zemlia v plenu*, a film released just before *Zhivoi trup*, which dramatized in stark and tragic terms the neo-feudal repression of the landless peasantry on the eve of the October Revolution. As I have argued elsewhere, the innovative treatment of the atmospheric insert renders this film a poetic masterpiece that deserves a markedly greater respect than it has merited hitherto.[154] By the same token, it would be wilful perversity to accuse either Otsep or Golovnia of pandering to a mainstream (German) audience. Not only is *Zhivoi trup* a serious work in terms of its direction and cinematography, it is comparable to Golovnia's earlier films alongside Pudovkin and contains a number of formal innovations, the most startling of which is the extended montage sequence that accompanies the singing and dancing of the gypsy choir.

As interpreted by Otsep, *Zhivoi trup* becomes a drama about the search for meaning in a world that does not understand the desire for escape. With the exception of the extended montage sequence and a number of scenes that involve abrupt movement – for example when Masha bursts suddenly into a room to prevent Protasov's suicide, or when his life as a vagrant among the drunken *narod* (people or folk) is dramatized through the use of rapid-fire montage and hand-held shots – *Zhivoi trup* is a film of restraint, contemplation and silence, with few words spoken between the characters, and the intensity of the emotional drama communicated largely by means of the eyes; this is a film conducted in a minor key and in a largely sombre mood which progressively darkens. Despite the imposing spaces that feature in the film, in particular the impressive interior of the diocesan bishop's office, the entrance and grandiose staircase leading to Protasov's apartment and the courts of justice in which the trial takes place, there is an austere quality about the sets which echoes the Spartan aesthetic informing Golovnia's earlier work with Pudovkin. The visual treatment of the trial sequence, for example, with its initial, axial angle of vision and symmetrical arrangements of figures, echoes the compositional mechanisms of the analogous sequence in *Mat'*. Despite the very different social milieu, the interiors are uncluttered and for the most part lacking in ostentation; indeed, there is a general feeling of emptiness about these interiors, this impression enhanced by the linear and tonal simplicity of Golovnia's compositions, which eradicate all unnecessary distractions.

The classical rigour of the frame reflects the formality of the relationships between the protagonists, the connections between them consisting of observations conducted at a distance, rather than direct, spontaneous communication. The number of instances in which characters observe each other through half-closed doors or windows, and where the actions in view are capable of being misinterpreted, is striking. The scene in which Liza espies Fedor and Masha during the gypsy-choir evening, for example, and mistakes his paternal gestures towards her as evidence of sexual intimacy, is an excellent illustration of the distance that separates the characters and their isolation in relation to one another. The film's overt lack of interest in dramatic momentum and its willingness to depict moments of quiet contemplation, if not alienation, are witnessed in two early scenes. The first is the moment when Fedor enters his apartment, stands in front of a hallway mirror and silently reflects on what he might find if he goes into the drawing room, which is nearby: here, unusually, his body stands at an angle to the camera and his head and shoulders are out of focus, but occupy the entire left-hand side of the frame, and only his profile is visible in the reflected glass. The second is the image that follows seconds later, a ruthlessly focussed composition that consists of a bright and narrow strip of light which stretches beneath the drawing-room door (apart from the frame of this door, nothing else is visible). The culmination of the interest in alienation occurs in the courts of justice, where the crowds who have packed the auditorium use lorgnettes or opera glasses to observe the proceedings, almost as if watching a theatre production. Otsep returns the camera repeatedly to these members of the bourgeois public, viewed either in isolation or in serried ranks. There could be no better example of the intrusiveness from which Fedor so obviously wishes to escape.

Those reviewers who criticized Pudovkin's acting for its 'emptiness' were misreading the intentions of the director and missing the subtle nuances of expression that hint at the suffering within. This is signalled by directed light sources which, unusually for Golovnia at this stage in his career, are positioned mostly in front of the actor in order to register the merest hint of emotional response. Although such arrangements were a conventional and mainstream strategy at this time, it is important to note the moments when Golovnia adjusts them, either to indicate the evolution of Protasov's character, or to reflect different dramatic emphases in relation to other protagonists. As far as the latter are concerned, it is worth drawing attention to the lighting procedures adopted for the low-life characters who stage adulterous scenes (Golovnia underscores their louche attributes by arranging for angled top-lighting to shroud their eye sockets in darkness); and the arrangements for the scene in which Liza inspects the dead body which she fears is her husband's (her wearing of a bonnet and veil almost completely blocks out light from her traumatized face). As far as Protasov himself is concerned, as witnessed in the diocesan bishop's office at the very beginning of the film, the frontal position of the lights and the heavy application of make-up, perhaps appropriately in view of the film's title, give the impression of a ghost. Subsequently, the intensity, position and angle of the arcs are altered in order to express a variety of different emotions, such as Protasov's disgust on being presented with the calling cards of the candidates whom he must select for the projected adultery scene, and his anguished moments in the tavern when he contemplates shooting himself with a revolver. These variations are also utilised in the sequence in which, while standing in a doorway, he observes his wife playing the piano and embracing Karenin; and in the parting scene with Masha after the simulated suicide, during which he explains to her that he cannot take her with him on his journey into anonymity (this is the first moment in which make-up is removed entirely). The two extremes of portraiture can be illustrated by the unusual portrait of Protasov, partially concealed by a chair, as he sits in the tavern contemplating suicide, which employs a single source of low-angle lighting, justified naturalistically by the presence of a small table lamp that throws an isolated pool of light on the floor; and his fighting speech to the panel of judges in the courts of justice, during which he berates them for their lack of understanding of complex human relationships. The plasticity of this later portrait, its quality of inner vibrancy and moral fibre, lies in stark contrast to the rigid, restrained and mask-like portraits of the other characters at earlier junctures in the film.

If the dictates of dramaturgy control the lighting arrangements in *Zhivoi trup*, they also determine the expressive devices applied for the visionary moments when Protasov glimpses the possibility of an alternative existence. These occur during the gypsy-choir sequence, a montage of rapidly edited images lasting several minutes which seeks to convey the haunting qualities of the songs he has requested and the increasing tempo of the dancing as the singers take to the floor. These images constitute a series of rhythmically orchestrated point-of-view shots that expresses the arc of Protasov's thoughts and emotions as he listens to the music, watches the dancers and attempts to finish a farewell letter to his wife. In its entirety, the sequence conforms to what Salt has described as the 'classical montage' sequence, which he traces to German Expressionist films of the early 1920s.[155] The structure of the sequence in *Zhivoi trup*, however, is a great deal more ambitious than the precursors cited by him. The duration of the sequence and the range of technical devices on display are impressive. The initial songs are accompanied by multiple exposures of hands plucking guitars. Further superimpositions follow in the shape of atmospheric inserts filmed by a slow-moving, gliding camera. These lyrical scenes are intercut with further 'flashed' images of fingers strumming guitars, tambourines being shaken, the faces of singers and a reprisal of the landscape scenes presented earlier. These are sufficiently energizing as a vision to compel Protasov to leap up from the sofa on which he has been lying, complete his letter to Liza and arrange for the letter to be sent home, after which he requests more music, this prompting the beginning of the dancing. After one singer has moved forward to perform, Otsep and Golovnia free the camera from its tripod and follow the dancing with a series of rapid, jagged movements; this captures the movements of a dancer's feet and the jewellery that adorns her body, and vibrates to the rhythms of her dancing and the movements of her hands and shoulders. As the momentum of this performance increases, the montage rhythm becomes more furious. The hand-held footage is followed by more 'flashed' images of musicians, singers and listeners, as well as superimposed images of dancers filmed with the camera removed from its tripod. As this performance increases in intensity, Otsep introduces a parallel narrative: Liza receives the letter from Fedor, dresses hurriedly and exits the family home in the company of Karenin. Interestingly, and unusually, the frenetic momentum of the dancing 'invades' this narrative, initially by means of a panning shot that follows the maidservant as she delivers the letter after having rapidly ascended the apartment staircase, and then by the hand-held shots that show Liza hurriedly putting on an overcoat, hat and fur wrap.

Apart from the hand-held footage which incorporates double exposure, the devices employed in this sequence are not breaking new ground. Tisse had removed the camera from its tripod for several scenes in *Stachka* and, although the material in question had not yet been released, for the scything sequences in *Staroe i novoe*. The FEKS cameraman Moskvin had also experimented with hand-held shots in *Shinel'* and would reprise this method of filming for the cabaret sequences in *Novyi Vavilon*, which was released at around the same time as *Zhivoi trup*.[156] Golovnia himself was no newcomer to this technique either, having removed the camera from its tripod for the fight sequence between strikers and strike-breakers in *Mat'*, and for the footage shot during Tsam ceremony in *Potomok Chingis-Khana*.[157] Nevertheless, the purpose for which the portable camera is employed in *Zhivoi trup* endows the scenes with a philosophical dimension absent in these earlier works. By implication, the emancipated movement of the camera is associated with the specific qualities of gypsy dance; namely exuberance, dynamism and freedom of expression. As the intertitles make clear, for Protasov the songs evoke the concept of *volia*, a term that can refer to the nomadic lifestyle of gypsies and the open spaces of the Russian steppe that they traditionally inhabit, which lie outside the zone of political authority. In their structuring of the choir sequence, Otsep and Golovnia rearrange the order of songs in Tolstoi's play in order to emphasize the upward trajectory of Protasov's thoughts. At the beginning of Act II, Scene I, for example, the choir in Tolstoi's play are singing 'Kon avela' ('Who is Coming?'), a song from the traditional gypsy repertoire which involves dance movements and is sung to the accompaniment of guitars, tambourines and violins. This is followed by a slow romance, 'Chas rokovoi' ('The Fateful Hour'), which is sung solo by Masha; 'Shel me versty' ('One Hundred Miles'), a song from the traditional repertoire which involves dance movements; 'Ne vecherniaia' ('Akh, ne vecherniaia zaria rano spotukhala' ('Ah, has not the evening sun set early')), an old Russian romance that tells the story of a young man who is contemplating leaving his wife and for this reason refuses to return home (this is a request from Protasov himself, and is also sung by a soloist); and finally 'Len' ('Flax'), a traditional Russian song for folk choir only. In *Zhivoi trup*, by contrast, although the songs are not named, the increasing montage rhythm and shift from song to song and dance suggest that the slower songs have been positioned earlier than the faster ones, mirroring the shifting register of Protasov's emotions from yearning and melancholy towards excitement and passionate hope.

Epilogue: The (Temporary) Parting of the Ways

It is curious that the gypsy-choir sequence in *Zhivoi trup* should match so precisely Pudovkin's observations in relation to the natural affinities between montage rhythm and music that had been articulated in 'Vremia v kinematografe' and 'Fotogeniia'. The explicit interest in the relationship between music and the rhythms of montage and image construction is demonstrated earlier in the film during the moment when Liza plays the piano in Karenin's presence: here, the images of her hands on the keys are multiplied by means of multiple exposure across the width and height of the frame, an anticipation of the technique that will be employed for the hands strumming guitars during the gypsy-choir sequence. If not for the credits, indeed, one could be mistaken for thinking that it was Pudovkin, not Otsep, who was responsible for the direction. It is perhaps noteworthy that it was Pudovkin, and not Otsep, who declared his love for Tolstoi's 'inherent realism' and the principle of 'maximum clarity' in his fiction while the film was in production.[158] In addition to the hand-held footage, the Spartan arrangements for the décor and the dramaturgical emphasis in the lighting arrangements, there are several moments in *Zhivoi trup* which echo the earlier films of Pudovkin and Golovnia. The use of double exposure coupled with camera movement during the choir sequence, despite the different landscapes, essentially reprises the Constructivist sequences in *Mat'*. Likewise, there are obvious parallels between the tranquil atmosphere of the riverbank scenes, which reveal the site of Protasov's simulated suicide, and the early-morning *pastorales* in *Mat'*, which act as a 'musical accompaniment' to the main narrative.

Shortly after the release of *Zhivoi trup*, Golovnia and Pudovkin experienced a disagreement that led to their working independently of each other. As indicated in Chapter One, Pudovkin's first experiment with sound, *Prostoi sluchai*, was based on a screenplay that broke conventional dramatic rules, but whereas the director himself was clearly excited by this challenge, Golovnia was unhappy about its dramatic imprecision and for this reason refused to work on the project, although as a personal favour, when Pudovkin began to experience difficulties, he generously agreed to act as a consultant alongside the first-choice camera operator, Kabalov.[159]

As Pudovkin struggled with the practical challenges of sound and the interventions of the studio, both of which delayed the film's eventual completion and release, Golovnia embarked on two expeditions under the aegis of Mezhrabpomfil'm which were clearly a response to the official command for films that would celebrate the first Five-Year Plan.[160] The result was two educational documentaries which he directed and edited himself. The first, which he also photographed, was entitled *Khleb* (Bread, 1929); this took as its subject the mechanization of agriculture and rapid construction of the Gigant collective farm, which had been established in 1928 and specialized in grain production.[161] Reviewers were impressed by the colossal scale of the enterprise, the vision of seemingly limitless fields of virgin wheat 'consumed' by harvesters, the relentlessly flowing rivers of grain as it was transported mechanically from harvester to collecting basin to goods wagons waiting on nearby railway tracks, and the elevators that had been erected at rapid speed during the previous year and were shown at different stages of their construction.[162] The second, entitled *Ryba* (Fish, 1929), was directed by Golovnia but shot by Vents. The subject of this film was a different kind of 'harvest', namely, the harvesting of the seas by collective fish-farms which had replaced the cottage industries specializing in the catching of herring, sturgeon and roach in the delta where the Volga River flows into the Caspian Sea. The references in reviews to the 'staged' nature of certain sequences, which showed locals reenacting the pre-revolutionary practice of illegal fishing, confirm the propagandistic nature of the exercise, although reviewers were impressed by the depth of immersion in the lives of the local fishermen and the attempts to convey the poetry of their surroundings.[163]

The making of these films confirms Golovnia's commitment to the genre of documentary and conveniently bookends his silent-era work. With the exception of *Kirpichiki*, the 'romance' based on a popular street song of the early revolutionary period, his career was launched by films in which explicit documentary material was included.[164] His next feature film, *Dezertir*, which was directed by Pudovkin on the basis of a screenplay by Agadzhanova-Shutko, could also boast a documentary-style underpinning in the sense that the plot was concerned with the experience of a prolonged strike by dockers during the Great Depression in the port of Hamburg.[165] Part of the shooting took place on location. Furthermore, the conceit of actuality was very much part of the film's acoustic environment. The sounds were recorded in genuine locations, rather than reproduced or imitated within the studio, although the time taken to make the film and cut the soundtrack separately (762 days in total, according to press reports) meant that, by the time of its release, the narrative had been overtaken by events and indeed was no longer 'actual'.[166] As an experiment with sound, *Dezertir* unfortunately falls outside the scope of this study. Nevertheless, because the sound was recorded non-synchronously, the camerawork was to a large extent free of the constraints usually associated with the transition to sound and employed a typical array of avant-garde techniques: extreme close-ups, truncation, *décadrage*, diagonal constructions, extreme angles of vision, *contre-jour* and 'washing'. *Dezertir* is the most Constructivist work of the Pudovkin and Golovnia partnership: set-piece sequences show the construction of a steamship (the *Piatiletka*, so named after the first Five-Year Plan); the manufacture of diesel generators in the Metallstroi factory in Leningrad; and May-Day demonstrations in the same city, with their carefully orchestrated cacophony of brass bands and planes droning overhead. While the dramaturgy can certainly be criticized for a degree of confusion, *Dezertir* is nevertheless a strikingly visual *tour-de-force*. The combination of syncopated sound with 'flashed' or stroboscopic images is the clear manifestation of Pudovkin's long-standing interest in the musical rhythms of montage; here, the 'blow' or 'accent' is physically present in the form of hammers striking iron surfaces and the juddering of pneumatic drills. In its combination of sound and image, *Dezertir* has parallels with *Entuziazm: Symfoniia Donbasy*, the Vertov documentary in which the method of editing visual and audio material separately was pioneered in the Soviet Union.[167]

Detailed investigation of Golovnia's camerawork during the silent era establishes him as one of the most searching and innovative of avant-garde camera operators. Like others of his generation, he was undoubtedly influenced by Tisse's work on *Stachka* and *Bronenosets Potemkin*, but his compositional approach in general is marked by a greater degree of restraint and precision.[168] Whereas Tisse preferred to work with wide-angle lenses in his films with

Eizenshtein, and sought to enhance the depth of the frame and fill it with meaningful detail, from *Konets Sankt-Peterburga* onwards Golovnia displayed a penchant for longer lenses, in the process narrowing the depth of field. The principle of maximum clarity meant that his compositions are for the most part austere and stripped to their bare essentials. The differences in 'signature' can be gauged by reference to the camera operators' different visual approach to similar materials. One might compare, for example, the visual depictions of monuments in *Konets Sankt-Peterburga* and *Oktiabr'*, both of which share the concept of symbolic desecration. In Golovnia's camerawork, because of the tighter angles of vision and long-distance lenses, the statues impose themselves more readily on the viewer. The presence of the frame is palpable, and the recourse to truncation at the edges of the frame creates a strong compositional tension. In *Oktiabr'*, by contrast, the monuments are presented as tangible but essentially marginal presences. One might further juxtapose the sheer weight of the equestrian statue of Alexander III in *Konets Sankt-Peterburga* with the impression of relative lightness in relation to the monument to the same tsar being dismantled in *Oktiabr'*, admittedly a challenging operation in view of the fact the monument in question was a reconstructed model. It could never be said of Golovnia, as Eizenshtein said in relation to the scene of Kerenskii ascending the Jordan staircase in *Oktiabr'*, that the marble grandeur and opulence had not been communicated. Whether filming in exterior or interior locations, Golovnia was capable of rendering the weight and volume of objects through the manipulation of light in a way that Tisse in general was not.

Notes

1. Cited in A. Golovnia, 'Molodoi chelovek velikoi epokhi', *Iskusstvo kino*, 1973.2, 58–72 (p. 58).
2. These words apparently belong to Béla Balázs, and were used as an epigraph to Golovnia's course at the camera operators' faculty at VGIK. See 'Broken Cudgels' [interview with Golovnia recorded in July 1965], in *Cinema in Revolution: The Heroic Era of the Soviet Film*, ed. by Jean and Luda Schnitzer and Marcel Martin, trans. with additional material by David Robinson (London: Secker and Warburg, 1973), pp. 133–49 (p. 141).
3. Volchek was a GTK graduate at the end of the 1920s who successfully partnered Mikhail Romm on a number of acclaimed films during the 1930s. Pudovkin directed two films with him and his assistant, Era Savel'eva, at this time. The first, co-directed with Iurii Tarich, was *Ubiitsy vykhodiat na dorogu* (1942); the second, co-directed with Dmitrii Vasil'ev, was *Vo imia Rodiny* (also known as *Russkie liudi*, 1943), a screen adaptation of a play by Simonov. Volchek's name

is revealed in the letter to Golovnia (undated) as published in Pudovkin, *Sobranie sochinenii*, III (1976), 274–75 (p. 274).

4.   Gromov, *Kinooperator Anatolii Golovnia*, p. 167.

5.   Cited in ibid., p. 51 (emphasis in the original). This is confirmed in Vladimir Golovnia [no relation], 'Vsevolod Pudovkin: Nekotorye vpechatleniia', in *Pudovkin v vospominaniiakh sovremennikov*, ed. by T. E. Zapasnik and A. Ia. Petrovich, introductory essay by Leonid Trauberg (Moscow: Iskusstvo, 1989), pp. 329–36 (p. 329).

6.   Anatolii Golovnia, 'Vsevolod Pudovkin na s"emke', *Iskusstvo kino*, 1968.8, 63–65 (pp. 63 & 64).

7.   Ibid., pp. 63–64.

8.   For the reception of Pudovkin's theoretical writings and his films both in the Soviet Union and abroad, see Amy Sargeant, *Vsevolod Pudovkin: Classic Films of the Soviet Avant-Garde* (London: I. B. Tauris, 2000), pp. vii–xxxi.

9.   R. Il'in, 'V laboratorii mastera', *Iskusstvo kino*, 1982.5, 131–35 (p. 132); and Gromov, *Kinooperator Anatolii Golovnia*, pp. 173–74.

10.   See, for example, his contribution to a round-table discussion of Mikhail Kalatozov's *Ia – Kuba* (1964), in '"Ia – Kuba"', *Iskusstvo kino*, 1965.3, 24–37 (pp. 24–25).

11.   Vance Kepley, Jr, *The End of St. Petersburg*, KINOfiles Film Companion 10 (London: I. B. Tauris, 2003), p. 1.

12.   Nikolai Iezuitov, *Pudovkin* (Moscow-Leningrad: Iskusstvo, 1937), p. 105.

13.   For further information on the 'literature of fact', see Halina Stephan, *"Lef" and the Left Front of the Arts* (Munich: Verlag Otto Sagner, 1981), pp. 158–66 & 182–86.

14.   A. Golovnia, 'Vsevolod Pudovkin', *Iskusstvo kino*, 1940.1–2, 92.

15.   Cavendish, *Soviet Mainstream Cinematography*, pp. 39–60.

16.   'Kak ia stal rezhisserom', in Pudovkin, *Sobranie sochinenii*, II, 33–40 (p. 34) (first publ. in V. Pudovkin, *Izbrannye stat'i* (Moscow: Iskusstvo, 1955), pp. 39–48).

17.   L. Kuleshov, 'Kak voznikla nasha masterskaia', *Kino*, 1923.5, 30.

18.   'Naturshchik vmesto aktera', in Pudovkin, *Sobranie sochinenii*, I, 181–84 (first publ. as 'Address to the Film Society: The Use of Types as Opposed to Actors', in *Pudovkin: On Film Technique*, ed. and trans. by Ivor Montagu (London: George Newnes, 1929)). For Kuleshov's recollection in later years, see Kuleshov and Khokhlova, *50 let v kino*, p. 40. For his 1929 account of the experiment, see Kuleshov, 'Iskusstvo kino', p. 172.

19.   'Predislovie', in Pudovkin, *Sobranie sochinenii*, I, 130–32 (p. 131) (first publ. as the preface to the German edition of *Kinorezhisser i kinomaterial* (Berlin: Verlag der Lichtbildbühne, 1928)).

20.   'Kinorezhisser i kinomaterial', in Pudovkin, *Sobranie sochinenii*, I, 95–129 (p. 100) (first publ. Moscow: Kinopechat', 1926).

21.   Ibid.

22.   Ibid., p. 124.

23.   Ibid., p. 126.

24.   Ibid., pp. 122–23.

25.   Pudovkin, 'Fotogeniia', p. 91.

26.   Ibid., p. 92.

27.   'Vremia v kinematografe', in Pudovkin, *Sobranie sochinenii*, II, 87–89 (first publ. in *Kino*, 1923.2, 7–10).

28.   Pudovkin, 'Fotogeniia', p. 93.

29.   Ibid.

30.   Ibid.

31. Delluc, 'Photogénie', p. 38.
32. Ibid., p. 34.
33. Ibid., p. 56.
34. Ibid., p. 37.
35. Ibid., pp. 37–38.
36. Ibid., p. 39.
37. Ibid., p. 55.
38. Ibid., p. 57.
39. Ibid., p. 58.
40. Leo Mur, 'Fotogeniia', *Kino-zhurnal A.R.K.*, 1925.6–7, 3–6. On early responses to the advent of photography, see Susan Sontag, *On Photography* (London: Penguin, 1979), pp. 97–98.
41. Mur, 'Fotogeniia', p. 3.
42. Ibid.
43. 'Kinoki: Perevorot', in *Kino-Eye: The Writings of Dziga Vertov*, ed. with introduction by Annette Michelson, trans. by Kevin O'Brien (Berkeley: University of California Press, 1984), pp. 11–21 (p. 14) (first publ. in *LEF*, 1923.3).
44. Pudovkin refers to the Leningrad edition in his booklet on screenplay writing. See 'Kinostsenarii', in Pudovkin, *Sobranie sochinenii*, I, 53–74 (p. 56) (first publ. Moscow: Kinoizdatel'stvo RSFSR, 1926)).
45. Balash, 'Vidimyi chelovek', pp. 67, 81–82, & 88–89.
46. 'Priamoi put': Diskussionno', in Kuleshov, *Stat'i: Materialy*, pp. 127–30 (p. 129) (first publ. in *Kino*, 1924.48, 2); and Kuleshov, 'Iskusstvo kino', p. 194.
47. See Golovnia's brief article to celebrate the thirtieth anniversary of the film in *Mat'*, ed. by Glagoleva, p. 201 (first publ. in *Sovetskaia kul'tura*, 28 January 1957). See also A. Golovnia, *Svet v iskusstve operatora* (Moscow: Goskinoizdat, 1945), p. 100.
48. Mur, 'Khudozhnik sveta'.
49. Cavendish, *Soviet Mainstream Cinematography*, p. 48.
50. Kuleshov, 'Vystuplenie na iubileinom vechere A. A. Levitskogo', p. 413. For the comparison with Velázquez, see Frelikh, 'Stil' operatora', p. 7.
51. Golovnia, *Svet v iskusstve operatora*, p. 100.
52. Ibid.
53. Ibid., pp. 114–15.
54. Ibid., pp. 117–18.
55. Ibid., p. 118.
56. Ibid., pp. 118–19.
57. S. Iutkevich, 'Rezhisserskoe masterstvo Vs. Pudovkina v fil'me "Mat'"', in *Mat'*, ed. by Glagoleva, pp. 238–46 (p. 243) (first publ. in *VGIK: Uchenye zapiski*, I (Moscow: Iskusstvo, 1958), pp. 35–48).
58. Sargeant, *Vsevolod Pudovkin*, pp. 1–28 & 29–54.
59. 'Montazh nauchnoi fil'my', in Pudovkin, *Sobranie sochinenii*, II, 43–45 (first publ. in *Kino-zhurnal A.R.K.*, 1925.9, 10–11); and V. F.,'Mekhanika golovnogo mozga (Beseda s rezhisserom V. Pudovkinym)', *Sovetskii ekran*, 1926.31, 6–7 (p. 6).
60. Pudovkin, 'Montazh nauchnoi fil'my', p. 45.
61. Operator [Anatolii] Golovnia, 'S"emki kartiny "Povedenie cheloveka"', *Sovetskii ekran*, 1926.40, 4.
62. Cited in Gromov, *Kinooperator Anatolii Golovnia*, pp. 27–28.
63. Professor [L. N.] Voskresenskii, 'O nauchnykh fil'makh', *Kino-zhurnal A.R.K.*, 1925.9, 12–13 (p. 13).

64. See, for example, the photographs published in E. D. Bogoliubov, *Mezhdunarodnyi shakhmatnyi turnir v Moskve 1925 g* [1927] <http://www.chess.ufnet.ru/history/foto01.htm> (accessed 30 September 2011).
65. Ibid.
66. Gromov, *Kinooperator Anatolii Golovnia*, pp. 23–24.
67. Pudovkin in conversation with I. Rostovtsev, in *Mat'*, ed. by Glagoleva, pp. 186–89 (p. 188) (first publ. in *Mosfil'm*, I (Moscow: Iskusstvo, 1959), pp. 244–48).
68. '"Mat'"': Beseda s rezhisserom V. Pudovkinym', in Pudovkin, *Sobranie sochinenii*, II, 49–50 (first publ. in *Sovetskii ekran*, 1926.35, 6).
69. Operator [Anatolii] Golovnia, 'Osnovy operatorskoi raboty: Dve tochki zreniia na rol' kino-aktera', *Sovetskii ekran*, 1927.44, 7.
70. Evgenii Dobrenko, *Stalinist Cinema and the Production of History*, trans. by Sarah Young (Edinburgh: Edinburgh University Press, 2008), pp. 172–77.
71. A. V. Lunacharskii, 'Iz stat'i "Pobedy sovetskogo kino"', in *Mat'*, ed. by Glagoleva, pp. 225–27 (p. 225).
72. Viktor Shklovskii, 'Poeziia i proza v kinematografii', in *Poetika kino*, ed. by Eikhenbaum, pp. 137–42 (p. 142).
73. Gromov, *Kinooperator Anatolii Golovnia*, p. 62.
74. Vera Baranovskaia, 'Akter dramy v kino', *Sovetskii ekran*, 1926.38, 4.
75. Kabalov, 'Glazami operatora', p. 96.
76. Mur, 'Verkhom na luche', p. 10.
77. Golovnia, *Svet v iskusstve operatora*, p. 120.
78. See the discussion of this portrait in Golovnia, *Masterstvo kinooperatora*, pp. 111–12. It is also the centrepiece of a poster produced by S. Kozlovskii to accompany the release of the film. See Pack, *Film Posters of the Russian Avant-Garde*, p. 63.
79. Mur, 'Verkhom na luche', p. 10.
80. Golovnia, *Svet v iskusstve operatora*, p. 122.
81. Cavendish, *Soviet Mainstream Cinematography*, pp. 180–83.
82. Pudovkin, 'Kak ia stal rezhisserom', p. 37.
83. Iutkevich, 'Rezhisserskoe masterstvo Vs. Pudovkina v fil'me "Mat'"', p. 246.
84. Gromov, *Kinooperator Anatolii Golovnia*, p. 48–49.
85. Cavendish, *Soviet Mainstream Cinematography*, pp. 125–27.
86. On *sdvig*, see Juliette R. Stapanian, *Mayakovsky's Cubo-Futurist Vision* (Houston, TX: Rice University Press, 1986), pp. 18–21.
87. Iutkevich, 'Rezhisserskoe masterstvo Vs. Pudovkina v fil'me "Mat'"', p. 242.
88. *Alexander Rodchenko: Photography, 1924–54*, ed. by Lavrentiev, p. 118.
89. G. Boltianskii, 'O noveishikh priemakh s"emki', *Kino*, 1927.6, 3. On the use of optical distortion for POV shots in European cinema in the early 1920s, see Salt, *Film Style and Technology*, pp. 166–67.
90. Frelikh, 'Stil' operatora'.
91. Ibid., p. 7.
92. Arlazorov, *Protazanov*, p. 56.
93. Ibid., p. 175.
94. They are: *Chelovek* (1912), directed by Władysław Starewicz; *V zhizni vse byvaet* (1916), directed by Viacheslav Viskovskii; *Doch' "cheloveka"* (1916), directed by Ivan Lazarev; and *Chelovek iz restorana* (1916), directed by Sigizmund Veselovskii. See Veniamin Vishnevskii,

Khudozhestvennye fil'my dorevoliutsionnoi Rossii: Fil'mograficheskoe opisanie (Moscow: Goskinoizdat, 1945), pp. 25, 86–87, 93, & 120.

95. 'Vystuplenie na dispute "Puti i politika Sovkino" (15 oktiabria 1927 goda)', in Vladimir Maiakovskii, *Polnoe sobranie sochinenii*, 13 vols (Moscow: Gosudarstvennoe izdatel'stvo khudozhestvennoi literatury, 1955–61), XII (*Stat'i, zametki i vystupleniia: Noiabr' 1917–1930*), ed. by A. M. Ushakov and others, 1959, 353–59 (p. 358).

96. Cited in Arlazorov, *Protazanov*, p. 177. An interview with the director of Mezhrabpom-Rus', published on 15 May 1927, states that the studio had managed to facilitate an energy supply of around two thousand amperes, which was average for a typical Moscow studio, but in the same breath mentions the need to import some 150 individual lighting units from abroad within the next two months. See 'Kino-fabrika aktsionernogo obshchestva Mezhrabpom-Rus'', *Kino-front*, 1927.5, 28; and Rakushev, 'Osveshchenie v kino-atel'e', p. 21.

97. Aleksandr Levitskii, *Rasskazy o kinematografe* (Moscow: Iskusstvo, 1964), p. 71.

98. Cited in Arlazorov, *Protazanov*, p. 174.

99. Cited in ibid., pp. 174–75.

100. 'Peterburg-Petrograd-Leningrad', in Pudovkin, *Sobranie sochinenii*, II, 53–54 (p. 53) (first publ. in *Sovetskoe kino*, 1927.2, 6).

101. For the still in question, see *Sovetskoe kino*, 1927.8–9, 27.

102. Gromov, *Kinooperator Anatolii Golovnia*, p. 65.

103. Elizabeth Kridl Valkenier, *Valentin Serov: Portraits of Russia's Silver Age* (Evanston, IL: Northwestern University Press, 2001), p. 138.

104. Ibid.

105. Pudovkin, 'Kak my delali fil'mu "Konets Sankt-Peterburga"', p. 56.

106. Clark, *Petersburg: Crucible of Revolution*, pp. 4–13.

107. Golovnia, *Svet v iskusstve operatora*, p. 126.

108. Ibid., p. 124.

109. Ibid.

110. For use of this colloquial term, see V. Pudovkin, 'Konets Sankt-Peterburga', *Sovetskii ekran*, 1927.46, 6–7 (p. 7).

111. John E. Bowlt, *Moscow and St. Petersburg in the Silver Age, 1900–1920* (London: Thames and Hudson, 2008), pp. 9–31.

112. Nilsen, *The Cinema as a Graphic Art*, pp. 67–107.

113. *Kino-zhurnal A.R.K.*, 1925.9, 5.

114. Although he does not refer explicitly to these scenes, Golovnia mentions the use of reflectors for the battlefield sequences. See Golovnia, *Svet v iskusstve operatora*, p. 126.

115. See, for example, *At the Moulin Rouge* (1892), in *Henri Toulouse-Lautrec*, ed. with introduction by Douglas Cooper (New York: Harry N. Abrams, 2004), p. 85.

116. Susan Layton, *Russian Literature and Empire: Conquest of the Caucasus from Pushkin to Tolstoy* (Cambridge: Cambridge University Press, 1994), pp. 1–14.

117. Golovnia, *Svet v iskusstve operatora*, p. 127.

118. The presence of British armed forces in this area – both Pudovkin's screenplay and the literary anecdote by Osip Brik on which it was based refer to the area being under British military control – would appear to be invented. See P. Novikov, *Grazhdanskaia voina v vostochnoi Sibiri, Rossiia zabytaia i neizvestnaia series* (Moscow: Tsentropoligraf, 2005), pp. 128–29.

119. Golovnia, 'Broken Cudgels', p. 148.

120. Ibid.

121. Ibid., pp. 128 & 129.
122. A. Valiuzhenich, *Osip Maksimovich Brik: Materialy k biografii* (Akmola: Niva, 1993), pp. 230–34.
123. Amy Sargeant, *Storm over Asia*, KINOfiles Film Companion 11 (London: I. B. Tauris, 2007), p. 2.
124. N. K. [Nikolai Kaufman], '"Potomok Chingis-Khana"', *Sovetskii ekran*, 1928.31, 5.
125. Golovnia, 'Broken Cudgels', p. 148.
126. Golovnia, *Svet v iskusstve operatora*, p. 128.
127. Ibid.
128. N. K. [Nikolai Kaufman], '"Potomok Chingis-Khana"', p. 5. In the screenplay, the British general and his wife visit a monastery in order to observe Buddhist monks at prayer and meet the lama. There is no mention of the dance festival of Tsam. See Osip Brik, 'Potomok Chingis-Khana (literaturnyi stsenarii)', in Valiuzhenich, *Osip Maksimovich Brik*, pp. 63–73 (pp. 67–68).
129. N. Kaufman, '"Potomok Chingis-Khana"', *Kino*, 1928.35, 5.
130. Valerii Inkizhinov, 'Bair i ia', *Sovetskii ekran*, 1928.33, 7–8.
131. Ibid.
132. N. Kaufman, '"Potomok Chingis-Khana" (Beseda s rezhisserom V. Pudovkinym)', *Kino*, 1928.9, 4.
133. Emma Widdis, *Visions of a New Land: Soviet Film from the Revolution to the Second World War* (London: Yale University Press, 2003), pp. 100 & 111. See also Sargeant, *Storm over Asia*, p. 13.
134. 'Kak snimalsia "Velikii Perelet": 1. Zametki rukovoditelia s"emki (V. Shneiderov); 2. Zametki operatora (Georgii Blium)', *Kino-zhurnal A.R.K.*, 1926.1, 28–29.
135. M. Kastorin, 'S kino-apparatom po Buriatii', *Sovetskoe kino*, 1927.3, 13–14.
136. Kh. Khersonskii, 'Nanuk', *Sovetskii ekran*, 1928.36, 8.
137. *Alexander Rodchenko: Photography, 1924–54*, ed. by Lavrentiev, pp. 44–45 & 82. Brik's first engagement was as assistant director on Abram Room's 1927 documentary *Evrei na zemle*.
138. Leo Mur, 'Na fabrike "Mezhrabpom-fil'm"', *Sovetskii ekran*, 1928.39, 15.
139. O. M. Brik, 'Pobeda fakta (diskussionno)', *Kino*, 1927.14, 3. For the paradox of his position within the studio and his public advocacy of documentary film, see O. M. Brik, 'Ostaius' veren!', ibid., 1927.45, 4.
140. See N. Kaufman 'Buria i gibel' korablia (Na s"emkakh fil'my "Stekliannyi glaz" na fabrike Mezhrabpom-Fil'm'), *Sovetskii ekran*, 1928.40, 8.
141. N. Kaufman, '"Stekliannyi glaz"', *Sovetskii ekran*, 1928.44, 8–9.
142. Brik, 'RING LEFA: "Odinnadtsatyi" Vertova; "Oktiabr'" Eizenshteina', p. 326.
143. Brik, 'Potomok Chingis-Khana (literaturnyi stsenarii)', pp. 67–68.
144. Ibid., p. 68.
145. Inkizhinov, 'Bair i ia', p. 8.
146. Sergei Eizenshtein, '"My dolzhny idti ne k osuzhdeniiu Pudovkina, a k izvlecheniiu pol'zy iz dannoi temy": Dve lektsii Sergeia Eizenshteina o fil'me "Potomok Chingis-Khana"' [1928], publ. by Svetlana Ishevskaia, *Kinovedcheskie zapiski*, 68 (2004), 26–63 (pp. 41–43).
147. The first public performance of this play was staged by Vladimir Nemirovich-Danchenko at the Moscow Arts Theatre in September 1911. When the film release was announced in the press, there was speculation as to how exactly R. Perskii & Co. had acquired a copy of the text, which had not yet been published by the Niva publishing house. The family itself was upset and requested the release to be cancelled, or at least postponed, until after the play had been performed. See the letter of Aleksandra Tolstoia dated 30 August 1911 to the editors of *Teatr i zhizn'*, in *Velikii kinemo: Katalog sokhranivshikhsia igrovykh fil'mov Rossii: 1908–1919*, ed. by V. Ivanova and others (Moscow: Novoe literaturnoe obozrenie, 2002), p. 81 (first publ. in *Teatr i zhizn'*, 1911.6).

148. For details of the release, see *Sovetskie khudozhestvennye fil'my: Annotirovannyi katalog*, ed. by A. V. Macheret and others, I-III (Moscow: Iskusstvo, 1961), III, 263. On Kholodnaia's role, see Cheslav Sabinskii [Czesław Sabiński], 'Iz zapisok starogo kinomastera', *Iskusstvo kino*, 1936.5, 60–63.

149. Lev Shatov, '"Zhivoi trup"', *Kino*, 1929.16, 4.

150. Prim, '"Zhivoi trup" Fedora Otsepa', *Sovetskii ekran*, 1929.16, 6.

151. Shatov, '"Zhivoi trup"'.

152. Prim, '"Zhivoi trup" Fedora Otsepa'.

153. Denise J. Youngblood, *Movies for the Masses: Popular Cinema and Soviet Society in the 1920s* (Cambridge: Cambridge University Press, 1992), pp. 50–67.

154. Cavendish, *Soviet Mainstream Cinematography*, pp. 176–92.

155. Salt, *Film Style and Technology*, p. 176. For the influence of the 'classical montage' sequence on earlier Soviet films, see Cavendish, *Soviet Mainstream Cinematography*, pp. 89–93 & 151–52.

156. See the production still in Butovskii, *Andrei Moskvin, kinooperator*, between pp. 160 and 161.

157. Golovnia, 'Broken Cudgels', p. 149.

158. 'Kak ia rabotaiu s Tolstym', in Pudovkin, *Sobranie sochinenii*, II, 58–59 (first publ. in *Sovetskii ekran*, 1928.37, 5).

159. 'Tvorchestvo literatora v kino: O kinematograficheskom stsenarii Rzheshevskogo', in Pudovkin, *Sobranie sochinenii*, I, 79–84 (first publ. in *Na literaturnom postu*, 1930.5–6). For Golovnia's response, see 'Broken Cudgels', p. 138.

160. For the difficulties experienced with *Prostoi sluchai* (originally entitled *Ochen' khorosho zhivetsia*), see Sargeant, *Vsevolod Pudovkin*, pp. 143–48.

161. Located in the Sal'skaia steppe, Rostov province, this farm had rapidly acquired the status of showcase industrial exhibit. Images of it had featured in Eizenshtein's *Staroe i novoe* (see previous chapter), and Gor'kii had visited the site during the harvest of 1929 as part of the official celebrations of its achievements.

162. B. Vl., 'Dve kul'turfil'my', *Kino i zhizn'*, 1929.4, 5–6 (p. 5).

163. N. Kaufman, 'Fil'ma o rybe', *Sovetskii ekran*, 1929.30, 5.

164. Gromov, *Kinooperator Anatolii Golovnia*, p. 25.

165. Golovnia, *Svet v iskusstve operatora*, p. 130.

166. '"Dezertir" gotov', *Kino*, 1933.17, 1. On Pudovkin's method of editing the sound material for *Dezertir*, see '"Asinkhronnost" kak printsip zvukovogo kino', in Pudovkin, *Sobranie sochinenii*, I, 158–62 (first publ. as 'Asynchronism as a Principle of Sound Film', in Pudovkin, *Film Technique*); and 'Problema ritma v moem pervom zvukovom fil'me', in Pudovkin, *Sobranie sochinenii*, I, 163–66 (first publ. as 'Rhythmic Problems in My First Sound Film', in Pudovkin, *Film Technique*).

167. Jeremy Hicks, *Dziga Vertov: Defining Documentary Film* (London: I. B. Tauris, 2007), pp. 71–89.

168. On the influence of Tisse, see '"Vstrecha na El'be": Stenogramma zasedaniia operatorskoi sektsii SRK, 1949, 9 marta', in A. D. Golovnia, *O kinooperatorskom masterstve* (Moscow: VGIK, 1970), pp. 103–08 (pp. 103–04).

CHAPTER FOUR

Andrei Moskvin and the Factory of the Eccentric Actor

He had perfect command of technology in order not to be a technician.[1]

Introduction

The films of the Factory of the Eccentric Actor (FEKS) are the least studied of the Soviet avant-garde. Although pamphlets and monographs on the careers of Kozintsev and Trauberg appeared during the Soviet era, and although the regeneration of interest in the movement since 1991 has spawned documents, memoirs and interviews which clarify its anarchic and surreal beginnings, the films released by this collective during the silent era have been relatively neglected in critical terms.[2] FEKS started life as an experimental theatre group committed to eccentric, improvised comedy which combined anti-bourgeois *épatage* with the staging of various types of fairground-style attraction and gag. The first FEKS manifesto, promulgated at a public meeting in December 1921 and subsequently expanded into a series of programmatic statements (the pamphlet entitled *Ekstsentrizm* (Eccentrism), which made its appearance in early 1922), cited a variety of influences: Marinetti's Futurist manifestos on theatre, Nat Pinkerton detective novels, variety performance, cabaret, *chanson*, jazz, the circus and poster art; in other words, what may generally be described as 'boulevard culture'.[3] The collective's particular fascination was reserved for Charlie Chaplin, who had been claimed by the Dadaist movement in Europe, and whose film *The Kid* (1921) had provoked a scandal by being banned in Germany and France.[4] Bulgakova, on the basis of statements published in *Ekstsentrizm*, has described the FEKS world view at this time in terms of 'life as a stunt'.[5] While the move into film was characterized by a greater degree of sobriety, the first works of the collective nevertheless preserved its interest in burlesque, pastiche, parody and the carnivalesque. Constantly exploring new territory in terms of content, form and style, subsequent FEKS productions were united by an attitude of generic playfulness, or what the Formalist literary theorist Iurii Tynianov described at the time as 'genre emancipation'.[6] By the end of the 1920s, having come under attack for their seeming reluctance to engage with contemporary issues, FEKS appeared to have exhausted their sources of invention. Boris Alpers, for example, a theatre specialist closely allied to Meierkhol'd during the 1920s, argued that FEKS had privileged aesthetics over social content to such an extent that their films had become mere 'album[s] of illustrations'. In his view, this was the very antithesis of cinema, and thus the most reactionary tendency in contemporary Soviet film.[7]

One does not need to share Alpers's brutal condemnation of FEKS in order to appreciate the pertinence of his observation that 'subject-matter for FEKS is simply a formal pretext for an exercise in stylization'.[8] Although his observation mostly applied to the films released after *Chertovo koleso*, Alpers's remarks in relation to the improvised theatrical performances of the early period, with their 'absence of social content and even logical sense', imply that, for him, the roots of the later malaise could be found at the movement's inception.[9] Certainly, with the release of *Shinel'*, the subversive screen adaptation of Gogol''s short story, the FEKS collective embarked on a journey that would take its members close to the Formalists and their interest in the literary text as a site for generic play. It is symptomatic of this unofficial alliance that Tynianov composed the screenplay for *Shinel'*, and that his conceptual approach may well have been influenced by the groundbreaking essay on 'Shinel'' by Eikhenbaum, his fellow Formalist theoretician, which had been published in 1919.[10] The 'elective affinity' is evidenced by Tynianov's subsequent involvement in the screenplay for *SVD*, the third full-length FEKS feature, and Moskvin and Mikhailov's contribution to the collection of essays on the poetics of cinema which Eikhenbaum edited in the same year.[11] In a later review of his collaborations with FEKS, Tynianov revealed that *Shinel'* and *SVD* had been conceived as weapons aimed at mainstream film culture: the first, which scandalized critics and confused viewers because it mixed themes, motifs and details from several Gogol' stories, assaulted the conventions of the screen adaptation as encapsulated by *Kollezhskii registrator*; while the second, which poeticized the ill-fated revolt in January 1826 by generals and officers of the Southern League, the more radical wing of the Decembrist movement, sought to subvert the conventions of the historical costume drama (what Tynianov disparagingly dismissed as 'moving picture galleries').[12] This interest in genre and form may have been anathema to commentators like Alpers, and indeed became acutely problematic in view of the denunciations of 'formalism' which began to surface in 1928, but for Tynianov the FEKS films were valuable vehicles by means of which historical events could be made comprehensible and relevant to modern-day audiences.[13] The Formalist 'adoption' of FEKS is further evidenced by Shklovskii's introduction to Vladimir Nedobrovo's 1928 pamphlet, the first study of FEKS, in which he (Shklovskii) defined eccentricity as a 'battle against the habitual in daily life'.[14]

This chapter concerns itself with the visual language of the FEKS films of the 1920s. Like the other avant-garde units, FEKS was collectivist in spirit, and the style of its films was undeniably the product of close collaboration between like-minded artists. The creative geniuses behind the formation of the collective, Kozintsev and Trauberg, while only fifteen and nineteen years old, respectively, when FEKS came into being, were gifted individuals who were largely responsible for its subsequent evolution. From its initial beginnings, FEKS consisted of a group of talented artists from the world of theatre and the circus who pioneered an eccentric approach to comic material which, while it may have failed to gain many adherents in the 1930s due to the restrictive practices of Socialist Realism, would nevertheless reemerge three decades later in the form of Aleksandr Alov and Vladimir Naumov's *Skvernyi anekdot* (A Nasty Story, 1966), a screen adaptation of the 'Gogolian' short story by Fedor Dostoevskii, and five decades later in the eccentric works of Kira Muratova. Several members of FEKS, most importantly Kozintsev and Iutkevich (who joined the collective in the summer of 1922), had received training in the visual arts.[15] Furthermore, FEKS could rely on the talents of Evgenii Enei, a Hungarian-born artist who designed many of the sets for Sevzapkino (later Leningradkino and Lenfil'm) during the 1920s, and whose career within the Soviet film industry spanned nearly five decades (the last production on which he worked was Kozintsev's screen adaptation of *King Lear* in 1971). Another crucial figure within the nucleus of FEKS was Moskvin, a cameraman who joined the movement relatively late, having been introduced to Kozintsev and Trauberg only in the summer of 1925, but whose career, like Enei's, would be associated with both directors for the next two decades, and with Kozintsev, after his split with Trauberg in 1946, for the following fifteen years. As close colleagues and kindred spirits, despite several moments of disagreement, Moskvin and Kozintsev would make seventeen films in total together before the former's death in 1961 (this number does not include projects which did not reach fruition or which, having been completed, were not released).

The importance of Moskvin for the creation of the FEKS visual style was universally acknowledged at the time. His influence and significance within

Lenfil'm are attested by the substantial number of memoirs dedicated to his life and career, as well as the recent publication of a critical biography.[16] This degree of attention, which goes well beyond the memorialization process prompted by the deaths of other camera operators of the avant-garde, demonstrates that Moskvin was a crucial figure not only within FEKS, but also within Leningradkino and later Lenfil'm, where he was regarded as the guiding spirit of the so-called 'Leningrad school' of cinematography. This 'school' consisted of friends and colleagues, most notably Mikhailov, Gordanov and Sviatoslav Beliaev, but also the younger generation of camera operators who emerged from the GTK in the late 1920s: Aleksandr Gintsburg, Vladimir Rapaport, Zhozef Martov and Evgenii Shapiro.[17] This closely knit group, as well as sharing expertise, advice and opinions, was united around a core set of values and beliefs. The memoirs of Gordanov are revealing about the collaborative spirit which existed within and between the film units operating in Leningrad at this time. His own close friendship with Moskvin, which began at the age of fourteen while they were at school, resulted in photographic experiments in the early 1920s, the evolution of shared artistic tastes and sensibilities, and mutual cooperation on their respective film projects.[18] Although the written testimony in relation to the evolution of this 'school' is solid, however, the physical evidence for its existence is comparatively fragile. Its great tragedy lies in the fact that a bomb dropped by the German air force on Pushkin, the settlement just outside Leningrad where the main storage facility for the film studios was located, destroyed many of the camera negatives struck during this period and consigned several works to oblivion.[19] At the time of writing, it would appear that five films shot by Moskvin during the 1920s, three of them in collaboration with the FEKS directors, have perished. They are: *Pokhozhdeniia Oktiabriny* (The Adventures of Oktiabrina, 1924), *Mishki protiv Iudenicha* (The Mishkas vs. Iudenich, 1925), *Bratishka* (Little Brother, 1926), *Turbina no. 3* (Turbine Nr. 3, 1927) and *Chuzhoi pidzhak* (Someone Else's Jacket, 1927).[20] Furthermore, two FEKS works from this decade are incomplete: *Chertovo koleso* is missing the third and sixth parts; and *SVD* has only recently been restored to full health, albeit with a 'happy end' intended only for export, courtesy of the Cinémathèque Royale de Belgique.[21]

The 'Leningrad school' was characterized by a particular fascination for the poetic properties of light. At the beginning of his career, Moskvin was recognized as someone influenced by the aesthetics of French Impressionism and, although this has not been emphasized to anything like the same extent, the Pictorialist movement in still photography.[22] If the 'Moscow school', represented by Tisse, was characterized by a preference for the graphic and linear, the 'Leningrad school' was painterly in temperament and evinced a strong interest in texture and tonal nuance. As Golovnia observed many years later, Moskvin tended to light not so much the object itself, but rather the space around the object, and in this way endeavoured to increase the perception of spatial depth within the frame: in painting and photography this is known as aerial or atmospheric perspective.[23] Some have credited Moskvin with the invention of 'zonal lighting'.[24] His innovations in the sphere of lighting were accompanied by experiments with the use of smoke within the studio, a technique for supplying aerial perspective which, as far as studio cinematography is concerned, is thought to have originated with G. W. 'Billy' Bitzer, the first-choice cameraman of Griffith for much of his career.[25] Although Moskvin made the discovery by accident while shooting *Chertovo koleso*, he quickly grasped that smoke has the capacity to alter the optical quality of air by changing the colours of objects and softening their contours. Applying smoke in varying densities, and with a subtle understanding of how colour translated onto orthochromatic film stock, Moskvin achieved an astonishingly varied saturation and richness of tone. Furthermore, he quickly established a reputation for portraiture and developed a series of lighting methods that would be imitated by his pupils in subsequent years. The evolution of these techniques became exceedingly complex with the passage of time; indeed, one account from the late 1930s describes his positioning of eight separate lighting units for a single close-up.[26]

Moskvin was a living legend, known to everyone employed at Leningradkino and Lenfil'm, not just those in the camera-operating department or the processing laboratories. At the same time, nevertheless, he has remained something of an enigma, a person who was paradoxical in his combination of personality traits. By all accounts he was taciturn, formal and dour in his relations with colleagues. He wore blue overalls while working on set and spat on the floor to indicate where he wanted actors to stand, both defiantly proletarian affectations, albeit thoroughly in tune with the spirit of the 1920s.[27] At the same time, he had a penchant for ironic wit and eccentricity, and a degree of quasi-aristocratic flamboyance. In his youth, for example, he belonged to a group of students whose behaviour and dress codes were modelled on the English dandy; their particular affection was reserved for Oscar Wilde, and the name they gave themselves (the 'Bunburyists') was drawn from the invented, sickly friend of Algernon Moncrieff in *The Importance of Being Earnest*.[28] Further testimony to Moskvin's eccentricity can be found in the strange contraption he drove around Leningrad in the 1930s, a 'sports car' that had been customized from various bits and pieces of scrap metal, and sprayed canary yellow, a provocative choice bearing in mind the sobriety for which the decade is famous. According to Bleiman (although he neglects a celebrated predecessor in the form of Maiakovskii's Renault), this was a time when private possession of a car was less a rarity than a 'myth'.[29] Furthermore, although it was jokingly christened 'Antilopa Gnu' (The Wildebeest) by friends after the car in Zolotoi telenok (The Golden Calf, 1931), the hugely popular novel by Il'f and Petrov, it was typical of Moskvin's fondness for collecting bric-a-brac and engineering bricolage in general.[30] This eccentric tendency, while certainly reflective of the public ethos of FEKS in the 1920s, did not apparently conflict with his attitude to his work, which was methodical, professional and disciplined. This attitude was encapsulated in his legendary catchphrase, 'Natura – dura!' ('Nature is a fool!'), which expressed his contempt for things that could not be controlled or manipulated, for example weather conditions on external locations, the unpredictability of which could waste valuable time.[31] Despite his terseness, defensiveness and, on occasion, rudeness, Moskvin was a loyal friend and encouraging mentor, someone who, when he recognized talent, protected and nurtured it.[32]

Moskvin: Background, Education and Early Photographic Experiments

Moskvin was born on 1 February 1901 (Old Style) into a respectable middle-class family. His father, an engineer by profession, had worked for forty-five years on the railways before becoming director of the Sormovo locomotive factory, one of the largest in Russia before the October Revolution. Moskvin was educated at the lyceum in Tsarskoe Selo, developed an interest in chemistry in his teenage years, and on leaving his gymnasium was accepted at the chemical faculty of the Petrograd Technological Institute. He studied there for three years, after which, in the autumn of 1921, he transferred to the Petrograd Institute of Railway Communications, where he stayed for a further three years before being expelled. The reasons for his expulsion are not clear, although it might be deemed indicative that during this same period the 'Bunburyists' were pursuing a lifestyle dedicated to the dandyish notion of lack of substance. Via his acquaintance with Gordanov, who was studying at the Petrograd Higher Photo-Technical Institute, and at that moment enjoying several weeks of work experience with the veteran camera operator Nikolai Efremov on *N + N + N* (*'Nini, nalog, nepriatnost'*) (N + N + N ('Nini, New Taxes and Nastiness'), 1924), Moskvin managed to minimize the damage of his expulsion by being accepted as an unpaid assistant at Sevzapkino. He was employed initially on *N + N + N*, where he ran errands for Efremov. In the same capacity, he worked on Aleksandr Ivanovskii's *Stepan Khalturin* (1925), this time alongside Ivan Frolov and Fridrikh (also known as Fedor) Verigo-Darovskii, both of whom had started their careers in the pre-revolutionary era, and then later alongside Beliaev, who was making his debut as a cameraman on Semen Tymoshenko's *Napoleon-gaz* (Napoleon-gas, 1925). Because of Beliaev's subsequent illness, Moskvin was invited to be second cameraman on Pudovkin's *Mekhanika golovnogo mozga*.³³ In his memoirs, Kozintsev describes Moskvin hanging around the studio at this time and touting his photographs in order to be taken seriously as a potential camera operator.³⁴ It was only on 15 June 1925, however, a few weeks after meeting Kozintsev and Trauberg for the first time, that Moskvin was invited to work on *Chertovo koleso*.

Photography had been one of Moskvin's passions from a relatively early age, and his amateur works offer important clues in relation to his particular artistic affiliations. His family possessed a portable Kodak from before the war, but this was abandoned in 1924 when he managed to purchase a Universal Palmos camera, albeit without a functioning lens. Having read about the very simplest kind of lens, the monocle lens, in a German photographic manual dating from the 1880s, Moskvin and Gordanov started experimenting with a magnifying glass combined with primitive lighting in the form of an electric light bulb and salt-print paper. An album of twenty-five photographs has survived which includes portraits of their fellow 'Bunburyists', one of whom is dressed like Sherlock Holmes, and a series of ten photographs given the collective title *Dom no. 13: Kinodrama* (House Nr. 13: Film-Drama), the contents of which suggest a parody of the 'low-life' dramas popular in cinemas at this time.³⁵ The amateur provenance of these photographs is obvious. Nevertheless, as Gordanov points out, some of them betray the guiding principles of their later camerawork by virtue of the detailed study of the effects of 'light patches'.³⁶ Having shown their work to Ivan Ponomarev, one of the lecturers at the Higher Photo-Technical Institute, the two students were directed to information on the so-called Pettsval lens for portraiture. At around the same time, via V. B. Beringer, who was also a lecturer at the college, but someone who specialized in artistic photography, they were introduced to the work of David Octavius Hill and Robert Adamson, two of the early pioneers of the calotype process whose photographs were characterized by a certain softness of image.[37] They were also recommended works by Eduard Steichen, presumably from his Pictorialist period. The lecturers defined the two students' photography as 'romantic' – a far cry, it would appear, from the eccentric tradition from which Moskvin's future partners had emerged a couple of years earlier.[38]

The Origins and Development of FEKS

Kozintsev and Trauberg became acquainted in the summer of 1920 at the Comic Opera Theatre, which had just been established by Konstantin Mardzhanov in Petrograd, and where they were both employed as assistants.[39] One year previously, Kozintsev had staged a pantomime at the Harlequin Theatre in Kyiv, the city of his birth, but he was better known as a decorator and designer of stage sets. He had briefly attended evening classes given by Aleksandra Ekster, the Cubo-Futurist artistic director of Aleksandr Tairov's Kamernyi Theatre. While these classes could not accurately be described as formal training, the contacts he acquired nevertheless led to Kozintsev's involvement in the decoration of agit-trains during the Civil War and an invitation to design sets for the Lenin Theatre under the supervision of Isaak Rabinovich. Here he collaborated on several productions directed by Mardzhanov and decided to follow the theatre director to Petrograd.[40] In the same year, Trauberg arrived from Odessa: he was writing verse plays and seeking entry into the world of theatre. His first attempt at dramatic writing, *Dzhin Dzhentl'men i rasputnaia butylka* (Djinn Gentleman and the Dissolute Bottle), was written in the summer of 1920 but deemed so absurd and provocative that Mardzhanov refused to stage it.[41] Partly on account of this refusal, the two young men decided to pursue their ambitions independently of their mentor. Along with Georgii Kryzhitskii, an artist associated with the Krivoe zerkalo (Crooked Mirror) cabaret, Kozintsev and Trauberg founded a 'Depot for Eccentrics' (Depo ekstsentrikov) and helped organize the now legendary 'Manifest ekstsentricheskogo teatra' ('Debate on Eccentric Theatre').[42] The formal inauguration of FEKS followed in the summer of 1922, after which preparations began for a stage spectacle based on the 'electrification' of Gogol''s *Zhenit'ba* (The Marriage, 1842). The première, which took place on 25 September 1922, was full of gags, stunts and circus-style attractions, and was for the most part improvised. The next FEKS stage production, *Vneshtorg na Eifelevoi bashne* (The

Foreign Export Co. on the Eiffel Tower) was better organized, but essentially another short-lived experiment, a one-off 'happening' in the Futurist mould, after which the group decided that their future lay in cinema. Their first libretto, *Zhenshchina Edisona* (Edison's Woman), took the subject of a female electrical robot, built by the well known American inventor, who decides to come to the Soviet Union and install herself as part of the Volkhovstroi power station; the libretto was offered to the studio management of Sevzapkino but rejected.[43] The second, *Pokhozhdeniia Oktiabriny*, was accepted, but only on the insistence of Boris Chaikovskii, a director of pre-revolutionary vintage who nevertheless appeared willing to support FEKS initiatives (he was nominally assigned the role of director, but essentially left the two novices to their own devices).[44] In the same year, FEKS released a short publicity film, *Krasnaia gazeta* (The Red Newspaper, 1924), fragments of which appear to have survived (the camera operator was V. Glass, prior to this moment an assistant working alongside Frolov at Sevzapkino).[45] This early period also included a comedy for children, *Mishki protiv Iudenicha*, which was intended as a parody of Perestiani's hugely popular *Krasnye d'iavoliata*.[46]

Although *Pokhozhdeniia Oktiabriny* has not survived, the details of the plot and its treatment in cinematic terms can be gauged by a number of sources: an interview with Kozintsev and Trauberg which appeared in the newspaper *Kino-nedelia* two weeks before the film's release;[47] a plot synopsis helpfully released by the publicity department of Sevzapkino as part of a well orchestrated advertising campaign in the same paper;[48] a number of production stills, some of which featured in this campaign;[49] and the various memoirs and interviews given by the directors and other members of the collective which appeared many years later.[50]

In the weeks before the release, Kozintsev and Trauberg emphasized the 'experimental' quality of the film, its 'demonstration of [eccentric] acting technique', its 'novelties in the sphere of the trick shot' and the 'new approach to the composition of the frame'.[51] They referred to the purely 'eccentric' connections between the individual episodes; the rapid tempo of the plot; the 'poster-like' use of political slogans; the resort to modern modes of transport; the activation of Leningrad's modern, industrial spaces, rather than its classical facades; the unconventional camera angles; the exploitation of high buildings as arenas for dangerous and eccentric stunts; and the adoption of reverse action, slow motion and speeded-up motion for comic effect.[52]

The plot synopsis released by the studio suggests an energetic combination of agitprop theatre, circus-style stunts and 'Red Pinkerton' chases. The three main characters are Oktiabrina, a model Komsomol member and head of a housing committee who is attempting to transform her local community along progressive Soviet lines and checks that the residents are community-spirited; a typical product of the NEP period, a so-called 'NEPman', who is resident in the building but pretends to be unemployed and refuses to pay his taxes; and a so-called 'minister-interventionist', Kullidzh Kerzonovich Puankare, a figure dressed in a clown's costume who is clearly a synthetic caricature of John Calvin Coolidge, Lord Curzon and Raymond Poincaré (he appears like a malevolent genie from a bottle of beer and is intent on robbing a bank in order to recoup international debts owed by the deposed tsar). Oktiabrina's attempt to bring these two reactionary figures to justice consists of several chase sequences that feature a camel advertising the Leningrad Food Trust; a fire engine, the ladder of which is used to ascend St Isaac's Cathedral; an aeroplane; industrial cranes; and the roofs of the cathedral and a state bank. The film is also characterized by a series of semi-surreal gags, the most striking of which is Oktiabrina's 'mobile office' (a motorbike equipped with megaphone and typewriter).

For all the comic invention of this film, and despite the claims made by the directors in advance, *Pokhozhdeniia Oktiabriny* appears to have been relatively conventional in terms of its visual aesthetic. Part of the problem lay in the choice of camera operator: Verigo-Darovskii was a product of the pre-revolutionary era and for this reason, according to the directors, insufficiently inventive. In terms of spirit and temperament, he was certainly eccentric enough to belong to the FEKS team. Like Zinaida Tarkhovskaia, the actress playing the role of the eponymous heroine, Verigo-Darovskii had trained in his youth as a ballet dancer. This doubtless explained his strange behaviour when introduced to the directors. According to Kozintsev, having asked in a thick Polish accent whether he (Kozintsev) was FEKS, but without waiting for a reply, Verigo-Darovskii danced into the middle of the room, stood on his head and exclaimed 'Voila!'.[53] In a similar vein, at the end of the day's shooting, it was apparently his custom to take a bow, retreat in the direction of the exit, blow kisses to everyone present and disappear from view.[54] Kozintsev has described his 'fakir-like pose' on preparing the camera for double exposures, which was followed by a few skips in the air, a capriole and his triumphant announcement that 'The trick shot, sirs, has been completed!'.[55] Verigo-Darovskii's intrepid and adventurous spirit was not open to question: he had taken serious risks while filming epidemics before the Revolution and actuality footage along various fronts during the First World War. Furthermore, unlike

Levitskii, he appeared unfazed by scenes filmed at great heights. Gordanov, for example, who witnessed the shooting of the film, recalls him standing on the roof of St Isaac's Cathedral, very near the edge of the cupola, with one foot resting on his tripod.[56] Although this particular moment has not been captured by any surviving production stills, there is an analogous image that shows Verigo-Darovskii sitting astride an iron railing that runs along the glass roof of a building, with both feet resting on the tripod, and presumably a steep drop behind him.[57]

Such composure, however, albeit coupled with a liberal recourse to expletives, was not a sufficient condition for fruitful collaboration. Gordanov, who had access to the rushes and watched the film after its release, has commented that very little of the cameraman's eccentric personality was detectable in the actual footage. Kozintsev subsequently dubbed him a 'child of the "Elektrobiograf"', a reference to the cinemas that sprung up like mushrooms in turn-of-the-century Russia, and thus an allusion to his outmoded way of thinking.[58] Despite their friendly relations, it was Verigo-Darovskii's lack of creative initiative, witnessed by his routine enquiry at the beginning of the day's shooting – 'So, what do you want me to do?' – which proved decisive; for Kozintsev and Trauberg, it was not a technician that they required, but rather a 'comrade' and 'inventor'.[59] The failure of the collaboration, although it was not necessarily reflected in the responses of critics and viewers, some of whom clearly appreciated the film's attempt to combine entertainment and propaganda, proved instructive. It marked the end of the FEKS passion for the bizarre as a self-sufficient artistic objective.[60] Furthermore, dissatisfaction with the relationship, which was confirmed after the making of *Mishki protiv Iudenicha*, prompted the directors to approach Moskvin, despite the fact that, for Kozintsev at least, the aspiring camera operator's experiments in the realm of still photography were not particularly impressive (in criticizing them for 'lack of focus', however, he was inadvertently revealing his ignorance of recent photographic trends).[61]

Chertovo koleso: Going around in Circles

The screenplay of *Chertovo koleso* was written by Adrian Piotrovskii, a literature and theatre specialist who was serving at the time as the head of the literary section of Sevzapkino. It was adapted from a short novel, *Konets khazy* (The End of the Dive), by Veniamin Kaverin, a young writer who at the time was a member of the Serapion Brothers.[62] The film tells the story of a young sailor from the *Avrora* – the epitome of Bolshevik rectitude because of its iconic role during the storming of the Winter Palace – and his enticement into a world of low-life characters inhabiting a decrepit building on the outskirts of Leningrad. Having decided to visit a fairground in the gardens of the House of Culture with his shipmates, the hero, Vania Shorin, finds himself seduced by the entertainments on offer, among them an attractive young woman named Valia, whose acquaintance he makes on a roller coaster. Vania loses contact with his crew, fails to return to the cruiser by the appointed hour and ends up spending the night and next few days in Valia's company. Their subsequent adventures bring them into the orbit of criminals, among them a magician, referred to only by his stage name, Chelovek-vopros (Mr Question-Mark), whom they have seen perform at the House of Culture, and who takes advantage of their relative naivety to entangle them in a web of low-level brigandage. The viewer is transported from the bustling fairground at the House of Culture, with its clowns, magicians, performers, head-spinning rides and firework displays, to the abandoned building that Mr Question-Mark and his accomplices have made their home. From there, the viewer is invited to the 'Institute of Plastic Arts', which turns out to be an illegal drinking and dancing den regularly raided by the authorities; a workers' beer hall; and a workers' club, which appears to be hosting an agitprop production. Troubled by his conscience, Vania gradually prises himself apart from Valia and the motley crew of robbers and decides to return to his cruiser just at the moment when a Bolshevik army unit arrives to purge the building of its disreputable element. After a violent shoot-out, Mr Question-Mark tries to escape along the rooftop of the building and drops a hand grenade on the troops below, inadvertently causing the whole building to collapse into a heap of rubble. The final intertitle suggests that, while such buildings may not be a rarity, all those that house similar criminal elements will slowly but surely meet the same fate.

Chertovo koleso clearly represents a development away from the circus-like stunts and surreal stylization of *Pokhozhdeniia Oktiabriny* towards a more sombre appreciation of contemporary realia. The counterparts of the low-life characters of Mr Question-Mark and his criminal accomplices are the conman Zhban and his gang of thugs in Kuleshov's *Neobychainye prikliucheniia,* and the *shpana* (riff-raff or tramps) in Eizenshtein's *Stachka*. The difference, however, lies in the fascination with fairground material and the particular way in which this material is represented. The scenes that take place in the House of Culture, for example, contain all the elements of the popular entertainments celebrated in the early FEKS manifestos. Furthermore, there is an energy and dynamism about the visual presentation of this material which seeks to communicate the exhilaration of this culture. The use of a mobile camera, rather than montage, is the main vehicle by which this sensation is achieved. Positioned on trucks as the couple hurtle along the 'American mountain' – the name given to the roller coaster in Russia in the early twentieth century – Moskvin's camera looks backwards, forwards and sideways with giddying effect. According to Leonid Kosmatov, a GTK graduate and later professional camera operator, the footage created something of a 'furore' at the time.[63] The camera is also positioned on the so-called 'Devil's Wheel' (a rotating platform) and records the blurred moments when bodies are flung off by the centrifugal force. Another revolving vantage point is supplied by a merry-go-round. Self-evidently, these scenes are attractions in the literal sense of the word; indeed, in several respects they evoke some of the earliest forms of actuality footage, the so-called 'phantom rides' or 'shoot-the-chutes', which sought to replicate the sensation of rapid movement and were highly popular with audiences in the early years of cinema.[64] Bearing in mind the known interest in popular culture, it is possible that FEKS was influenced by treatments of fairground material in U.S. comedies, for example Harold Lloyd's *Number, Please?* (1920), which takes place for the most part in an amusement park and also includes material shot from a roller coaster, albeit at a more sedate pace. A similar exploitation of a merry-go-round and the paraphernalia of the fair, while nevertheless combined with a more menacing dramatic tension, can be found in *Coeur fidèle* (A Faithful Heart, 1923), a film directed by Epstein which was certainly known to the FEKS collective, although it is not exactly clear when its members first had access to it.[65]

The symbolic associations of fairground material nevertheless distinguish *Chertovo koleso* from its actuality and fiction-film precursors. Most importantly, the revolving footage reflects the structural dynamic of the narrative itself in the sense that this follows a broadly cyclical pattern. The circle as a visual paradigm is signalled early in the film when Moskvin adopts a narrow iris for the shots of the *Avrora* and Mr Question-Mark's poster. The same shape is evoked by the porthole through which Vania looks ashore; the round faces of the clocks that remind the couple that time is ticking away; the 'Devil's Wheel' itself, which is later transformed into an imaginary clock; the shots of a spinning Catherine wheel, its fireworks fizzing and exploding, and at one point providing a scintillating halo behind the silhouetted couple which is emblematic of their 'exploding' feelings for each other; the scenes at the 'Institute of Plastic Arts', where the couple are shown dancing with each other while the rest of the hall appears to revolve around them; and the recourse to a multiple exposure, essentially Vania's drunken point of view, which involves a circular motion of the camera around the figures of dancing couples.

The second element that contributes to the fairground atmosphere is the use of chiaroscuro. This is consistent with the expressive approach to lighting generally in the film and distinguishes it markedly from its immediate predecessor, *Pokhozhdeniia Oktiabriny*. Many of the scenes at the House of Culture take place at night, in the dark (the roller-coaster sequence, because it was shot during a white night, apparently had to be tinted blue in order to maintain consistency with the rest of the sequence).[66] From the technical point of view, such scenes as those of the female tightrope walkers at the House of Culture were made possible by the availability of projector arcs. Although not a novelty at this time, as Levitskii's images of the Bronze Horseman for Eizenshtein's *1905 god* make starkly clear, their deployment by Moskvin is striking in the sense that they are aimed just above the heads of crowds, rather than directly at the photographed object, and are sometimes positioned so that they face the camera. This gives rise to a broad, flaring effect that accords naturally with the explosions provided by the fireworks. The composition showing the tightrope walkers, one of whom is illuminated by the rays of a projector positioned off-screen left and the other shot in silhouette by means of a second source placed in the depths of the frame, with the crowd puffing cigarette smoke into the air, has passed into legend because it was the first sequence to be filmed, and thus to some extent established the visual dynamics of the rest of the production.[67] The same scene also apparently triggered Moskvin's interest in the effects of smoke.[68] The most impressive feature of this image, however, is its metaphoric power, the distant position and high angle of the camera combining with the lighting to accentuate the jostling movements of the crowd, to the extent that the mass of bodies seems to swell and heave like an ocean tide. While it provides an ironic reversal of the smooth waters in the port where the *Avrora* lies at anchor, this impression is nevertheless perfectly in keeping with the ship-like, rocking effect produced by the shots from the roller coaster. The employment of a mobile spotlight for the 'Devil's Wheel' sequence – it seeks to pinpoint the bodies of the couple as they spin around like a mini-searchlight (Fig. 24) – was a masterstroke that predates by two years Tisse's adoption of the same device for the Finland Station sequence in *Oktiabr'*.

The fractured and fragmented quality of these images, with vision often obscured and sharp focus compromised, at times borders on the oneiric. Fairground material was part of the staple diet of German Expressionism, in both theatre and film, and it is interesting to observe the moments when *Chertovo koleso* moves self-consciously into this visual terrain. Two of the more obvious instances resort to grotesque exaggeration by means of optical distortion. The close-up in which one of Mr Question-Mark's associates holds up a bottle in front of the camera, for example, clearly involves use of a wide-angle lens in order to produce a distortion of perspective. Building on this device, Moskvin twice uses anamorphosis by means of a distorting mirror, as might be found in the fairground (exactly the same kind of mirror is exploited for comic purposes in *Number, Please?*). While optical distortion was relatively commonplace in the early 1920s – see, for example, Jacques Feyder's *Jérôme Crainquebille* (Coster Bill of Paris, 1922) and Murnau's *Der letzte Mann* – it was invariably adopted to evoke a hallucinatory vision and was thus essentially a subjective point of view, rather than the objective portrayal of something sinister and unappetizing.[69] The evocation of the uncanny and unedifying in *Chertovo koleso* is echoed in the low-angle lighting employed for the portraits of the clown and magician at the fairground (Fig. 25); the portraits of the *shpana* in their dilapidated abode; and the close-up of the man who threatens Vania with a knuckleduster outside the workers' club. This technique, while at times motivated by the light sources which might realistically be expected within the purported location (footlights in the case of the fairground and a fire around which the men are huddled in the case of the *shpana*), nevertheless has a sinister effect. Although the atmosphere is not quite as macabre, the FEKS presentation of fairground material has certain analogues in the sphere of German drama and film, for example Ernst Toller's 1923 play *Hinkemann*, in which the main protagonist, a demobilized soldier, ekes out a precarious existence as a fairground attraction by breaking the necks of rats and drinking their blood; or Paul Leni's *Das Wachsfigurenkabinett* (The Waxworks Museum, 1924), the fourth episode of which ('Jack the Ripper') positions the fairground as a menacing and hallucinatory hunting ground for the notorious British killer.

As a site for entertainment and excitement, but also one that carries the risk of ideological contamination, the fairground as treated by FEKS in *Chertovo koleso* constitutes an ambiguous comment on the attractions of the carnival. It is by no means untypical for the post-revolutionary period, however.[70] On the one hand, as the archetypal embodiment of street culture, the fairground is approached as the essence of modern urban experience, its assortment of rides producing the sensation of speed and movement that was celebrated by the Italian Futurists.[71] On the other hand, because it represented a type of popular culture still contaminated by vestiges of the backward, pre-revolutionary past, the fairground represented a potential threat to the new, revolutionary order. As depicted in *Chertovo koleso*, carnival is envisaged as a 'holiday' from Bolshevik rectitude which the hero must ultimately forsake in order not to be compromised by it. Furthermore, the amusements on offer can only be enjoyed once the more disreputable elements have been purged and replaced by a healthier and more obviously Soviet type of entertainment. This reinforces the idea, implied in *Pokhozhdeniia Oktiabriny*, that FEKS was engaged in the sovietization of boulevard culture, and therefore to some extent its neutering, rather than its straightforward and exuberant embrace. *Chertovo koleso* might thus be regarded as a meta-film about the FEKS fascination with this kind of material and the ideological pitfalls concealed within it.

The Dislocated View: The FEKS Adaptation of Nikolai Gogol''s 'Shinel''

As mentioned previously, Tynianov's screenplay for the FEKS adaptation of 'Shinel'' incorporated themes, details and characters from a number of Gogol''s prose works. The strategy of citation is implied by the full title of the film, *Shinel'*, *kino-p'esa v manere Gogolia* (The Overcoat, a Film-Play in the Manner of Gogol'), but this does not prepare the viewer for the astonishing range of allusions, some so subtle and microscopic that they are easily missed, some of which refer to unpublished fragments of texts with which only a literary specialist would be familiar, and some to works written by authors other than Gogol'.[72] Within the category of microscopic reference, one might invoke the commercial sign displayed above the barber's shop on Nevskii Prospekt which advertises 'blood-letting' – a deliberate allusion to 'Nos' ('The Nose', 1836), another of Gogol''s Petersburg tales – and that which advertises the rooms of a 'hotel' ('Rooms of the Foreigner Ivan Fedorovich'), which alludes to a similarly worded sign in *Mertvye dushi* (Dead Souls, 1842), the curiosity lying in the seemingly unmotivated emphasis on foreign ownership. These signs are referents in a dual sense because, apart from their commercial purpose within the diegesis, they raise the spectre of a Gogolian universe or 'master text' within which several distinct stories will be interwoven. At the very least, such allusions hint that fidelity to the narrative plot line of 'Shinel'' is not the overriding concern of the FEKS adaptation. This suspicion is reinforced by the opening sequence, the action of which is derived not from 'Shinel'', as might reasonably be expected from the film's title, but from another Petersburg tale altogether, 'Nevskii Prospekt' (1835). As the film progresses, it becomes clear that Tynianov's libretto, rather in the manner of a multiple exposure, is seeking to weave together several of the Petersburg tales in order to accentuate the themes they have in common – namely, Gogol''s interest in, if not obsession with, masculine sexual and erotic appetite. In relation to 'Shinel'', the short story, Tynianov's adaptation subtly insinuates that the purchase of the new overcoat by the main protagonist, Akakii Akakievich Bashmachkin, is primarily an erotically driven act to compensate for his social alienation and emasculation at the hands of male authority figures.

Although not well received for the most part by critics and the viewing public, one of whom called for the directors to be arrested on the grounds of wasting state funds, *Shinel'* is now regarded as a masterpiece of Soviet experimental cinema.[73] In part this owes to the eccentric acting styles of the FEKS ensemble, in particular the seemingly mechanized movements and strange, shuffling gait of Andrei Kostrichkin as Bashmachkin (this gait alludes to the fictional protagonist's unfortunate affliction with haemorrhoids) and the grotesque facial grimaces of Aleksei Kapler, who plays the role of the Unimportant (and later Important) Person. The stylized quality of the FEKS production can be gauged by comparison with Murnau and Freund's *Der letzte Mann*, which also takes as its subject the crushing of the 'little man' at the hands of a ruthless and brutally indifferent authority. Despite the innovative devices of this film, among them the absence of intertitles, the persistent recourse to tracking-shots and the use of optical distortion for fantasy sequences, the world it depicts is far less disturbing than the city which supplies the backdrop for *Shinel'*. Undeniably, the superficial luxury of the hotel in *Der letzte Mann* is deconstructed to expose the ruthlessly exploitative system that operates behind its facades, yet apart from the film's final sequence, a fantasy that mercilessly exposes the emptiness of U.S.-style happy endings, this world nevertheless looks and feels recognizably 'real'. By contrast, the world of Russia's capital during the reign of Nicholas I is depicted by FEKS as grotesque, surreal and hyperbolic. This is a world in which mannequins seem more human than people; in which eccentric modes of behaviour, while superficially comic, conceal menacing, violent intentions; and where the steam emanating from kettles, samovars and bathhouses seems more tangible than physical reality. Like the Gogol' stories on which it is based, in particular 'Nevskii Prospekt', where the author-narrator warns that 'everything is a deceit, everything is a dream, and nothing is what it seems', the atmosphere is ghostly and uncanny.[74] Moskvin's lighting techniques and compositional strategies are characterized by an edginess and unpredictability which evoke the conditions of a claustrophobic, existential void. Although its subject, the decadence, corruption and moral depravity which lay at the heart of the civil service during tsarist times, was ideologically impeccable from the official point of view, the overriding vision of Shinel' might be regarded as verging on the absurd.[75]

The challenge of defining the visual style of Shinel' lies primarily in its extraordinary eclecticism. In the absence of any dramaturgical principle that would explain the (sometimes abrupt) shifts, it might be speculated that the multiplicity of contrasting methods was chiefly designed to reflect the unnerving quality of Gogol''s prose style. In this respect, as suggested earlier, the FEKS team may well have been inspired by Eikhenbaum, who explored 'Shinel'' not so much in terms of narrative content as its manner of delivery; in other words, as a contrived skaz performance characterized by constant shifts in style, tone and register, persistent punning and a peculiar penchant for words that are 'strange, enigmatic, unusual sounding and acoustically striking'.[76]

The opening sequence of Shinel' gives a foretaste of this deliberate strategy of disorientation. Superficially, it might be described as an 'establishing shot': Akakii Akakievich stands beneath a street lamp on Nevskii Prospekt and waits for the emergence of the so-called 'Woman from the Rooms' from a coffee shop across the street. The first level of disorientation lies in the fact that this scene is taken not from 'Shinel'', as might be expected, but from the opening pages of 'Nevskii Prospekt'. These describe a young painter's feverish pursuit of a woman, a 'heavenly creature' whom he fleetingly glimpses while on his ritual afternoon promenade, only to discover on entering her 'home' that she is a prostitute. The subsequent shifts in camera position in relation to this scene are unmotivated and result in a lack of orientation on the part of the viewer. After the initial 'establishing shot', the camera assumes a bewildering array of positions and regularly alters its distance and angle of vision in relation to the two figures concerned. Thus a close-up profile of Akakii Akakievich as he stands beneath the streetlamp is followed by a shot of the doorway from which the young woman will eventually emerge; at this moment, the camera is too close for this image to be regarded straightforwardly as his point of view. This shot is followed by a further close-up of Akakii Akakievich; a long-shot of the young woman as she emerges from the doorway of the shop; a medium-shot of Akakii Akakievich which is taken from a different angle, and with the young woman out of focus in the background; another close-up of Akakii Akakievich as he looks towards the young woman; another close-up of the young woman as she stands on top of the steps leading down from the coffee shop; a long-shot of the street, during which pedestrians gradually dissolve into nothingness; a shot of Akakii Akakievich as he looks over towards the young woman again, but this time with the camera set further back from the previous shot (the woman is now within the field of focus); a long-shot of the empty street, but this time from a higher angle than the previous long-shot; a return to the earlier scene with both Akakii Akakievich and the young woman in focus, but with the figures of the crowd now returning; and a return to the relatively high-angled long-shot in which the pedestrians have resumed their habitual business. Apart from the establishment of the putative relationship, which at this stage exists solely in the form of voyeuristic gazing and an implicit allusion to the hero's erotic impulses, the treatment of this sequence would appear to be emphasizing the suspension of reality which occurs as a result of Bashmachkin's feverish anticipation of her appearance. At the same time, the shifting position of the camera lacks a dramatic rationale and coherence: spatial orientation is confirmed, but the extended nature of the sequence in temporal terms and the multiplicity of viewpoints are far in excess of conventional dramaturgical necessity.

A further example of the disorientating strategies employed in *Shinel'* lies in Moskvin's approach to the poetics of soft-focus cinematography. The adoption of varying degrees of diffusion and the effects achieved by different diffusing devices mark a radical departure from the poetics of *Chertovo koleso*, although it is a strategy with obvious links to Moskvin's amateur photographic interests before his move into film. It is important to emphasize that the application of soft-focus clearly functions as the antithesis of U.S.-style glamour photography; or rather, if it can be said to evoke the practices of this vogue, it does so in a subversive fashion.[77]

Judging by the instances in which diffusion is adopted most blatantly, it might be speculated that its main purpose lies in the evocation of a dream-like atmosphere which is associated with an erotic and corrupting decadence. The most striking example occurs in relation to Akakii Akakievich's first dream. During this extended sequence, which is also modelled on scenes in 'Nevskii Prospekt', he imagines being summoned to visit the 'Woman from the Rooms' by a smartly dressed footman. When he arrives at her 'residence' by horse-drawn carriage, however, he finds not a room, but a surreal version of the very civil service department in which he is employed: officials bustle about fulfilling their routine duties, and one or two request Akakii Akakievich's signature on legal documents. To add to the confusion, the object of his fantasy is lying seductively on a desk in the middle of the office and concealing her face behind a translucent fan. Furthermore, in the background the viewer is presented with a number of figures and objects which, it can safely be presumed, do not belong to the customary office décor: an official serenely playing a harp; another juggling skittles in the air; two naked mannequins positioned next to a window; and a life-sized model of Napoleon Bonaparte.

The compositional methods adopted by Moskvin for this extended sequence involve several devices for creating softness of focus in rapid succession; as a result, the fantasy in its entirety might be regarded as a subtle form of *mise en abîme*. The announcement of the invitation, for example, takes place as Akakii Akakievich stands next to an absurdly large, boiling kettle: the clouds of steam that emanate from this prop are so dense that when the footman marches through the door to present Akakii Akakievich with his invitation, he is almost completely obscured from view. The scene in the 'department', likewise, includes a portrait of the 'Woman from the Rooms' which is heavily diffused by means of the translucent material of her fan; the same technique is employed moments later, but from a reverse angle, when Akakii Akakievich is shown from her point of view dusting himself down and collecting his thoughts after he has recovered from a faint. This image is then intercut with a further portrait of the woman which narrows the depth of field and places the human figures and objects in the background out of focus. In turn, this is succeeded by a long-shot of the 'department' in which either petroleum jelly or some other form of lubricant has been smeared around the edges of the lens to soften the peripheries of the frame. There is a further close-up of the young woman, this time in profile, which appears to have been photographed with either a diffusion disk or an uncorrected lens. Finally, the dream sequence is brought to a close by a manual 'bringing out' of focus. It is worth stressing that while these substances, materials and optical methods were standard techniques during the 1920s, it is highly unusual to find them all employed in close temporal proximity to one another. The psychological motivation behind the display of soft-focus is further echoed in the scene in which Akakii Akakievich imagines his old and worn overcoat being replaced; this suggests that, as in the source text, which describes the new coat as his 'life's companion' (*podruga zhizni*), there is a sexual imperative that underpins the purchase.

Soft-focus as a vehicle for the creation of erotic fantasy does not exhaust its potential usefulness in *Shinel'*. Nevertheless, its application elsewhere, where fantasy is not the overriding rationale, confuses the viewer's understanding of Moskvin's strategy. The first occasion is the scene in which Akakii Akakievich is shown sitting at his desk copying documents with a quill (Fig. 26). Further (moderate) applications of diffusion occur in the scene of his humiliation at the impromptu party taking place in the 'rooms', during which drink and food are thrown over his face and clothes, his nose is flicked and he is brutally thrown to the floor; during his attendance at a tea party thrown by colleagues in honour of his new acquisition; during his meeting with the Important Person after the theft of his overcoat; and during the scene in which he is shown lying in bed, seriously ill and close to death. The particular emphasis on all four occasions would appear to lie in the creation of pathos, in other words, diffusion functions in these scenes as a vehicle with which to convey sentimental vision. In view of the fact that this strategy contrasts with the application of soft-focus in the dream or reverie sequences, it might be argued that the procedure is motivated by the desire to replicate the ambiguous attitude of the author-narrator in 'Shinel''; namely, as Eikhenbaum has identified, the abrupt and unexpected shifts in tone from ridicule and caricature to compassion.[78] The treatment of the main protagonist in the FEKS adaptation is equally ambivalent: on the one hand, he is presented as the emasculated, browbeaten victim of a corrupt and inhuman governmental machine; on the other, he is exposed as a weak individual who does not question his tormentors or openly rebel against them, and is himself guilty of erotic fetishization. In this respect, albeit *avant la lettre*, Bashmachkin might be regarded as someone whose existence is hollow and empty, much in the manner of the fictional protagonist created by Tynianov in his later screenplay and short story, 'Podporuchik Kizhe' ('Second Lieutenant Kizhe', 1927), the character in question invisible to those around him but nevertheless treated as if he were a real person.[79]

Optical distortion of varying degrees functions less as an aesthetic principle in *Shinel'* than as a specific method for creating disorientation in the mind of the viewer. In this respect, it belongs to a compositional strategy that seeks to exaggerate natural phenomena and to juxtapose objects of massively different dimensions. Evidence for this strategy can be found in the use of wide-angle lenses to produce an impression of perspectival distortion and the manipulation of lighting for the purpose of exaggerated effect. The best illustration of the former is the sideways portrait of the 'Woman from the Rooms' during the dream sequence, which shows her without her customary hat and with one of the buns in her hair looming disproportionately large before the camera. The most striking example of the latter is the sequence during which Akakii Akakievich is confronted by thieves intent on divesting him of his overcoat. The mise en scène here is ingenious in the sense that the robbers are presented primarily in terms of elongated shadows which supply a menacing presence within the frame and seek to convey the unnerving and destabilizing atmosphere of the source text, according to which the theft takes place at night and the identities of the thieves are unknown. The position of the camera in relation to this mise en scène and its relatively high angle stress the puny dimensions of Akakii Akakievich in relation to these shadows. Furthermore, the edges of the frame are brought into play as the boundaries of a visual 'cage' within which the hero is trapped and from which he initially tries to escape. Having moved cautiously towards the left-hand side of the frame to avoid his assailants, Akakii Akakievich is not permitted to exit the frame and is forced back towards the centre by the appearance of two additional shadows which penetrate more and more deeply into the frame (the function of the frame-edge as a 'barrier' is apparent only when the film is presented in its correct aspect ratio (Fig. 27)). The lighting for this sequence, because of the unusually low position of the arcs, is unmotivated in terms of the supposed location, an unnamed square somewhere on the periphery of the capital. It does, however, accord with a description of Nevskii Prospekt in the story of the same title. In the relevant passage, which describes the activities of pedestrians as dusk begins to fall, the author-narrator refers to the vast shadows cast by the 'enchanting and wondrous light' of a streetlamp along the pavement and the walls of nearby buildings, the heads of these shadows, or so it is claimed, 'sometimes reaching all the way to Policeman's Bridge' (the possibility of conscious allusion is suggested by the fact that, albeit retrospectively, this same passage has been cited by Kozintsev as evidence of Gogol''s 'unusual' prose style).[80] In both cases, while clearly striving for an effect of the uncanny and grotesque, the resulting images contradict the effects that would actually have been produced by the overhead gas lamps of the period.

The grotesque exaggeration of reality in the theft sequence has its visual counterpart in the set designs by Enei; while he never resorts to the extremes of

Expressionist abstraction, as displayed, for example, in *Das Kabinett des Dr Caligari* (The Cabinet of Dr Caligari, 1920), his vision of Petersburg does nevertheless involve a measure of perspectival distortion and Gogolian wonkiness, as if everything is not quite in its proper place or has been knocked slightly off kilter. Camera angle is exploited with something of the same effect in mind. As Kozintsev has confirmed, the play with dimension, with figures appearing larger or smaller depending on their position in relation to the camera, was a deliberate strategy with which to emphasize the existence of social and sexual hierarchies. This reaches its climax in the encounter between the humiliated Akakii Akakievich and the Important Person in the film's penultimate sequence: on Moskvin's initiative, an extremely high angle was adopted in order to underline the hero's relative insignificance in relation to the ruthless power structures of the state (Fig. 28).[81] The play with dimension is not solely confined to angle of vision, however. Even when the camera is placed in an axial position in relation to the mise en scène, for instance for the moment at the beginning of the film when three of the protagonists – the 'Woman from the Rooms', the Unimportant Person and the Cheat – are presented as minute (silhouetted) figures against the illuminated façade of a hotel, the play with dimension is also emphasized. The later shots that show Akakii Akakievich dwarfed by landmark monuments after the theft of his overcoat – the statue of General Kutuzov, the statue of the Sphinx located along University Embankment and the equestrian statue of Nicholas I which stands before St Isaac's Cathedral, none of which featured in Tynianov's screenplay – further attest to the use of this device.[82] The *reductio ad absurdum* of this strategy is revealed when Akakii Akakievich is dwarfed even by his new overcoat (Petrovich, the tailor, drapes it over him in such a way that the collar completely conceals his head).

'Romantic Melodrama': The Impairment of Vision in *SVD* (*Soiuz velikogo dela*)

Shinel''s vision of pre-revolutionary St Petersburg is the closest that Soviet cinema comes to replicating the disturbing narratives of German Expressionist films, with their tendency towards the grotesque distortion of the natural world, their interest in uncanny and delirious dream states, and their rejection of conventional plot in favour of *Stationendramen*, or 'station dramas'.[83] Recent attempts to narrow the definitions of this movement and to draw distinctions between the influence of Expressionist ideas from theatre and literature and the stock elements of horror borrowed from the Gothic tradition do not necessarily negate this observation.[84] As the Soviet theatre specialist Valentin Melik-Khaspabov observed in 1925, Expressionism in theatre and film was primarily characterized by an anti-naturalistic style which involved a desire to free the stage from the 'tyranny of the object' and a tendency towards abstraction.[85] According to Sokolov, one of the first reviewers of *Shinel'*, there were strong similarities between the FEKS adaptation and Robert Wiene's *Raskolnikow* (1923), a German adaptation of Dostoevskii's *Prestuplenie i nakazanie* (Crime and Punishment, 1866), which introduced perspectival distortion by means of wide-angle lenses, and the sets for which, perhaps unsurprisingly in view of the historical setting, were similarly designed.[86] In some quarters, Moskvin was accused of plagiarizing the work of German camera operators.[87] Kozintsev's violent repudiation of this accusation by claiming that the 'excessive theatricality' of Expressionism was alien to FEKS, and that the surreal vision of the film was inspired by the 'phantasmagoric' conditions of the Civil War, does not necessarily undermine the value of Sokolov's insight.[88] As Gordanov points out, although neither Moskvin nor Enei was familiar with the works of Expressionist cinema, like most of the employees at Leningradkino they were certainly *au fait* with the terminology associated with the phenomenon.[89]

Many of the visual experiments in *Shinel'* were reprised in Moskvin's subsequent work for FEKS, to the extent that they would come to be regarded as his personal 'signatures'. As will be shown, the soft-focus treatment and ethereal lighting of Akakii Akakievich's dream anticipated the restaurant and cabaret sequences at the beginning of *Novyi Vavilon*. By the same token, the gentle snow flurries picked out by arcs for the night-time theft scene in *Shinel'* later metamorphosed into the driving snowstorms which provide the crucial atmospheric accompaniment to the ill-fated mutiny by soldiers of the Chernigov regiment in *SVD*. Several of the devices Moskvin employed in the early films would, with the passage of time, acquire more complex nuances. This can be witnessed, for example, in his approach to *contre-jour*. Deployed initially for the tightrope-walking sequence in *Chertovo koleso*, the method of photographing against the light in *Shinel'* became a means with which to engineer images that uncannily resemble the genre of the silhouette portrait: see, for example, the scene in which Akakii Akakievich is framed by his illuminated window just before receiving his invitation from the 'Woman from the Rooms'. This effect may well have been inspired by the popularity of such portraits during the era of Romanticism, but it is worth pointing out that silhouetted drawings or photographs were very much part of the visual culture of the early twentieth century: they had featured on several occasions in Stieglitz's *Camera Work*; they were echoed in the stylized illustrations of certain 'Silver Age' artists, for example Georgii Narbut; and, as designed by Lotte Reiniger, who at the time was working at the theatre of Max Reinhardt, they had been deployed as part of the credit sequences for films directed by Paul Wegener from 1915 onwards.[90] By the time of *SVD* , when driving snow and wind were introduced, *contre-jour* had become a monument to the fleeting impressions created by flickering and shifting shapes. This evolution in Moskvin's personal style was noticed by his contemporaries, one of whom talked about the lightness of his photographic touch, his 'avoidance of colour' and the impression that his frames were sketched 'as if by an Italian pencil'.[91]

These continuities are intriguing in view of the fact that, despite the proximity in terms of historical epoch, *SVD* was planned as a very different kind of production, one that, in theory, should have resulted in a very different type of visual aesthetic. The action of the narrative is set in 1826 and, as indicated earlier, tells the story of the tragic mutiny of officers and soldiers of the Chernigov infantry regiment who belonged to the Decembrists' Southern League. The screenplay was written by Tynianov in collaboration with Iulian Oksman, an academic historian who, like Tynianov, was an expert in the 1820s. Two years previously, Tynianov had published *Kiukhlia: Povest' o dekabriste* (Kiukhlia: A Novel about a Decembrist), his fictional account of the life of the Decembrist poet Vil'gel'm Kiukhel'beker; and one year previously, Oksman had edited an important collection of documents and memoirs pertaining to the Chernigov uprising which had been published to coincide with its centenary.[92] The timing of the FEKS project was doubtless prompted by the official celebration of this centenary. As well as several officially sponsored commemorative events, the Decembrist uprisings had triggered a flurry of rival film productions at Leningrad studios, for example Ivanovskii's *Dekabristy* (The Decembrists, 1926) and Gardin's *Poet i Tsar'* (The Poet and the Tsar, 1927), the plot of which was based on the last years of Pushkin's life. It is possible, moreover, that both Tynianov and Oksman were aware of Pushkin's unfinished prose fragment, 'Povest' o praporshchike Chernigovskogo polka' ('A Novel about the Ensign of the Chernigov Regiment'), which was based on the poet's period of southern exile, during which he met several of the leading members of the Southern League, and which, it has been speculated, would have been dedicated to the uprising.[93]

The fact that the Southern League was regarded by historians as the more radical of the two conspiracies doubtless made it a subject of particular fascination for the FEKS collective. Its relatively peripheral importance in geographical terms (the revolt of the regiments organized by the Northern League on St Petersburg's Senate Square on 14 December (Old Style) is the event more central to the popular consciousness) may also have been a factor. Despite these obvious attractions, however, it is clear that the restaging of historical fact for a contemporary audience was not the primary objective of *SVD*. Even at the writing stage, Tynianov prejudiced the historical accuracy of the uprising by introducing events that took place at different times and in different locations. Medoks, for example, while a genuine historical figure, was not involved directly in the Chernigov uprising; in fact, his involvement was marginal in the extreme, lying solely in his blackmailing activities after the uprising's leaders had been exiled to Siberia.[94] A Casanova-style seducer, charlatan and ruthless blackmailer, the figure of Medoks undoubtedly contributes the ingredient of romantic melodrama to a narrative that could easily have become burdened by political correctness. In the hands of Tynianov, *SVD* moves into the zone of the 'thriller', or what one reviewer dubbed a 'Red adventure novel'.[95] This 'thriller' undoubtedly contains moments of tremendous pathos – the arrest and incarceration of General Vishnevskii after his exposure as one of the Southern League's leading conspirators, the brutal suppression of the uprising itself and the death of Ensign Sukhanov (although the names of the general and his ensign were altered, the characters were nevertheless based on real people who took part in the uprising) – but the circumstances that gave rise to the rebellion and the nature of the conspiracy itself are approached obliquely, so much so that the connection between the three letters of the film's title (SVD) and the secret society by which the Southern League was known to its members, itself a Tynianov fabrication, is never properly explained. This led to accusations that the uprising served merely as a colourful background to the romantic melodrama, and that indeed any uprising could have served the same purpose.[96]

The polemic against the historical costume drama is largely expressed through Moskvin's lighting and camerawork. As befits a narrative dominated by conspiracy, betrayal and mass murder, the visual style for the most part is resolutely low key. Around 70 per cent of the film takes place in low lighting conditions and only two spheres – the tavern, where Medoks is first seen playing cards, and the travelling circus, a vestige of the FEKS interest in popular forms of entertainment, to which Sukhanov escapes after the suppression of the uprising – are photographed in anything like high key. *SVD* is a vision of the human figure as silhouette or shadow, engulfed in darkness, mortally threatened by the elements and protected only by fragile and restricted pools of light. Everything in this world is flickering and unstable. Even the landscape for the most part is devoid of texture and volume, with everything material existing only in the form of stark outlines, or vapour, dust and wind, none of them tangible. The centrepiece of the storm that accompanies the uprising has prompted comparisons with a number of literary works, most importantly Aleksandr Blok's *Dvenadtsat'* (The Twelve, 1918), a narrative poem that dramatizes the pathos of the October Revolution, although the influence is found in the use of a snowstorm as the central motif, rather than the Cubo-Futurist illustrations by Iurii Annenkov which accompanied the poem's first publication. Another possible source, albeit not one acknowledged by the FEKS directors, is Pushkin's 'Besy' ('Demons', 1830), interpreted by some as a veiled reference to the Decembrist uprising, with its ghostly apparitions swarming past the passenger in their untold hundreds against the background of a snowy wasteland and howling storm.[97]

As Butovskii has observed, Moskvin's compositional strategies in relation to the visual rendering of the Chernigov uprising are present from the very opening shots of *SVD*.[98] A soldier stands guard in the depths of the frame by a frozen road; there is a wooden fence to his left, which rises gently on sloping ground from left to right, and a tree standing to his right, which leans slightly in the same direction. The fence and tree are silhouetted by a pool of light that illuminates the back and knapsack of the soldier, but leaves everything else in darkness apart from thick flurries of snow which are driven past and around this figure by a furious wind. The flickering arc seems to alter the boundaries of this pool of light and causes the shape of the storm to expand and contract with a strange, billowing effect, rather as if the film stock is in the process of decomposition. This opening scene is a powerful image of human solitude in the face of the threatening elements, the small dimensions of the soldier in relation to his surroundings accentuating the pathos of his situation: he is the guardian of emptiness, his job futile (what human traffic could there be along this road?) and his sense of duty a blind instinct. The storm continues for the exterior scenes up to and including the mutiny itself. Moskvin's approach to lighting this storm remains consistent, but for the scenes immediately afterwards, such as the encounter between Sukhanov and General Vishnevskii's wife as she tries to pass the checkpoint in order to retrieve her letters to Medoks, and for the scenes of the mutiny itself, the arcs have been moved around to face the camera either directly or from a three-quarters back position. Occasionally, when it is necessary to pick out significant detail amidst the all-encompassing gloom, such as the features of Sof'ia Magarill, the actress playing the general's wife, the projectors appear to have been replaced by spotlights. Where *contre-jour* is employed, the arcs produce silhouettes or greyish-black outlines, the expressions on the human faces opaque.

Atmospherically, the snowstorm is spellbinding and reaches its extraordinary climax during the scenes of the insurrection: the silhouette of the drummer boy who signals the beginning of the mutiny against the background of a blizzard; the shots of soldiers rushing out of their barracks into the heart of the storm, their shapes no longer recalling human bodies but rather ghostly apparitions that flit rapidly across the screen, reduced almost to abstraction; the brief sequences of the speech encouraging the insurrection, where the driving clouds of snow reduce the visibility of the speaker to nearly zero (Fig. 29); and the scene in which a survivor who escapes the mutiny rides off into the distance to warn his commanders of what is taking place.

No frame still can adequately capture the kinetic poetry of these sequences. Aesthetically, the softening of contours, obliteration of detail and extreme tonal contrast suggest the experiments of Pictorialist photographers with photogravure and the gum-bichromate print. Both processes sought to replicate the effects of the pencil and charcoal sketch. The former was a technique for reproducing the photographic image in printer's ink and is best illustrated by the works of Peter Henry Emerson in the latter part of the nineteenth century.[99] The second involved a process that washed away unwanted details and produced prints that often resembled wash drawings or watercolours: it is best illustrated by the works of George Davison, Robert Demachy and the photographers of the so-called 'Clover-Leaf' or 'Trifolium' group, Heinrich Kühn, Hans Watzek and Hugo Henneberg, who were based in Austria but whose works had appeared at international exhibitions and in *Camera Work*.[100] Bearing in mind the use of deep chiaroscuro, there are important precursors in the form of Steichen's portraits, for example his studies of Auguste Rodin, Gustav Maeterlink and the American art critic Sadakichi Hartmann, as well as his own self-portrait.[101] Although these works date for the most part from the fin-de-siècle period, it is more than likely that Moskvin was familiar with them. As already indicated, he had been directed towards Steichen by lecturers at the Higher Photo-Technical Institute. Furthermore, he had access to photographic almanacs of recent vintage courtesy of Mikhailov's uncle, Konstantin Somov, the well known painter and member of the 'Mir iskusstva' (World of Art) group, to whose well stocked library Moskvin paid regular visits.[102] Inevitably, such precursors lack the pictorial dynamism of *SVD* and its continual assault on the optic nerves as a result of flickering, elusive movement. It is the strength of these images in pictorial terms that gave rise to Balász's view of *SVD* as an 'optical ballad'.[103]

Although the use of inclement weather produces specific effects not seen in the other sections of *SVD*, both the application of diffusion and the use of shadow play are an intrinsic part of Moskvin's approach elsewhere. The smoky atmosphere of the tavern, where officers meet to discuss the conspiracy in a basement room, pursues with greater elaborateness the experiments in *Shinel'* which use wafting or billowing vapour, although here, as in the tightrope-walking sequence in *Chertovo koleso*, it is the smoke produced by cigarettes and cigars puffed by characters within the mise en scène which softens the image. A classic portrait of Medoks, one that perfectly encapsulates the melodramatic quality of *SVD*, involves several distinct smoke rings floating in front of his face (these were apparently produced by Ermler, who was observing the FEKS directors at work and invited to participate) (Fig. 30).[104] The use of shadow play on both interior and exterior sequences is also highly expressive. The moment when Sukhanov is directed downstairs to the conspirators' meeting place shows their elongated shadows projected against an interior wall of the tavern (Fig. 31). This moment is reprised after the mutiny with a hint of grotesque exaggeration when it is the shadows of dancers, brutally indifferent to the execution taking place upstairs, which are projected onto the same wall. In a brilliant stroke of invention, one without precedent in Soviet cinema, Moskvin incorporates mobile shadow play for the ice-rink sequence during which the conspiracy is unmasked and the leaders are placed under arrest. The swirling movements of the skaters, picked out as silhouettes by arcs facing directly towards the camera, produce a continually shifting backdrop to the tense encounter between Sukhanov and the general's wife, whom he recognizes as the woman who persuaded him to let her through the checkpoint in the opening minutes of the film (Fig. 32). For the moment of recognition itself, the image becomes diffuse, followed seconds later by Moskvin's resort to optical distortion, a kaleidoscope effect achieved by means of a lens which leaves the centre of the frame untouched while introducing hexagonally shaped sections around the edges that are subject to slight distortion of perspective (the image in the centre of the frame would appear to be inverted). This shattering moment, a point-of-view shot belonging to Sukhanov which marks the beginnings of a passion that will shape the rest of the narrative, is at the same time a subjective, dream-like vision.

To the Barricades: *Novyi Vavilon* and the Paris Commune of 1871

From the brutal suppression of the uprising of the Chernigov regiment in *SVD* to the tragic defeat of the Paris Commune in 1871 is clearly not a great distance in terms of genre, even if, for Kozintsev, *Novyi Vavilon* sought to correct what appeared in hindsight to be an unwelcome 'error', namely, that 'style had become transformed into stylization'.[105] Albeit in ways that differed from the dominant model, both films conformed to the emerging utopian-martyrological genre in the Soviet Union, one that sought to erect cinematic monuments to the fallen heroes of past uprisings as a historical prelude to the triumph of the October Revolution. Unlike *SVD*, however, *Novyi Vavilon* celebrates an event more closely associated with the revolutionary consciousness of the international proletariat, one which, for Lenin, was the first truly proletarian uprising (his 'Uroki kommuny' ('Lessons of the Commune'), published in an émigré gazette in 1908, demonstrates the ways in which this failed uprising influenced his thinking).[106] Furthermore, *Novyi Vavilon* is less melodramatic than *SVD* in its deployment of romantic liaison as a vehicle with which to individualise the impact of epic events and accentuate their tragic dimension. For the first time in their filmmaking practice, Kozintsev and Trauberg introduced a 'coming to consciousness' narrative through the character of Louise Poiret, the shop assistant in the New Babylon emporium who is the film's central protagonist. By the end, this character has been transformed from a naïve young woman into a determined defender of the Commune, possibly one of the women, known collectively as 'les pétroleuses' (literally, those who use petrol for arson attacks), who were prepared to die for their beliefs. Kozintsev himself observed that the path from the 'blue' smoke-filled dance floors of the restaurant to the 'dark bronze' of the execution scene symbolized an 'entire human life'.[107] In his view, Moskvin's great achievement in *Novyi Vavilon* lay in his painstaking rendering of this woman's personal trajectory; as he notes in an echo of Inkizhinov's comments in relation to Golovnia, the degree to which the camera operator not only 'fixed' the portrait of a character, but also created that character along with the actor, was still poorly understood in the Soviet Union at the time.[108] It was apparently Moskvin who, having executed some swift screen tests with the actress, Elena Kuz'mina, when she turned up for audition, insisted on her selection (she was a member of the collective but had never before been given a major role in a FEKS production).

The title of *Novyi Vavilon* was taken from Emile Zola's *Au bonheur des dames* (The Ladies' Paradise, 1883), the eleventh novel of the Rougon-Macquart series, which was set in the 1860s during the Second Empire of Napoleon III. As Nesbet has recently demonstrated, this novel provides much more than merely the name of the emporium after which the FEKS film is titled.[109] *Au bonheur des dames* is a trenchant deconstruction of the department store as the modern embodiment of a rapacious and exploitative capitalism. Zola describes in detail the destructive impact of such stores on neighbouring commercial outlets; the cynical marketing strategies on which they are based (modelled on Le Bon Marché in Paris, the department store in Zola's novel stocks a multiplicity of textiles and ready-made garments aimed primarily at women); and the ruthless exploitation of the largely female workforce that supplies the goods on sale. Zola's interest in the gender dimension of the capitalist workplace is also mirrored in *Novyi Vavilon*, although the introduction of a revolutionary context in the FEKS film gives rise to a different outcome. The heroine of *Au bonheur des dames*, Denise Baudu, a shop assistant from the rural provinces, is relentlessly pursued by the wealthy owner of the store and does ultimately submit to his advances once he manages to convince her of the genuine nature of his affections by offering to marry her. In the FEKS film, by contrast, although the owner is also sexually interested in Poiret, the main focus of romantic interest is Jean, a renegade French soldier, who falls in love with her but refuses to support the Commune and for this reason forfeits her love. In an explicit expression of revolutionary commitment, Poiret refuses to allow private emotion to triumph over ideological principle.

Preparations for the production involved a collective trip to Paris in February 1928 and the collecting of artworks which, it was felt, would aid in establishing a sense of historical authenticity. This trip took place after a brief stay in Berlin but for reasons that are not clear excluded Moskvin, who returned to the Soviet Union. His place was taken by Mikhailov, who filmed a number of landmark sites, most notably (although now a cliché of Parisian architectural topography) the chimeras that adorn the roof of Nôtre Dame, and the Place Vendôme, the site of the communard destruction of the monument to Napoleon I.[110] Kozintsev's account of this trip mentions photographs taken with Erenburg's Leica; regular visits to antique shops to buy copies of artworks dating from the period; and visits to key landmarks, for example the cemetery at Père Lachaise, where the last defenders of the Commune were executed and their remains interred.[111] Before the trip Kozintsev had apparently undertaken some preliminary research. This included study of Marx's *Class War in France* (1871) and careful perusal of contemporary lithographs by Daumier and Jean Grandville, in particular the former's hand-coloured portraits of Robert-Macaire, the Parisian 'business agent' and archetypal villain, which served as illustrations for Pierre-Joseph Rousseau's *Physiologie du Robert-Macaire* (1842), and Grandville's series of half-human, half-animal figures, which had appeared in his *Les Métamorphoses* (1864).[112] After the return from Paris, Kozintsev accompanied Moskvin on several visits to galleries in Leningrad in order to study works by contemporaneous French painters: he refers to drawings by Constantin Guys, the ultimate *flâneur*, according to Baudelaire; and oil paintings by Daumier, their 'figures ... sculpted by light'.[113] He also mentions the 'palpitating light of the Impressionists' and the 'glimmering gaslights' of paintings by Georges Seurat.[114]

Although the trip to Paris was clearly important to the FEKS team in relation to experiencing the geography and architecture of the city first-hand, it is difficult to assess the significance of the artworks that Kozintsev studied or brought back with him. The lithographs of Daumier and Grandville, for example, are essentially works of caricature.[115] It might be speculated, therefore, that their usefulness resided more in their value as historical artefacts, in other words, as illustrations of bourgeois 'types' and fashionable modes of dress during the Second Empire, rather than as stylistic or aesthetic guides. The same caveat applies to works apparently also brought back from Paris, but not mentioned in Kozintsev's memoirs, for example portraits by Nadar (real name: Gaspard-Félix Tournachon), a left-leaning caricaturist, magazine editor and society photographer whose studio hosted the first exhibition of Impressionist paintings, and works by Eugène Atget, a photographer who had documented the changing landscape of Parisian streets and buildings at the turn of the century.[116] Nadar was renowned for his society portraits, some of which were profoundly innovative examples of studio photography.[117] Nevertheless, as will become clear, while some of Moskvin's portraits bear traces of the formality associated with atelier-based photography, his lighting approach and tonal resolution, as might be expected, are quite different. The influence of Atget might be regarded as similarly peripheral. Although he had taken many photographs during the first decades of the twentieth century, none of them was pertinent to the period of the Second Empire, and very few had actually been published by the time the FEKS team visited Paris. The one exception is *Avenue des Gobelins* (1925), which shows a shop window filled with mannequins dressed in suits and top hats.[118] This photograph had recently been adopted by the French Surrealists (although not intended as a Surrealist work, it was first published by André Breton in *La Révolution surréaliste* in 1926), and to some extent offers a further conceptual link between Zola's *Au bonheur des dames* and FEKS's *Novyi*

Vavilon. As Nesbet has pointed out, mannequins feature on frequent occasions in both novel and film.[119] Furthermore, as reinterpreted by Breton, Atget's work has come to symbolize the spiritual void at the heart of modern consumerism, the mannequins functioning simultaneously as desirable objects (the attire they display) and mirror images of the purchasers who desire them. Something of this dialectic is present in *Novyi Vavilon* when a giant mannequin with a painted face is seen standing behind Poiret at the moment when she receives an invitation from the directorial board to attend a ball which is taking place in the restaurant later in the evening. This dummy functions as a metonymic substitute for the female consumers who, seconds before, have been shown frenetically shopping in Poiret's particular section of the store. It is also a deformed fantasy figure, a reminder of the predatory sexual impulse which underpins the invitation.

The relationship between the soft-focus cinematography in the opening sequences of *Novyi Vavilon* and the influence of Impressionist artists is also a problematic one. As noted earlier in this chapter, Moskvin was already familiar with the techniques of the French Impressionists and the works of their photographic disciples, the Pictorialists. As Golovnia recalls, his familiarity with the works of Degas and Auguste Renoir permanently exhibited in the Shchukinskaia Gallery in Moscow apparently prompted the reflection that 'painting did not always require sharpness of focus'.[120] The aesthetics of Impressionism are clearly relevant for *Novyi Vavilon* in the sense that, historically speaking, the events of the Commune coincided approximately with this movement's emergence into the public sphere. In this sense, the progressive tendencies of the period, which include the canvases of Daumier, who is usually regarded as belonging to the 'realist' tendency in French art but in fact was among the first experimenters with Impressionist techniques – see, for example, his *Famille sur une barricade pendant la commune* (Family at a Barricade during the Commune, 1871) – become part of the visual fabric of the era. Moskvin's adoption of the poetics of soft-focus for a limited number of episodes in *Novyi Vavilon* might thus be regarded as an investigation into his method's own creative 'myth'.

At the same time, it is important to point out that the promotion of this kind of aesthetic takes place within a specific ideological environment. If the surreal visions of Akakii Akakievich in *Shinel'* are essentially chimeras that lead him into a sphere of erotic sensuality and self-destruction, the paradox of the method in *Novyi Vavilon* lies in the fact that diffusion is invoked in an explicitly decadent and bourgeois context. Despite the undeniably scintillating nature of this spectacle, the association of soft-focus with corruption and debauchery – with a world nonchalantly indifferent to the catastrophic events taking place beyond its environs which ultimately takes revenge on those (the communards) who seek to challenge its dominance – endows these scenes with an ambiguous quality. It is noteworthy that in both cases the poetics of soft-focus are introduced in the context of sensuous materials, the translucent fan held by the 'Woman from the Rooms' in *Shinel'* mirrored by the sumptuous range of goods (including lingerie) on display in the New Babylon department store and the erotic attire of the can-can dancers who perform in the store's restaurant.

Viewed in relation to Moskvin's earlier experiments, the resort to diffusion in *Novyi Vavilon* witnesses him refining his practices and exploiting all manner of technical tricks in order to create the necessary effects. For some of the scenes in question, he applies tried and tested techniques: smoke-filled interiors, diffusion disks, Vaseline around the lens, materials placed in front of the lens, and various types of uncorrected lenses or so-called 'portrait lenses'. Different shots are characterized by one or other of these devices, or a combination of them, with clues lying in the ways in which, and the degrees to which, the areas around the frame and within the depths of the frame exhibit a uniform loss of focus. The portrait of Magarill as the cabaret *chanteuse*, for example, is characterized by a degree of diffusion only towards the edges of the frame; this suggests the use of lubricant around the peripheries of the lens. By contrast, the close-up of the female performer with a monocle who holds a glass of champagne and has a cigar clamped in her mouth betrays a uniform loss of focus across the entire area of the frame, which results from diffusion disks, or layers of silk placed in front of the lens, or an uncorrected lens, perhaps a monocle lens, the adoption of which was beginning to be commented upon in the film press at this time.[121] Several of the compositions in which the action takes place on a single plane, for example those that show drumsticks beating a drum, a musician playing a violin (Fig. 33) and dancing couples rushing into and out of the light; the scenes involving the can-can dancers; and the shots of the solo drunk, dancing in happy oblivion after the rest of the hall has been vacated, all conform to this kind of approach. The soft-focus effects are enhanced by smoke and Moskvin's 'zonal' lighting of the set. This method divides the stage into receding planes, with the action restricted to each plane lit differently. Numerous semi-illuminated lamps, ostensibly part of the décor for the emporium, are positioned within the frame and themselves constitute dazzling patches of light. The richness and saturation of tone, ranging from deep black to scintillating white, but with the greater part of the gradations concentrated towards the silver-white end of the spectrum, are particularly impressive. Like the champagne the customers are quaffing, the scenes in the restaurant are sparkling and light-headed. For Kozintsev, after several frustrating days of experimenting with different arrangements of lights and lenses, and seemingly on the verge of failure, the effect was mesmerizing: it was, in his words, the photographic realization of Maiakovskii's description of Paris in his play *Misteriia-Buff* (Mystery-Bouffe, 1918) as the 'delirium of an agitated sea'.[122]

One of Moskvin's key innovations within this opening sequence is the scenes that incorporate activity across a number of planes; these created the most difficulty from the compositional point of view. The typical example, the scene which, as Butovskii points out, supplies the imagistic keystone, is the portrait of the emporium owner sitting at a table, dressed in a tuxedo and top hat, his left hand holding a pair of white gloves, his right hand firmly clasped around a glass of wine, and his position in the foreground static but placed against a background of swirling and hazy shapes (Fig. 34).[123] The combination of sharp foreground and out-of-focus background was apparently achieved by means of a lens that had been specially constructed for Moskvin by Zababurin, the optical scientist who had supervised Gordanov's thesis on optical lenses.[124] This lens is analogous to the so-called 'portrait lens', a long-focus lens, usually about 400mm or more, which had been given this name because it was popular with Soviet camera operators for close-ups.[125] This was because the depth of field, depending on the level of available light, was usually restricted to a very narrow plane; in other words, the face and body of the human figure were separated from the décor and their contours were pleasingly softened around the edges, giving rise to a supposedly 'painterly' effect. The moment when the optical properties of Moskvin's lens are best illustrated occurs when the emporium owner holds up a menu in front of his face: the letters are almost fully in focus, but his face is a shimmering mirage, and the hand that holds the menu, falling just outside the narrow depth of field, is significantly softened. Such a lens necessarily carries implications for the formal composition of the frame. All the scenes in which it is employed are axial, and thus theatrical in resonance, this being the inevitable by-product of the difficulties of controlling the depth of field for shots where the angle of vision is oblique.

Moskvin's cinematographic explorations in *Novyi Vavilon* are not stylistically homogenous. The opening scenes of the New Babylon emporium and its restaurant stand in stark contrast to the sober and static portraits of the cobblers, washerwomen and seamstresses who make the goods that are sold at the store, and whose lives are characterized by crushing, demeaning and exploitative work. Moskvin's rendering of this suffering, which evolves in due course into his treatment of the Paris Commune more broadly, sharply contrasts with the world of heady inebriation in the emporium, even though there is a subtle hint of the connectedness of these worlds by means of the vapours that emerge from the hot water used by the washerwomen and drift across the frame. Two portraits stand out from this sequence: the medium close-up of a white-haired cobbler, and shortly afterwards, the medium close-up of an older washerwoman, her body bent with exhaustion. The oppressive mood is established in part by means of the darkened backgrounds. Compared to the sophisticated lighting techniques and multiple sources of illumination in the emporium – that multiplicity a reflection, if not an extension, of the material opulence on display there – the viewer may be struck by the relative poverty and economy of means in the areas occupied by the workers. In the case of the washerwoman, Moskvin applies two relatively modest light sources: the first strikes her figure from behind, illuminating her left shoulder; the second, positioned off-screen left in a relatively low position, accentuates her careworn, perspiring face, the furrows of her brow, the ungainly shape of her nose and chin and her dank hair. The strongly linear emphasis in this portrait evokes the kind of wretchedness and pathos associated with the lithographs, sketches and engravings of the German proletarian artist Käthe Kollwitz. It may be significant that her work had been exhibited in Russia only two years previously;[126] and that, according to Gordanov, this was a period when familiarity with the work of German left-wing artists generally was at its height within Lenfil'm (specifically, he mentions examining Kollwitz's works while collaborating with Petrov on *Frits Bauer* (1930)).[127]

These early images mark a significant departure for Moskvin in the sense that, for the first time in his career, he was photographing suffering proletarian 'types'. In relation to the communard sequences as a whole, Moskvin traces a compositional circle which moves from representations of misery (the scenes in the emporium basement) through to hopes of transformation (the scenes with the women and the soldiers in charge of the army artillery), the realization of that transformation (the communards take control of the city), and then tragic defeat (the communards' execution by the walls of Père Lachaise). At each stage the visual treatment is adjusted. The scenes of triumph, for example the fraternization that takes place between the working-class women of the Commune and the rank-and-file army soldiers, during which milk is exchanged for guns, are executed for the most part in a high-key mode. For these scenes Moskvin produced a series of portraits largely linear in design and reminiscent of Tisse's work with Eizenshtein. According to Ianina Zheimo, the actress who had joined the FEKS team for the role of the tailor's assistant in *Shinel'* and was playing one of the younger female communards, Moskvin used sheets of tin plate as a means of *podsvetka* for exterior portraiture.[128] There is also evidence that he resorted to mirrors for the same purpose.[129] The effects of this technique can be witnessed in the images of Zheimo as she exhorts the soldiers to exchange their guns (the reflectors, positioned behind her, produce a *contre-jour* effect to highlight the lower part of her head); the portraits of two older soldiers (the reflector is now positioned in front of the actors, giving rise to some subtle modelling along the right-hand side of their faces); and the close-up of one of the older female communards (her head is presented in quarter profile and the reflector, positioned at a diametrically opposed angle to the rays of the sun, causes a square of light to strike the lower part of her neck and left cheek). Although the effects in these portraits lack realism, they nevertheless accentuate the fact that, despite the different physiognomies and ages of these protagonists, they nevertheless share the same determined and indomitable spirit. By the end of the film, this approach has been abandoned. During the scenes of execution, the close-ups revert to the darker chiaroscuro of the workers who produce the goods on display in the emporium. Indeed, there is a direct quotation: among those waiting to be executed is the same washerwoman, albeit photographed from a different angle of perspective, and in slightly different lighting conditions, but with her hair again wet, this time because of the persistent rain.

Since she is one of the key proletarian figures in *Novyi Vavilon*, the portraiture for Kuz'mina as Poiret should in theory conform to this general pattern, but there are divergences which are explained partly by dramaturgical requirement and partly by shifting points of view in relation to her. The opening sequences on the shop floor, for example, differ from the images of suffering associated with the workers employed elsewhere; they seek to establish her as someone excited by her employment and proximity to the goods on display in the emporium. As Butovskii has observed, the scene in which Kuz'mina three times shakes out a piece of material for sale, each shake marked by an editing cut and an intertitle which exclaims that 'it's good value for money!', involves three adjusted images which vary the lighting accent produced by a unit positioned above and slightly to her left, culminating in a brighter overall level of illumination.[130] This recourse to lighting variation is reprised later in the film with a rapidly flashed and subtly adjusted series of portraits that show Kuz'mina in different guises. The posed stature, the relatively modest clothing (for example, the heavy, dark-grey shawl around her shoulders), the arrangement of her hair (a 'crow's nest', as she later described it) and the multiple perspectives, including, quite bizarrely, views from the rear, suggest that these are, in fact, the celebrated screen tests which the actress later recalled in their memoirs (Figs 35 & 36).[131] By virtue of the static poses, the series in question approaches the status of portfolio shots for the aspiring model or actor, the emphasis, it would appear, lying purely on the anatomical and physiological. In many respects, these portraits are textbook illustrations of the impact of different lighting arrangements on the modelling of the human face. In general, Moskvin appears to have employed a tripartite system of lighting, with two lights coming directly from the front, but one of them stronger than the other, and with a spotlight positioned behind the subject, either directly, or at an angle, for the purposes of *contre-jour*. It is important to emphasize that for each portrait the positioning and intensity of the lighting units have been subtly adjusted.

Unlike the many faces of Marfa Lapkina in *Staroe i novoe*, however, the close-ups of Kuz'mina, when viewed in dramatic context, are not motivated by the desire to show character development. In fact, the viewer's reception of them and their significance as guides to Moskvin's lighting procedures are complicated by the fact that they belong to the memories of the soldier, Jean, who is contemplating defection from the Republican armies based in Versailles and the possibility of joining the Commune; in this sense, they function as (retrospective) point-of-view shots. The classic three-point system, because it is prompted by dramaturgical considerations, must therefore be placed within inverted commas and regarded as a form of ironic stylization.[132] The series of nine shots represents Poiret as remembered by a putative lover, who the viewer may suspect is guilty of idealizing her memory, perhaps in order to give him the courage to defect, or who, as Nesbet has suggested, might be guilty of imagining her as a fetishized consumer item, much like a department-store mannequin.[133] At the same time, this person's political persuasions, as later becomes clear when he betrays the Commune, are confused. The series of portraits, therefore, rather than communicating important information about Poiret, is ultimately part of the characterization of Jean. At the end of the film, now soaked in rain, Poiret symbolically returns to the basement: her hair is wet, her face is crumpled, her skin is no longer smooth (Fig. 37), and her body is about to be buried in a trench which her former lover is digging.

Epilogue: The End of FEKS

Moskvin's application of the poetics of Impressionism and Pictorialism was one of the last incidences of its kind in Soviet cinematography and unconsciously anticipated their demise; having been declared a 'bourgeois' art form in the Soviet Union in 1928, Pictorialist photography became an anachronistic form of expression that was rarely encountered in official culture from that moment onwards.[134] What the film historian Nikolai Lebedev termed a 'festival of painterliness' in relation to *Novyi Vavilon* might therefore, with the benefit of hindsight, be regarded as a swansong or valedictory hymn.[135] It was subsequently denounced by Kozintsev at a conference of Leningrad camera operators in 1933, during which he urged the destruction of 'all those molar lenses and "Roshers" which have concealed in the vast majority of cases the inability of the operator to photograph simply and properly', arguing in favour of the 'line' at the expense of the 'patch of light', and hailing the scientific 'precision' and 'clarity' of the daguerreotype.[136]

Although hurtful for Moskvin personally, Kozintsev's denunciation is revealing in the sense that it implies that it was camera operators, rather than directors, who were responsible for the trend. Furthermore, although not intended as such, his remarks constitute a repudiation of the view expressed four years earlier by Piotrovskii, who argued that the painterly tendencies in FEKS works and other films shot by Leningrad camera operators were the product of dramaturgical considerations rather than personal aesthetic preferences.[137] Whatever the truth of the matter, *Novyi Vavilon* undeniably marked the end of the FEKS experiment in terms of new forms of visual expression. As the conclusion to this study aims to demonstrate, developments elsewhere, in particular the denunciation of 'formalism', the introduction of sound technology and the advent of Socialist Realism were changing approaches to the art of cinematography generally in the 1930s. As far as FEKS itself was concerned, the seeds of change were apparent already in *Odna* (Alone, 1931). Although this was a silent film in all but name – it was planned to take advantage of Aleksandr Shorin's newly developed recording equipment, but few of the scenes were actually filmed synchronously – it encapsulates nevertheless a shift towards a more prosaic and streamlined aesthetic.[138] Indeed, apart from the innovation of 'white-on-white' cinematography in the opening sequences, which proved highly influential as far as other cinematographers were concerned, *Odna* marks the end of Moskvin as an avant-garde camera operator.

Notes

1. Grigorii Kozintsev, 'Glubokii ekran', in his *Sobranie sochinenii*, ed. by S. A. Gerasimov and others, 5 vols (Leningrad: Iskusstvo, 1982–86), I (*Glubokii ekran: O svoei rabote v kino i teatre*), 17–356 (pp. 98–99) (first publ. Moscow: Iskusstvo, 1971).
2. See Vladimir Nedobrovo, *FEKS: Grigorii Kozintsev: Leonid Trauberg* (Moscow-Leningrad: Kinopechat', 1928); I. Vaisfel'd, *G. Kozintsev: L. Trauberg: Tvorcheskii put'* (Moscow: Goskinoizdat, 1940); and E. Dobin, *Kozintsev i Trauberg* (Moscow-Leningrad: Iskusstvo, 1963). On the neglect of FEKS outside Russia, see Ien Kristi [Ian Christie], 'Feksy za granitsei: Kul'turno-politicheskie aspekty vospriiatiia sovetskogo kino za rubezhom', trans. by N. Tsyrkun, *Kinovedcheskie zapiski*, 7 (1990), 172–75.
3. For Kozintsev's contribution to this pamphlet, see 'AB! Parad ekstsentrika', in Kozintsev, *Sobranie sochinenii*, III (*O rezhissure: O komicheskom, ekstsentricheskom i groteksnom iskusstve: Nash sovremennik Shekspir*), 72–75 (first publ. in *Ekstsentrizm* (Petrograd: Ekstsentropolis, 1922), pp. 3–5). See also 'Eshche odno D. E.', in Kozintsev, *Sobranie sochinenii*, III, 76–79 (first publ. in *Teatr*, 1923.7).
4. By the time of the emergence of FEKS, Chaplin had been proclaimed a Dadaist by Tristan Tzara, Fernand Léger had already produced his celebrated Cubist portrait, and Aleksei Gan, editor of *Kino-fot*, had signed up to the international campaign to have *The Kid* released in Germany and France. See *Kino-fot*, 1 (1922), 10.
5. O. L. Bulgakova, 'Bul'vardizatsiia avangarda – fenomen Feks', *Kinovedcheskie zapiski*, 7 (1990), 27–47 (p. 30). The principle of 'life as a stunt' is proclaimed in Sergei Iutkevich, 'EkstsentrizM – Zhivopis' – ReklamA', in *Ekstsentrizm*, pp. 12–15 (p. 13).
6. Iurii Tynianov, 'O feksakh', *Sovetskii ekran*, 1929.14, 10.
7. B. Alpers, 'Put' Feksov', *Kino i zhizn'*, 1929.4, 4–5 (p. 5).
8. Ibid., p. 4.
9. Ibid.
10. 'Kak sdelana "Shinel'" Gogolia' was first published in B. Eikhenbaum, *Poetika: Sbornik po teorii poeticheskogo iazyka* (1919). I will cite from the reprinted version as published in B. Eikhenbaum, *O proze: O poezii: Sbornik statei*, introduction by G. Bialyi (Leningrad: Khudozhestvennaia literatura, leningradskoe otdelenie, 1986), pp. 45–63. For the possible influence of this essay on Tynianov, see Ippolit Sokolov, '"Shinel'"', *Kino-front*, 1926.2–3, 28. It is perhaps noteworthy that Eikhenbaum mentions the FEKS film in his discussion of screen adaptations of classical literature in the same year in which *Shinel'* is released. See B. Eikhenbaum, 'Literatura i kino', *Sovetskii ekran*, 1926.42, 10.
11. Mikhailov and Moskvin, 'Rol' kino-operatora v sozdanii fil'my'.
12. Tynianov, 'O feksakh'.
13. Ibid.
14. Viktor Shklovskii, 'O rozhdenii i zhizni Feksov', in Nedobrovo, *FEKS*, pp. 7–11 (p. 8).
15. 'Istoki', in Sergei Iutkevich, *Sobranie sochinenii*, ed. by M. Z. Dolinskii, 3 vols (Moscow: Iskusstvo, 1990), I (*Molodost'*), 17–68.
16. *Kinooperator Andrei Moskvin*, ed. by Gukasian; and Butovskii, *Andrei Moskvin, kinooperator*. See also 'Andrei Nikolaevich Moskvin: Biofil'mobibliografiia', publ. by Ia. Butovskii, *Kinovedcheskie zapiski*, 27 (1995), 118–40.

17. According to Butovskii, the term was first used at a Leningrad conference of camera operators in June 1933. See Butovskii, *Andrei Moskvin, kinooperator*, pp. 130–31. For further details on this conference, see the concluding chapter to this monograph.

18. Viacheslav Gordanov, 'Moi drug Andrei Moskvin', in *Kinooperator Andrei Moskvin*, ed. by Gukasian, pp. 142–53.

19. Natalia Noussinova, 'Entretien avec Leonid Trauberg', in *Leonid Trauberg et l'excentrisme: Les Débuts de la Fabrique de l'Acteur Excentrique 1921–25*, ed. by Natalia Noussinova, trans. by Catherine Perrel (Crisnée/Leuven: Editions Yellow Now/Le Stuc, 1993), pp. 11–56 (p. 52); and Butovskii, *Andrei Moskvin, kinooperator*, pp. 74–75.

20. *Chuzhoi pidzhak* was scripted by Veniamin Kaverin, and put into production, but Kozintsev and Trauberg decided not to continue with the project. It was nevertheless photographed by Moskvin in association with Boris Spis and Rokhl Mil'man. See Butovskii, *Andrei Moskvin, kinooperator*, pp. 92–93.

21. Iu. M. Lotman and Iu. G. Tsiv'ian, 'SVD: Zhanr melodramy i istoriia', in *Tynianovskii sbornik: Pervye tynianovskie chteniia (g. Rezekne, mai 1982)*, ed. by M. O. Chudakova (Riga: Zinatne, 1984), pp. 46–78 (p. 52).

22. Anatolii Golovnia, 'O moem molchalivom druge', in *Kinooperator Andrei Moskvin*, ed. by Gukasian, pp. 164–69 (pp. 167–68).

23. Golovnia, *Masterstvo kinooperatora*, p. 114.

24. Leonid Kosmatov, 'Vstrechi', in *Kinooperator Andrei Moskvin*, ed. by Gukasian, pp. 206–15 (p. 209).

25. Gukasian's introduction ('Andrei Moskvin') in ibid., pp. 5–116 (pp. 33 & 44). See also Golovnia, 'O moem molchalivom druge', p. 167.

26. The anecdote in question relates to the 'Natasha's room' sequence in *Vyborgskaia storona* (1938). See Apollinarii Dudko, 'Algebra i poeziia sveta', in *Kinooperator Andrei Moskvin*, ed. by Gukasian, pp. 192–96 (pp. 193–95).

27. Elena Kuz'mina, *O tom, chto pomniu* (Moscow: Iskusstvo, 1989), p. 154.

28. Butovskii, *Andrei Moskvin, kinooperator*, p. 17.

29. Mikhail Bleiman, 'Vpechatlenie', in *Kinooperator Andrei Moskvin*, ed. by Gukasian, pp. 170–78 (p. 172). For photographs of Maiakovskii's Renault, see *Alexander Rodchenko: Photography, 1924–54*, ed. by Lavrentiev, p. 204.

30. Bleiman, 'Vpechatlenie', p. 172. See also Kozintsev, 'Glubokii ekran', pp. 97–98.

31. Gukasian, 'Andrei Moskvin', p. 44.

32. For a detailed discussion of Moskvin's tutelage of graduates from the GTK, and later VGIK, see Butovskii, *Andrei Moskvin, kinooperator*, pp. 125–27, and Ionas Gritsius, 'Starshii drug', in *Kinooperator Andrei Moskvin*, ed. by Gukasian, pp. 179–84.

33. Gukasian, 'Andrei Moskvin', p. 12.

34. Kozintsev, 'Glubokii ekran', p. 81.

35. Butovskii, *Andrei Moskvin, kinooperator*, p. 24.

36. Gordanov, *Zapiski kinooperatora*, p. 9.

37. Newhall, *The History of Photography*, pp. 46–48.

38. Gordanov, *Zapiski kinooperatora*, p. 12.

39. Noussinova, 'Entretien avec Leonid Trauberg', pp. 18–19.

40. Kozintsev, 'Glubokii ekran', p. 23.

41. Noussinova, 'Entretien avec Leonid Trauberg', pp. 29–30.

42. 'Manifest ekstsentricheskogo teatra', publ. by V. G. Kozintseva and Ia. L. Butovskii, *Kinovedcheskie zapiski*, 7 (1990), 73–74 (p. 74).

43. Noussinova, 'Entretien avec Leonid Trauberg', p. 45. For the libretto, see '"Zhenshchina Edisona": Pervyi stsenarii feksov', publ. by N. I. Nusinova, *Kinovedcheskie zapiski*, 7 (1990), 83–96.
44. Kozintsev, 'Glubokii ekran', p. 71.
45. N. I. Izvolov, 'Feks i "Krasnaia gazeta"', *Kinovedcheskie zapiski*, 7 (1990), 176–81.
46. Theodore van Houten, *Leonid Trauberg and his Films: Always the Unexpected* ('s-Hertogenbosch: Art and Research, 1989), p. 46.
47. '"Pokhozhdeniia Oktiabriny" (Beseda s avtorami-rezhisserami G. M. Kozintsevym i L. Z. Traubergom)', *Kino-nedelia*, 1924.43, 16.
48. See the photo-collage on the cover of ibid.; and also the double-page spread in ibid., 1924.44, 22–23 (p. 23).
49. Ibid., p. 22.
50. S. Gerasimov, 'Fabrika ekstsentricheskogo aktera', *Iskusstvo kino*, 1940.1–2, 96–97.
51. '"Pokhozhdeniia Oktiabriny" (Beseda s avtorami-rezhisserami G. M. Kozintsevym i L. Z. Traubergom)'.
52. Ibid.
53. Kozintsev, 'Glubokii ekran', p. 80.
54. Ibid.
55. Ibid.
56. Gordanov, *Zapiski kinooperatora*, pp. 16–17.
57. *Leonid Trauberg et l'excentrisme*, ed. by Noussinova, p. 6.
58. Kozintsev, 'Glubokii ekran', p. 80.
59. Ibid.
60. Ibid. For reviews, see Tril, 'Disput na prosmotre fil'ma "Pokhozhdeniia Oktiabriny"', *Kino-nedelia*, 1924.45, 7; A. D-skii, '"Pokhozhdeniia Oktiabriny"', *Kino-zhurnal A.R.K.*, 1925.3, 34; and Rabkor M. Shanlein, '"Pokhozhdeniia Oktiabriny"', *Kino-nedelia*, 1925.7, 9.
61. Kozintsev, 'Glubokii ekran', p. 81. For stills of *Mishki protiv Iudenicha*, see *Kino-nedelia*, 1925.12, 7, and 1925.13, 8.
62. The Serapion Brothers (Serapionovy brat'ia) was a literary grouping established in Petrograd in 1921. Its membership consisted of a number of aspiring writers who at the time were attending lectures at the House of Arts given by Iurii Tynianov, Evgenii Zamiatin, and Kornei Chukovskii.
63. Cited in Butovskii, *Andrei Moskvin, kinooperator*, p. 40.
64. Fred J. Balshofer and Arthur C. Miller, *One Reel a Week*, foreword by Kemp R. Niver (Berkeley: University of California Press, 1967), p. 15.
65. Noussinova, 'Entretien avec Leonid Trauberg', p. 50; and 'Kak ia stal rezhisserom', in Iutkevich, *Sobranie sochinenii*, I, 273–333 (p. 329).
66. Kozintsev, 'Glubokii ekran', p. 99.
67. Ibid.
68. Butovskii, *Andrei Moskvin, kinooperator*, pp. 39–40.
69. Salt, *Film Style and Technology*, pp. 166–67.
70. See Catriona Kelly, *Petrushka: The Russian Carnival Puppet Theatre*, Cambridge Studies in Russian Literature series (Cambridge: Cambridge University Press, 1990), pp. 179–211; and J. Douglas Clayton, *Pierrot in Petrograd: Commedia dell'Arte/Balagan in Twentieth-Century Russian Theatre and Drama* (Montreal: McGill-Queen's University Press, 1993), pp. 103–24.
71. Harte, *Fast Forward*, pp. 17–19.

72. Iu. N. Tynianov, 'Libretto kinofil'ma "Shinel'"', in *Iz istorii Lenfil'ma*, III (*Stat'i, vospominaniia, dokumenty: 1920–1930e gody*), ed. by N. S. Gornitskaia (Leningrad: Iskusstvo, leningradskoe otdelenie, 1973), 78–80 (first publ. by the publicity department of Leningradkino in 1926); and also Iu. G. Tsiv'ian, 'Paleogrammy v fil'me "Shinel'"', in *Tynianovskii sbornik 2*, ed. by M. O. Chudakova (Riga: Zinatne, 1986), pp. 14–27.

73. See the response of M. Padvo in *Zhizn' iskusstva*, the relevant fragment of which is reprinted in 'FEKS (1921–1929)', *Sovetskii ekran*, 1929.12, 6–7 (p. 7).

74. 'Nevskii Prospekt', in N. V. Gogol', *Sobranie sochinenii*, ed. by S. I. Mashinskii and M. V. Khrapchenko, 7 vols (Moscow: Khudozhestvennaia literatura, 1977), III (*Povesti*), 7–39 (p. 39).

75. In particular, there are similarities between the FEKS work and the plays of Arthur Adamov. See Martin Esslin, *The Theatre of the Absurd*, 3rd revised edn (London: Methuen Drama, 2001), pp. 92–127.

76. Eikhenbaum, 'Kak sdelana "Shinel'" Gogolia', pp. 54–55. Emphasis in the original. *Skaz* is a literary term which refers to any narrative in the first or third person in which there is an element of voice-play, or one in which the stylistic register tends towards the colloquial, and is thus 'spoken' rather than 'written'. On the reception of this and other aspects of Gogol''s short story in nineteenth- and twentieth-century criticism, see Julian Graffy, *Gogol's The Overcoat*, Critical Studies in Russian Literature series (Bristol: Bristol Classical Press, 2000), pp. 4–20.

77. Salt, *Film Style and Technology*, pp. 130–31 & 186.

78. Eikhenbaum, 'Kak sdelana "Shinel'" Gogolia', pp. 57–63.

79. For more on this, see Lotman and Tsiv'ian, 'SVD: Zhanr melodramy i istorii', pp. 48–50.

80. Gogol', 'Nevskii Prospekt', p. 12; and Kozintsev, 'Andrei Moskvin [glava iz knigi]', p. 125.

81. Kozintsev, 'Glubokii ekran', pp. 114–15.

82. Ibid., p. 55.

83. 'Station drama' is the term given to a certain type of German Expressionist play, the dramatic structure of which is organized according to discrete episodes. The principle is derived from the 'stations of the cross', which depict in artistic terms the different stages of Christ's Passion.

84. Dietrich Scheunemann, 'Activating the Differences: Expressionist Film and Early Weimar Cinema', in *Expressionist Film: New Perspectives*, ed. by Dietrich Scheunemann (Rochester, NY: Camden House, 2003), pp. 1–31.

85. V. Melik-Khaspabov, 'Ekspressionizm v kino', *Kino-nedelia*, 1925.11, 8.

86. Sokolov, '"Shinel'"'.

87. Leonid Trauberg, 'O Moskvine', in *Kinooperator Andrei Moskvin*, ed. by Gukasian, pp. 134–41 (pp. 137–38).

88. Kozintsev, 'Glubokii ekran', pp. 109–10.

89. Gordanov, *Zapiski kinooperatora*, pp. 62–63.

90. See, for example, J. B. Kerfoot's 1904 silhouettes of Stieglitz, Steichen, Coburn and Käsebier, in Stieglitz, *Camera Work*, ed. by Margolis, p. 20. For Narbut's silhouette illustrations for *Tri basni Krylova* (1913), see Bowlt, *Moscow and St. Petersburg in Russia's Silver Age*, p. 188. For Reiniger's silhouetted portraits, see <http://en.wikipedia.org/wiki/Lotte_Reiniger> (accessed 2 December 2011).

91. N. Efimov, 'O manere operatora Moskvina', *Kino* (Leningrad), 1927.40, 3.

92. *Dekabristy: Otryvki iz istochnikov*, ed. by Iu. G. Oksman (Moscow: Gosudarstvennoe izdatel'stvo, 1926).

93. Oksman wrote about this fragment four years after *SVD* was released. See Iu. Oksman, 'Nachalo povesti o praporshchike Chernigovskogo polka', in *Putevoditel' po Pushkinu* (Moscow-Leningrad: Gosudarstvennoe izdatel'stvo khudozhestvennoi literatury, 1931), pp. 252–53.

94. Lotman and Tsiv'ian, 'SVD: Zhanr melodramy i istoriia', pp. 57–66; and I. Sepman, 'Tynianov-stsenarist', in *Iz istorii Lenfil'ma*, III, 51–77.

95. Mikhail Shneider, '"SVD"', *Kino-front*, 1927.9–10, 19–20.

96. See Nedobrovo's review in *Zhizn' iskusstva*, 1927.36, cited in Lotman and Tsiv'ian, 'SVD: Zhanr melodramy i istoriia', p. 59.

97. Dmitrii Blagoi, *Tvorcheskii put' Pushkina* (Moscow: Sovetskii pisatel', 1967), pp. 470–84.

98. Butovskii, *Andrei Moskvin, kinooperator*, p. 81.

99. Newhall, *The History of Photography*, p. 142.

100. Ibid., p. 147.

101. Stieglitz, *Camera Work*, ed. by Margolis, pp. 3, 4, 18, 41, & 43, respectively.

102. E. Mikhailov, 'O stanovlenii operatorskogo iskusstva na studii "Lenfil'm"', *Iz istorii Lenfil'ma*, II (*Stat'i, materialy, dokumenty: 1920e gody*), ed. by N. S. Gornitskaia (Leningrad: Iskusstvo, leningradskoe otdelenie, 1970), 137–44 (pp. 140–41).

103. Bela Balash [Béla Balázs], 'Russkaia fil'ma i ee kritika (Po povodu fil'my "SVD")', trans. by N. Fridland, *Kino* (Leningrad), 1928.33, 3.

104. Kozintsev, 'Glubokii ekran', pp. 119–20.

105. Kozintsev, 'Andrei Moskvin', p. 39.

106. 'Uroki kommuny', in V. I. Lenin, *Polnoe sobranie sochinenii*, 55 vols (Moscow: Gosudarstvennoe izdatel'stvo politicheskoi literatury, 1958–1965), XIII (*Iun' 1907–mart 1908*), 1961, 451–54 (first publ. in *Zagranichnaia gazeta*, 23 March 1908).

107. Kozintsev, 'Andrei Moskvin', p. 40.

108. Ibid., p. 39.

109. Anne Nesbet, 'Émile Zola, Kozintsev and Trauberg, and Film as Department Store', *The Russian Review*, 69 (2009), 102–21.

110. Kozintsev, 'Glubokii ekran', p. 141.

111. Ibid., pp. 138–45.

112. Ibid., p. 139.

113. Ibid., p. 145. For Baudelaire on Guys, see Harte, *Fast Forward*, p. 16.

114. Kozintsev, 'Glubokii ekran', p. 145.

115. Ibid., p. 138.

116. Butovskii, *Andrei Moskvin, kinooperator*, p. 113.

117. Newhall, *The History of Photography*, pp. 66–69.

118. Ibid., pp. 192–93.

119. Nesbet, 'Émile Zola, Kozintsev and Trauberg, and Film as Department Store', pp. 108–09.

120. Golovnia, 'O moem molchalivom druge', p. 168.

121. 'S"emka pod monokl'', *Kino* (Leningrad), 1927.31–32, 3.

122. Kozintsev, 'Glubokii ekran', p. 146.

123. Butovskii, *Andrei Moskvin, kinooperator*, p. 99.

124. Moskvin, 'O svoei rabote i o sebe'.

125. Gordanov, *Zapiski kinooperatora*, pp. 67–68.

126. Elizabeth Prelinger, 'Kollwitz Reconsidered', in *Käthe Kollwitz*, ed. by Elizabeth Prelinger, essays by Alessandra Comini and Hildegard Bachert (New Haven, CT: Yale University Press, 1992), pp. 13–82 (pp. 81–82).

127. Gordanov, *Zapiski kinooperatora*, p. 63.
128. Butovskii, *Andrei Moskvin, kinooperator*, p. 105.
129. A still from the shooting of the barricade sequence shows two mirrors positioned to the left of the actors. See 'Sentiabr' 1928 goda: "Novyi Vavilon": Odessa', in the illustrations section of ibid.
130. Ibid., p. 108.
131. Kuz'mina, *O tom, chto pomniu*, pp. 153–54.
132. For discussion of the three-point system and the more sophisticated variations which emerged during and after the 1920s, see Salt, *Film Style and Technology*, pp. 152–55; and the third chapter in L. V. Kosmatov, *Operatorskoe masterstvo*, Biblioteka liubitelia series (Moscow: Iskusstvo, 1962), pp. 47–98.
133. Nesbet, 'Émile Zola, Kozintsev and Trauberg, and Film as Department Store', p. 109.
134. Barkhatova, 'Pictorialism: Photography as Art', p. 60.
135. N. A. Lebedev, *Ocherki istorii kino SSSR: Nemoe kino*, 2nd revised and enlarged edn (Moscow: Iskusstvo, 1965), p. 385.
136. 'Nastroenchestvo', in Kozintsev, *Sobranie sochinenii*, II (*Kritiko-publitsisticheskie stat'i i vystupleniia: Zametki ob iskusstve i liudiakh iskusstva*), 1983, 16–21 (pp. 20 & 21) (first publ. in *Kino*, 1933.39)
137. Adr[ian] Piotrovskii, 'Granitsy stilia operatora i khudozhnika', *Kino* (Leningrad), 1929.5, 2.
138. Lilya Kaganovsky, 'The voice of technology and the end of Soviet silent film: Grigorii Kozintsev and Leonid Trauberg's *Alone*', *Studies in Russian and Soviet Cinema*, 1.3 (2007), 265–81. See also Mikhail Kaplan, 'Andrei Moskvin', *Iskusstvo kino*, 1940.6, 47–53 (p. 51).

CHAPTER FIVE

Danylo Demuts'kyi and Oleksandr Dovzhenko

The secret of the camera operator's art lies above all in the soul of the artist who has been given his gifts by nature, and who loves his Motherland and his people with all his heart. It is from this feeling that the artist draws the strength of his creative inspiration.[1]

Who knows what miracles of visual quality would have been achieved had the rest of Dovzhenko's films been photographed by Demuts'kyi?[2]

The screen is able to bring alive in front of our very eyes objects that are inanimate: I am thinking of the close-ups of apples in Earth, *about which one may say, without the risk of appearing paradoxical, that whosoever has not seen these apples has never properly seen an apple.*[3]

The Beginning and the End

The relationship between Danylo Demuts'kyi and Oleksandr Dovzhenko was the most short-lived among the film units of the avant-garde. After meeting each other for the first time on *Vasia – reformator* (Vasia the Reformer, 1926) and subsequently forging a creative alliance on *Arsenal* (1928), *Zemlia* and *Ivan*, their professional partnership came to an abrupt end, never to be formally resurrected.[4] The reason for this rupture has until relatively recently remained opaque. Since the opening of secret-police archives in independent Ukraine, however, it has become clear that the cause was external rather than internal. According to Liber, Demuts'kyi was arrested by the Ukrainian state security police in December 1932 and held for four months on the grounds of promoting counter-revolutionary propaganda.[5] He was released due to lack of evidence, but was rearrested in December 1934 and charged with being a 'socially dangerous individual', this resulting in a sentence of three years' internal exile. Demuts'kyi left Ukraine on 29 April 1935 and travelled to Tashkent, where he was able to find employment in the Uzbek national film studio. On 11 January 1938, however, he was arrested again, this time by the Uzbekistan state security police, and sentenced to a period of imprisonment lasting seventeen months.[6] His release and the declaration of war in 1941 led to the reestablishment of his former links with the Ukrainian film industry, which had been evacuated to Ashgabat, the capital of Turkmenistan, to which Dovzhenko had also been moved.[7] Demuts'kyi photographed three films for Ukrainian directors during this period.[8] He also worked with Protazanov on *Nasreddin v Bukhare* (Nasreddin in Bukhara, 1943), which was produced under the aegis of Tashkent Studio; for this and other works, most importantly the two films based on folkloric subjects which he shot with the Uzbek director Nabi Ganiev, he was awarded the title of Honoured Practitioner of the Arts for the Uzbekistan Soviet Socialist Republic. Demuts'kyi was permitted to return to Ukraine at some point in 1946, settling in his old apartment in Kyiv and finding employment in the Kyiv Film Studio.[9] He was awarded Stalin prizes for cinematography on Boris Barnet's *Podvig rozvidnyka* (Podvig razvedchika, The Exploits of a Spy, 1947), Volodymyr Braun's *U myrni dni* (V mirnye dni, In Days of Peace, 1950) and Ihor Savchenko's *Taras Shevchenko* (1951). Despite these official accolades, and the director's attempts to involve him in the making of *Michurin: Zhizn' v tsvetu* (Michurin: A Life in Bloom, 1948), Demuts'kyi never again worked with Dovzhenko.[10] In 1954, on the day of his death, in fact within minutes of his death, it was announced over the radio that Demuts'kyi had been awarded Honoured Practitioner of the Arts for the Ukrainian Soviet Socialist Republic.[11]

The purpose of tracing the detail of Demuts'kyi's fate at the hands of the authorities during the 1930s and 1940s is two-fold. On the one hand, while no doubt comparable to the peregrinations forced upon other members of the intelligentsia during this period, his biography offers an illuminating insight into the destruction wrought by the repressions of the period as far as camera operators were concerned. If other avant-garde teams remained largely intact, albeit verging on the inactive in the sense that the realization of their projects was persistently hampered by officialdom, the creative team that coalesced around Dovzhenko after the release of *Zvenyhora* was irrevocably decimated by a deliberate campaign of harassment that culminated not only in Demuts'kyi's various arrests, but also Dovzhenko's enforced flight to Moscow, a temporary measure to avoid persecution in Ukraine which ended up becoming permanent (his body was not even allowed to be buried in his native land after his death in November 1956).[12] Unlike other camera operators of his generation, for example Nil'sen and Kaliuzhnyi, Demuts'kyi was fortunate enough to avoid the Gulag, and worse, execution.[13] In this respect, his fate was analogous to that of Aleksandr Grinberg, a fellow Pictorialist photographer and cameraman whose nude studies at a 1935 exhibition resulted in his arrest on grounds of obscenity and a six-year sentence in the Gulag which was later fortunately reduced.[14] Nevertheless, Demuts'kyi's three arrests and period of exile not only disrupted his creative alliance with Dovzhenko, it also curtailed his influence on a younger generation of cameramen who had started working in VUFKU in the early 1930s. Some, like Iurii Ekel'chyk, who had worked as Demuts'kyi's assistant on *Ivan*, would later also endure a degree of harassment, for example over his involvement in the making of *Suvoryi iunak* (Strogii iunosha, A Severe Youth, 1936), a film directed by Room but never released.[15] Kokhno, who observed Demuts'kyi during the shooting of *Fata Morgana* (1932), has paid handsome tribute to his importance as mentor to this younger generation.[16]

On the other hand, the motivation for this repression gives an important insight into the nature of the bond that originally brought the team together and explains the profound, spiritual kinship that characterized the relationship between Dovzhenko and Demuts'kyi. This was based on their shared love and knowledge of Ukrainian culture and their concern for the survival and autonomy of that culture in the new, revolutionary era. In similar ways, both men became embroiled in the complex web of national politics that took shape during the 1920s and 1930s, their rise and fall from grace closely mirroring the attempts on the part of the creative intelligentsia in Ukraine to preserve a form of cultural independence, albeit within a socialist framework. At the beginning of his career, Dovzhenko was identified as a nationalist artist and *Zvenyhora* was hailed as the first authentically Ukrainian film.[17] Nevertheless, the issue of his artistic influences is still obscure and complicated by the fact that his poetic vision was influenced as much by modernist aesthetics as by Ukrainian folk-religious culture. Dovzhenko was undoubtedly passionate about the visual arts; indeed, his ambition as a young man after his return from a diplomatic posting abroad in 1923 was to become a painter.[18] The relationship between the works of art he produced from 1923 to 1926 and his films, however, has not been subjected to detailed investigation. Furthermore, the assumption that, as a practising artist, albeit one who would abandon painting once his move into film had been secured, Dovzhenko was solely responsible for the visual construction of his films is belied by other sources which suggest that his working practices were a great deal more complex than he was prepared to admit and to a significant extent depended on the creative input of other members of his team. A revisionist approach would stress the visual eclecticism of his silent-era films and the fact that stylistic variations are apparent both within and between films made at different stages of his career. This suggests that their visual language does not depend solely on his artistic allegiances, although these were undeniably important. Since the collapse of the Soviet Union and the release of documents from his private archive, it has become possible to interrogate the Dovzhenko 'myth' more robustly. This applies not only to the omission of politically awkward facts from his 1939 autobiography, something that has been highlighted by Liber, but also to his complex personality, his capacity for self-deception and self-mythologization, his abandonment of long-standing friends when it suited him, and (for some) the baleful influence of his wife, the actress and director Iuliia Solntseva, in trying to preserve something of this 'myth' after Dovzhenko's death.[19]

Although the creative partnership of Dovzhenko and Demuts'kyi is the primary focus of this chapter, it will also investigate films that Dovzhenko directed with other camera operators and those that Demuts'kyi photographed with other directors. It seeks to identify the sources of Dovzhenko's artistic vision and to demonstrate the ways in which these manifest themselves in his silent-era works. It will, nevertheless, stress the creative initiative of Demuts'kyi, an award-winning photographer influenced by the poetics of Pictorialism, who was committed to artistic experiment in ways no less energetic than Dovzhenko. It will argue, for example, that the most memorable sequences in *Zemlia*, the film that confirmed Dovzhenko's reputation as a poet of the cinema and proved influential for the generation of directors that came to the fore in the 1960s as part of the Soviet 'new wave', were primarily the product of Demuts'kyi's creative intervention. This chapter will consider the ramifications of this aesthetic decision in relation to the philosophy of nature as articulated in the film. It will also argue that the films photographed by Demuts'kyi represent a significant departure from the aesthetic canons of works that Dovzhenko directed alongside other camera operators. According to Petro Masokha, an actor trained at the Berezil Theatre in Kyiv who worked on *Zemlia* and *Ivan*, Dovzhenko never again managed to emulate the poetry of the works he directed alongside Demuts'kyi.[20] Indeed, it is typical of the auteur bias in cinema studies that, although Demuts'kyi was identified as a dynamic presence within Dovzhenko's unit as early as 1930, the year in which the Russian poet and translator Nikolai Ushakov identified him as one of the key figures in an emerging Ukrainian 'school' of cinematography, his significance has remained more or less unacknowledged beyond a handful of specialists and aficionados of his camerawork.[21]

The Initial 'Romance': From Painting and Photography to Cinema

Dovzhenko's undeniable interest in the visual arts is suggested by a number of facts: his passion for drawing from an early age; his brief attendance at the Kyiv Academy of Arts in 1918; his activities in Charlottenburg, just outside Berlin, from 1922 to 1923, which included attendance at courses offered by the State Higher School of Visual Arts, private lessons with the Expressionist painter Willy Jaeckel, and the acquaintance of other well known German artists, among them Heinrich Zille, Grosz, Kollwitz and Otto Nagel; and the establishment of an atelier in his apartment in Kharkhiv, which signalled the serious nature of his painterly ambitions.[22]

Judging from the works produced during this period, Dovzhenko's artistic influences were many and varied. First and foremost, he was the author of satirical cartoons which appeared in various Ukrainian-language newspapers and magazines; it is generally acknowledged that their blend of hyperbole and the grotesque owes much to the influence of Grosz, a left-wing painter, illustrator and set designer whose satirical works were extremely fashionable at the time in the Soviet Union.[23] During this same period, Dovzhenko produced book illustrations for anthologies of new writing, designs for film posters, portraits of contemporary literary and cultural figures and some self-portraits, both painted and sketched. These exhibit a range of influences and suggest an artist in the process of formation. His very first drawing, a self-portrait, is obviously derived from Cubist procedures.[24] Some of the sketched portraits of literary figures and one unfinished self-portrait are clearly influenced by Iurii Annenkov, an artist whose Cubo-Futurist portraits of contemporaries had been published as a collection in 1922.[25] Other sketches dating from the same period are more traditional in design and execution.[26] The film posters, of which only five have survived, among them those for Favst Lopatyns'kyi's *Synii paket* (Sinii paket, The Blue Packet, 1926) and Viktor Turin's *Borot'ba veletniv* (Bor'ba gigantov, The Battle of the Giants, 1926), share the expressive colour and linear emphasis of Constructivist artists like Klutsis and the Stenberg brothers.[27] By contrast, the painted self-portraits, each of them displaying a different attitude and pose, ignore the colourful blocks and strident lines associated with Constructivism and Cubo-Futurism in favour of a relatively restrained brushwork and palette reminiscent of Van Gogh's 1888 *Self-Portrait*. It comes as little surprise to learn that, along with Raphael, Il'ia Repin, Serov, Dmytro Levyts'kyi and Serhii Vasyl'kivs'kyi, the last two of whom were Ukrainian landscape painters, Van Gogh was one of Dovzhenko's favourite artists in the early 1920s.[28]

The variety of stylistic influences on display in this body of work renders comparison with Dovzhenko's films a treacherous task; indeed, it is unsurprising that for the most part the connections between them have been sought in the relatively narrow (and neutral) realm of caricature.[29] Those drawings that relate specifically to the films, for example the sketches produced during the making of *Arsenal* and *Michurin: Zhizn' v tsvetu*, also offer little in the way of compelling evidence: either they are stylistically incongruous with the particular scene as depicted in the film, or they consist of images that are already in the process of being filmed. In other words, they constitute responses to that process, rather than the preparatory stages that precede it (the fact that Dovzhenko sketches the actor, Grigorii Belov, who plays the role of Michurin, tends to suggest this).[30]

A more productive line of enquiry would draw upon the influence of German artists, in particular Kollwitz, not so much in relation to compositional method, but rather in terms of the expressions, positions and attitudes of the subjects, as well as the situational context. The opening sequences of *Arsenal*, for example, with their emphasis on the poverty, exhaustion, desperation and suffering that has resulted from the experience of war, are powerfully reminiscent of several works by Kollwitz: the 'widescreen' etching entitled *Scene from Germinal* (1893), one of several modelled on episodes from Zola's novel; the pen-and-ink drawing *Poverty* (1895); *Help Russia!* (1921), a lithograph designed as part of the international campaign to raise money for the victims of famine in the Lower Volga region; her charcoal sketch *The Survivors* (1922–1923), with its unusual lighting from above, which leaves the eyes of the female figures as ghostly, grotesque and darkened sockets; and *Bread!* (1924), a lithograph which, in its depiction of a mother besieged by two hungry children, is almost exactly copied by Dovzhenko.[31] These similarities suggest the strong influence of the Naturalist School. Further echoes of works by German left-wing artists in the opening sequences of *Arsenal* include the image of the dead soldier with the rictus, which is hauntingly reminiscent of two 1924 war sketches by Otto Dix, *Wounded* and *Dead Man in the Mud*.[32]

Although the influence of the Naturalist School is not, by and large, felt in Dovzhenko's paintings and sketches, it is probably safe to assume that the vision of human suffering in *Arsenal* was influenced by his encounters with German left-wing art in the early 1920s. This assumption notwithstanding, however, the films made before and after *Arsenal* do not belong straightforwardly to this category of vision. As this chapter aims to demonstrate, the stylistic compass of Dovzhenko's silent-era films is wide-ranging. It embraces the comic high-key, the noirish low-key, and the lyrically intense and visually ravishing. One film in particular, *Zvenyhora*, is marked by a radical degree of stylistic eclecticism. If it can be argued that Dovzhenko found his 'voice' on *Zvenyhora* because it was the first film on which he was given creative licence – in other words, the freedom to create his own, idiosyncratic genre outside the strictures of commerce or ideology – this 'voice' is best described as choral. Some of the distinctive features of this film, for example its Constructivist treatment of industrial landscapes and use of the hand-held camera, are strikingly modern; others, for example the treatment of rural landscapes and the quasi-mythological material, have the texture of photographic gravure and for this reason may strike the viewer as antiquated. A further disjunction lies in the fact that the modernist tendency is characterized by an impression of agitation, dynamism and kinetic energy, while the antiquated tendency moves towards the statuesque. These opposing features are a persistent presence in Dovzhenko's work, but it is noticeable after *Zvenyhora* that the compositional handling of these two approaches changes and that new and different stylistic directions begin to be felt. These relate to the emotional intensity of the camera's gaze, a greater lyrical appreciation of the colours, contours and material textures of the natural world, sensitivity to the quality of light, greater variation in optical method, and a greater degree of compositional invention. It is conceivable that this may have reflected evolution in Dovzhenko's own artistic preferences during the period concerned and the shifting nature of dramaturgical imperatives, but it is too much of a coincidence that this new direction gains impetus after the establishment of Demuts'kyi as his camera-operating partner of choice.

Demuts'kyi's path into cinematography was a familiar one for a camera operator, but it was accompanied by an international reputation in the sphere of artistic photography that few of his contemporaries, with the exception of Grinberg, could boast.[33] Like Dovzhenko, he was born in the countryside. His parents were members of the rural intelligentsia: his father was a doctor, composer and collector of Ukrainian folksongs, and his mother a specialist in Ukrainian folklore. Demuts'kyi studied music at a local gymnasium and wanted to enter a conservatoire on graduation, but parental pressure forced him to enrol for medicine, the study of which he apparently abandoned after only one year. He never lost his interest in music, however. In fact, he once described his photography and cinematography in musical terms:

Whenever I create something important or serious, whether in the sphere of photography or cinema, I always feel a kind of music which acquires some kind of musical form in my photographs or film frames. In the logic of its development, I always find support for the realization of the creative tasks with which I am faced.[34]

Having been given a camera by his uncle while still a child, Demuts'kyi pursued photography as an early hobby and passion. Although none of his plates from before the First World War has survived (there were apparently around five thousand in total), it is instructive that he was invited to join the prestigious Daguerre Society, one of the leading photographic societies in the Russian empire at the turn of the century. Its secretary, Nikolai Petrov, had been instrumental in organizing the International Salon of Artistic Photography in Kyiv in 1911, the first event of its kind in Ukraine and one that marked the tenth anniversary of the society's inauguration, and was an enthusiastic promoter of the latest trends.[35]

Demuts'kyi achieved public recognition in 1913 when four of his landscapes were selected for display at the All-Russian Exhibition of Photographic Artists.[36] Ushakov, the only commentator to have seen and written about the plates from this period, indicates that Demuts'kyi's creative evolution moved through four phases. The first consisted of portrait studies under the tutelage of Klavdiia Romaniuk, one of the leading photographic artists of her generation. The second, which preceded his success at the 1913 exhibition, showed him experimenting with Pictorialist printing techniques, in particular ozobromide, gum-arabic printing and bromoil.[37] The third phase, which coincided approximately with the First World War, was prompted by his encounter with Pictorialist works by photographers based in Europe and North America; this period was characterized by his adoption of the monocle lens, which was uncorrected for aberration, and which had been recommended by Petrov as early as 1903 on the basis of the experiments by Watzek, Henneburg and Kühn.[38] The fourth, which lasted from 1917 to 1918, consisted of experiments in photo-collage: these predate the first experiments in this genre by El' Lisitskii and Rodchenko, and suggest that Demuts'kyi may have been familiar with the photo-collages of the Berlin Dadaists, which also date from 1918.[39] His experiments during this phase included some 'rayonist' studies. For example, his portrait of Vadim Meller, the Cubo-Futurist and Constructivist artist who at the time was serving as the artistic director of the Berezil Theatre, consisted of separate strips of the negative printed at different levels of exposure.[40]

Demuts'kyi's commitment to photography was total even after the move into cinematography. According to Kokhno, he was never without his camera, and frequently took pictures as part of the preparatory process for his film work.[41] His camera accompanied him to Tashkent for his period of internal exile; indeed, some of his photographs from this period have survived.[42]

In order to appreciate the controversial nature of Pictorialist techniques during the early part of the twentieth century, it is sufficient to chart the debates in the pages of *Fotograf liubitel'*, the photographic journal in which Pictorialist landscapes were routinely denounced in terms of 'fog' or 'diffused mud'.[43] Surprisingly, echoes of this conservative response can still be found in the mid-1920s. Demuts'kyi's adoption of the monocle lens for photographic portraits of cast members of the Berezil Theatre, for example, was rudely dismissed by colleagues as 'blancmange'. Despite the fact that, in the very same year (1925), he was awarded a gold medal at the International Exhibition of Modern and Industrial Arts in Paris, they even questioned whether he knew how to take photographs properly.[44]

The early years of the Revolution witnessed Demuts'kyi working in a variety of different capacities and gravitating slowly towards cinematography. In 1921, he was appointed director of the photo-laboratory at the All-Ukrainian Academy of Sciences; during his tenure there he produced a number of nudes and several 'white-on-white' studies.[45] Two years later, he was working in the historical museum of the Berezil Theatre, one of the leading avant-garde theatres of the time, which had been founded by Lopatyns'kyi and Les' Kurbas. The arrival of Kas'ian Goleizovskii for the staging of *Iosif Prekrasnyi* (Joseph the Beautiful), the ballet which scandalized the management at the Bolshoi Theatre because of its innovative choreography and provocative costume designs, prompted a portfolio of some sixty photographs, all of them taken with a monocle lens.[46] In all likelihood, this was part of the fashionable interest among Soviet photographers in the poetics of the moving body, testimony to which is given by the various 'Art in Movement' exhibitions held in the Soviet Union from the mid-1920s onwards.[47] Demuts'kyi subsequently moved to VUFKU's Odessa studio, where he was put in charge of publicity shots for posters and photographed portraits of actors during casting sessions. His first official credit was for the feature film *V pazurakh Radvlady* (V kogtiakh sovetskoi vlasti, In the Claws of Soviet Power, 1926), a comedy in eight reels directed by Panteleimon Sazonov.[48] From here it was only a short step to camera operation itself, although the transition was apparently hampered by the resistance of the studio's professionals, who refused to let him near their cameras.[49] According to his autobiography, it was only after being given a camera by Kaliuzhnyi for one night in order to study its mechanisms that Demuts'kyi acquired the necessary rudiments of his craft.[50]

On Demuts'kyi's own admission, Kaliuzhnyi acted very much as his mentor during these early years.[51] This may partly be explained by their similar creative trajectories. Like Demuts'kyi, Kaliuzhnyi had worked as a photographer prior to his move into cinematography: he had published several portraits in collaboration with Petrov during the First World War and was familiar with the contemporary vogue for the monocle lens.[52] Ushakov describes him as one of the most experimental camera operators of his generation in Ukraine, yet so few of his works have survived that it is difficult to corroborate this reputation with any degree of confidence. For the most part, it appears to rest on a single work, *Zlyva*, which he photographed for Kavaleridze, who was an artist and sculptor before moving into film direction.[53] Judging by the reviews, which criticized the film's 'painterly excesses' and its 'statuesque', 'non-cinematic' acting, this film was undeniably an experimental work, but the specific target of these criticisms suggests that its visual poetics may have been heavily indebted to the Varangian sequence in *Zvenyhora*.[54] Furthermore, because this work has survived only in the form of stills, and it is not clear from the published examples whether these are frame or production stills, it is difficult to assess Kaliuzhnyi's specific contribution.[55] The same problem arises in relation to his other non-extant works, for example *Synii paket*, the screenplay for which was written by the 'Pan-Futurist' Geo Shkurupii, and Hryhorii Hrycher-Cherykover's *Pidozrilyi bagazh* (Podozritel'nyi bagazh, The Suspect Luggage, 1926).[56] Those films shot by Kaliuzhnyi that have survived offer little evidence in support of Ushakov's contention, although it could be argued that the directors in charge and their dramaturgies may have stifled his creative ingenuity. For example, the camerawork and lighting on *Benia Kryk* (Benia Krik, Benny Krik, 1926), the screen adaptation of Babel''s Odessa tales directed by Volodymyr Vil'ner, are relatively undistinguished. There is little evidence of the lighting innovations for which Kaliuzhnyi has been credited by contemporaries.[57] Furthermore, although some of the interior sequences feature unusual, jagged movements of the camera (Kaliuzhnyi later described these abrupt track-ins and track-outs as 'montage within the camera'), their *raison d'être* from the dramaturgical point of view is not immediately obvious.[58]

Iahidki kokhannia: The Pregnant Pause

When exactly Demuts'kyi and Dovzhenko came together for the first time as a formal creative partnership is not entirely clear. Conventional wisdom hitherto has dated this moment to the time when Dovzhenko was editing *Zvenyhora*, at which point it was agreed on the basis of their shared enthusiasms that they would collaborate on his next project.[59] Demuts'kyi's participation in the shooting of *Vasia – reformator*, however, and his official crediting on Dovzhenko's directorial debut, *Iahidki kokhannia* (Iagodka liubvi, Love's Little Berry, 1926), suggest that their acquaintance may have been earlier, although there is still confusion about the precise distribution of responsibilities on these productions. On *Vasia – reformator*, for example, which had been scripted by Dovzhenko, it would appear that Demuts'kyi was certainly employed as the main camera operator.[60] Nevertheless, he was working alongside Joseph Rona, an Austrian-born cameraman with many years' experience in Germany who had also worked as a director before joining VUFKU. Furthermore, at a certain point in the production, after the first-choice candidate, Lopatyns'kyi, had been removed, allegedly for altering the script, Rona was promoted to the position of director, a decision that apparently filled the actors with despair because of his uninspiring character and conventional methods.[61] Dovzhenko's involvement in the production was also apparently limited: although he was invited to join the unit in order to 'strengthen the creative input', and was present during a small number of rehearsals, his influence was firmly resisted by Rona. When completed, the film was not regarded as a success by the studio management and was instantly shelved (sadly, it is no longer extant).[62]

A similar confusion arises in relation to *Iahidki kokhannia*, which was also scripted by Dovzhenko. Despite Demuts'kyi's accreditation on this film, Shvachko is adamant that the two-reel comedy was photographed by Rona (Demuts'kyi at this time had apparently already begun shooting *Svizhyi viter* (Svezhii veter, A Breath of Fresh Air, 1926) with Heorhii Stabovyi).[63] It is possible that Rona's involvement in the production was prompted by studio nervousness in relation to a directorial 'novice'. As Liber and others have stressed, while Dovzhenko could boast a reasonably extensive knowledge of cinema at this time, having become acquainted with several household names in the German film industry while working and studying in Berlin, and having visited cinemas there on regular occasions, he had no actual theatre- or film-directing experience.[64] Judging from the sources available, moreover, it would appear that he experienced considerable difficulties when editing the material and was disappointed to discover that what had seemed amusing and comic when the scenes were being rehearsed and filmed did not translate well onto the screen. It is symptomatic of Dovzhenko's relative lack of experience that Hrycher-Cherykover was pressed into editing the material alongside him, although the latter's attempt to render the film more effective as comedy by reducing its length from three reels to two was not ultimately successful.[65]

It would not be appropriate to judge the artistic inclinations of Dovzhenko on the basis of *Iahidki kokhannia*: it has all the hallmarks of an apprenticeship work, and it is symptomatic of its relative unimportance to him that he later described the film as a 'directorial try-out' (*rezhisserskaia proba*).[66] It is essentially a comedy of manners in the style of Harold Lloyd, and very much a typical product of the Odessa studio of VUKFU at this time. It tells the story of a hairdresser and barber, Zhan Kovbasiuk, who is presented with a newborn baby by his current lover and spends the rest of the film trying to absolve himself of his paternal responsibilities by trying to foist the baby onto a variety of bystanders. He is eventually forced to accept his obligations by an official from the People's Tribunal, after which he discovers, much to his chagrin, that the baby in fact belongs to his lover's aunt, and that the lover has simply exploited the existence of the child to force him to sign a marriage certificate.

Although the film is primarily a comedy with traditional stock elements, for example a watermelon fight and several chases, it is not completely devoid of contemporary relevance. The inability of Zhan to feed and entertain the baby constitutes an ironic comment on the persistence of certain gender norms in the post-revolutionary era. Furthermore, the appearance of a street urchin towards the end of the film, while treated primarily as comic material, may serve as a poignant reminder to the viewer of the widespread problem of homeless children and orphans in the immediate post-revolutionary years. The film demonstrates Dovzhenko's assured handling of acting technique, as well as his familiarity with certain stock-in-trade tricks, for example slow-motion and speeded-up action for comic effect. Indeed, *Iahidki kokhannia* succeeds in imitating the Hollywood import to such an extent that, if not for the director's known passion for U.S. comedies of this kind, it might be suspected that the film was conceived as a pastiche or parody.[67] Certain elements of the plot, for example the multifarious attempts to dispense with the baby, appear to have been borrowed directly from

Chaplin's *The Kid*. The approach to make-up, moreover, which is heavily applied in the case of the male lead, and the choice of costumes (straw boaters and neckties) are strongly reminiscent of the romantic farces of the pre-revolutionary era, for example Bauer's *Prikliucheniia Liny v Sochi* (The Adventures of Lina in Sochi, 1916), which was shot by Zavelev. Only the scenes in the People's Tribunal hint at anything like the new political order.

It was presumably this anachronistic and retrograde aspect of the production that explained the funereal silence that greeted its studio screening, a reaction that apparently almost resulted in Dovzhenko's premature departure from the studio.[68] The same might be said about the cinematography, which, while undeniably professional, is conservative and less inventive in some respects than the pre-revolutionary camerawork of Zavelev for Bauer in the films set along the Black Sea coast. Predictably for a comedy, Rona elected to shoot in high key. Furthermore, like Zavelev, he appears to have relished the dazzlingly white tones produced by the southern sun. This is reinforced by the persistent deployment of white objects and materials on exterior and interior locations: prams, babies' bonnets and blankets; Zhan's boater; summer flowers dotted around the city's gardens; the sheets, napkins and shaving foam in Zhan's salon; and the white horse that transports him to the tribunal. In the interest of reinforcing this high-key mode, and perhaps inspired by Tisse's example on *Bronenosets Potemkin*, which of course had also been shot in the south, Rona twice resorts to mirrors or reflectors. The first occasion is after the watermelon fight when a street photographer, keen to capture the two protagonists in a typical scene 'from around the world' (this is the title of the magazine for which he works), asks them to pose for a picture: judging by the quality of the light that strikes Zhan's face from below at an oblique angle, and the ethereal reflection of the same light source in the glasses of the elderly man standing next to him, a mirror or some other reflector has been placed in front of the actors at a low position slightly to their right. The second occasion is when the same elderly man, now burdened with Zhan's unwanted baby, stops to rest and orders a drink from a street vendor: here, due to the awning that protects the two protagonists from the sun, mirrors or reflectors have been used to ensure exposure in the shadow areas. By contrast, lighting for interiors appears to be relatively conventional. Like Golovnia in *Shakhmatnaia goriachka*, but with considerably greater illumination at his disposal, Rona devises arrangements for interiors that generally involve a combination of arcs and mercury-vapour lamps: the former are positioned for the most part relatively high in relation to the actors, and usually slightly behind them and at an angle; the latter provide weak fill-light from the front. For the most part, Rona strives for an impression of naturalness within these interiors. In the lighting for the sequence which takes place in a toy shop, for example, where the arrangements can be gauged by the patches of light reflected in the body of a doll that sits on a shelf just behind the owner's counter, there has clearly been an attempt to simulate the effect of sunlight streaming through the window (off-screen right). Within this general framework, depending on the position of the actor, the lighting for portraiture tends to be diffuse rather than directed. Thus in Zhan's salon, which betrays the positioning of arcs to the left and right of the actor, the face itself, rather as on the exterior locations, where his boater acts as a form of protection from the sun, is not subjected to modelling and appears relatively flat.

Six Degrees of Separation: *Sumka dypkur'era, Dva dni* and *Zvenyhora*

The fact that Dovzhenko's embryonic partnership with Demuts'kyi did not develop into anything substantial at this stage indicates the prevailing conditions within the VUFKU studios. The demand for box-office hits to compete with foreign imports, and the tendency to move camera operators around between directors irrespective of their *mode d'emploi*, probably explain why, although they were clearly aware of each other, no creative partnership was forged.[69] Over the next two years, Demuts'kyi shot three films with Stabovyi; only two of them are extant. At one point he was filming with the director Petr Chardynin, an 'old hand', whose costume drama based on the life of Catherine the Great, *Prymkhy Kateryny II* (Kaprizy Ekateriny II, The Caprices of Catherine the Great, 1927), apparently filled him with frustration and despair.[70]

Dovzhenko, meanwhile, had started working on *Sumka dypkur'era* (Sumka dipkur'era, The Diplomatic Pouch, 1927), the plot for which was based on the circumstances of Teodor Nette's assassination by anti-Bolshevik Russian émigrés in Latvia. For the first time he was working alongside Nikolai Kozlovskii, an actuality specialist who had moved into cinematography for the shooting of *Sten'ka Razin* (1908), the first Russian film to be released for domestic consumption, which was produced by Aleksandr Drankov. Kozlovskii could boast considerable experience in the spheres of both direction and camera operation during the pre-revolutionary period. From 1907 to 1917 he photographed a number of films with different directors before settling with an established team within the studio of A. Taldykin & Co. He is also credited with the direction of three other films and later established his own private film company.[71] Zheliabuzhskii has described him as a 'great artist' and a 'master of chiaroscuro' who paid a great deal of attention to the composition of the frame.[72] From 1918 onwards, having decided not to emigrate, Kozlovskii was employed by the Moscow Cinema Committee. Like other camera operators working for this committee, he shot actuality footage and worked on a number of agitprop productions, among them Aleksandr Ivanov-Gai's *Golod* (Hunger, 1921), a screen adaptation of Leonid Andreev's Expressionist drama, *Tsar' Golod* (King Hunger, 1908), which was given a contemporary resonance and urgency by the inclusion of harrowing newsreel footage of the 1921 famine in the Lower Volga region (although he was not specifically credited, this footage was very probably shot by Kozlovskii himself).[73] Although Kozlovskii photographed several features during the 1920s, few of them have survived. Sobolev's observation that he worked coldly and mechanically alongside 'hacks', but enthusiastically and inventively with directors keen to experiment, may explain the unevenness of his extant works.[74] It may be significant in generic terms that one of the productions on which he was engaged before *Sumka dypkur'era*, namely, *Ego prevoskhoditel'stvo* (His Excellency, 1926), was based on the true-life assassination attempt on the Governor of Vilnius by a town cobbler called Girsh Lekhert on 5 May 1902.[75]

In stylistic terms, *Sumka dypkur'era* is markedly different from *Iahidki kokhannia*. This is partly explained by the fact that its narrative conforms very transparently to the spy thriller or 'Red detective' genre popular in the Soviet Union during the 1920s.[76] The first and second reels, which dramatize the attempted murder of two Soviet diplomatic couriers on their way by train to Dover from London on an important political assignment, have not survived, but the four following reels, which are extant, demonstrate the radically different visual aesthetic.[77] The third reel, for example, begins with several low-key and expressive moments. The bodies of the two couriers, one of them dead, lie on a railway embankment, their prostrate forms picked out by a single projector arc amidst driving rain and darkness. After the survivor has been rescued by a British signalman sympathetic to the Bolshevik cause, the viewer is presented with a 'classic montage' sequence in which the courier's confused recollection of the events leading up to his attempted murder, and his effort to understand where he is located, are communicated by means of disorientating and fragmented point-of-view shots. All of these images involve some mode of distortion: a portrait of an unknown protagonist, presumably one of the courier's attackers, which is initially out of focus and then, after it has been brought into and out of focus again, superimposed over a jagged horizontal pan both left and right as the courier's eyes agitatedly survey the objects in the room; a portrait of Lenin hanging on the wall which has been multiplied and fractured by use of a kaleidoscopic lens; a truncated, extreme close-up of a face which gradually moves away from the camera and out of focus; and an extreme close-up of a person (later revealed to be a British Government investigator called White), which is multiplied and spirals towards to the camera. The use of these special-effects lenses, the psychological justification admittedly dubious (even a hallucinating mind does not trigger fragmentation of this kind), is unparalleled in the Soviet cinema of this period.[78] Certainly, when viewed in its entirety, this sequence represents the nearest that the film comes to replicating the quasi-hallucinatory visions of German Expressionism.

Elsewhere in *Sumka dypkur'era* there are further signs of experimental tendencies. The insertion of documentary material showing the Dover docks – this is presumably archival footage – anticipates the use of actuality material in *Zvenyhora*, for example the agricultural and industrial sequences, although in the case of the latter this has clearly been filmed by a studio cinematographer – in other words, with much greater attention given to composition and the position of this material within the larger episodic whole. Furthermore, *Sumka dypkur'era* contains two sections of Soviet-style montage. The first consists of a rapid succession of expressive close-ups of determined sailors – these will be reprised in the Civil War sequences in *Zvenyhora*, albeit with camera angles that are not axial; and the second is encountered during the 'erotic' dance of the main female protagonist, the ballerina Elena, on board the HMS *Victoria* – here the frenetic movements of her body, sometimes truncated, are intercut with images of the ship's pistons working furiously, the lascivious gazes of her audience and the faces of jazz musicians. Multiple exposures of the players are included in this sequence. Dovzhenko and Kozlovskii also deploy occasional out-of-focus images, a 'vibrating' camera and a brief rocking motion to approximate the movements of the ship in a storm. The ugly and grotesque portraits of the members of the audience can be compared to the expressions of those watching with frenzied anticipation as Pavlo, in a scam to raise money for political ends while exiled in Prague, threatens to shoot himself on stage during the penultimate episode of *Zvenyhora*. Furthermore, with its angular compositions and selective lighting, *Sumka dypkur'era* is much more dynamic from the visual point of view than *Iahidki kokhannia.* Examples of this more modern aesthetic would include: the portrait of Elena at the beginning of the third reel which shows her inside a train compartment with 'realistic' top-lighting splashing across the top of her head, leaving her face darkened, and slashing rain striking the glass in front of her; the resort to chiaroscuro and multiple exposure for the portraits of Dovzhenko himself as the ship's boilerman, a typical piece of 1920s mobile sculpture which, albeit an undeniable act of self-publicizing narcissism, aims to accentuate the musculature of his body; and the spraying of the camera with a hose as British sailors clean the decks of the *Victoria* before it sets sail for Leningrad with the all-important communiqué on board.

Demuts'kyi's creative path was evolving in parallel with Dovzhenko's at this time, albeit within a series of slightly different generic contexts. From 1926 to 1927, for example, he shot three films for Stabovyi: the previously mentioned *Svizhyi viter*, *Dva dni* (Dva dnia, Two Days, 1927) and *Liudyna z lisu* (Chelovek iz lesa, The Man from the Forest, 1927). According to Ushakov, Stabovyi gave Demuts'kyi complete freedom as far as lighting and composition were concerned.[79] This is revealing in the case of *Dva dni*, a drama in six reels about the impact of the Civil War in Ukraine, large sections of which were shot at night. The central conflict in this film is handled with refreshing honesty by Stabovyi. The plot concerns a manservant, left to guard an aristocratic mansion and the young son of its owners after they have fled in the face of Bolshevik advances, who experiences a conflict of loyalties on the appearance of his own son, who has joined a Bolshevik regiment that briefly occupies the mansion. *Dva dni* is rare among Soviet films of the silent period in the sense that it evinces real sympathy for people who find themselves ensnared in political events beyond their understanding and are ill-prepared for the conflicts of interest that ensue. The dogged loyalty of the manservant, which is repaid with treachery when the Bolsheviks evacuate the area and the Whites return, has prompted comparisons with *Der letzte Mann*; undeniably, there is a startling physical resemblance between the actor playing the manservant, Ivan Zamychkovs'kyi, and Emil Jannings, who played the porter in Murnau's film. Ushakov has argued that the camerawork is partly indebted to *Der letzte Mann*, but also to the cinematography of James van Trees on *Lilies of the Field* (1924), a film directed by John Francis Dillon which apparently made a big impact in Ukraine.[80] These similarities notwithstanding, there are several sequences in which Demuts'kyi displays a distinctive approach. The opening scene, for example, an essentially static tableau showing a wounded horse, a dead soldier and an empty village, bears comparison with the opening *paysages* in *Arsenal*. In the second reel, moreover, when the manservant contemplates his memories of his son, who at this stage is presumed a victim of the war, the cinematography moves into sentimental soft-focus, with both portraits (the father and son) photographed with an uncorrected lens. The lighting arrangements, with arcs positioned in three-quarters back positions and only weak fill-light from the front, betray the influence of Tisse and Golovnia, rather than Freund's more conventional, frontal technique. The expressive treatment of the night sequences, with careful sculpting of the mansion exteriors, in particular its trees and iron railings, and the tendency to depict soldiers moving into and out of patches of light, contributed to Demuts'kyi's burgeoning reputation at this relatively early stage. A reviewer in *Kino*, one of the leading Ukrainian-language film publications at this time, hailed his 'taste', 'temperament' and 'exclusively artistic excellence'; it added that 'in his hands the camera lens is as obedient as a brush in the hands of a painter'.[81]

The year 1927 marked a turning point in the commercial strategies of VUFKU and permitted a greater degree of freedom for the more experimental directors within its studios. While Demuts'kyi was languishing alongside Chardynin, Dovzhenko was entrusted with the adaptation of a controversial screenplay by two émigrés, one of whom had returned to Ukraine in the mid-1920s after the declaration of an amnesty.[82] Entitled *Zvenyhora*, the film based on this screenplay is an extraordinarily complex work in terms of its narrative structure and vast historical canvas. The difficulty of the film resides primarily in the principle of ellipsis, as a result of which key events, in particular those belonging to the First World War and Civil War, are subjected to a fragmented and sometimes oblique treatment. The different narrative strands are nominally linked by the presence of a supra-historical and essentially symbolic figure, an old man, and the 'folk legend' with which he is associated; namely, the treasure buried in the hills of Zvenyhora, which gives the film its title and endows it with a historiosophical and mythological dimension. The symbolic meaning of this treasure, which according to the film's poetic conceit is the product of legendary events during the Varangian invasion of pre-Christian Rus', has been the source of much dispute. Some argue that it stands for a conservative national identity rooted in the past which must be rejected in the new, progressive era (it is protected by an evil monk, and the old man, while ultimately siding with the new regime after having tried to blow up a Bolshevik train, is superstitious and God-fearing). Others take the view that it asserts the continuity and autonomy of Ukraine's one-thousand-year history, with the three epochs featured in the narrative – the Varangian invasion, the supremacy of the Haidamaky in the sixteenth and seventeenth centuries, and the modern period of revolt – constituting moments of political and cultural independence free from external interference. Whatever view is taken, it is clear that *Zvenyhora* represents a vision that lies beyond genre. It offers a version of history that eschews the epic and borders at times on dream fantasy, a patchwork quilt of memorable and at times dazzling images which, while they may not ultimately cohere into a clear and easily comprehensible narrative, nevertheless encapsulate the modernist fascination for fragmented and non-teleological 'stream-of-consciousness'. The ambition of the film can be gauged by Dovzhenko's own comment in a brochure published shortly after the film's release that it expressed 'in two thousand metres, a millennium'.[83]

The complex politics that informed Dovzhenko's treatment of the screenplay and his disputes with its authors need not be discussed here; they have been admirably investigated by Liber.[84] It is the visual aesthetic of the film that requires this study's attention. The degree to which *Zvenyhora* represents a compromise between two creative personalities, both of them forceful but very different in terms of their aesthetic inclinations, has not been sufficiently appreciated in the critical writing on this film hitherto. Liber, for example, who refers to the problems encountered during the production – in particular, the disagreements between Dovzhenko, Zavelev and the production artist Vasyl' Krychevs'kyi, which resulted in open rebellion on the part of the latter two, sometimes on a daily basis, and the directing of complaints to the studio management – evinces little interest in their ramifications for the visual structure of the film.[85]

To view these disagreements purely in terms of a conflict between old and new ways of thinking would be an injustice to Zavelev. There can be little doubt that, like Levitskii, he was unimpressed by the more radical forms of avant-garde poetics; this is suggested by his guarded embrace of Kurbas during the making of *Vendetta* (Vendetta, 1924), an anti-religious satire that marked the theatre director's first foray into the realms of cinema.[86] This did not mean, however, that he was an ultra-orthodox cameraman who was hostile to any form of experiment. Zavelev's complaints about Dovzhenko need proper contextualization. His reproach that Dovzhenko 'does not understand montage', for example, was potentially perceptive in the sense that it anticipated the bafflement of audiences on the film's release: the jumps between historical epochs and the radical use of ellipsis proved a quite serious impediment to comprehension even on the part of sophisticated viewers, and remain so to this day.[87] Zavelev's objection to a whole section being filmed in soft-focus, allegedly on the grounds that this would 'discredit' him throughout the Soviet Union, also needs to be approached with caution. If the objection was principled, it reflected a position little different from Kuleshov, hardly a conservative figure, but someone who, as mentioned in Chapter Three, rejected the vogue for Impressionism, or what he dubbed 'antique gravure', on the grounds that it compromised clarity of vision and therefore understanding.[88] The crucial point here may have been Zavelev's reluctance to shoot a *whole section* out of focus. There is only one part of the film to which such an anxiety could potentially apply – the 'mythical' invasion by Varangian warriors – yet, as a close viewing will demonstrate, this lengthy sequence was not photographed entirely out of focus. This suggests that, while undeniably the site of creative conflict, *Zvenyhora* must also have been the product of artistic compromise. It is interesting to note that there are compositional approaches in this film which are not echoed in the works directed by Dovzhenko either before or afterwards, but which do resurface, the positioning and angle of vision of the camera virtually identical, in Zavelev's work for other directors. Most strikingly, this can be witnessed in his treatment of the industrial sequences in Oleksandr Soloviov's *Zirvani dni* (Vzorvannye dni, Days of Explosion, 1930), a film that satirizes the collectivization of agriculture and constitutes a meta-commentary on the function of documentary at the time of the first Five-Year Plan (unsurprisingly, it was never released in the Soviet Union). Interestingly, *pace* his protest in 1927, Zavelev appears to have been willing in this film to shoot brief scenes with a degree of diffusion.[89]

The stylistic eclecticism of *Zvenyhora* was noted by several early reviewers.[90] There is clearly an attempt to photograph different episodes in different visual styles, depending on their subject matter, dramaturgy and generic status. Confusingly, however, the complex narrative structure of the film results in these episodes sometimes being intermingled. On occasion, individual sequences find themselves divorced from their initial, episodic context and positioned cheek-by-jowl with sequences belonging to a different episode and thus exhibiting different visual characteristics. Furthermore, the viewer sometimes encounters stylistic incongruities within individual episodes. As a pertinent example, one might point to the *paysage* fragment which introduces the Ivan Kupalo (St John's Eve) episode and shows trees and the sun reflected in the calm waters of a stream or small river, the mirror-clear reflections compromised by the occasional drop of rain (Fig. 38). In terms of its narrative position, this landscape belongs to the series of bucolic images which poeticize the ancient rituals and pastimes of the Ukrainian folk. In terms of tonal arrangement, with its restricted range of deep blacks and brilliant whites, and the classical precision of its composition, the landscape belongs aesthetically (and presumably also geographically) to the images of the river which provide the backdrop for the performing of ancient rituals, for example the round dances associated with the festival of Ivan Kupalo and the placing of juniper wreaths in the water to foretell the identity of future husbands. The recourse to *contre-jour* for the moment when three young women rush to the riverbank to see their wreaths floating downstream produces an identical set of tonalities to those in the *paysage* fragment, a similar kind of solar glare, and the balancing of the whole in compositional terms, in particular as a result of the careful arrangement of the human figures and their precise positioning in relation to nearby trees (Fig. 39). A very traditional kind of visual aesthetic can be detected here, perhaps even the kind of 'beautiful scene' which Dovzhenko, according to Nechesa, the VUFKU studio head, feared would 'destroy' his film.[91] Paradoxically, however, a very similar kind of composition and visual aesthetic can be witnessed in a brief moment from the Civil War episode. This is also a *paysage* fragment, one that shows the silhouetted reflections of soldiers crossing a ford, and looks as if it has been photographed in exactly the same location (Fig. 40).

A further paradox becomes apparent in this episode in the sense that the scenes showing the dancers have been photographed in a quasi-Pictorialist style, the sharpness of the image compromised by the use of non-anastigmatic lenses, the dust that rises from the ground, and the smoke of a small fire around which the dancers are moving. This may have reflected Dovzhenko's belief that the simulation of antique gravure might best illustrate the ancient pedigree of these rituals and their deep roots in Ukrainian folk culture, but it undoubtedly compromises the unity of stylistic vision as established in the other sequences from this episode.[92] The recourse to such poetics for these images offers further support for the idea that Zavelev was not in principle opposed to soft-focus cinematography. Furthermore, it indicates that Dovzhenko must have been familiar with Pictorialist concepts before the making of *Zemlia*, although of course, bearing in mind Demuts'kyi's photographic activities during the 1920s, and their acquaintance as a result of working on *Vasia – reformator*, he could hardly have been unaware of them.

Such compositions are graphically juxtaposed with the Constructivist-style images of the industrial sequences. Here, perhaps ironically, the tonalities of the river and stream landscapes are similar, with *contre-jour* and glaring sunlight employed to accentuate them, but the compositional approach is fundamentally different, with diagonals predominating, and the largely axial position of the camera abandoned in favour of extreme *rakurs* and the occasional 'Dutch tilt'. The adoption of multiple exposure, which occurs after the Bolsheviks are stirred into action to save the Revolution from reactionary bourgeois forces, signals this different aesthetic. The superimposition in question produces a collage-like effect that shows coal being lifted diagonally by conveyer belts against a background of factory chimneys, each one photographed at a different angle and with different sets of parallel electric cables criss-crossing the frame (Fig. 41). The absence of camera movement aside, these images are strikingly similar to the montage sequences in *Mat'* discussed in Chapter Three. The idea that links the frames is the centrality of the extraction of coal, Ukraine's national 'treasure', which fires the furnaces in steel foundries. In due course, this sequence gives way to images of steel being pressed, the mechanization of industrial processes and the production of tractors. The audacious culmination of this montage combination witnesses the camera rising slowly in an industrial lift, the scaffolding in the foreground moving past hypnotically in shadow, and the lift carrying the spectator higher and higher until a God-like perspective overlooking a massive construction project is achieved.

The only self-contained episode in the entire film is the Varangian invasion. Visually, this is the most experimental section in *Zvenyhora*, its realization from the technical point of view complicated to the extent that it is not immediately clear how the effects have been achieved. Close analysis reveals that the sequence consists of a series of superimposed images: the human action is photographed for the most part in reasonably sharp focus, but the landscape through which the human figures move is diffuse. This gives rise to a general imprecision in relation to the visual presentation of the material which resonates with the highly symbolic, semi-ritualized nature of the action and the deliberately retarded gestures and movements (Fig. 42). In essence, this section constitutes the cinematic equivalent of ritual theatre, the revival of which had been associated with the Symbolist movement in the pre-revolutionary era, and which in the modern period included the staging of genuine folk rituals, such as wedding ceremonies, suitably adapted or modernized.[93] The historical, mythical context explains the surreal quality of the sets. Indeed, although shot largely out of focus, the props are clearly not intended to be realistic representations of actual objects, as can be seen from the stylized depiction of a tree in the background of one of the early scenes, which has been photographed in long-shot. Other shapes are vague and verge on the abstract, to the extent that they are unrecognizable (production stills suggest that the 'trees' in question may have been painted in an impressionistic style before being placed in position).[94] The overt presence of a stage – the section in its entirety looks very much as if it has been filmed on a theatre set, rather than within a studio – explains the static position of the camera, which frames the action from an axial position at the conventional height for the pre-revolutionary era, and for the most part in medium- or long-shot, with only rare incursions into the zone of the medium close-up. Such 'anachronism', while undeniably redolent of silent cinema in its early, 'primitive' phase, may be regarded as entirely appropriate in view of the mythological subject. Those, like Sobolev, who regard the *longueurs* of this sequence as the product of Zavelev's conservative instincts, and note their retrograde character when compared to montage theory in its Soviet manifestation, are missing the point entirely.[95] The unvarying position of the camera and the stylized attitudes of the actors are clearly designed to allude to antiquated forms of artistic expression: the episodic arrangements of frescoes; the tableaux that depict episodes from saints' lives; and the horizontal narratives of tapestries celebrating epic events. Dovzhenko treats the invasion cinematically as if it were an archaeological artefact raised from a newly exhumed barrow. Furthermore, while clearly seeking to promote an embryonic myth of nationhood, the Varangian episode is at the same time a poetic expression of the principle of violence that motivates human history. Despite its antique stylization, the repeated shots of blows and beheadings by means of swords serve as a displaced substitute for the bloodshed that is implied, but never explicitly shown, as part of the First World War and Civil War sequences elsewhere. It belongs to a whole series of visual tropes that describe events by means of substitution, for example the haystacks that metamorphose into rifles to signal the onset of war, or the bayonet point of a rifle stuck into sand to indicate the refusal to serve at the Front.

Domestic Violence: *Arsenal*

In view of the eclecticism of *Zvenyhora*, it is difficult to isolate with confidence the emerging principles of Dovzhenko's aesthetic inclinations. Certain ideas exist in embryonic form and are developed in a more sustained manner in *Arsenal*. The use of the freeze-frame, for example, adopted briefly in *Zvenyhora* for the moment when the old man mounts his horse in the opening sequence, suggests Dovzhenko's interest in history as a 'frozen' or 'petrified' category, perhaps even a form of death, and yet the non-linear structure of *Zvenyhora*, with its vision of past events as continuously present in the Ukrainian national consciousness, suggests otherwise. Certainly, the next two films he directed, but this time alongside Demuts'kyi, evince a persistent interest in static forms, one which, in radical defiance of cinema's kinaesthetic essence, brings the moving image into the zone of the still photograph. In *Arsenal*, the viewer is presented on several occasions with images of human figures locked into petrified, statuesque poses which function as metaphors for political stagnancy and deadlock. Such compositions coincide with moments – the effects of war on rural communities, the nervous waiting period during the strike of the munitions factory – when the conditions of normal life have been suspended. Indeed, it is the static sequence and sustained gaze associated with it that form the basis of what some commentators have defined as the very essence of Dovzhenko's art. Shklovskii, for example, has observed that the Ukrainian director's use of the 'extended take' (*dlinnyi plan*) anticipated the montage rhythms of sound film.[96] Other commentators have referred to the emotional intensity of Dovzhenko's images and what Perez has described in relation to *Zemlia* as the 'self-sufficient fragment'.[97] In this context, it is worth drawing attention to the fact that the 'extended take' involves a shift from the highly dynamic and edited image, with its requirement of distinct and immediate impressions, towards the static and thus 'photographed' image, with a sense of enclosed space, absence of movement within the frame and the possibility of sustained investigation by the viewer.

It is remarkable how many incidental characters are obliged to hold the attention of the camera's gaze in *Arsenal*. The woman during the strike who is shown concentrating on her knitting, the woman who has been unfaithful to her husband during the First World War, and the Red Cross nurse who seeks to understand the meaning of death are just three of the many images which, because they are static, approach the condition of still photography. Repeatedly, the viewer is confronted with sustained and disturbing portraits of physical and mental anguish: the opening image of the mother who has lost her three sons; the German soldier convulsed hysterically by laughing gas; and the dead soldier lying prostrate in mud. By necessity, these shots are meticulously staged, yet the ways in which they have been composed, and the particular lighting treatment by Demuts'kyi, imbue them with a tremendous pathos. There is suffering elsewhere in the films of the avant-garde released to celebrate the tenth anniversary of the October Revolution, but there is nothing as powerful or heart-rending as *Arsenal*.

The tendency towards the static is best illustrated by one of the most haunting images in *Arsenal*: the execution of the munitions worker. His portrait is presented as part of the film's concluding section, which shows Rada forces overwhelming the strikers and launching reprisals in the form of extrajudicial executions. The sequence begins with scenes of Cossack soldiers celebrating victory. At a certain moment, however, Dovzhenko cuts to a close-up of a young man, his head inclined upwards and his eyes staring vacantly and rightwards out of the frame. The meaning of this shot and the identity of the protagonist are not immediately clear, but the expression is unforgettable. This man, as the viewer subsequently learns, is about to be executed: a series of cuts moves the camera further and further away from him in staggered jumps until it becomes clear that he is lined up against a wall, moments from death. With the benefit of hindsight, the qualities of the initial portrait which hint at impending death become more obviously perceptible. This is the only close-up in the film in which all extraneous detail (at least initially) has been stripped away. In addition, the lighting has been manipulated so that shadow areas hug the curves of the young man's face, in particular the left-hand side of the face, as if he is wearing a head garment pulled tightly against his cheeks. When the camera pulls back, it becomes clear that the actor has been positioned next to a large shadow cast against the wall, the vertical lines of which encroach upon his face. The suggestiveness of the arrangement is calculated. The lighting accentuates the structure of his cheekbones, and imbues his face with a prematurely cadaverous aspect, as if he were already dead, or nearly dead. Kepley Jr notes perceptively that this image constitutes something of a 'death-mask', but does not recognize that the man is not yet dead.[98] The idea of a Christ-like martyrdom is insinuated when, in long-shot, seconds before the man is executed, his arms are shown extending outwards, ostensibly in a gesture of surrender, but with clear overtones of crucifixion. Furthermore, the theatricality of his collapse to the ground is reprised by the four executions that follow in swift succession shortly afterwards. In the relatively long time that the bodies take to fall, one is reminded of the highly poeticized executions that constitute the culmination of the Varangian episode in *Zvenyhora*. In these sequences and others like them in *Arsenal*, one senses the birth of a foundation myth.

Scenes of death are so frequent in *Arsenal* that it might almost be described as a *danse macabre*. Images of lifelessness punctuate the film at periodic intervals.

They include motionless bodies at rest, as well as moments of trauma associated with suffering, whether physical or emotional, which appear to paralyse the protagonists in question. By varying their compositional strategies in each case, Dovzhenko and Demuts'kyi treat each death and each trauma as a uniquely individual moment. Thus Demuts'kyi adopts an extremely unusual angle of lighting for the mother whose son has been executed during the pacification of the strike: here, in a direct reversal of the Kollwitz portrait mentioned earlier, but with a similar effect, a spotlight has been positioned directly beneath her chin to produce a disturbing, ghost-like appearance, with only dark sockets representing her eyes (Fig. 43). Elsewhere, it is the method of composition and the lighting arrangements that distinguish the shot. The depiction of the dead soldier half-buried in earth, introduced in the 'landscape during battle' sequence, is a diagonal composition of uniformly grey tonality in which natural light, striking the subject from the side, emphasizes the rictus into which his face is contorted. This 'death-mask' is then ironically juxtaposed with the reaction of the laughing-gas victim, his hysterical laughter the very mirror of the dead man's grin. For the death of the soldier who has dictated a letter home in the makeshift hospital, Dovzhenko and Demuts'kyi invert the image so that his lifeless head faces downwards at a slight angle to the camera. The woman who has been killed by a sniper just prior to the Red Cross sequence receives yet another visual treatment. The truncation is brutal here: only part of this woman's prostrate body, with its arms outstretched, lies across the top of the frame. This is a most unusual composition in the sense that, by placing significant objects (her body, her abandoned basket and earthernware jug) around the peripheries of the frame and positioning only the textures of the cobbled street in the centre, Demuts'kyi radically subverts the principle of *cadrage* (centering). By relegating the key picture information to the margins of the frame, it is insinuated that this victim belongs to the category of collateral damage.

For the scenes of collective injury and death, Demuts'kyi and Dovzhenko operate in a no less inventive manner. Among the most powerful images of internecine conflict is the beginning of the makeshift hospital sequence. The compositions that show the bodies in this hospital – three in total, or four if the establishing shot that shows the Red Cross nurse moving among the dead or dying soldiers is included – seem suspended between life and death. The documentary conceit is so powerful that it is not immediately obvious whether the footage is actuality or not. Furthermore, irrespective of their formal status, it is not immediately clear whether the images are freeze-frames, authentic photographs or simply well staged cinematic images in which a total absence of movement has been achieved. On the one hand, the deliberately 'poor' technical quality and the haunting realism of the facial expressions suggest the non-staged. On the other, the compositional organization of the frame indicates a degree of artifice far removed from the informal spontaneity usually associated with actuality footage. The ideas insinuated through such manipulation are disturbing in the extreme. The first image disorientates the viewer by virtue of truncation and fragmentation: hands, a head (partly in shadow), feet and arms all intrude into the frame, but the rest of the bodies have been removed from view (the establishing shot for the sequence anticipates this compositional mechanism by having a pair of anonymous legs and boots protrude into the lower third of the frame). The impression of disorientation is enhanced by visual inversion: a boot lies at the top of the frame, whereas a shoulder is positioned at the bottom. The image that follows immediately afterwards shows three bodies lying against a wall in a loosely diagonal formation. This time the truncation is achieved by means of the positioning of the bodies in relation to one another, and the lighting strategy, which 'truncates' parts of the faces by leaving them in shadow; untouched by light, their expressions are invisible. In the third image, a man with a moustache, presumably dead but perhaps simply wounded and exhausted, lies at a slight angle to the camera across the bottom of the frame; a hand from a body lying on a wooden bunk above him dissects the frame, and again the body itself is removed from view. The use of truncation in these compositions hints at the theme of dismemberment which has already been introduced in the opening scenes through the peasant who has lost an arm and the son who has lost the use of both of his legs, except that here it is not the limbs that are missing but the bodies. All the portraits discussed above, as visions of death or fatal injury, verge on the grotesque.

There are other moments in *Arsenal* when the camerawork approaches the condition of still photography in the sense that the figures within the frame remain more or less stationary, and where the emphasis on the static suggests the realm of death, sterility or disability. In some of the early rural scenes, for example, the peasant figures seem rooted to the spot; where movement occurs, it is halting and tentative. The compositional procedures adopted for these scenes are illustrated most readily by the scene that follows the intertitle 'Once upon a time there was a war': the woman in the foreground, silhouetted against a background of snow, is positioned along a simple diagonal from her *khata* or hut, which is positioned centre-right, but in the depths of the frame. A more complex realization of this scheme becomes apparent in the frames that follow the editing cut. Now there are three women: one is pushed up against the right-hand side of the frame; the second is positioned further away, on the left-hand side of the frame; and the third is standing further away still but closer to the centre of the frame. Taking the first woman as the visual cue, the eye of the viewer is drawn in a zig-zag fashion into the depths of the frame and then follows the line of a fence jutting into the frame from the right, which leads to a *khata* in the background; it is from this area that a man on crutches, presumably a victim of the war, will shortly intrude, walking tentatively across the centre of the frame. A further echo of this compositional method occurs just prior to the prolonged tracking-shot across snow-bound terrain which follows Bolshevik riders as they return a fallen comrade to his village: here a peasant woman stands at the right-hand edge of the frame, a fence and its shadow protrude into the frame, another woman stands on the left-hand side and a *khata* is again positioned in the background (variation lies in the fact that a large area of shadow fills the lower third of the frame). After the next cut, the Bolshevik soldiers on horseback will burst abruptly into the frame.

The series of frozen attitudes presented by Demuts'kyi and Dovzhenko in these scenes has its antipode in the extended tracking-shots which follow the riders after they have burst into this frame. In place of the static and statuesque peasant figures, evidence of the mortal decay into which the rural community has fallen as a result of the war, the male population presumably having been conscripted or, as in the case of the invalid, disabled, the viewer is presented with the dynamic, constantly shifting, unsteady viewpoint of the Bolshevik soldiers as they gallop through a bleak and wintry terrain on their way to deliver their comrade to his final resting place. Although it is customary to emphasize the exhilarating effects of these images – at times filming with a portable camera, and at times with a conventional camera on a tripod clearly fixed to a carriage or cart, Demuts'kyi presents a multiplicity of rapidly shifting and head-spinning viewpoints – the vision of nature which this sequence offers is no less compelling. As well as tracking the pounding progress of the horses, Demuts'kyi's camera is equally preoccupied with the landscape in the background, its monotony broken only by the silhouetted trees that line the country road and the occasional crow or raven that rises from the ground and flaps nonchalantly across the frame. The importance of landscape for the series of tracking-shots is suggested by the 'still life' with which it has been introduced, an expressive *tour-de-force* that depicts the stark outlines of trees punctuating the distance along the slightly sloping brow of an incline. This in turn produces a downward momentum that is continued into a circular whole by the elongated shadow of a tall tree which wriggles its way rightwards into the foreground, where it is met by an area of leafy shade. Kepley Jr describes this image as the sole instance of 'pastorale' in *Arsenal*, but it is worth commenting that these are landscapes of death: the fallen are conveyed back to the earth at a time when nature itself is dormant.[99]

Zemlia: The Transcendental Embrace

Zemlia is renowned for its series of static tableaux, as well as for a number of scenes in which human movement within the frame is reduced to a minimum. These moments have an important structuring and rhythmic function within the film as a whole: they open and close the narrative, giving rise to the perception of a symbolic circularity, and punctuate the rest of the work at certain intervals, appearing in meaningful clusters and establishing a series of static motifs to balance the film's interest in different types of motion: the hysterical response of the Bilokin' family to reports that the ownership of their land is under threat; the montage sequence that shows the mechanized harvesting; Vasyl''s dance; the agitated sprinting and parody of that dance by his kulak murderer, Khoma; and the desperate reaction of Natalka, Vasyl''s fiancée, while the funeral itself is taking place.

Although the essence of Dovzhenko's visual poetics has been located in a variety of different practices – his elliptical editing procedures, for example, or his use of jump-cuts – it is the moments of stillness, suffused with an astonishingly intense, lyrical poetry, which have been suggested as the most salient feature of his directorial vision, expressing some of his key philosophical ideas, in particular in relation to nature. Marcel Martin's words on the visual impact of the penultimate sequence, cited as the third epigraph to this chapter, give a flavour of the kind of ecstatic responses that they have elicited among both Soviet and non-Soviet audiences. Such scenes have also proved highly influential in the formation of subsequent visual aesthetics, giving rise in the 1960s to an informal school within the Soviet Union which Bleiman classified as 'poetic' or 'archaic' and associated with neo-nationalist tendencies in the Armenian, Georgian and Ukrainian Soviet republics.[100] This 'school' celebrated cinema as a visually poetic rather than dramatic medium. In its most extreme forms, for example Sergei Paradzhanov's

Tsvet granata (The Colour of Pomegranates, 1969), where the camera is completely static and the gestures of the actors are theatrical and symbolic, if not ritualized, much in the manner of the Varangian sequence in *Zvenyhora*, the filmmaking process consciously embraces the condition of painting and still photography.

The implications of the static scenes in *Zemlia* are markedly different from those in *Arsenal*, however. If immobility in the latter indicates death or proximity to death, in *Zemlia* the *natures mortes* seek to encapsulate truths that are equally mysterious, but which possess associations of richness, abundance and harmony between people and nature. The crucial element, one that has been neglected in discussion of *Zemlia* hitherto, lies in the decision to adopt a monocle lens for these sequences. It is important to appreciate that the use of soft-focus has important aesthetic and ideological implications. It is clearly erroneous, for example, to insist upon the tactile quality or solidity of these images in a context which, by virtue of the monocle lens, accentuates the elusive nature of that which appears on screen, to the extent that the outlines and textures of objects and human figures lack concrete definition.[101] The adoption of a lens uncorrected for sharp focus stresses intangibility, rather than tangibility, and has a tendency to push the image towards abstraction. This is not to deny the sensuous ways in which the monocle registers the caressing action of sunlight: North American practitioners of soft-focus in the 1920s drew attention precisely to this facet of these lenses.[102] The same quality has also been remarked upon by Soviet commentators with a solid understanding of the photographic tradition, for example Antypenko, who draws attention to the creation of 'aureoles' in *Zemlia* where normally there would be ordinary light patches.[103]

Because Pictorialist tendencies in photography had been officially denounced in 1928, Demuts'kyi's proposal to adopt the monocle lens was obviously risky. It is symptomatic of this risk that *Zemlia* went into production just as the leading vehicle for Pictorialist photography in the Soviet Union, the journal *Fotograf*, was liquidated, leading to the dispersal of the movement and its disappearance 'underground'.[104] The contemporary distaste for such aesthetics on the part of the radical intelligentsia was reflected in Sokolov's review of *Zemlia*, in which he criticized its impressionistic tendencies for being 'anachronistic', for failing to express the 'bravery' and 'severity' of the new revolutionary epoch, and for producing a series of 'mask-like, flat *natures mortes*' (the review indicates that Sokolov was aware of Demuts'kyi's previous incarnation as a Pictorialist photographer).[105] By resorting to a monocle lens, whether consciously or subconsciously, Demuts'kyi was aligning the poetics of *Zemlia* with a certain artistic tradition, one which had developed as a result of several decades of debate within photographic societies about the ways in which the human eye perceives contours, and the desire, through the creative intervention of the photographer, to counter the perception that photography was essentially a mechanical process.[106] One of these early interventions, sometimes combined with the application of alternative printing procedures, was the use of non-anastigmatic lenses or specially constructed soft-focus lenses.[107] Uncorrected lenses were fashionable among experimental photographers in Europe and North America at the turn of the century, and this vogue eventually infiltrated the world of moving pictures. Struss, for example, developed his own 'Pictorial Lens' as early as 1915; one year later, it was customized and adopted by the cameraman John Leezer for a film directed by Griffith.[108] Another stills photographer and cinematographer, Charles Rosher, the preferred cameraman of Mary Pickford, developed his 'Kino Portrait' lens in association with a German optical company in the mid-1920s; he employed it on Pickford's last silent film, *My Best Girl* (1927), directed by Sam Taylor, as did the German camera operator Günther Rittau for the close-ups of Marlene Dietrich in Josef von Sternberg's *Der blaue Engel* (The Blue Angel, 1930).[109] Another example was the so-called 'miracle lens' developed by the fashion photographer Hendrik Sartov for the close-ups of Lillian Gish in *Broken Blossoms*. According to Karl Brown, the assistant to 'Billy' Bitzer at this time, this was little more than a 'yellowed spectacle lens' with both chromatic and spherical aberrations which was little dissimilar in appearance to the bottom of a beer bottle. This primitive lens, nevertheless, caused something of a sensation when the film was released.[110]

Demuts'kyi's application of the monocle lens occurs at six main junctures in *Zemlia*: the portraits of the grandfather, Semen, as he lies in an orchard surrounded by fallen apples; the portraits of young couples in the village after the harvest, which serve as a prelude to Vasyl''s 'nocturnal' dance; the dance itself, which leads to his murder; Natalka's reaction to his funeral; the images of apples hanging from trees and lying on the ground next to watermelons as they are gently caressed by rain; and the medium close-ups of Natalka and her new lover, with which the film concludes.

The sequence that precedes Vasyl''s dance consists of seventeen individual portraits, the vast majority of them completely static. This section intersperses landscape scenes – a cloudscape, a single tree, a river or marsh shrouded in mist, and a clouded sky broken by angled rays of the sun – with shots of immobile young couples, some standing next to each another (Fig. 44), while others, for example Vasyl' and his fiancée, are positioned in a motionless embrace. These moments are clearly illuminated by the setting sun rather than the moon, despite the specific instruction given in the film novella that Dovzhenko composed many years later on the basis of the original libretto.[111] This suggests that Dovzhenko may have wanted to evoke parallels with the landscape paintings of Arkhip Kuindzhi, most famously *Ukrainskaia noch'* (Ukrainian Night, 1876) and *Lunnaia noch' na Dnepre* (Moonlight on the Dnieper, 1880), but that the technical difficulty of shooting in low lighting conditions due to the film stock's insufficient sensitivity prompted a different solution. Antypenko, indeed, suggests that this sequence constitutes one of the first examples of *rezhimnaia rabota* ('magic hour' cinematography) in the history of Soviet cinema.[112]

As far as the landscape scenes themselves are concerned, the choice of subject matter and manner of composition reflect the influence of the Barbizon school and Itinerant and Pictorialist precursors. The scene showing the night mist over silvery water, despite the absence of colour, is reminiscent of Théodore Rousseau's *A Marsh on the Landes* (1842), a characteristic product of the Barbizon school which proved influential for French *plein-airistes*, and also three paintings by Aleksei Savrasov: *Lunnaia noch'* (Moonlit Night, 1870); *Zakat nad bolotom* (Sunset over the Marshes, 1871); and *Proselok* (The Country Road, 1873). The choice of a solitary tree as a subject for study, coupled with a large expanse of sky, also belongs to a rich Itinerant and Pictorialist tradition. Although there are differences in terms of compositional emphasis and atmospheric conditions, Savrasov's *Duby* (Oaks, 1855), Ivan Shishkin's *Molodye duby* (Young Oaks, 1886), Kuindzhi's *Duby* (Oaks, 1900–1905) and Watzek's *Poplars and Clouds* (1906) may be identified as precursors. The image of an empty terrain shrouded in darkness and illuminated only by the slanting rays of the sun suggests the strong influence of Kuindzhi's *Posle dozhdia* (After the Rain, 1879), although the lighting conditions here, as the title indicates, are quite specific.

As confirmed by the film-novella, this section is designed to express the wonder and strangeness of the Ukrainian evening, a moment of defamiliarization when, as Dovzhenko writes, a 'poetry full of new and exciting meanings' becomes possible.[113] It is undeniably a visionary statement, yet what informs this vision requires elucidation. The adoption of the monocle lens not only heightens the dream-like quality of these images and accentuates the indistinctness of the outlines, thus giving rise to a sense of estrangement, but also contains within itself the concept of merging with surrounding reality; in other words, a sense of unity, harmony, completeness and connectedness. This is particularly important in relation to the visual presentation of the couples. For all the supposed naturalism of these scenes, the poses of the couples and the expressions on their faces are devoid of sensuality or passion. Indeed, they are extremely unnatural, as if the human figures are mesmerized by what they perceive around them. Demuts'kyi composes the images to emphasize the proximity of the couples to nature, rather than their proximity to each other. None of the couples look into each other's eyes, and in certain cases their eyes are closed, as if they are experiencing a hypnotic trance. In one case, the eyes are looking in completely different directions, the separation of the human figures in question, despite the consoling arm around the shoulder glimpsed later, emphasized by the vertical lines of a window frame in the background. The impression of a trance-like state is reinforced by the inclusion of two images of older couples asleep in their beds. The overwhelming sense of stasis is ruptured only by Vasyl' and his fiancée, who move apart in a prelude to their parting, and the former's decision to walk home along a stretch of dusty track between the village dwellings.

If these twilight sequences imply themes of stasis and rest, the shots of Vasyl' walking home and breaking suddenly into dance accentuate frenetic movement and restlessness. Despite the insistence in the film-novella that this dance takes place at night, the intensity of the illumination, and the angle of what is very obviously sunlight, suggest that filming must have taken place in the early hours of the morning (this is confirmed by Svashenko's account of the preparations for the dance).[114] The shots that follow inevitably focus on the mechanics of this dance, yet they too are landscapes in their own right, the monocle lens continuing the sensation of a dream-like trance in which everything is diffuse and mysterious. This impression is reinforced by the fact that Vasyl' initially closes his eyes, an allusion to the mesmerized stance of one of the couples in the previous sequence. I have written elsewhere about the semiotics of this dance – an improvised series of movements modelled on the *hopak*, a Cossack dance associated with riding into battle – and the symbolic importance of the dust that rises from the earth as Vasyl' pounds his feet on the ground.[115] The light throughout the sequence, however, which strikes the dirt track, the wooden palisades and the buildings at a low angle from the side, also plays a crucial role. Not only does it catch the dust that rises from the ground, causing it to glint, but on various occasions it illuminates Vasyl''s face, his peaked cap and his traditional shirt as he moves towards the camera, making them gleam (Fig. 45). The physical configuration of the village – that is, its blocking of the sun's rays at discrete intervals – divides each scene into patches of dark shadow and intense light and constitutes a continuously mobile, dynamic and structuring element within the frame. The fleeting nature of these compositions suggests transience rather than permanence: the dust, which has previously lifted into a billowing cloud that envelopes him, blows away rapidly after his murder (in effect, he himself becomes a cloud of dust); and the horse, which has jerked its head abruptly upwards on hearing the 'sound' of the gunshot, resumes its grazing unaffected.

The scenes of the apples are the most celebrated in the film, and yet they, too, occupy a curious terrain halfway between outright abstraction and fleshy, tangible sensuousness. This reflects the varied compositional treatment to which they are subjected. Photographically, the episode in its entirety can be divided into two parts which describe a circular pattern: the initial shots are presented in reasonably sharp focus, after which the images are subjected to increasing degrees of diffusion, before returning to relatively sharp focus. The compositional arrangement of each part tends to bring the apples nearer and nearer to the camera, with each part ending with a close-up of a single apple. Whether diffuse or sharp, however, each composition involves a degree of deception that produces an ethereal quality. In the case of the impressionistic images, it is the adoption of the monocle lens that constitutes the deception, giving rise to a spectral quality in the areas struck by light. In the case of the non-diffuse images, it is the manipulation of natural light to communicate roundness of form and surface texture. The degree of artifice can be gauged by the fact that, for the scenes of random fruit lying on the ground, bright sunlight and pouring rain have been combined, which is manifestly unrealistic (Fig. 46). When they are inspected closely, moreover, it becomes clear that nearly all the scenes with apples hanging from branches involve lighting effects that cannot be the product of nature; all of them are subtly differentiated in terms of lighting and compositional strategy. In many respects, Demuts'kyi's approach is a textbook illustration of the effects that can be achieved by directing either single or multiple sources of light towards a spherical object from different angles. Several compositions involve a natural source striking the fruit from above at an angle, but also a reflection of that source from below; this can happen in nature, but not with the intensity seen here, which is suggestive of a mirror or some other reflecting surface (Fig. 47). The most striking illustration of this procedure, which may have prompted Martin's observation, constitutes the culminating point of the second series. Here the viewer is presented with a close-up of a single apple with droplets of water still clinging to its surface. In this composition, light strikes from below, above and behind, giving a powerful sense of texture and volume, as well as capturing the speckled tones of the skin. It is an astonishing image of a succulent fruit and a ravishing assault on the senses.

Taken as a whole, the images in this sequence must constitute one of the most sustained studies of fruit in the history of photography. On the one hand, the series glances back in time to the celebrated *natures mortes* by Nikolai Svishchev-Paola, a Russian photographer who came to prominence at the turn of the century, for example his intricately patterned *Cabbage* (1908).[116] On the other hand, looking forward in time, Demuts'kyi's compositions anticipate the atmospheric inserts of blossoming trees and shrubs in *Michurin: Zhizn' v tsvetu*, which was photographed by Kosmatov, and where exactly the same kind of mesmerizing effect is sought.

Anatolii Trapani, a photographer who belonged to the Pictorialist movement, jokingly compared the 'realists with the anastigmats' with the 'mystics with the monocle'.[117] Dovzhenko's philosophy of nature has been described variously, but the essence of his quest is encapsulated by Svashenko in his recollection of the preparations for the dance: 'My surroundings were so dazzlingly beautiful that I wanted to merge with them'.[118] The idea of human beings as an intrinsic part of the natural world, their deaths part of an endless cycle of birth, death and rebirth, is pagan rather than Orthodox Christian in origin. The sense of awe and wonder in relation to nature that underpins folk beliefs and rituals perhaps explains Dovzhenko's definition of the artistic impulse in relation to cinematography. As he observed on one occasion: 'If the (camera) operator is an artist, he ought to be able to see and capture the sacred moment of nature'.[119] It may also explain his remarks in conversation with Masokha during the making of *Zemlia*, which appear to mourn the passing of Ukraine's 'rich' folkloric heritage and its current status as something 'unfortunately, growing sickly and dying'.[120]

The imaginative power of the penultimate section of *Zemlia* was probably the reason why Dovzhenko sought to involve Demuts'kyi in the making of *Michurin: Zhizn' v tsvetu*. The initial approach took the form of a letter written in Ukrainian in 1944 while Demuts'kyi was still resident in Tashkent.[121] For reasons that are not clear, Demuts'kyi declined to accept this offer. Nevertheless, he was approached a second time by Dovzhenko in April 1947, this time for supplementary landscape footage which, for reasons that are also not clear, he was unable to organize with

Kosmatov (the shooting of the exterior sequences for the film had ostensibly already been completed by this stage). Although the request did not produce the desired result, the letter is eloquent about Dovzhenko's trust in the skills and sensitivities of his former camera operator:

> Work on Zhizn' v tsvetu *is difficult and laborious. I am asking you, Danylo, to help me. Shoot landscapes for me in the way that only you know how. Shoot the cataracts of the Dnieper, so that there is breadth, so that everything is joyous, so that everything is propelled forward: the water, the trees, the* khaty, *the clouds. Shoot the floods with feeling, with the joy of a young boy...*
>
> *Get in a boat, Danylo, take your camera in your hands and make your way quickly to a submerged village. Imagine that you are a knight, that you are riding to its rescue, and that you are not Danylo, but Vasco da Gama or Magellan, and that the awareness of your strength and skill as a master of your craft fills you with happiness.*[122]

The reasons for Demuts'kyi's inability to fulfil this request are unknown. However, the scenes of buds and flowers opening in spring in *Michurin: Zhizn' v tsvetu*, while undeniably impressive in terms of their recourse to time-lapse photography, lack the careful patterning and sustained gaze of the analogous images in *Zemlia*. Antypenko's paradoxical remark that the monochrome images of *Zemlia* seem more authentically colourful than the 'unnatural' and 'dyed' images of post-war colour cinematography – he was referring specifically to the images of the sunflowers and the 'golden' dust disturbed by Vasyl''s feet during the dance sequence – is pertinent here.[123] Even allowing for the fact that *Michurin: Zhizn' v tsvetu* was produced during an era of severe censorship restrictions, it might be offered as evidence that, without Demuts'kyi, Dovzhenko's vision became progressively uninspired, impaired and impoverished.

Epilogue: The Parting of the Ways

Despite the closeness of their relationship at the beginning of their respective careers, Dovzhenko made little public comment on his partnership with Demuts'kyi during his lifetime. The one exception is a lecture given to aspiring directors at GIK on 17 December 1932, in which he outlined his artistic methods and, in passing, offered a few observations on the relationship between directors and camera operators. His comments, because of their controversial nature, are worth citing at length.

> For me, of course, all operators are like Demuts'kyi. I always compose the frame myself because I like to work quickly, but the more you can take from the camera operator, the better for you; the less you take, the worse it will be ... .
>
> You can only depend on the camera operator to the extent that you are confident that he understands the film in the same way that you do, that he inhabits the film as seriously and deeply from the creative point of view as you ... .
>
> If this is not the case, the operator can be dangerous, especially if he is stronger than you, a director at the beginning of his career. Perhaps in the beginning he will help you, but you always have to remember that you should not fall under his influence. You should express in the film your own personality, your own feelings ... .
>
> For me in my film work the camera operator has a purely technical function ... .
>
> In my view, you future directors should be lord and master of everything that appears in your film ... . I do everything myself. There is nothing in my films that is not created by my own hands.[124]

These comments are striking in their lack of generosity and reluctance to insist on the special nature of the relationship with Demuts'kyi. Two possible reasons have been advanced for this: first, Dovzhenko's anxieties in relation to his camera operator's tenuous position within the studio (this was the month in which Demuts'kyi was arrested, and it has been speculated that Dovzhenko was distancing himself from his former colleague for political reasons);[125] and second, the possibility that Dovzhenko was jealous of the reception Demuts'kyi had received during their trip abroad in 1930, ostensibly to investigate the potential of sound technology – in some places this was more enthusiastic than Dovzhenko's own reception, and it has been argued that from this moment onwards their 'great friendship' began to sour.[126] In fairness, it should be remembered that Dovzhenko himself was in a precarious position at the time of the lecture: he was waiting nervously in Moscow while the authorities in Kyiv decided his fate, and rumours were circulating that his own arrest was imminent.[127] However, it would appear that even he realized that the remarks in his lecture were controversial. This is suggested by the fact that this particular section of the lecture was revised and toned down for publication in his *Collected Works* (the original comments, as cited by Masokha, are even more self-aggrandizing and dismissive of cameramen).[128] With the benefit of hindsight, bearing in mind Demuts'kyi's difficult position, and comparing them with other, more supportive statements that were emerging at this time, for example a brief celebration of Demuts'kyi's career in the newspaper *Kino*, the comments in this lecture might be regarded as unhelpful at best, and slightly treacherous at worst.[129]

Whatever the motivation for the remarks, their general tenor is robustly contradicted by accounts that describe Dovzhenko's methods at close quarters. Masokha, for example, who worked closely with him on the cusp of the 1930s (he plays the role of Khoma in *Zemlia*), has expressed incredulity at his assertion that the camera operator has only a 'technical function'.[130] Kokhno, moreover, while noting Dovzhenko's painterly appreciation of landscape, nevertheless stresses Demuts'kyi's decisive contributions. Thus, for example, in his recollection of the shooting of the opening sequence of *Ivan*, which involved the film crew travelling down the Dnieper by steamboat, he points out that, although Dovzhenko periodically checked the image through the camera's viewfinder, it was Demuts'kyi who took the all-important step of switching from a conventional to a wide-angle lens, which had the effect of dramatically opening out the scene and stretching the expanse of water that stood before them. He also points out that, as part of the preparations for shooting this sequence, Demuts'kyi had instructed his assistants to read the famous passage from Gogol''s 'Strashnaia mest'' ('A Terrible Vengeance', 1832), in which the calm, glassy surface of the river and its tremendous expanse are described as a 'magical space which has no rival'.[131] Another telling moment occurred in relation to the establishing shots of the hydroelectric dam complex. Although both men spent several days studying the site, it was left to Demuts'kyi to analyse the light conditions that prevailed at various times of the day, which led to his decision to shoot early in the morning, *contre-jour*, with a long-distance Dallmeyer-Ross lens and coloured filter.[132] It is clear from Kokhno's account that Dovzhenko had little or no involvement in the lighting arrangements for the scenes within interiors.[133]

The fact that this monograph is concerned solely with the poetics of silent-era works precludes discussion of Dovzhenko's and Demuts'kyi's projects after the release of *Ivan*. Even a cursory review, however, suggests that Dovzhenko experienced tremendous creative frustration and floundered during the era of

Socialist Realism. Like others, he was forced into artistic compromises and the humiliation of writing directly to Stalin in order to secure official patronage and support for his projects.[134] Like others pressured into conformity, Dovzhenko directed films during the 1930s and 1940s which were regarded as lacking his earlier mastery and vision. Even those works officially regarded as triumphs, for example *Shchors* (1939), the 'Ukrainian *Chapaev* [1934]', which was made with Stalin's explicit support and approval, took a terrible toll on Dovzhenko's mental and physical health, to the extent that it gave rise to thoughts of suicide.[135] Dovzhenko himself was well aware of the tragic waste of his talents. His outbursts at meetings and his remarks recorded by informers working for the NKVD suggest someone both bitter about his treatment and utterly disillusioned with the Soviet project.[136]

Demuts'kyi, by contrast, although inactive for most of the 1930s because of his various arrests and internal exile, and doubtless experiencing just as much in the way of private torment, nevertheless produced some outstanding camerawork which deserves much greater recognition than it has enjoyed hitherto. Ironically, part of the reason for his success may well have been his residence in Tashkent, a relative backwater in terms of the Soviet film industry, and thus peripheral in relation to the controlling centres of cultural and ideological life. The regional provenance of the productions on which he worked – *Nasreddin v Bukhare, Takhir i Zukhra* (1945) and *Pokhozhdeniia Nasreddina* (The Adventures of Nasreddin, 1946), the last two of which were directed by Ganiev, a major figure in the development of Uzbek cinema in the 1930s and 1940s – should not distract from their interest as professional and at times inspired expressions of national culture.[137] These narratives are modelled on sources rooted in the ancient history and folklore of the region. Hodja Nasreddin, for example, was a legendary trickster famous in the thirteenth century throughout the Middle East for his aphoristic wit; and the narrative of *Takhir i Zukhra* was based on a well known fourteenth-century folk epic (*dastans*) sung by wandering minstrels. Very probably as a result of the relaxation of censorship during the Second World War, which permitted the expression of nationalist feeling as a mobilizing, anti-Nazi force, neither film features Soviet-style ideological posturing or a 'coming-to-consciousness' narrative.

Despite their different generic frameworks and directors, these films can nevertheless be regarded as a triptych, the visual interest of which lies in the response of the outsider, Demuts'kyi, to the landscapes of traditional Uzbekistan. This response is contained in the films and photographs he produced during his period of exile.[138] These images belong to a rich seam of photographic exploration which stretches back to the years shortly after the unauthorized conquest of Tashkent in 1865 by regiments of the Russian imperial army. The fashion for 'Eastern' pictures during the next sixty years can be witnessed in N. Nekhoroshev's *Turkestan Album* (1871–72); the photographs of Tashkent by Dmitrii Nazarov, which won international prizes in the first decade of the twentieth century; the photo-album *10 let Uzbekistana* (Ten Years of Uzbekistan), which was compiled by Rodchenko in 1933; the photo-reportage of Maks Penson, who worked for *Pravda vostoka* for much of the 1920s and 1930s; the photographs of Iurii Ier'omin, a Ukrainian Pictorialist, which he took as part of an eastern expedition during the 1920s (see, for example, his *Vulytsia u Bukhari* (Ulitsa v Bukhare, Street in Bukhara, 1930)); and Tisse's footage of the Uzbekistan desert during the making of *Bol'shoi ferganskii kanal*.[139]

Although Demuts'kyi's poetic appreciation of landscape is apparent in all his three films for Tashkent Studio, it is displayed most ambitiously in *Takhir i Zukhra*. This work contains a great deal of exterior cinematography and, in its attempt to evoke a bygone era, creates a surreal, dream-like atmosphere. This is achieved through a variety of different means, but most strikingly by Demuts'kyi's 'signature', namely, resorting to diffusion by means of a monocle lens. This is witnessed during an extended sequence in which the main male protagonist, Takhir, who has been sentenced to death by Emir Bobakhan, the father of his beloved Zukhra, is shown being locked into a trunk, after which he is cast from a high cliff into the waters of a rapidly moving river. This particular form of execution, one with an ancient pedigree in Eastern myth, prompts a series of poetic manoeuvres on Demuts'kyi's part which attempt through manipulation of depth of field to underline the dramatic significance of the event. The sequence in question begins with an unorthodox 'washing' of the image as the trunk is nailed shut; for this moment, Demuts'kyi places the two warriors and the trunk in the medium foreground, in semi-silhouette but out of focus, behind which are pictured the streaming white lines of the downward-rushing water. This is followed by two compositions that reprise visual strategies first explored in *Zemlia*. After the trunk has been thrown into the water and a flash of lightning, emblematic of divine wrath, has illuminated the sky, the viewer is presented with images of scattering warriors and onlookers that have been shot through a dream-like curtain of rain with bright rays of sunshine in the background. Several of these compositions have been shot with a monocle lens. The same lens is adopted again, seconds later, after a brief series of shots of the trunk floating along the calm surface of the water, for images of the same trunk propelled by rapids. Here, as in the image of the evening mist rising above the surface of a river or pond in *Zemlia*, the tonal range is restricted between the dark-grey zone of the body of water and the greyish white zone of the foaming surf. The composition and chemical manipulation of the print bear all the hallmarks of Demuts'kyi's fondness for impressionistic image-making; indeed, this extended sequence may well constitute the death knell of the Pictorialist mode of vision in the Soviet Union.

Notes

1. Demuts'kyi, cited in L. Kokhno, 'Operator-poet: Vospominaniia o D. P. Demutskom', *Iskusstvo kino*, 1961.12, 52–56 (p. 52).
2. Petr Masokha, '"Ia ne boius' sporit' s vami, Aleksandr Petrovich...": Neotoslannoe pis'mo k M. M. Kovalenko', publ. by Sergei Trimbach, *Kinovedcheskie zapiski*, 31 (1996), 131–39 (p. 135).
3. Marcel Martin, *Le Langage cinématographique*, 3rd edn (Paris: les éditeurs français réunis, 1977), p. 42. Emphasis in the original.
4. Demuts'kyi is usually credited with the camerawork on Dovzhenko's directorial debut, *Iahidki kokhannia*, but for reasons which will be discussed later in this chapter this accreditation must be regarded as suspect.
5. Liber, *Alexander Dovzhenko*, p. 153n105.
6. Ibid.
7. On Dovzhenko's sojourn in Ashgabat, see ibid., pp. 187–88.
8. The three films are: *Ostannia cherha* (Posledniaia ochered', 1941), a film novella in two reels directed by Heorhii Tasin for the Tashkent and Odessa Film Studios; *Syni skeli* (Sinie skaly, 1942), an episode within the three-part *Boevoi kinosbornik, no. 9*, which was directed by Volodymyr Braun for the Kyiv Film Studio based in Ashgabat; and *Roki molodii* (Gody molodye, 1942), a vaudeville in nine reels directed by Hryhorii Hrycher-Cherykover for the same studio.
9. Liber, *Alexander Dovzhenko*, p. 153n105.
10. Antipenko, 'Moi Demutskii', pp. 97–98. See also Mykola Kutsenko, *Storinky zhyttia i tvorchosti O. P. Dovzhenka* (Kyiv: Dnipro, 1975), pp. 228–29; and Liber, *Alexander Dovzhenko*, p. 235.
11. Antipenko, 'Moi Demutskii', p. 98.
12. Liber, *Alexander Dovzhenko*, pp. 132–36 & 257.
13. For information on the career of Nil'sen, who was arrested by security police while filming on set, see Arkadii Bernshtein, 'Gollivud bez kheppi-enda: Sud'ba i tvorchestvo Vladimira Nil'sena', *Kinovedcheskie zapiski*, 60 (2002), 213–59. On the fate of Kaliuzhnyi, see Ushakov, 'Tri operatora', p. 160.
14. Grinberg was arrested by the NKVD in 1936 on charges of circulating pornography and sentenced to five years imprisonment in the Gulag. He was released in 1938, however, and later rehabilitated in the 1950s. See <http://www.kino-teatr.ru/kino/operator/38780/bio> (accessed 9 November 2011).

15. Milena Michalski, 'Promises Broken, Promise Fulfilled: The Critical Failings and Creative Success of Abram Room's *Strogii iunosha*', *Slavonic and East European Review*, 82.4 (2004), 820–46. See also R. N. Il'in, *Iurii Ekel'chik* (Moscow: Iskusstvo, 1962), pp. 14–30.

16. Kokhno, 'Operator-poet', p. 52.

17. K. Fel'dman, 'Ukrainskie kino-rezhissery', *Sovetskii ekran*, 1928.44, 7.

18. 'Avtobiografiia' [1939], in A. P. Dovzhenko, *Sobranie sochinenii*, ed. by I. L. Andronikov and others, 4 vols (Moscow: Iskusstvo, 1966–69), I, ed. by S. S. Ginzburg, 33–56 (p. 43) (first publ. in *Dnipro*, 1957.12).

19. On Dovzhenko's 'disappearance' in 1921 and the complex politics of the civil war in Ukraine, see Liber, *Alexander Dovzhenko*, pp. 31–41 & 52–53.

20. Masokha, '"Ia ne boius' sporit' s vami, Aleksandr Petrovich…"', p. 135.

21. A rare exception within the literature on Dovzhenko is A. G. Rutkovskii in conversation with Oleg Aronson. See O. V. Aronson, 'Kinoantropologiia "Zemli"', *Kinovedcheskie zapiski*, 23 (1994), 141–48 (pp. 147–48).

22. Dovzhenko, 'Avtobiografiia', pp. 40–41. For the period in Germany, see Khans-Ioakhim Shlegel' [Hans-Joachim Schlegel], 'Berlin i Germaniia Aleksandra Dovzhenko', trans. by L. S. Maslova, *Kinovedcheskie zapiski*, 31 (1996), 139–46 (pp. 143–44).

23. *Dovzhenko: Khudozhnyk*, ed. by I. Zolotoverkhova and H. Konovalov (Kyiv: Mystetstvo, 1968), p. 10.

24. Reproduced in Liber, *Alexander Dovzhenko*, p. 101.

25. *Dovzhenko: Khudozhnyk*, ed. by Zolotoverkhova and Konovalov, pp. 62–64 & 73.

26. Ibid., pp. 63 & 67.

27. Ibid., pp. 79 & 80.

28. Ibid., p. 14.

29. Ibid., pp. 78–84.

30. Ibid.

31. *Käthe Kollwitz*, ed. by Prelinger, pp. 139, 123, 130, & 129, respectively.

32. Ibid., p. 57.

33. Grinberg had been a member of the Russian Photographic Society since 1907, after which he became one of the leading exponents of Pictorialism. See <http://www.kino-teatr.ru/kino/operator/38780/bio> (accessed 10 November 2011) and <http://artpages.org.ua> (accessed 10 November 2011). After the Revolution, he worked in the camera operation department of the GTK and shot several films as a camera operator. These included two agit-films, the negatives of which were destroyed by White counter-intelligence. Only two examples of his feature-film work in the 1920s have survived: *Fed'kina pravda* (1925), a drama in three reels directed by Ol'ga Preobrazhenskaia for the first factory of Goskino; and *Dva druga, model' i podruga* (1927), a comedy in six reels directed by Aleksei Popov for the Moscow branch of Sovkino.

34. Cited in V. Antropov, 'D. Demutskii', in *Desiat' operatorskikh biografii*, ed. by Goldovskaia, pp. 86–105 (p. 96).

35. Barkhatova, 'Pictorialism: Photography as Art', pp. 52 & 53–54. Although the plates have not survived, Antypenko claims to have seen photographic reproductions from this early period. See Antipenko, 'Moi Demutskii', p. 98. See also his article under the same title, essentially a shortened version of the earlier article in *Iskusstvo kino*, but with additional illustrations, in *Fotografiia*, 6 (1995) <www.photoweb.ru/prophoto/biblioteka> (accessed 9 November 2005). Henceforth, in order to avoid confusion, this will be referred to as 'Moi Demutskii' (*Fotografiia*).

36. Antipenko, 'Moi Demutskii', p. 93.

37. Barkhatova, 'Pictorialism: Photography as Art', pp. 53–54.
38. For further information on the emergence of this group, see Margaret Harker, *The Linked Ring: The Secession in Photography in Britain 1892–1910* (London: Heinemann, 1979), p. 162. See also F. Matthies-Masuren, 'Hugo Henneberg – Heinrich Kühn – Hans Watzek', in *Camera Work*, 13 (1906), 21–41.
39. On photo-montage as a Dadaist 'anti-art' procedure, see Lodder, *Russian Constructivism*, p. 186.
40. Ushakov, 'Tri operatora', p. 163.
41. Kokhno, 'Operator-poet', p. 52.
42. See, for example, the photograph entitled 'Uzbekskii dvorik', in Antipenko, 'Moi Demutskii', p. 96.
43. Barkhatova, 'Pictorialism: Photography as Art', pp. 53–54.
44. Ushakov, 'Tri operatora', p. 163.
45. Ibid.
46. Ibid. A portrait of Goleizovskii himself, the only surviving image from the collection, is published in Antipenko, 'Moi Demutskii' (*Fotografiia*).
47. Barkhatova, 'Pictorialism: Photography as Art', p. 58.
48. Stills from this film appeared in the film press at the time, but it is not clear whether they are frame stills or production stills. See, for example, *Sovetskii ekran*, 1926.12, 8–9.
49. See the relevant excerpt from Demuts'kyi's 'Avtobiografiia', cited in Antipenko, 'Moi Demutskii', p. 95.
50. Ibid.
51. Cited in ibid.
52. Ushakov, 'Tri operatora', p. 175.
53. For further information on Kavaleridze, see P. Masokha, 'Velykyi nimyi na Frantsuz'komu byl'vari', in *Kriz' kinoob'ektyv chasu: Spohady veteraniv ukrains'koho kino*, ed. by L. D. Hoholev (Kyiv: Mystetstvo, 1970), pp. 87–159 (pp. 123–25).
54. Khr[isanf] Khersonskii, '"Zlyva"', *Sovetskii ekran*, 1929.27, 6.
55. Khr. Kh. [Khrisanf Khersonskii], '"Liven'"', ibid., 1929.7, 13.
56. '"Sinii paket"', *Sovetskii ekran*, 1926.11, 8–9; and '"Podozritel'nyi bagazh"', ibid. For the reception of *Synii paket*, see O. Shvachko, 'Spohady pro nezabutne', in *Kriz' kinoob'ektyv chasu: Spohady veteraniv ukrains'koho kino*, ed. by Hoholev, pp. 53–85 (p. 66).
57. For example, in ibid., p. 65.
58. Ushakov, 'Tri operatora', p. 177.
59. Ibid., p. 165.
60. Shvachko, 'Spohady pro nezabutne', pp. 67–68.
61. Ibid.
62. Ibid. See also L. Bodyk, 'Kinokadry zhittia i strichky', in *Kriz' kinoob'ektyv chasu: Spohady veteraniv ukrains'koho kino*, ed. by Hoholev, pp. 213–77 (pp. 238–39).
63. Shvachko, 'Spohady pro nezabutne', p. 71.
64. Liber, *Alexander Dovzhenko*, pp. 64–72. See also Shlegel', 'Berlin i Germaniia Aleksandra Dovzhenko', pp. 143–44.
65. Shvachko, 'Spohady pro nezabutne', pp. 71–72.
66. Dovzhenko, 'Avtobiografiia', p. 46.
67. Liber, *Alexander Dovzhenko*, p. 67.
68. Ibid., p. 76.
69. Fel'dman, 'Ukrainskie kino-rezhissery'. Also I. Ivanitskii, 'Ukrainskaia sovetskaia kinematografiia za 15 let', *Sovetskoe kino*, 1934.11–12, 84–93 (pp. 84–85).

70. Ushakov, 'Tri operatora', p. 165.

71. See the relevant entries under his name in *Velikii kinemo* and Vishnevskii, *Khudozhestvennye fil'my dorevoliutsionnoi Rossii*.

72. Iurii Zheliabuzhskii, 'Masterstvo sovetskikh operatorov: Kratkii ocherk razvitiia' [1948], publ. by Svetlana Izhevskaia and A. S. Deriabin, *Kinovedcheskie zapiski*, 69 (2004), 246–73 (p. 258).

73. A copy of this film is held in the British Film Institute, although it has been wrongly catalogued under the title *Golod... golod... golod....* As indicated in Chapters Two and Three, this is the title of a different film directed by Pudovkin and shot by Tisse in the same year.

74. R. Sobolev, *Aleksandr Dovzhenko*, Zhizn' v iskusstve series (Moscow: Iskusstvo, 1980), p. 35.

75. *Sovetskie khudozhestvennye fil'my*, I, 193–94.

76. Youngblood, *Movies for the Masses*, p. 77.

77. For a brief résumé of these two missing reels, see '"Sumka dipkur'era"', *Sovetskii ekran*, 1927.13, 8–9.

78. This lens might well have been specially customized, since neither Nil'sen (*The Cinema as a Graphic Art*, pp. 59–60) nor Zheliabuzhskii (*Iskusstvo operatora*, pp. 76–88) mentions such a lens in their respective discussions of optical equipment.

79. Ushakov, 'Tri operatora', p. 164.

80. Ibid., pp. 164–65.

81. Cited in Antipenko, 'Moi Demutskii', p. 96.

82. Liber, *Alexander Dovzhenko*, pp. 86–87.

83. 'Moia fil'ma – bol'shevistskaia fil'ma', in Dovzhenko, *Sobranie sochinenii*, I, 253–54 (p. 253) (first publ. in *Zvenyhora: Zbirnyk: Statti pro fil'my O. Dovzhenka, ta in.* (Kyiv: VUFKU, 1928)).

84. Liber, *Alexander Dovzhenko*, pp. 86–87.

85. See ibid., pp. 87–88; and Vance Kepley, Jr, *In the Service of the State: The Cinema of Alexander Dovzhenko* (Madison: University of Wisconsin Press, 1986), p. 49.

86. On Zavelev's 'aesthetic' resistance to Kurbas, see O. Pereguda, 'Kinematograf i Les' Kurbas', in *Kriz' kinoob'ektyv chasu: Spohady veteraniv ukrains'koho kino*, ed. by Hoholev, pp. 39–51 (pp. 40–41 & 46). See also Irena R. Makaryk, 'Dissecting Time/Space: The Scottish Play and the New Technology of Film', in *Modernism in Kyiv: Jubilant Experimentation*, ed. by Irena R. Makaryk and Virlana Tkacz (Toronto: University of Toronto Press, 2010), pp. 443–77 (pp. 454–61).

87. For example, see Eizenshtein's recollection of his first viewing of the film, '[Rozhdenie mastera]', in Eizenshtein, *Izbrannye proizvedeniia*, V, 438–42 (first publ. in *Iskusstvo kino*, 1940.1–2, 94–95).

88. Kuleshov, 'Priamoi put': Diskussionno', p. 129.

89. These observations are based on the copy held in Gosfil'mofond. For production details, see *Sovetskie khudozhestvennye fil'my*, I, 361.

90. See, for example, K. Fel'dman, '"Arsenal"', *Sovetskii ekran*, 1929.11, 11.

91. Cited in Liber, *Alexander Dovzhenko*, p. 88.

92. For the use of *paysage* generally during this period, see Cavendish, *Soviet Mainstream Cinematography*, pp. 180–83.

93. For discussion of these issues in the immediate post-revolutionary context, see Evgenii Zamiatin, 'Narodnyi teatr', in his *Sochineniia*, ed. by Evgeniia Zhiglevich and Boris Filippov, 4 vols (Munich: Neimanis, 1970–88), IV, 424–29 (first publ. in *Blokha: Igra v 4 d. Evg. Zamiatina* (Leningrad: Academia, 1927), pp. 3–11).

94. See the production still in Dovzhenko, 'Avtobiografiia', p. 41.

95. Sobolev, *Aleksandr Dovzhenko*, pp. 42 & 48.

96. Viktor Shklovskii, 'Sashko Dovzhenko', in V. Shklovskii, *Za 60 let: Raboty o kino*, ed. by E. Levin (Moscow: Iskusstvo, 1985), pp. 293–304 (p. 297) (first publ. in V. Shklovskii, *Zhili-byli* (Moscow: Sovetskii pistatel', 1964), pp. 461–81).

97. Gilberto Perez, 'All in the Foreground: A Study of Dovzhenko's *Earth*', *Hudson Review*, 28 (1975), 68–86 (p. 78).

98. Kepley, Jr, *In the Service of the State*, p. 68.

99. Ibid., p. 70.

100. Mikhail Bleiman, 'Chto segodnia? Chto zavtra? 1967–71', in M. Bleiman, *O kino: Svidetel'skie pokazaniia, 1924–71* (Moscow: Iskusstvo, 1973), pp. 477–569.

101. Perez, for example, has written of the way in which the images in *Zemlia* 'render the fullness and self-sufficiency, the rounded steadiness of solid forms'. See Perez, 'All in the Foreground', p. 77.

102. The remark by the American cinematographer Joseph Walker may be regarded as typical: 'Sunlight through a soft-focus lens doesn't actually move, but you feel it's somehow alive. It's probably due to the little aura, the little halo that comes out around it.' Cited in *Karl Struss: Man with a Camera*, ed. by John and Susan Harvith, p. 7.

103. Antipenko, 'Moi Demutskii', p. 96.

104. Barkhatova, 'Pictorialism: Photography as Art', p. 59.

105. Ippolit Sokolov, '"Zemlia"', *Kino*, 1930.21, 4–5 (p. 5).

106. Peter Henry Emerson, cited in Newhall, *The History of Photography*, p. 142.

107. Helmut Gernsheim, *The History of Photography from the Earliest Use of the Camera Obscura in the Eleventh Century up to 1914* (London: Oxford University Press, 1955), p. 463.

108. *Karl Struss: Man with a Camera*, ed. by John and Susan Harvith, pp. 1–3.

109. Kevin Brownlow, *The Parade's Gone by...* (London: Secker & Warburg, 1968), p. 234.

110. Karl Brown, *Adventures with D. W. Griffith*, ed. by Kevin Brownlow, afterword by John Boorman (London: Faber & Faber, 1988), p. 206.

111. The libretto for *Zemlia* was published in the Kyiv journal *Avanhard* in 1930, but in 1952 Dovzhenko decided to expand this treatment into a *kino-povest'*. See 'Zemlia', in Dovzhenko, *Sobranie sochinenii*, I, 111–38 (p. 129) (first publ. in *Dnipro*, 1957.1).

112. Antipenko, 'Moi Demutskii', p. 96.

113. Dovzhenko, 'Zemlia', p. 129.

114. Semen Svashenko, 'Kak rozhdalsia tanets', in *Dovzhenko v vospominaniiakh sovremennikov*, ed. by Solntseva and Pazhitnova, pp. 85–90 (p. 88).

115. Phil Cavendish, 'Zemlia/Earth', in *The Cinema of Russia and the Former Soviet Union*, 24 frames series, ed. by Birgit Beumers (London: Wallflower, 2007), pp. 57–67 (pp. 63–64).

116. Reproduced in *Photography in Russia*, ed. by Elliott, p. 159.

117. Cited in Anatolii Chulko, 'Intimnaia nota v svetopisi', *Fotomagazin*, 7–8 (1998) <http://www.photoweb.ru/prophoto/biblioteka/Photograph/Eremin/01.htm> (accessed 9 November 2005).

118. Svashenko, 'Kak rozhdalsia tanets', p. 88.

119. Cited in Il'in, *Aleksandr Dovzhenko*, p. 48.

120. Cited in Alexander Dovzhenko, *The Poet as Filmmaker: Selected Writings*, ed. and trans. by Marco Carynnyk (Cambridge: MIT Press, 1973), p. xlviii.

121. See the letter from Dovzhenko to Demuts'kyi dated 18 January 1944, cited in Kutsenko, *Storinky zhyttia i tvorchosti O. P. Dovzhenka*, p. 223.

122. Cited in Antipenko, 'Moi Demutskii', pp. 97–98. The date of the letter, 10 April 1947, is confirmed in Kutsenko, *Storinky zhyttia i tvorchosti O. P. Dovzhenka*, p. 228.

123. Antipenko, 'Moi Demutskii', p. 97.
124. A. P. Dovzhenko, 'Moi tvorcheskii metod (Lektsiia vo VGIKe, 17 dekabria 1932)', in Dovzhenko, *Sobranie sochinenii*, IV, 381–93 (pp. 391–92).
125. Masokha, "'Ia ne boius' sporit' s vami, Aleksandr Petrovich...'", p. 134.
126. Ibid., pp. 134 & 137.
127. Liber, *Alexander Dovzhenko*, pp. 133–36.
128. One deleted passage reads as follows: 'The operators created a huge fuss about me in this regard, saying that, as they put it, "Dovzhenko is destroying our style". This is what happened during the making of *Zemlia*.' The second paragraph of the original address also read slightly differently: 'For me, of course, all operators are like Demuts'kyi, because I compose the frame myself insofar as I like to work quickly. I don't like the pedantry of operators and I always carry the camera around and position it myself. This is the moment when I formulate my thoughts; when I am dragging the camera around, this is when the greatest part of my work is done. And then I say to the operator "just put everything in focus and start filming!"'. Cited in Masokha, "'Ia ne boius' sporit' s vami, Aleksandr Petrovich...'", pp. 135 & 138n2.
129. D. Mar'ian, 'Odin iz luchshikh', *Kino*, 1932.29, 2.
130. Masokha, "'Ia ne boius' sporit' s vami, Aleksandr Petrovich...'", p. 135.
131. Kokhno, 'Poeziia truda', pp. 79–80. For the passage in question, see Gogol', 'Strashnaia mest'', in his *Sobranie sochinenii*, I, 139–76 (p. 163).
132. Kokhno, 'Poeziia truda', p. 84.
133. Ibid., pp. 80 & 84.
134. Liber, *Alexander Dovzhenko*, p. 136.
135. Ibid., pp. 162–63.
136. Ibid., p. 217.
137. D. Teshabaev, *Puti i poiski: Voprosy stanovleniia uzbekskoi kinorezhissury i kinodramaturgii* (Tashkent: Izdatel'stvo literatury i iskusstva im. Gafura Guliama, 1973), pp. 40–83.
138. Antipenko, 'Moi Demutskii', p. 96.
139. Evgenii Skliarevskii, 'Iz istorii fotoiskusstva Tashkenta', <http://sklyarevskij.livejournal.com/1884055> (accessed 21 November 2011). *Vulytsia u Bukhari* is reproduced in Chulko, 'Intimnaia nota v svetopisi'. For images from Nekhoroshev's *Turkestan Album*, see *Photography in Russia*, ed. by Elliott, pp. 126–27.

The End of the Golden Age

If the 1920s can be regarded as a 'golden age' for Soviet camera operators, during the early years of the next decade the profession became subject to a diverse range of pressures which meant that, in essence, this age was drawing to a close. Although the avant-garde units, with the exception of Dovzhenko's team, remained more or less intact during the 1930s and 1940s, there were several developments that conspired to transform radically the nature of the camera operator's task and to curtail severely the experimentation which had been a hallmark of the previous decade. The first was the gradual move to 'talkies'. Broadly speaking, this shifted the emphasis of the screened image away from the visual towards the acoustic and impeded the camera operator's creative initiative to the extent that, both within the Soviet Union and abroad, it was regarded within the profession as little short of a catastrophe.[1] The second was the move towards a 'cinema understood by the millions' and the increasingly vocal criticisms of formalism and montage theory, culminating in the embrace of Socialist Realism, which was announced at the Congress of Writers in 1934.[2] Another pressure, which paralleled and may indeed have been triggered by these developments, was the failure of the profession, despite very strenuous efforts, to be accorded formal authorship rights within the industry. This campaign concerned itself primarily with the payment of royalties, but it was symptomatic of an extremely important conceptual issue; namely, the question of how authorship can be attributed to a product that has been created collaboratively. The rhetoric that accompanied this campaign suggests that it furnished an opportunity for camera operators to voice their dissatisfaction in relation to a whole host of issues concerning their working conditions. Defeat, therefore, was a blow to the profession on a practical level, but it was also damaging psychologically in the sense that it acted as a general disincentive to work creatively. Eizenshtein's public intervention in March 1933 implies that, behind the surface bonhomie, the campaign for creative recognition had provoked significant tensions between directors and camera operators, and given rise to some unpleasant mutual recrimination. In short, the early 1930s was a period of tremendous uncertainty for camera operators, one that witnessed significant changes in their working practices and deepening anxieties in relation to their isolation within the industry as a whole.

The campaign for recognition of camera operators' creative rights appears to have been launched by the editors of *Kino*, who convened a special meeting in their offices on 9 June 1932 to air the relevant grievances. Complaints were voiced about the critical neglect of camerawork in the film press and the situations of colleagues who had been dismissed from their posts for daring to remonstrate about their poor working conditions. There were also claims that the lack of protection within the industry as a whole was leading to a 'brain drain', in other words, the defection of high-profile members of the profession into the more recognized sphere of direction.[3] Because this meeting was not well attended by the leading lights of the profession, a second meeting was organized on 25 July which attracted, among others, Tisse, Kaufman, Blium and Evgenii Slavinskii. Tisse denounced the injustice of films being shelved on the grounds of directorial incompetence when the contribution of the camera operator had been 'unimpeachable' (all too often, he complained, the camerawork on a given production was regarded by the studio management as a mere 'detail' and something 'trivial').[4] Kaufman pointed to the iniquity of camera operators like him filming and editing their own documentaries, but not receiving royalties for their work. Kosmatov demanded that cinematographers should be given the same amount of time as directors to draw up their scenarios. There were also numerous complaints about working conditions, in particular the state of processing laboratories, which Blium dismissed as little better than those of a 'Chinese laundry'. Answering calls from the participants of this meeting to 'destroy the conspiracy of silence' around the profession, the editors of *Kino* duly published a manifesto on authorial rights crafted by Zheliabuzhskii, a respected figure within the film industry who had combined direction and camera operation in his films of the 1920s.[5] This manifesto was accompanied by the voicing of further complaints in relation to professional marginalization, but also by several profiles of camera operators, two of which were penned by directors or screenplay writers with whom they had collaborated in recent years.[6] This was clearly a response to the appeal by the editors of *Kino* for directors to become actively involved in the campaign for recognition.[7]

The momentum created by this campaign appears to have galvanized the profession into action. Two conferences of camera operators were organized to discuss the general situation, the first held in Moscow in April 1933 and the second in Leningrad three months later, both of them unprecedented events in those cities.[8] Without exception, the speakers at the Moscow conference denounced the injustice of a situation in which writers, directors and composers could claim authorial status, and thus enjoy royalties, but camera operators could not. Golovnia's opening address, while acknowledging the importance of avant-garde directors in encouraging camera operators to view their profession creatively in the early 1920s, argued that the weight of responsibility had shifted very much towards the latter in the intervening period.[9] Tisse claimed that the creative input of the camera operator was often deliberately undermined or disparaged by directors in the public sphere because it was perceived as a threat to their own status. Rehearsing the main points of his manifesto, Zheliabuzhskii argued that the 'camera operator's scenario' was a crucial part of the production process and that it should therefore be regarded as a creative document in its own right; in his experience, neither the screenplay nor the director's shooting scenario indicated how particular scenes should be realized from a visual point of view. Concerns were also expressed about the recent trend towards what one delegate described as a 'film library' (fil'moteka) of camera operators, by which he meant a pool of personnel attached to individual studios, but unaffiliated to particular creative teams, who could be assigned to productions at a moment's notice. This, he argued, ran counter to the principle of stability, the importance of durable partnerships with individual directors, and the recognition that camera operators had a highly intuitive way of working which should not be assigned on the basis of management whim or the urgent need to fulfil production quotas. The speakers at the conference in Leningrad, while focussed more on aesthetic issues and questions relating to the existence of an emerging 'Leningrad school' of cinematography, nevertheless also passed a resolution that directly echoed the positions in relation to creative rights which had been agreed earlier in Moscow. This is confirmed in the article published two months later by Tisse and Nil'sen in *Sovetskoe kino*.[10] In part, they endeavoured to show that the argument about the creative rights of the camera operator belonged to a much wider debate about the distinctiveness, or otherwise, of the Soviet film product itself.

The general tenor of the remarks at the Moscow and Leningrad conferences hints at the existence of significant tensions between directors and camera operators. The lack of solidarity is also suggested by the claim that earlier attempts to appeal to the union of cinematographers had been thwarted by the refusal of directors to attend the relevant meetings, and by the fact that, despite the open invitation, only two directors attended the Moscow conference.[11] It is important to stress that the existence of tensions behind the façade of collective solidarity was not necessarily something new in Soviet cinema. A humorous cartoon, published in 1925, depicts a screenplay writer, a production artist, a director and a cameraman all arguing about their unique importance within the production process (the cameraman claims that 'without me, you might as well be without hands!').[12] Furthermore, it would appear that the issue of authorship rights did not solely concern the camera-operating fraternity; several articles in 1933 also raise the issue of rights in relation to living authors and the writers of screenplays.[13]

These facts notwithstanding, Eizenshtein's intervention just one month before the April conference in Moscow paints a picture of an industry in disarray, sinking beneath the weight of mutual recrimination.[14] In fairness, despite the provocative language employed, his article might be regarded as a perfectly reasonable attempt to define the meaning of authorship in relation to a collective process. Furthermore, perhaps unsurprisingly in view of his own disagreements in the past, for example with Pletnev, which have been mentioned in Chapter Two, Eizenshtein appears just as preoccupied by the legal disputes between screenplay writers and directors (everywhere you look, he claims, there seems to be a prosecutor involved). Nevertheless, his article contains a number of quite specific and provocative references to the camera-operating fraternity. He refers to the 'bickering over the cameraman's pretensions to direction', the 'repressed anger' making 'the handles of the camera quiver as they are cranked', and rumours that 'in the country that is building socialism it is nonetheless possible to "buy out" a cameraman from another creative collective ... in return for a few small crumbs from the co-authorship payments'.[15] The resulting tensions had produced letters of angry protest to studio executives and press editors, many of them unpublishable on grounds of obscenity, or so he mischievously claimed, and unprecedentedly high levels of scurrilous rumour and personal invective.[16] For Eizenshtein, these 'squabbles' over creative rights were a 'stinking wave' which had been unleashed by 'schoolboys'. Furthermore, they were 'bourgeois atavism', a kulak-style vestige of the era of private property, which was bringing the industry into disrepute.[17] As the title of his article makes clear ('Po mestam!' means 'Everyone to their Places!'), while he recognized the creative endeavours of camera operators, he took the view that, unless they were involved in the genesis of the screenplay, they did not have any special claim to authorship.

The tensions revealed by the conferences in Moscow and Leningrad were merely one facet of the increasing marginalization experienced by the camera-operating profession during the transition to sound. As I have explained elsewhere, the introduction of sound technology posed a number of technical challenges which, as well as limiting the creative ambitions of camera operators, frequently gave rise to frustration and, at times, significant stress.[18] The sense of marginalization was symbolically reflected in their confinement, or perhaps better to say 'incarceration', within soundproofed booths, so that the noisy whirring of the cameras was not picked up by microphones; trapped in these 'tanks', as they were dubbed in Hollywood, apart from the discomfort of the excessive heat, the camera operators could hear nothing and were unable to communicate with the directors.[19] Even when he finally managed to free himself from this physical restriction, the camera operator was confronted by a further impediment; namely, the encasement of their cameras in so-called wooden 'blimps', which rendered the apparatus to all intents and purposes immobile (unlike their U.S. equivalents, the early Soviet 'blimps' were so heavy that standard tripods could barely withstand their weight).[20] The dependence on a new breed of sound engineers was physically manifested in the electric cables that connected the now cumbersome cameras umbilically to the sound recording equipment; although stationed in close proximity, this was also heavy and essentially immobile. The symbolism of the camera's anchored position was further aggravated by restrictions on the placing of lighting units owing to the need to avoid the shadows of microphones falling into the frame. The standard arcs themselves were no longer viable because they hummed. Moreover, the carbons that produced the illumination, when about to burn out, had a tendency to 'hiss' or 'sing', further compromising the soundtrack.[21] In due course, studios would become equipped with tungsten (incandescent) filament lamps, but the process of transformation was slow, and the alternating current which supplied Soviet studios had a pulsation rate equivalent to the new speed of filming (twenty-four frames per second), which meant that there was a constant danger of 'technical deficiency' (brak).[22] On top of these challenges, and completely separately, camera operators were struggling with the move towards domestic self-sufficiency, which had been announced as part of the first Five-Year Plan. The prohibition on the purchase of foreign equipment was particularly disastrous in relation to film stock. Although the industry, with the help of French specialists, had developed orthochromatic and panchromatic film stock, to be manufactured in Shostka, it was not supplied in sufficient quantities and there were numerous complaints about its chemical reliability. In due course, this gave rise to a fully fledged film-stock crisis in 1932.[23]

Synchronous filming was a nightmare in the early years; indeed, it was only thanks to what Gordanov has called the 'miracles of resourcefulness' on the part of cameramen and lighting technicians that any synchronous shooting took place at all.[24] The impact of the technical challenges posed by the new method of filming can be gauged by the fact that nearly all the films commissioned as sound or partially sound productions in the late 1920s and early 1930s either were not released as sound films, contained very little in the way of synchronously shot material, or consisted simply of silent images to which a musical soundtrack or some other sound effects were added. For this reason, a distinction was drawn between films that contained sound effects only (*shumovye*) and those that incorporated dialogue (*govoriashchie*).[25] Kabalov's account of the first experiment with recording equipment on the streets of Moscow on 2 October 1929 with the Tagefon, a camera that recorded visual images and sound simultaneously according to Pavel Tager's system of optical printing, confirmed suspicions that the new method of filming might pose insurmountable problems: the apparatus was huge and could only be transported on the back of a truck; it was equipped with only a single lens which could not be changed; and when Kabalov placed his eye next to the viewfinder to focus the image, he was surprised to receive a 400-volt shock because the metal casing of the apparatus was 'live'.[26] Problems with recording on exterior locations, where the equipment either did not capture the authentic quality of natural sound, and was therefore 'unphotogenic', or could easily be compromised by interference, meant that sequences with dialogue invariably took place in studios which had been soundproofed.[27] The problems of soundproofing the studios, the constant danger of acoustic interference during the filming process, the mumbling or mispronunciation of words by actors and numerous other potential 'defects' in the soundtrack have passed into cinematic legend. It is symptomatic of these problems that, for example, although there were dramatic and ideological shortcomings in Pudovkin's *Prostoi sluchai*, it was largely for technical reasons that the film was not released in a sound version. A more cautious approach was adopted by the FEKS team when they came to work with the system developed by Aleksandr Shorin in Leningrad for the production of *Odna*. Nevertheless, their declaration that the film would not be characterized by a random series of sounds which reflected 'various kinds of purely naturalistic moments', but rather by a series of sound sequences that were properly combined and edited with silent sequences into an organic whole, was not ultimately realized.[28]

It was only when new methods of combining sound and vision began to be explored that camera operators were liberated from the tyranny of sound equipment. In 1930, adopting the methods pioneered by Edwin Hopkins in North

America, Vertov recorded and edited the soundtrack independently of the visual image for his first sound documentary, *Symfoniia Donbasy*. Furthermore, he advocated the use of acoustic material in a variety of experimental ways and was one of the earliest Soviet exponents of authentic sound recording.[29] The possibility of separate sound editing gave rise to a number of experimental projects on the part of the avant-garde. As already mentioned in Chapter Two, it was the method employed by Eizenshtein and Aleksandrov for the making of *Romance sentimentale*. Furthermore, the aspect ratio of the surviving footage of *Que Viva Mexico!* suggests that, although this was shot in the absence of sound-recording equipment, sufficient space had been left along the left-hand margin of the film stock to permit the addition of acoustic material if required. As already indicated in Chapter Three, Pudovkin's *Dezertir* also exploited this new method of optical sound-editing. Like Vertov, Pudovkin proposed a conceptual approach that retained the shooting and editing freedom associated with the silent era while at the same time experimenting with a more inventive use of sound than was common practice at the time. This included the use of local asynchrony, the manipulation of the acoustic environment in order to communicate subjective experience, and the orchestration of acoustic material and the musical accompaniment for the purposes of rhythmic contrast rather than purely for aural amplification.[30] His essays from 1933 and 1934 represent a significant development when compared to the 'Declaration on Sound' which he had signed with Eizenshtein and Aleksandrov in 1928.[31] In his own words, Pudovkin 'cut' the phonogram for *Dezertir* as freely as he did the visual material.[32] Furthermore, like Vertov, and much against the grain of current practice, he recorded authentic sounds on location rather than artificially within the studio. The mini-'symphony' of ship-whistles and sirens that constitutes the introductory 'overture' to *Dezertir*, for example, was recorded in the Leningrad docks, at night, in order to ensure that there was no interference from other sources.[33] In the same way, the rich chorus of shouts, songs, cheers, banging drums, brass bands and aircraft propellers that accompanies the May-Day demonstrations in the second half of the film was recorded non-synchronously during two genuine processions (Pudovkin explains that he treated the individual sounds as 'musical instruments' within a large, orchestrated ensemble).[34] The decision to circumnavigate the problem of synchronous filming by recording and editing the sound materials separately presumably explains why, in his retrospective account of the shooting of *Dezertir*, Golovnia does not mention the soundtrack as having posed a significant impediment as far as the visual language of the film was concerned.[35]

If the works cited above suggest that the technical challenges posed by sound did not de facto necessitate a repudiation of avant-garde poetics, the gradual shift towards 'sound thinking' and the increasing emphasis on cinema's accessibility did eventually render them moribund. Apart from the emergence of new genres, such as the musical and musical comedy or melodrama, the privileging of dialogue over montage produced a more emotionally accessible and prosaic form of narrative in which the psychology of the individual and the nuanced treatment of character became decisive. This development necessitated a reevaluation of visual imperatives in favour of more simplified and less expressive styles. At the Leningrad conference of camera operators, as mentioned in Chapter Four, Kozintsev called for an end to *nastroenchestvo* – in other words, the tendency towards Impressionism – which he argued had constituted 'three-quarters' of what camera operators had contributed to Soviet cinema since its infancy.[36] He rejected the recent tendency towards what he described as a 'phantasmagoria of (light) spots', which verged on outright abstraction and ran the risk of 'deforming the object'. He called instead for more realistic forms of expression which, by returning cinematography to the 'scientific precision' and 'purity' of the daguerreotype, would build on the profound interest of the pioneers of still photography in 'human character'.[37] Two years later, at the 1935 All-Union Creative Conference of Workers in Soviet Cinema, his aesthetic position was echoed by Trauberg:

> *My fervent ambition is for how a film has been shot to be invisible … . This means that certain devices beloved of camera operators, but excessively showy, are going to have to be made redundant.*[38]

Moskvin's attempt to clarify his words, or perhaps to put a favourable gloss on them, expressed this ambition slightly differently:

> *I don't want to act as Trauberg's defence lawyer, but I want to say that by simplicity both of us mean not a vulgarization of photography, or the other elements of the film, but rather a more perfect photographic form, as well as a perfection of the screenplay and the direction.*[39]

Despite this intervention, however, the ominous import of Trauberg's remark was not lost on certain delegates. Piotrovskii, for example, warned of the dangers of 'disarming the [camera] operator'.[40] He was supported by Golovnia, who argued in the context of *Dezertir* that, while he had been forced to seek new visual devices which perhaps had not been as 'striking' as before, this did not necessarily mean that 'photography, and camera operators, were no longer necessary'.[41]

As detailed in the previous chapters, three of the creative teams associated with the Soviet avant-garde continued to work throughout the Stalinist period, but at different times they experienced difficulties with the realization of certain projects, and to a great extent the inventiveness of the 1920s came to an end. Undeniably, there are vestiges of the earlier period of experimentation, but it should be emphasized that these are mostly confined to the works of Eizenshtein and can be witnessed within relatively narrow aesthetic categories. They are mostly associated either with the innovative use of sound or with the advent of colour technology, which offered new possibilities on the basis of which the visual language of film could be reformulated and renewed. Furthermore, these experiments took place within a very different cultural environment and were analogous to the gradual evolution in expressive means which characterized world cinema generally. As Kaplan points out, the transition to sound produced a marked shift away from expressiveness and compositional dynamism towards a much more 'unassuming' and 'thoughtful' camerawork, one devoted solely to the creation of character.[42] Some, like Moskvin, engineered a complete transformation; others, like Tisse, retained some of their former 'signatures' but were still forced to adapt to the new situation and thus limit the field of exploration. To all intents and purposes, the avant-garde chapter in Soviet cinema had come to a close.

Notes

1.   Cavendish, *Soviet Mainstream Cinematography*, pp. 194–96.
2.   Peter Kenez, *Cinema and Soviet Society from the Revolution to the Death of Stalin* (London: I. B. Tauris, 2001), pp. 143–45.
3.   M. Shch., 'Khudozhniku sveta – tvorcheskie prava!' (Na soveshchanii operatorov v redaktsii gazety "Kino")', *Kino*, 1932.27, 3.
4.   For Tisse's remarks and those by other participants cited later in this paragraph, see N., 'Operator – soavtor fil'my', ibid., 1932.37, 2.
5.   [Iurii] Zheliabuzhskii, 'Avtorskoe pravo operatora: V poriadke postanovki voprosa', ibid.
6.   For example, see Mark Donskoi, 'Rabotal uporno i nastoichivo', ibid. (on Nikolai Ushakov); and S. Ermolinskii, 'Zateinik i khudozhnik', ibid. (on Kosmatov).
7.   M. Shch., 'Khudozhniku sveta – tvorcheskie prava!'. See also the articles under the section entitled 'Razreshite vyskazat'sia', in ibid.
8.   Butovskii, *Andrei Moskvin, kinooperator*, pp. 130–33.

9. For these remarks and the comments of other delegates at the conference cited later in this paragraph, see Alina, 'Spory o besspornom voprose'.

10. Nil'sen and Tisse, 'O tvorchestve kinooperatora: K itogam moskovskoi i leningradskoi konferentsii operatorov'.

11. Alina, 'Spory o besspornom voprose'.

12. *Kino*, 1925.28, 1.

13. For example, see A. Macheret, 'Tvorcheskaia podopleka iuridicheskikh nepoladok', ibid., 1933.13, 3.

14. S. Eizenshtein, 'Po mestam!', ibid.

15. Ibid.

16. Ibid.

17. Ibid.

18. Cavendish, *Soviet Mainstream Cinematography*, pp. 193–219.

19. Leo Mur, 'Novosti kino-tekhniki: Zvukovoe kino v Amerike', *Sovetskii ekran*, 1929.19, 12–13. See also L., 'Kak snimaetsia zvuchashchaia fil'ma', *Sovetskii ekran*, 1929.41, 12.

20. Gordanov, *Zapiski kinooperatora*, p. 104.

21. Mur, 'Novosti kino-tekhniki: Zvukovoe kino v Amerike', p. 12.

22. Kabalov, 'Glazami operatora', p. 99.

23. Gordanov, *Zapiski kinooperatora*, p. 90.

24. Ibid., p. 104.

25. Mur, 'Novosti kino-tekhniki: Zvukovoe kino v Amerike', p. 13.

26. Kabalov, 'Glazami operatora', p. 98.

27. Gervinus, 'Po tainikam zvukovoi fil'my', *Sovetskii ekran*, 1929.41, 13–14.

28. Cited in Butovskii, *Andrei Moskvin, kinooperator*, p. 116.

29. Hicks, *Dziga Vertov: Defining Documentary Film*, pp. 71–89.

30. Pudovkin, 'Asinkhronnost' kak printsip zvukovogo kino', and 'Problema ritma v moem pervom zvukovom fil'me'.

31. Sergei Eizenshtein, Grigorii Aleksandrov and Vsevolod Pudovkin, 'Zaiavka', in *The Film Factory: Russian and Soviet Cinema in Documents 1896–1939*, ed. by Richard Taylor and Ian Christie, trans. by Richard Taylor (London: Routledge, 1988), pp. 234–35 (first publ. in *Zhizn' iskusstva*, 5 August 1928).

32. Pudovkin, 'Problema ritma v moem pervom zvukovom fil'me', p. 165.

33. Ibid., p. 166.

34. Ibid.

35. Golovnia, *Svet v iskusstve operatora*, pp. 129–31.

36. Kozintsev, 'Nastroenchestvo', p. 16.

37. Ibid., p. 18.

38. Cited in Butovskii, *Andrei Moskvin, kinooperatora*, pp. 135–36.

39. Cited in ibid., p. 136.

40. Cited in ibid.

41. Cited in ibid.

42. M. Kaplan, 'Kul'tura operatora', *Iskusstvo kino*, 1940.1–2, 63–67 (p. 65).

Fig. 1 – Frame still from the Odessa mist sequence in *Bronenosets Potemkin*.

Fig. 2 – The risks of war-time filming: the actuality specialist Petr Novitskii shoots at the Front wearing a gas mask.

Fig. 3 – 'Budushchee vperedi' ('Le grand pisdagiste Tissé'): scandalous 'secret drawing' by Sergei Eizenshtein.

Fig. 4 – *Stachka*: strikers are doused with jets of water during the hosing sequence.

Fig. 5 – *Stachka*: grid-pattern composition for the agitation sequences on the factory floor.

Fig. 6 – *Stachka*: diagonal composition and staging in depth for the tenement-block sequence.

Fig. 7 – *Bronenosets Potemkin*: the sailors start agitating.

Fig. 8 – *Bronenosets Potemkin*: Giliarovskii (Grigorii Aleksandrov) issues the order to shoot.

Fig. 9 – *Oktiabr'*: a bourgeois member of the crowd during the 'July Days' episode.

Fig. 10 – *Oktiabr'*: a bourgeois citizen of St Petersburg celebrates the overthrow of the monarchy in February 1917.

Fig. 11 – *Oktiabr'*: the Cossack Savage Division – a close-up portrait.

Fig. 12 – *Staroe i novoe*: a peasant onlooker during the cream-separator sequence.

Fig. 13 – *Staroe i novoe*: a female peasant onlooker during the cream-separator sequence.

Fig. 14 – *Mat'*: portrait of the mother, Pelageia Nilovna Vlasova (Vera Baranovskaia), during the arrest sequence.

Fig. 15 – *Mat'*: portrait of the mother during the court sequence.

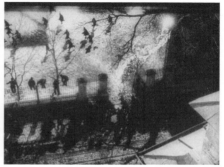

Fig. 16 – *Mat'*: Bolshevik demonstrators are dispersed and flee for their lives.

Fig. 17 – *Mat'*: portrait of the drunken father, Mikhail Vlasov (Aleksandr Chistiakov).

Fig. 18 – *Mat'*: portrait of the arresting colonel.

Fig. 19 – *Mat'*: portrait of the presiding judge.

Fig. 20 – *Konets Sankt-Peterburga*: example of *rakurs* (extreme angled shot) during the patriotic sequence.

Fig. 21 – *Konets Sankt-Peterburga*: the Winter Palace during a white night.

Fig. 22 – *Konets Sankt-Peterburga*: the foundry worker in goggles at the Lebedev factory.

Fig. 23 – *Konets Sankt-Peterburga*: truncated image of the crowd during the 'Rodina zovet' (Motherland Calls) sequence.

Fig. 24 – *Chertovo koleso*: mobile spotlight for the 'Devil's Wheel' sequence.

Fig. 25 – *Chertovo koleso*: low-angle lighting for the figure of the clown at the House of Culture (Narodnyi dom).

Fig. 26 – *Shinel'*: soft-focus portrait of Akakii Akakievich (Andrei Kostrichkin).

Fig. 27 – *Shinel'*: use of shadow play during the theft sequence.

Fig. 28 – *Shinel'*: use of *rakurs* for the shot before Akakii Akakievich's audience with the Important Person.

Fig. 29 – *SVD*: the call to insurrection.

Fig. 30 – *SVD*: portrait of Medoks (Sergei Gerasimov).

Fig. 31 – *SVD*: shadow play on the tavern wall where the conspiracy takes place.

Fig. 32 – *SVD*: *contre-jour* and shadow play during the ice-skating sequence.

Fig. 33 – *Novyi Vavilon*: violin player during the opening sequence.

Fig. 34 – *Novyi Vavilon*: the owner of the emporium (David Gutman).

Fig. 35 – *Novyi Vavilon*: portrait of Louise Poiret (Elena Kuz'mina).

Fig. 36 – *Novyi Vavilon*: portrait of Poiret.

Fig. 37 – *Novyi Vavilon*: portrait of Poiret moments before her execution at Père Lachaise cemetery.

Fig. 38 – *Zvenyhora*: landscape composition which introduces the Ivan Kupalo (St John's Eve) sequence.

Fig. 39 – *Zvenyhora*: young maidens watch their wreaths float down the river during the celebration of Ivan Kupalo.

Fig. 40 – *Zvenyhora*: soldiers cross a ford during the Civil War sequence.

Fig. 41 – *Zvenyhora*: Constructivist-style multiple exposure.

Fig. 42 – *Zvenyhora*: Varangian invasion sequence – the opening shot.

Fig. 43 – *Arsenal*: portrait of the mother whose son is executed in the final sequence.

Fig. 44 – *Zemlia*: portrait of a young couple during the post-harvest sequence.

Fig. 45 – *Zemlia*: the 'nocturnal' dance of Vasyl' (Semen Svashenko).

Fig. 46 – *Zemlia*: apples and watermelons on the ground during the penultimate sequence.

Fig. 47 – *Zemlia*: composition with apples using mirror reflectors.

Filmography

The list of film titles below includes the following information: title, translated title (if necessary), director, camera operator, year of production/year of release (if different), and name of the studio or production company. Those films released in Ukraine have been given Ukrainian titles with Russian and English translations in parenthesis. Where Ukrainian and Russian titles are identical, the latter have not been given.

Aelita (Aelita, Queen of Mars), Iakov Protazanov, Iurii Zheliabuzhskii, 1924, Mezhrabpom-Rus'

Arsenal, Oleksandr Dovzhenko, Danylo Demuts'kyi, 1928, VUFKU

Ballet mécanique (Mechanical Ballet), Fernand Léger and Dudley Murphy, Man Ray and Dudley Murphy, 1924, France

Benia Kryk (Benia Krik, Benny Krik), Volodymyr Vil'ner, Oleksii Kaliuzhnyi, 1926, VUFKU

Bezhin lug (Bezhin Meadow), Sergei Eizenshtein, Eduard Tisse, 1935–37, Gosudarstvennoe upravlenie kinematografii

Bol'shoi ferganskii kanal (The Great Ferghana Canal), Sergei Eizenshtein, Eduard Tisse, 1939

Borot'ba veletniv (Bor'ba gigantov, The Battle of the Giants), Viktor Turin, Fridrikh (Fedor) Verigo-Darovskii, 1926, VUFKU

Bratishka (Little Brother), Grigorii Kozintsev and Leonid Trauberg, Andrei Moskvin, 1926, Sovkino (Leningrad)

Broken Blossoms, D. W. Griffith, G. W. 'Billy' Bitzer and Hendrik Sartov, 1919, D. W. Griffith Productions and Paramount

Bronenosets Potemkin (Battleship Potemkin), Sergei Eizenshtein, Eduard Tisse, 1925, Goskino (First Factory)

Brumes d'automne (The Mists of Autumn), Dimitri Kirsanoff, Jean de Miéville, 1928, Mentor Film

Chapaev, Georgii Vasil'ev and Sergei Vasil'ev, Aleksandr Sigaev, 1934, Lenfil'm

Chelovek (The Man), Władysław Starewicz (director and camera operator), 1912, Khanzhonkov & Co.

Chelovek iz restorana (The Man from the Restaurant), Sigizmund Veselovskii, Petr Mosiagin, 1916, G. Libken & Co.

Chelovek iz restorana (The Man from the Restaurant), Iakov Protazanov, Anatolii Golovnia, 1927, Mezhrabpom-Rus'

Chelovek s kinoapparatom (Man with the Movie Camera) [documentary], Dziga Vertov, Mikhail Kaufman, 1929, VUFKU

Chertovo koleso (The Devil's Wheel), Grigorii Kozintsev and Leonid Trauberg, Andrei Moskvin, 1926, Leningradkino

Chuzhoi pidzhak (Someone Else's Jacket), Grigorii Kozintsev and Leonid Trauberg, Andrei Moskvin, 1927, Sovkino (Leningrad)

Coeur fidèle (A Faithful Heart), Jean Epstein, Léon Donnot and others, 1923, Pathé Consortium Cinéma

Danton, Dimitri Buchowetzki, Arpad Viragh, 1921, Wörner-Filmgesellschaft

Das Kabinett des Dr Caligari (The Cabinet of Dr Caligari), Robert Wiene, Willy Hameister, 1920, Decla-Bioscop A.G.

Das Wachsfigurenkabinett (The Waxworks Museum), Paul Leni, Helmar Lerski, 1924, Neptune Film A.G.

Dekabristy (The Decembrists), Aleksandr Ivanovskii, Ivan Frolov, 1926, Sovkino (Leningrad)

Der blaue Engel (The Blue Angel), Josef von Sternberg, Günther Rittau, 1930, Universum Film (UFA)

Der letzte Mann (The Last Laugh), F. W. Murnau, Karl Freund, 1924, Universum Film (UFA)

Dezertir (The Deserter), Vsevolod Pudovkin, Anatolii Golovnia, 1933, Mezhrabpomfil'm

Dnevnik Glumova (Glumov's Diary), Sergei Eizenshtein, Boris Frantsisson, 1923, Goskino

Doch' "cheloveka" (The Daughter of a "Man"), Ivan Lazarev, Mikhail Vladimirskii, 1916, A. Khanzhonkov & Co.

Dva dni (Dva dnia, Two Days), Heorhii Stabovyi, Danylo Demuts'kyi, 1927, VUFKU

Dva druga, model' i podruga (Two Friends, a Model and a Girlfriend), Aleksei Popov, Aleksandr Grinberg, 1927, Sovkino (Moscow)

Ego prevoskhoditel'stvo (His Excellency), Grigorii Roshal', Nikolai Kozlovskii, 1926, Belgoskino

Ein Lichtspiel: Schwarz-weiß-grau (Light Spill: Black-White-Grey), László Moholy-Nagy (director and camera operator), 1929, Germany

Entuziazm: Symfoniia Donbasy (Entuziazm: Simfoniia Donbassa, Enthusiasm: Symphony of the Donbas), Dziga Vertov, Boris Tseitlin, 1931, Ukrainfil'm

Evrei na zemle (The Jew on Earth), Abram Room, Albert Kühn, 1927, VUFKU

Evreiskoe schast'e (Jewish Luck), Aleksandr Granovskii, Eduard Tisse, 1925, Goskino (First Factory)

Fata Morgana, Boris Tiahno, Danylo Demuts'kyi, 1932, Ukrainfil'm

Fed'kina pravda (Fed'ka's Truth), Ol'ga Preobrazhenskaia, Aleksandr Grinberg, 1925, Goskino (First Factory)

Frauennot-Frauenglück (Misery and Fortune of Women), Eduard Tisse (direction and camera operation), 1930, Praesens Film

Frits Bauer, Vladimir Petrov, Viacheslav Gordanov, 1930, Sovkino (Leningrad)

Giftgas (Poison Gas), Mikhail Dubson, Akos Farkas, 1929, Levfilm

Golod (Hunger), Aleksandr Ivanov-Gai, Nikolai Kozlovskii, 1921, Petrogradskii Okruzhnoi Foto-Kino-Komitet

Golod... golod... golod... (Hunger... Hunger... Hunger...), Vladimir Gardin and Vsevolod Pudovkin, Eduard Tisse, 1921, VFKO/GTK

Iahidki kokhannia (Iagodka liubvi, Love's Little Berry), Oleksandr Dovzhenko, Joseph Rona, 1926, VUFKU

Ia – Kuba (I am Cuba), Mikhail Kalatozov, Sergei Urusevskii, 1964, Mosfil'm and ICAIC (Cuba)

In der Nacht: Eine musikalische Bildphantasie (In the Night: A Musical Picture Fantasy), Walter Ruttmann, Reimar Kuntze, 1931, Tobis-Melodiefilm GmbH

Intolerance: Love's Struggle Throughout the Ages, D. W. Griffith, G. W. 'Billy' Bitzer, 1916, Triangle Film Corporation and Wark Producing Corp.

Ivan, Oleksandr Dovzhenko, Danylo Demuts'kyi, 1932, Ukrainfil'm

Ivan Groznyi (Ivan the Terrible), Sergei Eizenshtein, Eduard Tisse, 1944–46, Mosfil'm/ Tsentral'naia ob"edinennaia kinostudiia (Alma-Ata)

Jérôme Crainquebille (Coster Bill of Paris), Jacques Feyder, Léonce-Henri Burel and Maurice Foster, 1922, Films A. Legrand

Kat'ka bumazhnyi ranet (Kat'ka's Reinette Apples), Fridrikh Ermler and Eduard Ioganson, Evgenii Mikhailov, 1926, Sovkino (Leningrad)

Khleb (Bread) [documentary], Anatolii Golovnia (direction and camera operation), 1929, Mezhrabpomfil'm

Kinoglaz (Ciné-Eye), Dziga Vertov, Mikhail Kaufman, 1924, Goskino

Kirpichiki (Little Bricks), Leonid Obolenskii and Mikhail Doller, Anatolii Golovnia, 1925, Mezhrabpom-Rus'

Kollezhskii registrator (The Collegiate Assessor), Iurii Zheliabuzhskii and Ivan Moskvin, Iurii Zheliabuzhskii, 1925, Mezhrabpom-Rus'

Komissar (The Commissar), Aleksandr Askol'dov, Valerii Ginzburg, 1967, Gor'kii Film Studio

Konets Sankt-Peterburga (The End of St Petersburg), Vsevolod Pudovkin, Anatolii Golovnia, 1927, Mezhrabpom-Rus'

Korol' Lir (King Lear), Grigorii Kozintsev, Ionas Gritsius, 1971, Lenfil'm

Krasnaia gazeta (The Red Newspaper) [publicity film], Grigorii Kozintsev and Leonid Trauberg, V. Glass, 1924, Sevzapkino

Krasnye d'iavoliata (The Little Red Devils), Ivan Perestiani, Aleksandr Digmelov, 1923, Kinosektsiia Narkomprosa Gruzii

Kreml' v proshlom i v nastoiashchem (The Kremlin – Past and Present) [documentary], Grigorii Boltianskii and Eduard Tisse, 1925, Goskino (First Factory)

La Chute de la maison Usher (The Fall of the House of Usher), Jean Epstein, Georges Lucas and Jean Lucas, 1928, Films Jean Epstein

Lillies of the Field, John Francis Dillon, James van Trees, 1924, Corinne Griffith Productions

Liudyna z lisu (Chelovek iz lesa, The Man from the Forest), Heorhii Stabovyi, Danylo Demuts'kyi, 1927, VUFKU

Luch smerti (The Death Ray), Lev Kuleshov, Aleksandr Levitskii, 1925, Goskino (First Factory)

Mat' (Mother), Vsevolod Pudovkin, Anatolii Golovnia, 1926, Mezhrabpom-Rus'

Mekhanika golovnogo mozga (Mechanics of the Brain), Vsevolod Pudovkin, Anatolii Golovnia, 1926, Mezhrabpom-Rus'

Ménilmontant, Dimitri Kirsanoff (director and camera operator), 1926, France

Michurin: Zhizn' v tsvetu (Michurin: A Life in Bloom), Oleksandr Dovzhenko, Leonid
  Kosmatov, 1948, Mosfil'm
Mishki protiv ludenicha (The Mishkas vs. ludenich), Grigorii Kozintsev and Leonid
  Trauberg, Fridrikh (Fedor) Verigo-Darovskii, 1925, Sevzapkino
Miss-Mend (Miss-Mend/The Adventures of Three Reporters), Boris Barnet and Fedor
  Otsep, Evgenii Alekseev, 1926, Mezhrabpom-Rus'
My Best Girl, Sam Taylor, Charles Rosher and David Kesson, 1927, Mary Pickford Company
Nanook of the North [documentary], Robert J. Flaherty (direction and camera operation),
  1922, Les Frères Revillon/Pathé Exchange
Napoleon-gaz (Napoleon-gas), Semen Tymoshenko, Sviatoslav Beliaev, 1925, Sevzapkino
Nasreddin v Bukhare (Nasreddin in Bukhara), Iakov Protazanov, Danylo Demuts'kyi, 1943,
  Tashkent Studio
Neobychainye prikliucheniia mistera Vesta v strane bol'shevikov (The Extraordinary
  Adventures of Mr West in the Land of the Bolsheviks), Lev Kuleshov, Aleksandr
  Levitskii, 1924, Goskino (First and Third Factories)
N + N + N ('Nini, nalog, nepriatnost'') (N + N + N ('Nini, New Taxes and Nastiness')),
  Vladimir Shmidtgof, Nikolai Efremov, 1924, Sevzapkino
Nosferatu, eine Symphonie des Grauens (Nosferatu, a Symphony of Horrors), F. W.
  Murnau, Fritz Arno Wagner, 1922, Jofa-Atelier Berlin-Johannisthal, Prana-Film GmbH
Novyi Vavilon (The New Babylon), Grigorii Kozintsev and Leonid Trauberg, Andrei
  Moskvin, 1929, Sovkino (Leningrad)
Number, Please?, Harold Lloyd, Walter Lundin, 1920, Rolin Films
Odna (Alone), Grigorii Kozintsev and Leonid Trauberg, Andrei Moskvin, 1931, Lensoiuzkino
Oktiabr' (October), Sergei Eizenshtein and Grigorii Aleksandrov, Eduard Tisse, 1927,
  Sovkino (Moscow and Leningrad)
Ostannia cherha (Posledniaia ochered', The Last Burst of Fire), Heorhii Tasin, Danylo
  Demuts'kyi, 1941, Tashkent and Odessa Film Studios
Ot stali do rel's (From Steel to Rails) [documentary], Eduard Tisse (direction and camera
  operation), 1923, Goskino
Padenie dinastii Romanovykh (The Fall of the Romanov Dynasty) [documentary], Esfir'
  Shub, 1927, Sovkino
Pidozrilyi bagazh (Podozritel'nyi bagazh, The Suspect Luggage), Hryhorii Hrycher-
  Cherykover, Oleksii Kaliuzhnyi, 1926, VUFKU
Podvig rozvidnyka (Podvig razvedchika, The Exploits of a Spy), Boris Barnet, Danylo
  Demuts'kyi, 1947, Ukrainfil'm
Poet i Tsar' (The Poet and the Tsar), Vladimir Gardin, Sviatoslav Beliaev, 1927, Sovkino
  (Leningrad)
Pokhozhdeniia Nasreddina (The Adventures of Nasreddin), Nabi Ganiev, Danylo
  Demuts'kyi, 1946, Tashkent Studio
Pokhozhdeniia Oktiabriny (The Adventures of Oktiabrina), Grigorii Kozintsev and Leonid
  Trauberg, Fridrikh (Fedor) Verigo-Darovskii, 1924, Sevzapkino
Potomok Chingis-Khana (The Descendent of Genghis-Khan/Storm Over Asia), Vsevolod
  Pudovkin, Anatolii Golovnia, 1928, Mezhrabpomfil'm

Potselui Meri Pikford (The Kiss of Mary Pickford), Sergei Komarov, Evgenii Alekseev, 1927, Mezhrabpom-Rus'

Po zakonu (By the Law), Lev Kuleshov, Konstantin Kuznetsov, 1926, Goskino (First Factory)

Prikliucheniia Liny v Sochi (The Adventures of Lina in Sochi), Evgenii Bauer, Boris Zavelev, 1916, Khanzhonkov & Co.

Proekt inzhenera Praita (The Project of Engineer Prait), Lev Kuleshov, Mark Naletnyi, 1918, Khanzhonkov & Co.

Prostoi sluchai (A Simple Case), Vsevolod Pudovkin, Grigorii Kabalov, 1932, Mezhrabpomfil'm

Prymkhy Kateryny II (Kaprizy Ekateriny II, The Caprices of Catherine the Great), Petr Chardynin, Danylo Demuts'kyi, 1927, VUFKU

Que Viva Mexico!, Sergei Eizenshtein and Grigorii Aleksandrov, Eduard Tisse, 1932, The Mexican Picture Trust

Raskolnikow, Robert Wiene, Willy Goldberger, 1923, Leonardo-Film, Neumann-Filmproduktion

Roki molodii (Gody molodye, The Years of Youth), Hryhorii Hrycher-Cherykover, Danylo Demuts'kyi, 1942, Kyivskaia fil'mstudiia (Ashgabat)

Romance sentimentale (A Sentimental Romance), Sergei Eizenshtein and Grigorii Aleksandrov, Eduard Tisse, 1930, Sequana Films

Ryba (Fish) [documentary], Anatolii Golovnia, Konstantin Vents, 1929, Mezhrabpomfil'm

Salamandra (The Salamander), Grigorii Roshal', Louis Forestier, 1928, Mezhrabpomfil'm and Prometeusfilm (Berlin)

Serp i molot (Hammer and Sickle), Vladimir Gardin, Eduard Tisse, 1921, Goskinoshkola/VFKO (Third Factory)

Shakhmatnaia goriachka (Chess Fever), Vsevolod Pudovkin, Anatolii Golovnia, 1926, Mezhrabpom-Rus'

Shchors, Oleksandr Dovzhenko and Iuliia Solntseva, Iurii Ekel'chyk, 1939, Kyivskaia kinostudiia

Shestaia chast' mira (A Sixth Part of the World) [documentary], Dziga Vertov, Mikhail Kaufman and others, 1926, Goskino

Shinel', kino-p'esa v manere Gogolia (The Overcoat, a Film-Play in the Manner of Gogol'), Grigorii Kozintsev and Leonid Trauberg, Andrei Moskvin, 1926, Leningradkino

Signal (The Signal), Aleksandr Arkatov, Eduard Tisse, 1918, Moskovskii kinokomitet

Skvernyi anekdot (A Nasty Story), Aleksandr Alov and Vladimir Naumov, Anatolii Kuznetsov, 1966, Mosfil'm

Slesar' i kantsler (The Locksmith and the Chancellor), Vladimir Gardin and Vsevolod Pudovkin, Evgenii Slavinskii, 1923, VUFKU

Stachka (Strike), Sergei Eizenshtein, Eduard Tisse, 1924, Goskino (First Factory)

Starets Vasilii Griaznov (The Elder Vasilii Griaznov), Czesław Sabiński, Eduard Tisse, 1924, Goskino (First Factory)

Staroe i novoe ("General'naia liniia") (The Old and the New ("The General Line")), Sergei Eizenshtein and Grigorii Aleksandrov, Eduard Tisse, 1929, Sovkino (Moscow)

Stekliannyi glaz (The Glass Eye) [documentary], Lilia Brik and Vitalii Zhemchuzhnyi, Anatolii Golovnia and Konstantin Vents, 1928, Mezhrabpomfil'm

Sten'ka Razin, Vladimir Romashkov, Aleksandr Drankov and Nikolai Kozlovskii, 1908, Atel'e A. Drankova

Stepan Khalturin, Aleksandr Ivanovskii, Ivan Frolov and Fridrikh (Fedor) Verigo-Darovskii, 1925, Sevzapkino

Sumka dypkur'era (Sumka dipkur'era, The Diplomatic Pouch), Oleksandr Dovzhenko, Nikolai Kozlovskii, 1927, VUFKU

Suvoryi iunak (Strogii iunosha, A Severe Youth), Abram Room, Iurii Ekel'chyk, 1936, Ukrainfil'm

SVD (Soiuz velikogo dela) (The Union of the Great Cause), Grigorii Kozintsev and Leonid Trauberg, Andrei Moskvin, 1927, Sovkino (Leningrad)

Svizhyi viter (Svezhii veter, A Breath of Fresh Air), Heorhii Stabovyi, Danylo Demuts'kyi, 1926, VUFKU

Synii paket (Sinii paket, The Blue Packet), Favst Lopatyns'kyi, Oleksii Kaliuzhnyi, 1926, VUFKU

Syni skeli (Sinie skaly, The Blue Cliffs), Volodymyr Braun, Danylo Demuts'kyi, 1942, Kyivskaia fil'mstudiia (Ashgabat)

Tabu: A Story of the South Seas, F. W. Murnau and Robert J. Flaherty, 1931, Murnau-Flaherty Productions

Takhir i Zukhra, Nabi Ganiev, Danylo Demuts'kyi, 1945, Tashkent Studio

Taras Shevchenko, Ihor Savchenko, Arkadii Kol'tsatyi and Danylo Demuts'kyi, 1951, Kyivskaia kinostudiia

Teplaia kompaniia (Zhizn' besprizornykh) (A Cosy Crowd (The Lives of Street Children)), Leo Mur, Eduard Tisse and Aleksandr Ryllo, 1924, Goskino (First Factory)

The Kid, Charlie Chaplin, Roland Totheroh, 1921, Charlie Chaplin Productions

Thunder over Mexico, Sol Lesser [Sergei Eizenshtein, Eduard Tisse], 1933, The Mexican Film Trust

Tret'ia Meshchanskaia (Bed and Sofa), Abram Room, Grigorii Giber, 1927, Sovkino (Moscow)

Tsvet granata (The Colour of Pomegranates), Sergei Paradzhanov, Suren Shakhbazian, 1969, Armenfil'm

Turbina no. 3 (Turbine Nr. 3), Semen Tymoshenko, Andrei Moskvin and Sviatoslav Beliaev, 1927, Sovkino (Leningrad)

Ubiitsy vykhodiat na dorogu (The Murderers Go out onto the Road), Vsevolod Pudovkin and Iurii Tarich, Boris Volchek, 1942, Tsentral''naia ob'edinennaia kinostudiia (Alma-Ata)

U myrni dni (V mirnye dni, In Days of Peace), Volodymyr Braun, Danylo Demuts'kyi, 1950, Kyivskaia kinostudiia

Vasha znakomaia (Your Acquaintance), Lev Kuleshov, Konstantin Kuznetsov, 1928, Sovkino (Moscow)

Vasia – reformator (Vasia the Reformer), Favst Lopatyns'kyi/Joseph Rona, Joseph Rona, 1926, VUFKU

Velikii perelet (The Great Flight) [documentary], Vladimir Shneiderov, Georgii Blium, 1925, Proletkino

Vendetta (Vendetta), Les' Kurbas, Boris Zavelev, 1924, VUFKU

Vo imia Rodiny (In the Name of the Motherland) [also known as *Russkie liudi* (Russian People)], Vsevolod Pudovkin and Dmitrii Vasil'ev, Boris Volchek, 1943, Tsentral'naia ob"edinennaia kinostudiia (Alma-Ata)

Voina i mir (War and Peace), Iakov Protazanov, Aleksandr Levitskii, 1915, Thiemann and Reinhardt

V pazurakh Radvlady (V kogtiakh sovetskoi vlasti, In the Claws of Soviet Power), Panteleimon Sazonov, Fridrikh (Fedor) Verigo-Darovskii, 1926, VUFKU

Vsem na radost' (To Everyone for Luck), Aleksandr Anoshchenko, Boris Frantsisson, 1924, Goskino (Kul'tkino)

Vyborgskaia storona (The Vyborg Side), Grigorii Kozintsev and Leonid Trauberg, Andrei Moskvin, 1938, Lenfil'm

V zhizni vse byvaet (In Life Anything Can Happen), Viacheslav Viskovskii, camera operator unknown, 1916, A. Drankov & Co.

Way Down East, D. W. Griffith, G. W. 'Billy' Bitzer, 1920, D. W. Griffith Productions

Zakroishchik iz Torzhka (The Tailor from Torzhok), Iakov Protazanov, Petr Ermolov, 1925, Mezhrabpom-Rus'

Zemlia (Earth), Oleksandr Dovzhenko, Danylo Demuts'kyi, 1930, VUFKU

Zemlia v plenu (The Captive Earth), Fedor Otsep, Louis Forestier, 1927, Mezhrabpom-Rus'

Zheleznaia piata (The Iron Heel), Vladimir Gardin and others, Grigorii Giber and Aleksandr Levitskii, 1919, Goskinoshkola and VFKO

Zhivoi trup (The Living Corpse), Boris Chaikovskii, [first name unknown] Noske, 1911, R. Perskii & Co.

Zhivoi trup (The Living Corpse), Czesław Sabiński, Vladimir Siversen and Aleksandr Ryllo, 1918, Kharitonov & Co.

Zhivoi trup (The Living Corpse), Fedor Otsep, Anatolii Golovnia, 1929, Mezhrabpomfil'm and Prometeusfilm (Berlin)

Zirvani dni (Vzorvannye dni, Days of Explosion), Oleksandr Soloviov, Boris Zavelev, 1930, Ukrainfil'm

Zlyva (Liven', Downpour), Ivan Kavaleridze, Oleksii Kaliuzhnyi, 1929, VUFKU

Zvenyhora (Zvenigora), Oleksandr Dovzhenko, Boris Zavelev, 1927, VUFKU

Bibliography

The entries below have been organized alphabetically. This applies to articles in the Soviet press where authorship is indicated by initials only; in these cases, the initialled surname has been listed first, followed by the initialled first name. In the cases of names with multiple entries, these entries have been organized in chronological order according to the date of first publication or composition. In the case of the former, the date is indicated in parentheses at the end of the entry; in the case of the latter, the date is indicated in square brackets immediately after the title. Edited volumes have been listed by title, followed by the name of the editor(s). Entries which consist of chapters or essays in edited volumes give the title and shortened publication details of the volume in question. The full publication details are given under the entry for the volume. Articles where authorship is not indicated are listed by title only.

Agden, V., 'Kino-khudozhnik na Zapade i v S.S.S.R.', *Kino-zhurnal A.R.K.*, 1926.3, 16–18

Albera, François, *Eisenstein et le constructivisme russe* (Lausanne: L'Age d'homme, 1990)
    'Eisenstein: The Graphic Question', in *Eisenstein at Ninety*, ed. by Christie and Elliott, pp. 119–27

Aleksandrov, Grigorii, letter to Sergei Eizenshtein dated 27 November 1925, in *Brononosets Potemkin*, ed. by Kleiman and Levina, p. 83
    Epokha i kino (Moscow: Politizdat, 1976)

Alexander Rodchenko: Photography: 1924–54, ed. with introduction by Alexander Lavrentiev (Cologne: Könemann, 1995)

Alexander Rodchenko: Revolution in Photography, ed. by Alexander Lavrentiev (Moscow: Multimedia Complex of Actual Arts/Moscow House of Photography Museum, 2008)

Alina, G., 'Spory o besspornom voprose', *Kino*, 1933.21, 4

Alpers, B., 'Put' Feksov', *Kino i zhizn'*, 1929.4, 4–5

'Andrei Nikolaevich Moskvin: Biofil'mobibliografiia', publ. by Ia. Butovskii, *Kinovedcheskie zapiski*, 27 (1995), 118–40

Anon, 'Photography of the Month: "Thunder over Mexico"', *American Cinematographer*, 16.3 (1933), 92–93

Anoshchenko-Anod., A., 'O naplyvakh', *Kino-zhurnal A.R.K.*, 1925.1, 20

Anoshchenko, Nikolai, 'Shtaakenskii gigant', *Kino-front*, 1926.1, 24–26
    'Germanskaia kinematografiia nashikh dnei', *Kino-front*, 1926.2–3, 35–36
    'Novinki kino-s"emochnoi apparatury', *Kino-front*, 1927.2, 16–18
    'Khudozhestvennaia kino-s"emka s dobavochnymi linzami', *Kino-front*, 1927.7–8, 18–23
    'Zametki operatora', *Kino-front*, 1928.2, 27

'Pochemu na iuge severnye operatory inogda delaiut... nedoderzhki', *Kino-front*, 1928.2, 27–28

'Novyi shtativ dlia s"emochnykh kamer', *Sovetskii ekran*, 1929.29, 12

'Prozhektora s poluvattnymi lampami', *Sovetskii ekran*, 1929.29, 12

'Novinki kinotekhniki: Novosti liubitel'skoi apparatury,' *Sovetskii ekran*, 1929.31, 12

'Kombinirovannye kadry', *Sovetskii ekran*, 1929.42, 12

'Triuki troinoi prizmy', *Sovetskii ekran*, 1929.43, 10

Antipenko, Aleksandr, 'Moi Demutskii', *Iskusstvo kino*, 1972.9, 93–98

'Moi Demutskii', *Fotografiia*, 6 (1995), http://www.photoweb.ru/prophoto/biblioteka (accessed 9 November 2005)

Antropov, V., 'D. Demutskii', in *Desiat' operatorskikh biografii*, ed. by Goldovskaia, pp. 86–105

Aranovich, D., 'Sovremennyi kinoplakat', *Sovetskii ekran*, 1927.28, 13–14

Arlazorov, Mikhail, *Protazanov, Zhizn' v iskusstve* series (Moscow: Iskusstvo, 1973)

Aronson, O. V., 'Kinoantropologiia "Zemli"', *Kinovedcheskie zapiski*, 23 (1994), 141–48

Attasheva, P., 'Geroi "General'noi"', *Sovetskii ekran*, 1929.6, 8

Aumont, Jacques, *Montage Eisenstein*, Theories of Representation and Difference series, ed. by Teresa de Lauretis, trans. by Lee Hildreth, Constance Panely and Andrew Ross (London: BFI, 1987)

Avladga, 'Kino-s"emochnyi apparat "Ekler"', *Kino-front*, 1926.9–10, 20

'Avtomaticheskaia kino-kamera', *Sovetskii ekran*, 1926.8, 15

Balázs, Béla, 'Vidimyi chelovek' [Russian translation of *Der sichtbare Mensch*], trans. by K. I. Shutko, *Kinovedcheskie zapiski*, 25 (1995), 61–121 (first publ. in Moscow: Izdatel'stvo Vserossiiskogo Proletkul'ta, 1925)

'Stil'naia fil'ma, stil' fil'my i stil' voobshche (Stat'ia Bela Balasha)', *Kino-zhurnal A.R.K.*, 1926.2, 13–14

'O budushchem fil'my', *Kino*, 1926.27, 3 (first publ. in *Die Filmtechnik*, 1926.6)

'Russkaia fil'ma i ee kritika (Po povodu fil'my "SVD")', trans. by N. Fridland, *Kino* (Leningrad), 1928.33, 3

Balshofer, Fred J., and Arthur C. Miller, *One Reel a Week*, foreword by Kemp R. Niver (Berkeley: University of California Press, 1967)

Baranovskaia, Vera, 'Akter dramy v kino', *Sovetskii ekran*, 1926.38, 4

Barkhatova, Elena, 'Pictorialism: Photography as Art', in *Photography in Russia*, ed. by Elliott, pp. 51–60

Bergan, Ronald, *Sergei Eisenstein: A Life in Conflict* (Woodstock, NY: The Overlook Press/ Peter Mayer, 1999)

Bernshtein, Arkadii, 'Gollivud bez kheppi-enda: Sud'ba i tvorchestvo Vladimira Nil'sena', *Kinovedcheskie zapiski*, 60 (2002), 213–59

Blagoi, Dmitrii, *Tvorcheskii put' Pushkina* (Moscow: Sovetskii pisatel', 1967)

Bleiman, Mikhail, 'Chto segodnia? Chto zavtra? 1967–71', in M. Bleiman, *O kino: Svidetel'skie pokazaniia, 1924–71* (Moscow: Iskusstvo, 1973), pp. 477–569

'Vpechatlenie', in *Kinooperator Andrei Moskvin*, ed. by Gukasian, pp. 170–78

Blium, Georgii, 'Zametki operatora', in 'Kak snimalsia "Velikii perelet"', *Kino-zhurnal A.R.K.*, 1926.1, 28–29 (p. 29)

Bliumberg, M., 'Osveshchenie kino-atel'e', *Kino-zhurnal A.R.K.*, 1925.11–12, 17–18

Bodyk, L., 'Kinokadry zhittia i strichky', in *Kriz' kinoob'ektyv chasu: Spohady veteraniv ukrains'koho kino*, ed. by Hoholev, pp. 213–77

Bogoliubov, E. D., *Mezhdunarodnyi shakhmatnyi turnir v Moskve 1925 g.* [1927], http://www. chess.ufnet.ru/history/fotoo1.htm (accessed 12 June 2011)

Boltianskii, Grigorii, 'Kino-khronika i kino-agitka', *Kino*, 1922.3, 18–20
  'O noveishikh priemakh s"emki', *Kino*, 1927.6, 3
  Kul'tura kino-operatora: Opyt issledovaniia, osnovannyi na rabotakh E. K. Tisse (Moscow: Kinopechat', 1927)
  Sovetskaia fotografiia za desiat' let (Moscow: Izdanie komiteta vystavki, 1928)

Bordwell, David, *The Cinema of Eisenstein* (Cambridge, MA: Harvard University Press, 1993)

Bosenko, Valerii, 'Staryi "Sentimental'nyi romans"', *Kinovedcheskie zapiski*, 54 (2001), 285–94

Bowlt, John E., *Moscow and St. Petersburg in the Silver Age, 1900–1920* (London: Thames and Hudson, 2008)

Brik, Osip, 'Chego ne vidit glaz', *Sovetskoe kino*, 1926.2, 22–23
  'Foto i kino', *Sovetskoe kino*, 1926.4–5, 23
  'Poslednii krik', *Sovetskii ekran*, 1926.7, 3–4
  'Kino v teatre Meierkhol'da', *Sovetskii ekran*, 1926.20, 6–7
  'Pobeda fakta (diskussionno)', *Kino*, 1927.14, 3
  'Ostaius' veren!', *Kino*, 1927.45, 4
  'RING LEFA: "Odinnadtsatyi" Vertova; "Oktiabr'" Eizenshteina', in Osip Brik, 'Kinopublitsistika 20-kh godov', publ. by A. V. Valiuzhenich, *Kinovedcheskie zapiski*, 69 (2004), 274–332 (pp. 326–32) (first publ. in *Novyi LEF*, 1928.4)
  'Potomok Chingis-Khana (literaturnyi stsenarii)' [1928], in Valiuzhenich, *Osip Maksimovich Brik: Materialy k biografii*, pp. 63–73

Broening, H. Lyman, '"How It All Happened": A Brief Review of the Beginnings of the American Society of Cinematographers', *American Cinematographer*, 2.20 (1921), 13

'"Bronenosets Potemkin": Fil'my-iubiliary', publ. by V. P. Korshunova and G. D. Endzina, *Iskusstvo kino*, 1986.1, 129–37

Bronenosets Potemkin, Shedevry sovetskogo kino series, ed. by N. Kleiman and K. Levina (Moscow: Iskusstvo, 1969)

Brown, Karl, *Adventures with D. W. Griffith*, ed. by Kevin Brownlow, afterword by John Boorman (London: Faber & Faber, 1988)

Brownlow, Kevin, *The Parade's Gone by...* (London: Secker & Warburg, 1968)

Bulgakova [Bulgakowa], Oksana, 'Bul'vardizatsiia avangarda – fenomen Feks', *Kinovedcheskie zapiski*, 7 (1990), 27–47
  Sergei Eisenstein: A Biography, trans. by Anne Dwyer (Berlin: Potemkin Press, 2001)

Butovskii, Ia. L., *Andrei Moskvin, kinooperator* (St Petersburg: Dmitrii Bulanin, 2000)

Cavendish, Philip, 'The Hand that Turns the Handle: Camera Operators and the Poetics of the Camera in Pre-Revolutionary Russian Cinema', *Slavonic and East European Review*, 82.2 (2004), 201–45

'Zemlia/Earth', in *The Cinema of Russia and the Former Soviet Union*, 24 frames series, ed. by Birgit Beumers (London: Wallflower, 2007), pp. 57–67

Soviet Mainstream Cinematography: The Silent Era, 3rd edn (London: UCL Arts and Humanities Publications, 2010)

'From "Lost" to "Found": The "Rediscovery" of Sergei Eizenshtein's *Dnevnik Glumova* and its Avant-Garde Context', http://www.kinokultura.com/2013/issue41.shtml

Christie, Ian, 'Feksy za granitsei: Kul'turno-politicheskie aspekty vospriiatiia sovetskogo kino za rubezhom', trans. by N. Tsyrkun, *Kinovedcheskie zapiski*, 7 (1990), 172–75

'Rediscovering Eisenstein', in *Eisenstein Rediscovered*, ed. by Christie and Taylor, pp. 1–30

Chulko, Anatolii, 'Intimnaia nota v svetopisi', *Fotomagazin*, 7–8 (1998), http://www.photoweb.ru/prophoto/biblioteka/Photograph/Eremin/01.htm (accessed 9 November 2005)

Cinema in Revolution: The Heroic Era of the Soviet Film, ed. by Luda and Jean Schnitzer and Marcel Martin, trans. with additional material by David Robinson (London: Secker & Warburg, 1973)

Clark, Katerina, *Petersburg: Crucible of Revolution* (Cambridge, MA: Harvard University Press, 1995)

Dekabristy: Otryvki iz istochnikov, ed. by Iu. G. Oksman (Moscow: Gosudarstvennoe izdatel'stvo, 1926)

Delluc, Louis, 'Photogénie', in Delluc, *Ecrits cinématographiques: Le Cinéma et les cinéastes*, ed. by Pierre Lherminier, 3 vols ([Paris]: Cinémathèque Française, 1985–90), I, 34–77 (first publ. Paris: Brunoff, 1920)

Desiat' operatorskikh biografii, ed. by M. Goldovskaia (Moscow: Iskusstvo, 1975)

'"Dezertir" gotov', *Kino*, 1933.17, 1

'Diskussiia o kartine "Bronenosets Potemkin" v ARK (7 ianvaria 1926 goda)', in *Bronenosets Potemkin*, ed. by Kleiman and Levina, pp. 198–200

Dobin, E., *Kozintsev i Trauberg* (Moscow-Leningrad: Iskusstvo, 1963)

Dobrenko, Evgenii, *Stalinist Cinema and the Production of History*, trans. by Sarah Young (Edinburgh: Edinburgh University Press, 2008)

Donskoi, Mark, 'Rabotal uporno i nastoichivo', *Kino*, 1932.37, 2

Douglas Clayton, J., *Pierrot in Petrograd: Commedia dell'Arte/Balagan in Twentieth-Century Russian Theatre and Drama* (Montreal: McGill-Queen's University Press, 1993)

Dovzhenko, Oleksandr, 'Moia fil'ma – bol'shevistskaia fil'ma', in Dovzhenko, *Sobranie sochinenii*, I, 253–54 (first publ. in *Zvenyhora: Zbirnyk: Statti pro fil'my O. Dovzhenka, ta in.* (Kyiv: VUFKU, 1928))

'Moi tvorcheskii metod (Lektsiia vo VGIKe, 17 dekabria 1932)', in Dovzhenko, *Sobranie sochinenii*, IV, 381–93

'Avtobiografiia' [1939], in Dovzhenko, *Sobranie sochinenii*, I, 33–56 (first publ. in *Dnipro*, 1957.12)

'Zemlia' [1952], in Dovzhenko, *Sobranie sochinenii*, I, 111–38 (first publ. in *Dnipro*, 1957.1)

Sobranie sochinenii, ed. by I. L. Andronikov and others, 4 vols (Moscow: Iskusstvo, 1966–69)

The Poet as Filmmaker: Selected Writings, ed. and trans. by Marco Carynnyk (Cambridge: MIT Press, 1973)

Dovzhenko: Khudozhnyk, ed. by I. Zolotoverkhova and H. Konovalov (Kyiv: Mystetstvo, 1968)

Dovzhenko v vospominaniiakh sovremennikov, ed. by Iu. I. Solntseva and L. I. Pazhitnova (Moscow: Iskusstvo, 1982)

D-skii, A., '"Pokhozhdeniia Oktiabriny"', *Kino-zhurnal A.R.K.*, 1925.3, 34

Dudko, Apollinarii, 'Algebra i poeziia sveta', in *Kinooperator Andrei Moskvin*, ed. by Gukasian, pp. 192–96

Efimov, N., 'O manere operatora Moskvina', *Kino* (Leningrad), 1927.40, 3

Eikhenbaum, Boris, 'Kak sdelana "Shinel'" Gogolia' [1919], in Eikhenbaum, *O proze: O poezii: Sbornik statei*, introduction by G. Bialyi (Leningrad: Khudozhestvennaia literatura, leningradskoe otdelenie, 1986), pp. 45–63

'Literatura i kino', *Sovetskii ekran*, 1926.42, 10

Eisenstein at Ninety, ed. by Ian Christie and David Elliott (Oxford: Museum of Modern Art, Oxford, 1988)

Eisenstein Rediscovered, ed. by Ian Christie and Richard Taylor (London: Routledge, 1993)

Eisenstein Revisited: A Collection of Essays, ed. by Lars Kleberg and Håkan Lövgren (Stockholm: Almquist & Wiksell International, 1987)

Eizenshtein: Bronenosets Potemkin (Moscow: Kinopechat', 1926)

Eizenshtein, Sergei, 'Teatral'nye tetradi S. M. Eizenshteina' [1919–24], publ. by M. K. Ivanova and V. V. Ivanov, *Mnemozina: Istoricheskii al'manakh*, ed. by V. V. Ivanov, II (Moscow: Editorial URSS, 2000), 190–279

'Montazh attraktsionov', in Eizenshtein, *Izbrannye proizvedeniia*, II, 269–73 (first publ. in *LEF*, 1923.3)

'The Montage of Film Attractions' [1925], in Eisenstein, *Selected Works*, I, 39–58

'Beseda s rezhiss. S. M. Eizenshteinom', *Kino-nedelia*, 1925.4, 17

'Tezisy k vystupleniiu na diskussii v ARKe' [1926], publ. by N. I. Kleiman, *Kino i zritel'*, 2 (1985), 31–37

'Konstantsa (Kuda ukhodit "Bronenosets Potemkin")' [1926], in *Bronenosets Potemkin*, ed. by Kleiman and Levina, pp. 290–92

'Eisenstein on Eisenstein, the Director of "Potemkin"', in Eisenstein, *Selected Works*, I, 74–76 (first publ. in *Berlin Tageblatt*, 7 June 1926)

'Dva cherepa Aleksandra Makedonskogo', in Eizenshtein, *Izbrannye proizvedeniia*, II, 280–82 (first publ. in *Novyi zritel'*, 1926.35, 10)

'"General'naia liniia" (Beseda s S. M. Eizenshteinom)', *Kino*, 1927.11, 3

'"My dolzhny idti ne k osuzhdeniiu Pudovkina, a k izvlecheniiu pol'zy iz dannoi temy": Dve lektsii Sergeia Eizenshteina o fil'me "Potomok Chingis-Khana"' [1928], publ. by Svetlana Ishevskaia, *Kinovedcheskie zapiski*, 68 (2004), 26–63

'O "General'noi linii" (Beseda s S. Eizenshteinom i G. Aleksandrovym)', *Kino*, 1929.5, 2

'The Dramaturgy of Film Form (The Dialectical Approach to Film Form)' [1929], in Eisenstein, *Selected Works*, I, 161–80 (first publ. (and translated) in *Sergei Eisenstein, Film Form: Essays in Film Theory*, ed. and trans. by Jay Leyda (New York: Harcourt, Brace & World, 1948))

'Za kadrom', in Eizenshtein, *Izbrannye proizvedeniia*, II, 283–96 (first publ. as the afterword to N. Kaufman, *Iaponskoe kino* (Moscow: Tea-kino-pechat', 1929), pp. 72–92)

'Chetvertoe izmerenie v kino', in Eizenshtein, *Izbrannye proizvedeniia*, II, 45–59 (first publ. [first half only] as 'Kino chetyrekh izmerenii' in *Kino*, 1929.34, 4)

'The Dynamic Square', in Eisenstein, *Selected Writings*, I, 206–18 (first publ. in *Close Up*, 8.1 (1931), 3–16, and 8.2 (1931), 91–94)

'Po mestam!', *Kino*, 1933.13, 3

'"E!": O chistote kinoiazyka', in Eizenshtein, *Izbrannye proizvedeniia*, II, 81–92 (first publ. in *Sovetskoe kino*, 1934.5, 25–31)

'Sredniaia iz trekh', in Eizenshtein, *Izbrannye proizvedeniia*, V, 53–78 (first publ. in *Sovetskoe kino*, 1934.11–12, 54–83)

'The Prometheus of Mexican Painting' [1935], in *Mexico According to Eisenstein*, ed. by Karetnikova, pp. 159–67

'[Montazh] (1937)', in Eizenshtein, *Izbrannye proizvedeniia*, II, 329–484

'Predsedateliu torzhestvennogo zasedaniia v chest' XXV-letiia tvorcheskoi deiatel'nosti E. Tisse' [1939], publ. by L. F. Gudieva, *Kinovedcheskie zapiski*, 32 (1996–97), 171–72

'25 i 15', in Eizenshtein, *Izbrannye proizvedeniia*, V, 422–25 (first publ. in *Kino*, 1939.24, 2)

'O stroenii veshchei', in Eizenshtein, *Izbrannye proizvedeniia*, III, 37–71 (first publ. in *Iskusstvo kino*, 1939.6, 7–20)

'Fil'm o ferganskom kanale', in Eizenshtein, *Izbrannye proizvedeniia*, I, 187–88 (first publ. in *Pravda*, 13 August 1939)

'[Rozhdenie mastera]', in Eizenshtein, *Izbrannye proizvedeniia*, V, 438–42 (first publ. in *Iskusstvo kino*, 1940.1–2, 94–95)

'Pervoe pis'mo o tsvete' [1946], in Eizenshtein, *Izbrannye proizvedeniia*, III, 487–91

'Kak ia uchilsia risovat' – Glava ob urokakh tantsa' [1946], in Eizenshtein, *Izbrannye proizvedeniia*, I, 257–72 (first publ. in *Kul'tura i zhizn'*, 1957.6)

'Books on the Road' [1946], in Eisenstein, *Selected Works*, IV, 390–402

'Iz neokonchennogo issledovaniia o tsvete' [1946–47], in Eizenshtein, *Izbrannye proizvedeniia*, III, 500–67

'(Pri vstrechi moei s Meksikoi...)' [1946–47], in Eizenshtein, *Izbrannye proizvedeniia*, I, 442–45

'Pafos' [1946–47], in Eizenshtein, *Izbrannye proizvedeniia*, III, 37–233

'Tsvetnoe kino' [1948], in Eizenshtein, *Izbrannye proizvedeniia*, III, 579–88 (first publ. in S. M. Eizenshtein, *Izbrannye stat'i* (Moscow: Iskusstvo, 1956), pp. 311–20)

'Dvenadtsat' apostolov', in Eizenshtein, *Izbrannye proizvedeniia*, I, 122–35 (first publ. in Sergei Eizenshtein, *Izbrannye stat'i* (Moscow: Iskusstvo, 1956), 366-78)

Izbrannye proizvedeniia, ed. by S. I. Iutkevich, 6 vols (Moscow: Iskusstvo, 1964–71)

Selected Works, ed. and trans. by Richard Taylor, 4 vols (London: BFI, 1988–95)

'"Mudrets" S. M. Eizenshteina: Opyt slovesnoi rekonstruktsii spektaklia', publ. by N. Kleiman, *Kinovedcheskie zapiski*, 39 (1998), 54–110

Dessins secrets, texts by Jean-Claude Marcadé and Galia Ackerman (Paris: Editions de Seuil, 1999)

Eizenshtein, S., and Gr. Aleksandrov, 'Eksperiment, poniatnyi millionam', in Eizenshtein, *Izbrannye proizvedeniia*, I, 144–47 (first publ. in *Sovetskii ekran*, 1929.6, 6–7)

Eizenshtein, Sergei, Grigorii Aleksandrov and Vsevolod Pudovkin, 'Zaiavka' [Declaration on Sound], in *The Film Factory*, ed. by Taylor and Christie, pp. 234–35 (first publ. in *Zhizn' iskusstva*, 5 August 1928).

Eizenshtein, Sergei, and Sergei Iutkevich, 'The Eighth Art: On Expressionism, America and, of course, Chaplin', in Eisenstein, *Selected Works*, I, 29–32 (first publ. in *Ekho*, 7 November 1922)

Eizenshtein v vospominaniiakh sovremennikov, ed. by R. N. Iurenev (Moscow: Iskusstvo, 1974)

Ekstsentrizm [FEKS manifesto with contributions by Grigorii Kozintsev, Leonid Trauberg, Georgii Kryzhitskii and Sergei Iutkevich] (Petrograd: Ekstsentropolis, 1922)

Elliott, David, 'Taking a line for a walk', in *Eisenstein at Ninety*, ed. by Christie and Elliott, pp. 19–40

Erenburg, Il'ia, *Materializatsiia fantastiki* (Moscow-Leningrad: Kinopechat', 1927)

Ermilov, Professor N. E., 'Pechal'noe polozhenie russkoi foto-kino-literatury', *Vestnik fotografii i kinematografii*, 1923.2, 43–46

Ermitazh: Istoriia stroitel'stva i arkhitektura zdanii, ed. by B. B. Piotrovskii (Leningrad: Stroiizdat, leningradskoe otdelenie, 1989)

Ermolinskii, Sergei, 'Zateinik i khudozhnik', *Kino*, 1932.37, 2

Erofeev, Vl., 'Proizvodstvo plenki', *Sovetskoe kino*, 1925.4–5, 63–67

Esslin, Martin, *The Theatre of the Absurd*, 3rd revised edn (London: Methuen Drama, 2001)

F., V., 'General'naia liniia (Beseda s S. M. Eizenshteinom)', *Kino*, 1926.2, 1

'Mekhanika golovnogo mozga (Beseda s rezhisserom V. Pudovkinym)', *Sovetskii ekran*, 1926.31, 6–7

'General'naia liniia (Beseda s S. M. Eizenshteinom)', *Kino-front*, 1927.4, 29–30

Fefer, V., '"Povedenie cheloveka" ("Mekhanika golovnogo mozga")', *Sovetskoe kino*, 1926.1, 10–12

'Operator khroniki', *Sovetskoe kino*, 1926.6, 14–15

'FEKS (1921–1929)', *Sovetskii ekran*, 1929.12, 6–7

Fel'dman, K., 'Razval frantsuzskogo "levogo avangarda"', *Sovetskii ekran*, 1928.24, 8

'Ukrainskie kino-rezhissery', *Sovetskii ekran*, 1928.44, 7

'"Arsenal"', *Sovetskii ekran*, 1929.11, 11

Figes, Orlando, *The Whisperers: Private Life in Stalin's Russia* (London: Penguin, 2008)

Film und Foto der zwanziger Jahre [catalogue of the 1929 'Film and Photo' exhibition in Stuttgart], published by the Württembergischer Kunstverein, with articles by Ute Eskildsen and Jan-Christopher Horak (Stuttgart: Hatje, 1979)

Fogel'man, Iu., 'Pankhromaticheskaia plenka', *Kino i kul'tura*, 1929.3, 45–48

'Fotograficheskie obshchestva', *Vestnik fotografii i kinematografii*, 1923.1, 21–22

Frelikh, Oleg, 'Stil' operatora', *Sovetskii ekran*, 1927.10, 6–7

Freund, Karl, 'Revoliutsiia v kino-s"emkakh', *Sovetskii ekran*, 1927.31, 4

'Just What Is "Montage"?', *American Cinematographer*, 15.8 (1934), 204 & 210

G., A., 'Novosti kino-liubitel'skoi apparatury', *Kino-front*, 1926.1, 16–17

Gal'perin, A., '120-metrovoi s"emochnyi apparat "Amata" firmy "Inzh. Linkhof Miunkhen"', *Kino-front*, 1926.2–3, 14

'Kino-s"emochnyi apparat "Mitshel'"', *Kino-front*, 1927.1, 16–20

'Perechen' chastei kino-s"emochnogo apparata "Mitshel'"', *Kino-front*, 1927.2, 18

'Vosstanovlenie pozitiva', *Kino-front*, 1927.2, 20–22

'Novinki liubitel'skoi kinos"emochnoi apparatury', *Kino-front*, 1927.3, 22–23

'Novoe o patente Shiuftana', *Kino-front*, 1927.3, 24–25

'Stsenarii tekhnicheskogo triuka', *Kino-front*, 1927.5, 19–22

Gan, Aleksei, 'Kinematograf i kinematografiia', *Kino-fot*, 1 (1922), 1

Gerasimov, Sergei, 'Fabrika ekstsentricheskogo aktera', *Iskusstvo kino*, 1940.1–2, 96–97

Gernsheim, Helmut, *The History of Photography from the Earliest Use of the Camera Obscura in the Eleventh Century up to 1914* (London: Oxford University Press, 1955)

Gervinus, 'Po tainikam zvukovoi fil'my', *Sovetskii ekran*, 1929.41, 13–14

Gil'berseimer, Liudvig, 'Dinamicheskaia zhivopis' (bespredmetnyi kinematograf)', *Kino-fot*, 1 (1922), 7

Gogol', N. V., 'Strashnaia mest'' (1832), in Gogol', *Sobranie sochinenii*, I, 139–76

'Nevskii Prospekt' (1835), in Gogol', *Sobranie sochinenii*, III, 7–39

Sobranie sochinenii, ed. by S. I. Mashinskii and M. V. Khrapchenko, 7 vols (Moscow: Khudozhestvennaia literatura, 1977)

Goldovskii, E. M., *Osveshchenie kino-atel'e* (Moscow: Kinopechat', 1927)

'O primenenii poluvattnykh lamp pri s"emke v kinoatel'e', *Kino i kul'tura*, 1929.3, 34–44

Golovnia, Anatolii, 'S"emki kartiny "Povedenie cheloveka"', *Sovetskii ekran*, 1926.40, 4

'Osnovy operatorskoi raboty: Dve tochki zreniia na rol' kino-aktera', *Sovetskii ekran*, 1927.44, 7

'Vsevolod Pudovkin', *Iskusstvo kino*, 1940.1–2, 92

Svet v iskusstve operatora (Moscow: Goskinoizdat, 1945)

Masterstvo kinooperatora (Moscow: Iskusstvo, 1965)

'Broken Cudgels' [interview given in July 1965], in *Cinema in Revolution*, ed. by Schnitzer, Schnitzer and Martin, pp. 133–49

'Vsevolod Pudovkin na s"emke', *Iskusstvo kino*, 1968.8, 63–65

O kinooperatorskom masterstve (Moscow: VGIK, 1970)

Ekran – moia palitra (Moscow: Biuro propagandy sovetskogo kinoiskusstva, 1971)

'O moem molchalivom druge', in *Kinooperator Andrei Moskvin*, ed. by Gukasian, pp. 164–69

'Molodoi chelovek velikoi epokhi', *Iskusstvo kino*, 1973.2, 58–72

Golovnia, Vladimir, 'Vsevolod Pudovkin: Nekotorye vpechatleniia', in *Pudovkin v vospominaniiakh sovremennikov*, ed. by Zapasnik and Petrovich, pp. 329–36

Goodwin, James, *Eisenstein, Cinema, and History* (Urbana: University of Illinois Press, 1993)

Gordanov, Viacheslav, *Zapiski kinooperatora* (Leningrad: Iskusstvo, leningradskoe otdelenie, 1973)

'Moi drug Andrei Moskvin', in *Kinooperator Andrei Moskvin*, ed. by Gukasian, pp. 142–53

Graffy, Julian, *Gogol's The Overcoat*, Critical Studies in Russian Literature series (Bristol: Bristol Classical Press, 2000)

Grinberg, A., 'Tekhnika pavil'onnoi s"emki', *Kino-zhurnal A.R.K.*, 1926.3, 13–14

Gritsius, Ionas, 'Starshii drug', in *Kinooperator Andrei Moskvin*, ed. by Gukasian, pp. 179–84

Gromov, E., *Kinooperator Anatolii Golovnia: Fil'my: Svidetel'stva: Razmyshleniia* (Moscow: Iskusstvo, 1980)

Groys, Boris, 'The Birth of Socialist Realism from the Spirit of the Russian Avant-Garde', in *Laboratory of Dreams*, ed. by Bowlt and Matich, pp. 193–218

Gukasian, F. G., 'Andrei Moskvin', in *Kinooperator Andrei Moskvin*, ed. by Gukasian, pp. 5–116

Harker, Margaret, *The Linked Ring: The Secession in Photography in Britain 1892–1910* (London: Heinemann, 1979)

Harte, Tim, *Fast Forward: The Aesthetics and Ideology of Speed in Russian Avant-Garde Culture, 1910–1930* (Wisconsin: University of Wisconsin Press, 2009)

Henri Toulouse-Lautrec, ed. with introduction by Douglas Cooper (New York: Harry N. Abrams, 2004)

Hicks, Jeremy, *Dziga Vertov: Defining Documentary Film* (London: I. B. Tauris, 2007)

Hoberman, J., 'A face to the *shtetl*: Soviet Yiddish cinema, 1924–36', in *Inside the Film Factory*, ed. by Taylor and Christie, pp. 124–50

Horak, Jan-Christopher, *Making Images Move: Photographers and Avant-Garde Cinema* (Washington, D.C.: Smithsonian Institution Press, 1997)

'"Ia – Kuba"', *Iskusstvo kino*, 1965.3, 24–37

I., A., 'Litso "Stachki"', *Sovetskii ekran*, 1925.7, 7–8

Ialovyi, Ar., 'Trekhfaznye dugovye lampy', *Kino-zhurnal A.R.K.*, 1923.3, 29

Iezuitov, Nikolai, *Pudovkin* (Moscow-Leningrad, 1937)

Il'in, R. N., *Iurii Ekel'chik* (Moscow: Iskusstvo, 1962)

'V laboratorii mastera', *Iskusstvo kino*, 1982.5, 131–35

Inkizhinov, Valerii, 'Bair i ia', *Sovetskii ekran*, 1928.33, 7–8

Inside the Film Factory: New Approaches to Russian and Soviet Cinema, ed. by Richard Taylor and Ian Christie (London: Routledge, 1991)

Iudin, N., 'Amerikanskoe osveshchenie v kino', *Kino-front*, 1926.1, 12–13

Iurenev, R., *Sergei Eizenshtein: Zamysly: Fil'my: Metod (Chast' pervaia: 1898–1929)* (Moscow: Iskusstvo, 1985)

Iutkevich, Sergei, 'EkstsentrizM – Zhivopis' – ReklamA', in *Ekstsentrizm*, pp. 12–15

'Rezhisserskoe masterstvo Vs. Pudovkina v fil'me "Mat'"', in *Mat'*, ed. by Glagoleva, pp. 238–46 (first publ. in *VGIK: Uchenye zapiski*, I (Moscow: Iskusstvo, 1958), 35–48)

'Istoki', in Iutkevich, *Sobranie sochinenii*, I, 17–68

'Kak ia stal rezhisserom', in Iutkevich, *Sobranie sochinenii*, I, 273–333

Sobranie sochinenii, ed. by M. Z. Dolinskii, 3 vols (Moscow: Iskusstvo, 1990)

Ivanitskii, I., 'Ukrainskaia sovetskaia kinematografiia za 15 let', *Sovetskoe kino*, 1934.11–12, 84–93

Ivanov-Barkov, Evgenii, 'Ural'skaia promyshlennost' na fil'me', *Kino*, 1922.3, 23–24
Izvolov, N. I., 'Feks i "Krasnaia gazeta"', *Kinovedcheskie zapiski*, 7 (1990), 176–81
Kabalov, Grigorii, 'Tsvetochuvstvitel'nost' kino-plenki', *Kino-front*, 1927.1, 20
　　'Glazami operatora', *Iskusstvo kino*, 1983.2, 95–100
Kaganovsky, Lilya, 'The voice of technology and the end of Soviet silent film: Grigorii
　　Kozintsev and Leonid Trauberg's *Alone*', *Studies in Russian and Soviet Cinema*, 1.3
　　(2007), 265–81
'Kak snimalsia "Velikii Perelet": 1. Zametki rukovoditelia s"emki (V. Shneiderov); 2.
　　Zametki operatora (Georgii Blium)', *Kino-zhurnal A.R.K.*, 1926.1, 28–29
Kaplan, Mikhail, 'Kul'tura operatora', *Iskusstvo kino*, 1940.1–2, 63–67
　　'Andrei Moskvin', *Iskusstvo kino*, 1940.6, 47–53
Karl Struss: Man with a Camera, ed. with introduction by John and Susan Harvith (Ann
　　Arbor, MI: Cranbrook Academy of Art, 1976)
Kastorin, M., 'S kino-apparatom po Buriatii', *Sovetskoe kino*, 1927.3, 13–14
Käthe Kollwitz, ed. with introduction by Elizabeth Prelinger, essays by Alessandra Comini
　　and Hildegard Bachert (New Haven, CT: Yale University Press, 1992)
Kaufman, Mikhail, 'Foto i kino', *Sovetskoe kino*, 1926.6, 11
Kaufman, N., '"Potomok Chingis-Khana" (Beseda s rezhisserom V. Pudovkinym)', *Kino*,
　　1928.9, 4
　　'"Potomok Chingis-Khana"', *Sovetskii ekran*, 1928.31, 5
　　'"Potomok Chingis-Khana"', *Kino*, 1928.35, 5
　　'Buria i gibel' korablia (Na s"emkakh fil'my "Stekliannyi glaz" na fabrike Mezhrabpom-
　　Fil'm')', *Sovetskii ekran*, 1928.40, 8
　　'"Stekliannyi glaz"', *Sovetskii ekran*, 1928.44, 8–9
　　'Foto-kino vystavka v Shtutgardte', *Sovetskii ekran*, 1929.16, 10
　　'Fil'ma o rybe', *Sovetskii ekran*, 1929.30, 5
Kelly, Catriona, *Petrushka: The Russian Carnival Puppet Theatre*, Cambridge Studies in
　　Russian Literature series (Cambridge: Cambridge University Press, 1990)
Kenez, Peter, *Cinema and Soviet Society from the Revolution to the Death of Stalin* (London:
　　I. B. Tauris, 2001)
Kepley, Jr, Vance, *In the Service of the State: The Cinema of Alexander Dovzhenko* (Madison:
　　University of Wisconsin Press, 1986)
　　'The origins of Soviet cinema: a study in industry development', in *Inside the Film
　　Factory*, ed. by Taylor and Christie, pp. 60–79
　　The End of St. Petersburg, KINOfiles Film Companion 10 (London: I. B. Tauris, 2003)
Khersonskii, Khrisanf, 'Komicheskaia i komediia', *Kino-zhurnal A.R.K.*, 1925.11–12, 27–28
　　'Nanuk', *Sovetskii ekran*, 1928.36, 8
　　'"Liven'"', *Sovetskii ekran*, 1929.7, 13
　　'"Zlyva"', *Sovetskii ekran*, 1929.27, 6
　　'"Staroe i novoe"', *Kino*, 1929.41, 5
Kino-Eye: The Writings of Dziga Vertov, ed. with introduction by Annette Michelson, trans.
　　by Kevin O'Brien (Berkeley: University of California Press, 1984)
'Kino-fabrika aktsionernogo obshchestva Mezhrabpom-Rus'', *Kino-front*, 1927.5, 28

'"Kino i ego tekhnika"', *Kino-zhurnal A.R.K.*, 1925.1, 32

Kinooperator Andrei Moskvin: Ocherk zhizni i tvorchestva: Vospominaniia tovarishchei, ed. with introduction by F. G. Gukasian (Leningrad: Iskusstvo, leningradskoe otdelenie, 1971)

Knoke, G., 'Protsess obrashcheniia kino-negativov v pozitivy', *Kino-zhurnal A.R.K.*, 1925.4–5, 33

Kokhno, Leonid, 'Operator-poet: Vospominaniia o D. P. Demutskom', *Iskusstvo kino*, 1961.12, 52–56

'Poeziia truda', in *Dovzhenko v vospominaniiakh sovremennikov*, ed. by Solntseva and Pazhitnova, pp. 79–85

Korn, Ia., 'Tekhnicheskoe oborudovanie 1-i Goskino-fabriki', *Kino-zhurnal A.R.K.*, 1925.9, 14

Korotkii, V. M., *Operatory i rezhissery russkogo igrovogo kino 1897–1921* (Moscow: NII kinoiskusstva, 2008)

Kosmatov, Leonid, 'Sovershenstvuia khudozhestvennuiu formu...', *Iskusstvo kino*, 1957.12, 23–26

Operatorskoe masterstvo, Biblioteka liubitelia series (Moscow: Iskusstvo, 1962)

'Vstrechi', in *Kinooperator Andrei Moskvin*, ed. by Gukasian, pp. 206–15

Kovalov, Oleg, 'Opticheskaia fantaziia no. 5', *Iskusstvo kino*, 1998.7, 35–42

Kozintsev, Grigorii, 'AB! Parad ekstsentrika', in Kozintsev, *Sobranie sochinenii*, III, 72–75 (first publ. in *Ekstsentrizm*, pp. 3–5)

'Eshche odno D. E.', in Kozintsev, *Sobranie sochinenii*, III, 76–79 (first publ. in *Teatr*, 1923.7)

'"Pokhozhdeniia Oktiabriny" (Beseda s avtorami-rezhisserami G. M. Kozintsevym i L. Z. Traubergom)', *Kino-nedelia*, 1924.43, 16

'Nastroenchestvo', in Kozintsev, *Sobranie sochinenii*, II, 16–21 (first publ. in *Kino*, 1933.39)

'Andrei Moskvin', *Sovetskoe kino*, 1935.11, 35–43

'Andrei Moskvin [glava iz knigi]', in *Kinooperator Andrei Moskvin*, ed. by Gukasian, pp. 119–33

'Glubokii ekran', in Kozintsev, *Sobranie sochinenii*, I, 17–356 (first publ. Moscow: Iskusstvo, 1971)

Sobranie sochinenii, ed. by S. A. Gerasimov and others, 5 vols (Leningrad: Iskusstvo, 1982–86)

Kresin, Mikhail, 'Kinematografiia i Sevzapkino', *Vestnik fotografii i kinematografii*, 1923.2, 34–36

Kridl Valkenier, Elizabeth, *Valentin Serov: Portraits of Russia's Silver Age* (Evanston, IL: Northwestern University Press, 2001)

Kriz' kinoob'ektyv chasu: Spohady veteraniv ukrains'koho kino, ed. by L. D. Hoholev (Kyiv: Mystetstvo, 1970)

Kuleshov, Lev, 'Iskusstvo, sovremennaia zhizn' i kinematografiia', *Kino-fot*, 1 (1922), 2

'Kak voznikla nasha masterskaia', *Kino*, 1923.5, 30

'Priamoi put': Diskussionno', in Kuleshov, *Stat'i: Materialy*, pp. 127–30 (first publ. in *Kino*, 1924.48, 2)

'Volia: Uporstvo: Glaz', in Kuleshov, *Sobranie sochinenii*, I, 111–13 (first publ. in
  Eizenshtein: Bronenosets Potemkin (Moscow: Kinopechat', 1926))
'Pochemu plokho sniali voinu', *Sovetskii ekran*, 1928.30, 5
'Iskusstvo kino', in Kuleshov, *Sobranie sochinenii*, I, 161–225 (first publ. Moscow-
  Leningrad: Tea-kino-pechat', 1929)
'Nashi pervye opyty', *Sovetskoe kino*, 1936.11–12, 126–37
'Vystuplenie na iubileinom vechere A. A. Levitskogo' [22 December 1960], in Kuleshov,
  Sobranie sochinenii, II, 413–16
Stat'i: Materialy, ed. by A. S. Khokhlova, introduction by E. Gromov,
  Kinematograficheskoe nasledie series (Moscow: Iskusstvo, 1979)
Sobranie sochinenii, ed. by R. N. Iurenev, 3 vols (Moscow: Iskusstvo, 1987–88)
Kuleshov, L., and A. Khokhlova, *50 let v kino* (Moscow: Iskusstvo, 1975)
Kutsenko, Mykola, *Storinky zhyttia i tvorchosti O. P. Dovzhenka* (Kyiv: Dnipro, 1975)
Kuz'mina, Elena, *O tom, chto pomniu* (Moscow: Iskusstvo, 1989)
L., 'Kak snimaetsia zvuchashchaia fil'ma', *Sovetskii ekran*, 1929.41, 12
Laboratory of Dreams: The Russian Avant-Garde and Cultural Experiment, ed. by John E.
  Bowlt and Olga Matich (Stanford, CA: Stanford University Press, 1996)
Lavrentiev, A. N., 'The Photo Eye/Das Photo-Auge/L'Oeil de l'appareil', in *Alexander
  Rodchenko: Photography, 1924–1954*, ed. by Lavrentiev, pp. 10–37
Layton, Susan, *Russian Literature and Empire: Conquest of the Caucasus from Pushkin to
  Tolstoy* (Cambridge: Cambridge University Press, 1994)
Lebedev, N. A., *Ocherki istorii kino SSSR: Nemoe kino*, 2nd revised and enlarged edn
  (Moscow: Iskusstvo, 1965)
Lenin, V. I., 'Uroki kommuny', in Lenin, *Polnoe sobranie sochinenii*, 55 vols (Moscow:
  Gosudarstvennoe izdatel'stvo politicheskoi literatury, 1958–1965), XIII (*Iun' 1907–
  mart 1908*), 1961, 451–54
Leonid Trauberg et l'excentrisme: Les Débuts de la Fabrique de l'Acteur Excentrique 1921–25,
  ed. by Natalia Noussinova, trans. by Catherine Perrel (Crisnée/Leuven: Editions
  Yellow Now/Le Stuc, 1993)
Lesnaia, Klavdiia, 'Khudozhnik v kino', *Sovetskii ekran*, 1929.38, 11
Lesser, Julian 'Bud', 'Tisse's Unfinished Treasure: *Que Viva Mexico*', *American
  Cinematographer*, 72.7 (1991), 34–40
Levitskii, Aleksandr, *Rasskazy o kinematografe* (Moscow: Iskusstvo, 1964)
Levshin, Aleksandr, 'Na repetitsiiakh "Mudretsa"', in *Eizenshtein v vospominaniiakh
  sovremennikov*, ed. by Iurenev, pp. 136–50
Leyda, Jay, *Kino: A History of the Russian and Soviet Film*, 3rd edn (Princeton, NJ: Princeton
  University Press, 1983)
'Eisenstein and Tisse', supplementary material on the Criterion DVD release of *Ivan the
  Terrible* and *Alexander Nevsky* ('Special Materials'/*Bezhin lug*/Important Texts)
Liber, George O., *Alexander Dovzhenko: A Life in Soviet Film* (London: BFI, 2002)
Lista, Giovanni, *Futurism and Photography* (London: Merrell, 2001)
Lium'er, A. and L. [Auguste and Louis Lumière], and A. Zeivetts, 'Usilenie negativov
  okrashivaniem', *Kino-front*, 1926.4–5, 16

Lodder, Christina, *Russian Constructivism* (New Haven, CN: Yale University Press, 1983)

Lotman, Iu. M., and Iu. G. Tsiv'ian, 'SVD: Zhanr melodramy i istoriia', in *Tynianovskii sbornik: Pervye tynianovskie chteniia (g. Rezekne, mai 1982)*, ed. by M. O. Chudakova (Riga: Zinatne, 1984), pp. 46–78

Lubich, Ernst [Ernst Lubitsch], 'Amerikanskie kinooperatory', *Sovetskii ekran*, 1926.27, 14

Lunacharskii, A. V., 'Iz stat'i "Pobedy sovetskogo kino"', in *Mat'*, ed. by Glagoleva, pp. 225–27

Macheret, A., 'Tvorcheskaia podopleka iuridicheskikh nepoladok', *Kino*, 1933.13, 3

Maiakovskii, Vladimir, *Polnoe sobranie sochinenii*, 13 vols (Moscow: Gosudarstvennoe izdatel'stvo khudozhestvennoi literatury, 1955–61)

Makaryk, Irena R., 'Dissecting Time/Space: The Scottish Play and the New Technology of Film', in *Modernism in Kyiv: Jubilant Experimentation*, ed. by Irena R. Makaryk and Virlana Tkacz (Toronto: University of Toronto Press, 2010), pp. 443–77

Malevich, Kazimir, 'O vyiaviteliakh', *Kino-zhurnal A.R.K.*, 1925.6–7, 6–8

 'I likiut liki na ekranakh (V poriadke diskussii)', *Kino-zhurnal A.R.K.*, 1925.10, 7–9

 'Khudozhnik i kino', *Kino-zhurnal A.R.K.*, 1926.2, 15–17

'Manifest ekstsentricheskogo teatra', publ. by V. G. Kozintseva and Ia. L. Butovskii, *Kinovedcheskie zapiski*, 7 (1990), 73–74

Mar'ian, D., 'Odin iz luchshikh', *Kino*, 1932.29, 2

Martin, Marcel, *Le Langage cinématographique*, 3rd edn (Paris: les éditeurs français réunis, 1977)

Masokha, Petro, 'Velykyi nimyi na Frantsuz'komu byl'vari', in *Kriz' kinoob'ektyv chasu: Spohady veteraniv ukrains'koho kino*, ed. by Hoholev, pp. 87–159

 '"Ia ne boius' sporit' s vami, Aleksandr Petrovich..."': Neotoslannoe pis'mo k M. M. Kovalenko', publ. by Sergei Trimbach, *Kinovedcheskie zapiski*, 31 (1996), 131–39

Mat', ed. by N. A. Glagoleva, Shedevry mirovogo kino series (Moscow: Iskusstvo, 1975)

Matthies-Masuren, F., 'Hugo Henneberg – Heinrich Kühn – Hans Watzek', *Camera Work*, 13 (1906), 21–41

Melik-Khaspabov, V., 'Ekspressionizm v kino', *Kino-nedelia*, 1925.11, 8

Merkel', Maiia, *V sto sorok solnts* (Moscow: Iskusstvo, 1968)

Mexico According to Eisenstein, ed. with introductory essay by Inga Karetnikova in collaboration with Leon Steinmetz (Albuquerque: University of New Mexico Press, 1991)

Michalski, Milena, 'Promises Broken, Promise Fulfilled: The Critical Failings and Creative Success of Abram Room's *Strogii iunosha*', *Slavonic and East European Review*, 82.4 (2004), 820–46

Mikhailov, Evgenii, 'O stanovlenii operatorskogo iskusstva na studii "Lenfil'm"', *Iz istorii Lenfil'ma*, II (*Stat'i, materialy, dokumenty: 1920e gody*), ed. by N. S. Gornitskaia (Leningrad: Iskusstvo, leningradskoe otdelenie, 1970), 137–44

 'Vospominaniia ob A. N. Moskvine', in *Kinooperator Andrei Moskvin*, ed. by Gukasian, pp. 154–63

Mikhailov, E., and A. Moskvin, 'Rol' kino-operatora v sozdanii fil'my', in *Poetika kino*, ed. by Eikhenbaum, pp. 171–91

Mikhin, Boris, 'Pervoe znakomstvo', in *Eizenshtein v vospominaniiakh sovremennikov*, ed. by
    Iurenev, pp. 168–74
Moskvin, A., 'O svoei rabote i o sebe', *Sovetskii ekran*, 1927.38, 10
Mur, Leo [Leopol'd Murashko], 'Operator: Ocherk iz serii "rabotniki kino"', *Kino*, 1925.4, 3
    'Fotogeniia', *Kino-zhurnal A.R.K.*, 1925.6–7, 3–6
    'S"emki na nature i v atel'e', *Kino-front*, 1926.2–3, 2–7
    'Verkhom na luche', *Kino-zhurnal A.R.K.*, 1926.3, 7–10
    Fabrika serykh tenei (Moscow-Leningrad: Kinopechat', 1927)
    'Na fabrike "Mezhrabpom-fil'm"', *Sovetskii ekran*, 1928.39, 15
    'Operator Kinok', *Sovetskii ekran*, 1929.4, 10
    'Khudozhnik sveta', *Sovetskii ekran*, 1929.5, 10
    'Eduard Tisse', *Sovetskii ekran*, 1929.5, 12
    'Iz Parizha v Moskoviiu', *Sovetskii ekran*, 1929.7, 10
    'S vintovkoi i kino-apparatom', *Sovetskii ekran*, 1929.8, 6–7
    'Veteran kino-khroniki', *Sovetskii ekran*, 1929.9, 10
    'Uchenik svoego uchitelia', *Sovetskii ekran*, 1929.11, 10
    'Novosti kino-tekhniki: Zvukovoe kino v Amerike', *Sovetskii ekran*, 1929.19, 12–13
N., 'Operator – soavtor fil'my', *Kino*, 1932.37, 2
Nedobrovo, Vladimir, *FEKS: Grigorii Kozintsev: Leonid Trauberg* (Moscow-Leningrad:
    Kinopechat', 1928)
Nel'son, V., 'Voprosy osvetitel'noi tekhniki', *Kino-front*, 1928.2, 28–29
Nesbet, Anne, *Savage Junctures: Sergei Eisenstein and the Shape of Thinking* (London: I. B.
    Tauris, 2003)
    'Émile Zola, Kozintsev and Trauberg, and Film as Department Store', *The Russian
    Review*, 69 (2009), 102–21
Neuberger, Joan, 'Strange circus: Eisenstein's sex drawings', *Studies in Russian and Soviet
    Cinema*, 6.1 (2012), 5–52
Newhall, Beaumont, *The History of Photography from 1839 to the Present*, revised and
    enlarged edn (New York: The Museum of Modern Art, 1982)
Nikol'skaia, Tat'iana, 'Gruzinskie futuristy v kino (ranniaia stat'ia M. Kalatozishvili)', in *Ot
    slov k telu: Sbornik statei k 60-letiiu Iuriia Tsiv'iana*, ed. by Aleksandr Lavrov, Aleksandr
    Ospovat and Roman Timenchik (Moscow: Novoe literaturnoe obozrenie, 2010), pp.
    238–42
Nil'sen [Nilsen], Vladimir, *The Cinema as a Graphic Art (On the Theory of Representation in
    the Cinema)*, appreciation by S. M. Eisenstein, trans. by Stephen Garry ([London]:
    Newnes Limited, 1937)
Nil'sen, V., and E. Tisse, 'O tvorchestve kinooperatora', *Sovetskoe kino*, 1933.7, 58–65
Noussinova, Natalia, 'Entretien avec Leonid Trauberg', in *Leonid Trauberg et l'excentrisme*,
    ed. by Noussinova, pp. 11–56
Novikov, P., *Grazhdanskaia voina v vostochnoi Sibiri*, Rossiia zabytaia i neizvestnaia series
    (Moscow: Tsentropoligraf, 2005)
Novitskii, Petr, 'Kino na voine (Iz lichnykh vospominanii operatora P. K. Novitskogo)',
    Sovetskii ekran, 1925.6, 4

'Operator-rezhisser (Iz besedy s P. K. Novitskim'), *Sovetskii ekran*, 1925.8, 3
'Russkie i inostrannye operatory (Iz vospominanii operatora), *Kino-front*, 1926.1, 31–32
'Saft-fokus', *Kino-front*, 1927.5, 22–23
Novoselov, Vl., 'Vysshii Foto-Kino-Institut', *Art-EKRAN*, 1923.2, 8–9
'Novyi ob"ektiv "Plasmat"', *Vestnik fotografii i kinematografii*, 1923.1, 23
Oksman, Iu., 'Nachalo povesti o praporshchike Chernigovskogo polka', in *Putevoditel' po Pushkinu* (Moscow-Leningrad: Gosudarstvennoe izdatel'stvo khudozhestvennoi literatury, 1931), pp. 252–53
P., 'Usovershenstvovannyi ob"ektiv', *Sovetskii ekran*, 1925.7, 10
P., B., 'Russkoe fotograficheskoe obshchestvo (pri Gosudarstvennoi Akademii Khudozhestvennykh Nauk)', *Kino-front*, 1926.9–10, 34–35
Pack, Susan, *Film Posters of the Russian Avant-Garde* (Cologne: Taschen, 1995)
Pavlov, P., 'Novosti kino-s"emochnoi apparatury', *Kino-zhurnal A.R.K.*, 1926.1, 15–16
  'Novosti proektsionnoi apparatury' [two parts], *Kino-front*, 1926.1, 10–12, and 1926.2–3, 12–13
Pereguda, O., 'Kinematograf i Les' Kurbas', in *Kriz' kinoob'ektyv chasu: Spohady veteraniv ukrains'koho kino*, ed. by Hoholev, pp. 39–51
Perestiani, Ivan, *75 let zhizni v iskusstve* (Moscow: Iskusstvo, 1962)
Perez, Gilberto, 'All in the Foreground: A Study of Dovzhenko's *Earth*', *Hudson Review*, 28 (1975), 68–86
Pertsov, V., 'Mif o fotogenii', *Kino-front*, 1926.2–3, 4–7
  'Mest' zarezannykh kadrov (Zagranichnaia kartina na sovetskom ekrane)', *Sovetskoe kino*, 1926.2, 16–17
Petrić, Vlada, *Constructivism in Film: The Man with the Movie Camera: A Cinematic Analysis* (Cambridge: Cambridge University Press, 1987)
Photography in Russia 1840–1940, ed. by David Elliott (London: Thames and Hudson, 1992)
Piotrovskii, Adr[ian], 'Granitsy stilia operatora i khudozhnika', *Kino* (Leningrad), 1929.5, 2
'Pis'mo N. F. Agadzhanova-Shutko k S. M. Eizenshteinu', dated 14 October 1925, in *Bronenosets Potemkin*, ed. by Kleiman and Levina, p. 179
Pletnev, V., 'Otkrytoe pis'mo v redaktsiiu zhurnala "Kino-nedelia"', *Kino-nedelia*, 1925.6, 9
'"Podozritel'nyi bagazh"', *Sovetskii ekran*, 1926.11, 8–9
Poetika kino, ed. by B. M. Eikhenbaum, foreword by K. Shutko (Leningrad: Kinopechat', 1927; repr. [Berkeley, CA]: Berkeley Slavic Specialities, 1984)
Prelinger, Elizabeth, 'Kollwitz Reconsidered', in *Käthe Kollwitz*, ed. by Prelinger, pp. 13–82
Prim, '"Zhivoi trup" Fedora Otsepa', *Sovetskii ekran*, 1929.16, 6
Pudovkin, Vsevolod, 'Vremia v kinematografe', in Pudovkin, *Sobranie sochinenii*, II, 87–89 (first publ. in *Kino*, 1923.2, 7–10)
  'Fotogeniia', in Pudovkin, *Sobranie sochinenii*, I, 90–94 (first publ. in *Kino-zhurnal A.R.K.*, 1925.4–5)
  'Montazh nauchnoi fil'my', in Pudovkin, *Sobranie sochinenii*, II, 43–45 (first publ. in *Kino-zhurnal A.R.K.*, 1925.9, 10–11)
  'Kinostsenarii', in Pudovkin, *Sobranie sochinenii*, I, 53–74 (first publ. Moscow: Kinoizdatel'stvo RSFSR, 1926)

'"Mat'"': Beseda s rezhisserom V. Pudovkinym', in Pudovkin, *Sobranie sochinenii*, II, 49–50 (first publ. in *Sovetskii ekran*, 1926.35, 6)

'Kinorezhisser i kinomaterial', in Pudovkin, *Sobranie sochinenii*, I, 95–129 (first publ. Moscow: Kinopechat', 1926)

'Peterburg-Petrograd-Leningrad', in Pudovkin, *Sobranie sochinenii*, II, 53–54 (first publ. in *Sovetskoe kino*, 1927.2, 6)

'Konets Sankt-Peterburga', *Sovetskii ekran*, 1927.46, 6–7

'Kak my delali fil'mu "Konets Sankt-Peterburga"', in Pudovkin, *Sobranie sochinenii*, II, 56–58 (first publ. in *Konets Sankt-Peterburga* (Moscow: Teakinopechat', 1928))

'Predislovie', in Pudovkin, *Sobranie sochinenii*, I, 130–32 (first publ. as the preface to the German edition of *Kinorezhisser i kinomaterial* (Berlin: Verlag der Lichtbildbühne, 1928))

'Kak ia rabotaiu s Tolstym', in Pudovkin, *Sobranie sochinenii*, II, 58–59 (first publ. in *Sovetskii ekran*, 1928.37, 5)

'Naturshchik vmesto aktera', in Pudovkin, *Sobranie sochinenii*, I, 181–84 (first publ. as 'Address to the Film Society: The Use of Types as Opposed to Actors', in *Pudovkin: On Film Technique*, ed. and translated by Ivor Montagu (London: George Newnes, 1929))

'Tvorchestvo literatora v kino: O kinematograficheskom stsenarii Rzheshevskogo', in Pudovkin, *Sobranie sochinenii*, I, 79–84 (first publ. in *Na literaturnom postu*, 1930.5–6)

'Pervaia fil'ma', in *Mat'*, ed. by Glagoleva, pp. 184–85 (first publ. in *Kino*, 1932.44, 2)

Film Technique, ed. and trans. by Ivor Montagu (London: George Newnes, 1935)

'Asinkhronnost' kak printsip zvukovogo kino', in Pudovkin, *Sobranie sochinenii*, I, 158–62 (first publ. as 'Asynchronism as a Principle of Sound Film', in Pudovkin, *Film Technique*)

'Problema ritma v moem pervom zvukovom fil'me', in Pudovkin, *Sobranie sochinenii*, I, 163–66 (first publ. as 'Rhythmic Problems in My First Sound Film', in Pudovkin, *Film Technique*)

Letter to A. D. Golovnia (undated), in Pudovkin, *Sobranie sochinenii*, III, 274–75

'Kak ia stal rezhisserom', in Pudovkin, *Sobranie sochinenii*, II, 33–40 (first publ. in V. Pudovkin, *Izbrannye stat'i* (Moscow: Iskusstvo, 1955), pp. 39–48)

Sobranie sochinenii, ed. by A. Golovnia and others, 3 vols (Moscow: Iskusstvo, 1974–76)

Pudovkin v vospominaniiakh sovremennikov, ed. by T. E. Zapasnik and A. Ia. Petrovich, introductory essay by Leonid Trauberg (Moscow: Iskusstvo, 1989)

Radetskii, P., 'Perenosnaia dugovaia lampa "Atom" dlia kino-s"emki', *Kino-nedelia*, 1924.29, 6

Rakushev, Nikolai, 'Osveshchenie v kino-atel'e', *Kino-zhurnal A.R.K.*, 1925.6–7, 20–22

'Razreshite vyskazat'sia', *Kino*, 1932.37, 2

Rediscovering Eisenstein, ed. by Richard Taylor and Ian Christie (London: Routledge, 1993)

Rodchenko, Aleksandr, 'Khudozhnik i "material'naia sreda" v igrovoi fil'me: Beseda s khudozhnikom A. M. Rodchenko', *Sovetskoe kino*, 1927.5–6, 14–15

Rossiia v kinokadre, 1896–1916, ed. by V. N. Batalin and others (Moscow: ROSSPEN, 2007)

Rozenfel'd, Mikhail, 'Zolotoi potok', *Kinovedcheskie zapiski*, 84 (2007), 219–22 (first publ. in *Komsomol'skaia pravda*, 16 July 1935)

Rozental', L., review of Delluc's *Photogénie*, *Kino-zhurnal A.R.K.*, 1925.4–5, 43

'Russkoe fotograficheskoe o-vo', *Kino*, 1923.1, 25–26

S., T., 'Kino na Vsemirnoi Khudozhestvennoi Vystavke v Parizhe', *Kino-zhurnal A.R.K.*, 1925.9, 28

Sabinskii, Cheslav [Czesław Sabiński], 'Iz zapisok starogo kinomastera', *Iskusstvo kino*, 1936.5, 60–63

Salazkina, Masha, *In Excess: Sergei Eisenstein's Mexico* (Chicago, IL: University of Chicago Press, 2009)

Salt, Barry, *Film Style and Technology: History and Analysis*, 2nd (expanded) edn (London: Starword, 1992)

Sargeant, Amy, *Vsevolod Pudovkin: Classic Films of the Soviet Avant-Garde* (London: I. B. Tauris, 2000)

Storm over Asia, KINOfiles Film Companion 11 (London: I. B. Tauris, 2007)

Scheunemann, Dietrich, 'Activating the Differences: Expressionist Film and Early Weimar Cinema', in *Expressionist Film: New Perspectives*, ed. by Dietrich Scheunemann (Rochester, NY: Camden House, 2003), pp. 1–31

Seeber, Guido, 'Die taumelnde Kamera', *Die Filmtechnik*, 1925.5, 92–93

'Novoe v kino-s"emochnoi apparature', *Kino-zhurnal A.R.K.*, 1925.9, 15–17

'S"emka pod monokl'', *Kino* (Leningrad), 1927.31–32, 3

Sepman, I., 'Tynianov-stsenarist', in *Iz istorii Lenfil'ma*, III (*Stat'i, vospominaniia, dokumenty: 1920–1930e gody*), ed. by N. S. Gornitskaia (Leningrad: Iskusstvo, leningradskoe otdelenie, 1973), 51–77

Seton, Marie, *Sergei M. Eisenstein: A Biography*, revised edn (London: Dennis Dobson, 1978)

Sh., N., 'O fotogenii', *Sovetskii ekran*, 1925.6, 8–9

Shanlein, M. (Rabkor), '"Pokhozhdeniia Oktiabriny"', *Kino-nedelia*, 1925.7, 9

Shatov, Lev, '"Zhivoi trup"', *Kino*, 1929.16, 4

Shch., M., 'Khudozhniku sveta – tvorcheskie prava! (Na soveshchanii operatorov v redaktsii gazety "Kino")', *Kino*, 1932.27, 3

Shklovskii, Viktor, 'Gore ot shpagi', *Kino*, 1925.40, 3

'Eizenshtein', *Kino-zhurnal A.R.K.*, 1926.2, 5–6

'Poeziia i proza v kinematografii', in *Poetika kino*, ed. by Eikhenbaum, pp. 137–42

'O zakonakh stroeniia fil'my S. Eizenshteina' [Part 2], *Sovetskii ekran*, 1928.7, 7

'O rozhdenii i zhizni Feksov', in Nedobrovo, *FEKS*, pp. 7–11

'Piat' fel'etonov ob Eizenshteine', in *Bronenosets Potemkin*, ed. by Kleiman and Levina, pp. 296–98 (first publ. in *Gamburgskii schet* (Leningrad: Izdatel'stvo pisatelei v Leningrade, 1928))

'Sashko Dovzhenko', in V. Shklovskii, *Za 60 let: Raboty o kino*, ed. by E. Levin (Moscow: Iskusstvo, 1985), pp. 293–304 (first publ. in V. Shklovskii, *Zhili-byli* (Moscow: Sovetskii pisatel', 1964), pp. 461–81)

Eizenshtein (Moscow: Iskusstvo, 1973)

Shlegel', Khans-Ioakhim [Hans-Joachim Schlegel], 'Berlin i Germaniia Aleksandra Dovzhenko', trans. by L. S. Maslova, *Kinovedcheskie zapiski*, 31 (1996), 139–46

Shletser, Boris, "'Sentimental'nyi romans'", publ. by Rashit Iangirov, *Kinovedcheskie zapiski*, 54 (2001), 297–98 (first publ. in *Poslednie novosti*, 4 July 1930)

Shneider, Mikhail, 'Litso k ob"ektivu', *Kino*, 1927.6, 3

"'SVD'", *Kino-front*, 1927.9–10, 19–20

Shneiderov, V., 'Bor'ba za kachestvo sovetskoi foto-kino produktsii', *Kino-front*, 1926.4–5, 32

Shpinel', Iosif, 'Tvorcheskoe edinstvo', in *Dovzhenko v vospominaniiakh sovremennikov*, ed. by Solntseva and Pazhitnova, pp. 76–79

Shtraukh, Maksim, 'Iz s"emochnogo dnevnika M. M. Shtraukha' [1925], in *Bronenosets Potemkin*, ed. by Kleiman and Levina, p. 67

'V poiskakh akterov "General'noi" (Iz zapisok assistenta)', *Sovetskii ekran*, 1928.7, 4–5

'Vstrechi', *Iskusstvo kino*, 1940.1–2, 89–91

Shvachko, O., 'Spohady pro nezabutne', in *Kriz' kinoob'ektyv chasu: Spohady veteraniv ukrains'koho kino*, ed. by Hoholev, pp. 53–85

"'Sinii paket'", *Sovetskii ekran*, 1926.11, 8–9

Skliarevskii, Evgenii, 'Iz istorii fotoiskusstva Tashkenta', http://sklyarevskij.livejournal.com/1884055 (accessed 21 November 2011)

Sobolev, R., *Aleksandr Dovzhenko*, Zhizn' v iskusstve series (Moscow: Iskusstvo, 1980)

Sokolov, Ippolit, 'Skrizhal' veka', *Kino-fot*, 1 (1922), 3

"'Shinel'", *Kino-front*, 1926.2–3, 28

"'Zemlia'", *Kino*, 1930.21, 4–5

Sol'skii, V., 'V polose perevorotov', *Kino*, 1927.36, 3

Sontag, Susan, *On Photography* (London: Penguin, 1979)

Sovetskie khudozhestvennye fil'my: Annotirovannyi katalog, ed. by A. V. Macheret and others, I–III (Moscow: Iskusstvo, 1961)

Spiridovskii, N., 'O novykh sposobakh okrashivaniia pozitiva', *Kino-front*, 1926.9–10, 18

"'Standartizuite svet'", *Kino-front*, 1926.2–3, 8–9

Stanke, A., 'Rabota kino-operatora v Germanii', *Kino-zhurnal A.R.K.*, 1926.3, 29

Stapanian, Juliette R., *Mayakovsky's Cubo-Futurist Vision* (Houston, TX: Rice University Press, 1986)

Stephan, Halina, *"Lef" and the Left Front of the Arts* (Munich: Verlag Otto Sagner, 1981)

Stieglitz, Alfred, *Camera Work: A Pictorial Guide*, ed. by Marianne Fulton Margolis (New York: Dover Publications/International Museum of Photography, George Eastman House, 1978)

Stirk, David, and Elena Pinto Simon, 'Jay Leyda and *Bezhin Meadow*', in *Eisenstein Rediscovered*, ed. by Christie and Taylor, pp. 41–52

"'Sumka dipkur'era'", *Sovetskii ekran*, 1927.13, 8–9

Surkova, Ol'ga, *Tarkovskii i ia: Dnevnik pionerki* (Moscow: ZebraE/Eksmo/Dekont+, 2002)

Svashenko, Semen, 'Kak rozhdalsia tanets', in *Dovzhenko v vospominaniiakh sovremennikov*, ed. by Solntseva and Pazhitnova, pp. 85–90

Swallow, Norman, *Eisenstein: A Documentary Portrait* (London: George Allen & Unwin, 1976)

Taylor, Richard, *The Battleship Potemkin*, KINOfiles Film Companion 1 (London: I. B. Tauris, 2000)

October, BFI Film Classics series (London: BFI, 2002)

Teshabaev, D., *Puti i poiski: Voprosy stanovleniia uzbekskoi kinorezhissury i kinodramaturgii* (Tashkent: Izdatel'stvo literatury i iskusstva im. Gafura Guliama, 1973)

The Film Factory: Russian and Soviet Cinema in Documents 1896–1939, ed. by Richard Taylor and Ian Christie, trans. by Richard Taylor (London: Routledge, 1988)

Tikhonov, N., 'Fotografiia', *Kino-fot*, 2 (1922), 4

'Novosti zapadnoi kino-tekhniki', *Kino-zhurnal A.R.K.*, 1925.1, 8–9

Tisse, Eduard, 'Perepiska druzei', *Kino*, 1926.5, 6

'Eduard Tisse: "Rabotali my s nagruzkoi 100%"' [letters to Eizenshtein, 1925–44], publ. by G. R. Maslovskii, *Kinovedcheskie zapiski*, 8 (1990), 97–117

'Tekhnika s"emki "Bronenostsa Potemkina"', *Kino-zhurnal A.R.K.*, 1926.2, 10–11

'Novaia model' kino-s"emochnogo apparata', *Kino-front*, 1926.4–5, 15

'"General'naia liniia"', *Sovetskii ekran*, 1926.50, 10

'"General'naia liniia"', *Sovetskii ekran*, 1927.36, 12

'S"emki "Oktiabria"', *Sovetskii ekran*, 1927.46, 4

'"Na tom my stoim"', publ. by G. Maslovskii, trans. by Naum Kleiman, *Iskusstvo kino*, 1979.2, 100–04 (first publ. in *Die Filmtechnik*, 1927.6)

'Na s"emkakh "General'noi"', *Sovetskii ekran*, 1929.5, 13

'Na frontakh grazhdanskoi voiny: Vospominaniia operatora-boitsa', *Kino*, 1933.10, 2

'"VGIK: Tvorcheskii vecher, posviashchennyi t. Tisse E.K." 20 fevralia 1940g. (Stenograficheskii otchet)', publ. by L. F. Gudieva, *Kinovedcheskie zapiski*, 32 (1996–97), 172–79

'Budushchie mastera', *Kino*, 1940.1, 1

'Nezabyvaemye gody', *Iskusstvo kino*, 1940.1–2, 83–84

'Stranitsy proshlogo', *Iskusstvo kino*, 1941.6, 48–50

'Kak snimalsia "Bronenosets Potemkin"' [1945], in *Bronenosets Potemkin*, ed. by Kleiman and Levina, pp. 292–95

'Tvorcheskaia biografiia' [1952], publ. by L. F. Gudieva, *Kinovedcheskie zapiski*, 32 (1996–97), 161–68

'Doklad E. K. Tisse na seminare operatorov kinostudii "Mosfil'm" 27 aprelia 1956 goda', *Iskusstvo kino*, 1979.2, 104–13

Tissé, Eleonora, 'Some Notes on the Work of the Cameraman in "Ivan the Terrible": The Visual Construction of the Film Image Form', in *Eisenstein Revisited: A Collection of Essays*, ed. by Kleberg and Lövgren, pp. 133–44

Tolchan, Iakov, 'O negativnoi plenke i negative', *Kino-front*, 1926.4–5. 19

Trauberg, Leonid, 'O Moskvine', in *Kinooperator Andrei Moskvin*, ed. by Gukasian, pp. 134–41

Tret'iakov, Sergei, '"General'naia liniia"', in Tret'iakov, 'Izbrannye teksty 20-kh godov', *Kinovedcheskie zapiski*, 34 (1997), 6–19 (pp. 10–12) (first publ. in *Prozhektor*, 1927.6)

'Perevoploshchenie odnoi fil'my', in Tret'iakov, 'Izbrannye teksty 20-kh godov', *Kinovedcheskie zapiski*, 34 (1997), 6–19 (pp. 16–19) (first publ. in *Literaturnaia gazeta*, 1 July 1929)

Tril, 'Disput na prosmotre fil'ma "Pokhozhdeniia Oktiabriny"', *Kino-nedelia*, 1924.45, 7

'Tsikl lektsii o foto i kino', *Kino*, 1922.4, 29

Tsikounas, Myriam, 'Eisenstein and the theory of "models"; or, how to distract the spectator's attention', in *Eisenstein Rediscovered*, ed. by Christie and Taylor, pp. 189–99

Tsiv'ian, Iurii [Yuri Tsivian], 'Paleogrammy v fil'me "Shinel'"', in *Tynianovskii sbornik 2*, ed. by M. O. Chudakova (Riga: Zinatne, 1986), pp. 14–27

'Eisenstein and Russian Symbolist culture: An unknown script of *October*', in *Eisenstein Rediscovered*, ed. by Christie and Taylor, pp. 79–109

Tupitsyn, Margarita, *The Soviet Photograph: 1924–37* (New Haven, CT: Yale University Press, 1996)

El Lissitzky: Beyond the Abstract Cabinet (New Haven, CT: Yale University Press, 1999)

Malevich and Film, with essays by Kazimir Malevich and Victor Tupitsyn (New Haven, CT: Yale University Press, 2002)

Tynianov, Iurii, 'Libretto kinofil'ma "Shinel'"', in *Iz istorii Lenfil'ma*, III (*Stat'i, vospominaniia, dokumenty: 1920–1930e gody*), ed. by N. S. Gornitskaia (Leningrad: Iskusstvo, leningradskoe otdelenie, 1973), 78–80 (first publ. by the publicity department of Leningradkino in 1926)

'O feksakh', *Sovetskii ekran*, 1929.14, 10

Urusevskii, Sergei, 'Vynuzhdennoe vystuplenie kak demonstratsiia protiv otsutstviia doklada ob izobrazitel'nom reshenii fil'ma', in Urusevskii, *S kinokameroi i za mol'bertom* (Moscow: Algoritm, 2002), pp. 173–75

Ushakov, Nikolai, 'Tri operatora: Kniga 1930-goda', publ. by A. S. Deriabin and E. Ia. Margolit, trans. by E. A. Movchan, *Kinovedcheskie zapiski*, 56 (2002), 157–83 (first publ. as *Try operatory* (Kyiv: Ukrteakinovydav, 1930))

Vaisfel'd, I., *G. Kozintsev: L. Trauberg: Tvorcheskii put'* (Moscow: Goskinoizdat, 1940)

Valiuzhenich, A., *Osip Maksimovich Brik: Materialy k biografii* (Akmola: Niva, 1993)

van Houten, Theodore, *Leonid Trauberg and his Films: Always the Unexpected* ('s-Hertogenbosch: Art and Research, 1989)

Velikii kinemo: Katalog sokhranivshikhsia igrovykh fil'mov v Rossii: 1908–1919, ed. by V. Ivanova and others (Moscow: Novoe literaturnoe obozrenie, 2002)

Vertov, Dziga, 'Kinoki: Perevorot', in *Kino-Eye: The Writings of Dziga Vertov*, ed. with introduction by Annette Michelson, trans. by Kevin O'Brien (Berkeley: University of California Press, 1984), pp. 11–21 (first publ. in *LEF*, 1923.3)

Villi Frerk, Fr., 'Sovremennoe sostoianie germanskoi fotograficheskoi optiki', *Foto-kino*, 1923.2–3, 22–24

Vishnevskii, Veniamin, 'Kino-tekhnika i kino-iskusstvo', *Art-EKRAN*, 1923.2, 3–4

Khudozhestvennye fil'my dorevoliutsionnoi Rossii: Fil'mograficheskoe opisanie (Moscow: Goskinoizdat, 1945)

Vl., B., 'Dve kul'turfil'my', *Kino i zhizn'*, 1929.4, 5–6

von Geldern, James, *Bolshevik Festivals 1917–1920* (Berkeley: University of California Press, 1993)

Von Ingenieur Friess, 'Neues uber Aufnahmetechnik', *Die Filmtechnik*, 1925.12, 260–61

Vorkapich, Slavko, '*Motion* and the Art of Cinematography', *American Cinematographer*, 7.9 (1926), 15, 16, & 17

Voskresenskii, Professor [L. N.], 'O nauchnykh fil'makh', *Kino-zhurnal A.R.K.*, 1925.9, 12–13

Widdis, Emma, *Visions of a New Land: Soviet Film from the Revolution to the Second World War* (London: Yale University Press, 2003)

Youngblood, Denise J., *Movies for the Masses: Popular Cinema and Soviet Society in the 1920s* (Cambridge: Cambridge University Press, 1992)

Zamiatin, Evgenii, 'Narodnyi teatr', in Zamiatin, *Sochineniia*, ed. by Evgeniia Zhiglevich and Boris Filippov, 4 vols (Munich: Neimanis, 1970–88), IV, 424–29 (first publ. in *Blokha: Igra v 4 d. Evg. Zamiatina* (Leningrad: Academia, 1927), pp. 3–11)

Zheliabuzhskii, Iurii, '"Za grosh – piatak"', *Kino*, 1922.2, 17

Iskusstvo operatora (Moscow: Gosudarstvennoe izdatel'stvo legkoi promyshlennosti, 1932)

'Avtorskoe pravo operatora: V poriadke postanovki voprosa', *Kino*, 1932.37, 2

'Masterstvo sovetskikh operatorov: Kratkii ocherk razvitiia' [1948], publ. by Svetlana Izhevskaia and A. S. Deriabin, *Kinovedcheskie zapiski*, 69 (2004), 246–73

'"Zhenshchina Edisona": Pervyi stsenarii feksov', publ. by N. I. Nusinova, *Kinovedcheskie zapiski*, 7 (1990), 83–96

Index